TANZANIA *and* NYERERE

ORBIS BOOKS

Maryknoll, New York 10545

TANZANIA *and* NYERERE

A Study of Ujamaa and Nationhood

WILLIAM REDMAN DUGGAN
and
JOHN R. CIVILLE

Acknowledgment is gratefully given to President Julius K. Nyerere for permission to quote extensively from the following works, published by Oxford University Press, for which the president controls the copyright: *Freedom and Unity* (1967); *Freedom and Socialism* (1968); *Ujamaa: Essays on Socialism* (1971); *Freedom and Development* (1974).

Library of Congress Cataloging in Publication Data

Duggan, William Redman.
    Tanzania and Nyerere.

    Bibliography: p.
    Includes index.
    CONTENTS: Duggan, W.R. A study of ujamaa and nationhood.—Civille, J.R. Ujamaa socialism, an analysis of the socialism of Julius K. Nyerere in the light of Catholic Church teaching.
    1.   Tanzania—Politics and government.   2.   Nyerere, Julius Kambarage, Pres. Tanzania, 1922–   3.   Socialism in Tanzania.   4.   Socialism and Catholic Church.
I.   Civille, John R., 1940–   joint author.   II.   Title.
DT448.2.D84   320.9'678'14   76-18121
ISBN 0-88344-475-5

Contents

PART ONE
A Study of *Ujamaa* and Nationhood
by William Redman Duggan

PART TWO

Ujamaa Socialism: An Analysis of the Socialism of Julius K. Nyerere in the Light of Catholic Church Teaching
by John R. Civille

INTRODUCTION

At 12:01 A.M. on December 9, 1961, the British Union Jack was lowered over the United Nations Trust Territory of Tanganyika. In its stead rose the black, green, and yellow banner of this newly independent country, twelfth member of the British Commonwealth and ninety-ninth member of the United Nations.

The flag ceremony and attendant constitutional changes took place in Tanganyika's capital city of Dar es Salaam (meaning "Haven of Peace" in Swahili). At the ceremonies Prince Philip represented the British Crown. Present also were a host of world celebrities.

As the new flag rose and the new nation came into being, there acceded to its prime ministership a diminutive and colorful figure, the country's founding father, Julius Kambarage Nyerere. The new prime minister, then aged thirty-eight, was the son of a minor chief and a graduate of Makerere and Edinburgh universities. A herdboy in childhood, Julius Nyerere grew up to become first a schoolmaster, teacher of history and science, then a politician.

Nyerere was founder of his country's dominant and now sole political party, the Tanganyika African National Union (TANU). With a few faithful political lieutenants, he made that party into a national movement and, with it, led his country from colonialism into independence. That independence had been attained peaceably within a short span of seven years.

Nyerere and his political colleagues were not content to let the sovereignty of the British Crown remain for long. Thus, in its second year of nationhood, Tanganyika became a republic and Nyerere became its first president. Tanganyika, however, remained within the Commonwealth.

In 1964, after many vicissitudes described in later pages of this book, there was formed the United Republic of Tanzania, combining the Tanganyika mainland with the offshore, newly independent islands of Zanzibar/Pemba. Nyerere became president of that Union. As this book is written, more than a decade later, Nyerere continues as president of Tanzania. Today, in affectionate recognition of nearly two decades of his wise leadership and devotion to that land, his people call him *Mwalimu*, "Respected Teacher."

In the wake of World War I and again following World War II, there was global agitation for the end of colonialism. Particularly in Africa and in Asia, after 1945 there arose militant demands for independence and nationhood for all colonial peoples. These demands resulted in swift fragmentation and dissolution of most of the world's great empires—British, French, Belgian, Italian, and German. Only the Portuguese empire remained more or less intact, but this, too, is now in flux, a venue for nationalism, civil strife, and eventual nationhood.

When the charter of the United Nations Organization was proclaimed in San Francisco in 1945, only forty-six nations signed that accord. Yet, today, three decades later, there are 140 sovereign members of that organization.

This sweeping nationalism produced massive changes on the continental land mass of Africa. Here, prior to 1950, only four countries—Egypt, Ethiopia, Liberia, and South Africa—were independent. Today in Africa there are forty-five independent nation-states. These range in size from the large and thinly populated nations of Zaire and Sudan, containing more than 900,000 square miles each, to the small countries of Togo and Lesotho, containing only 22,000 and 11,000 square miles respectively. Populations of the new African nations, too, are disparate, ranging from 75 million people in Federal Nigeria to less than 600,000 residents of Botswana or Swaziland.

The gestation periods, birth pangs, and early years of these many new nations of Africa varied remarkably. The birth of Ghana in March 1957 was jubilant and optimistic. Yet the turbulence and internal agonies of Ghana's first years of statehood under the schizophrenic and often tyrannical leadership of Kwame Nkrumah both dissipated and belied that original optimism. Ghana's present leaders have had to shoulder unusual burdens, economic and political, in order to restore even a semblance of Ghana's earlier promise.

The birth pangs of the former Belgian Congo (now Zaire) in 1960 were torturous. The tragedies of its afterbirth are well known, necessitating immense international diplomatic energies, finances, and goodwill to keep that country independent and united. Dag Hammarskjöld's martyrdom remains a costly testament to the importance which Free World officials placed on making the Congo succeed as a viable nation-state.

Some among the new African nations were, in economic terms, virtually stillborn. Some of these even now remain politico-economic satellites of their former European colonial mentors. Yet others have become economic and even political appendages of more powerful African neighbor-states. A few, by dint of great effort and imaginative leadership, have been able to develop clear-cut independence in both political and economic spheres. Certain nations of great promise, like Nigeria, the Sudan, and Zambia, either have been plunged into grave internecine warfare or have encountered such massive and unexpected difficulties from external sources as to endanger their very nationhood, despite their fair beginnings. Still other nations have successfully, at least thus far, combined a modicum of stability and growth with sagacious leadership and internal order. Others have been the venue of unexpected, often cruel, military coups. Since 1961 more than forty successful or abortive coups and illegal takeovers of government have occurred among the new states of Africa. For most of these latter, it has proved difficult, if not impossible, to return to civilian constitutional rule.

The many irregular changes of power and the great disparities in development of these new African countries have brought on both misunderstanding and criticism from external sources. Those criticisms have centered, first, on the capabilities of these new nations to become viable; and second, on the roles of their leaders. Foreign observers have tended to be overly critical of the efforts, even of the capabilities of these African leaders to weld diverse peoples and poverty-stricken economies into stable nations. Such critics have neglected to measure the time and travail which necessarily accompany the process of welding people into nations. It is well for those critics to recall that even after the American Declaration of Independence in 1776, it took the far-sighted leaders of the infant republic some thirteen years to adopt a constitution and some eighty years of tortuous controversy and civil war before national unity was accomplished. Even today, the most powerful and viable democracies are constantly required to refurbish and rehabilitate their governmental institutions and their economies in order to progress.

The more discerning among Africa-watchers have sensed that certain of the newly emergent leaders of Africa have been authors of, and their countries laboratories for, new and imaginative theories of government. These observers have perceived that some of the more dedicated leaders are attempting to fashion new and effective social, political, and economic institutions out of their weakened colonial heritage and their shattered indigenous past.

Some of the new political and economic theories given birth in Africa have been tried and found wanting. Many of the new leaders, as well, were tried and found wanting. Some of their new-formed theories and institutions have been only ill-fitting imitations of former colonial systems or poor replicas of archaic tribal traditions. Yet from this melange of new and old political institutions, of new or time-tested social doctrine, there have emerged on the African continent some valuable lessons in the science of government and the development of nations.

The pragmatic, even inspiring, leadership of a number of the new African rulers is worthy of more detailed study. Notable among contempory chieftaincies in Africa is the balanced intellectual leadership of Léopold Senghor of Senegal; the surprising strength and unexpected conservatism of Jomo Kenyatta of Kenya; the innate sagacity of Ahmadou Ahidjo of Cameroon; and the steady hand of Habib Bourguiba of Tunisia.

Among the plethora of new nations and new leaders of Africa, one country and one leader have provoked increasing international attention and debate over the past decade. That country is Tanzania and that man is Julius K.

Nyerere. In no other African state today is the character, dynamism, even lifeblood, of the founder-leader so interwoven with his country's interests, direction, and fiber.

It has long been evident that Nyerere and his colleagues are attempting to develop new socio-economic values within the context of a novel political philosophy. They seek to meld the best of their remaining tribal values with the demands of modern life. Within the constrictions of a poverty-stricken economy, they seek to pair the beginnings of an urbanized, industrial society with a strengthened and diversified agricultural sector. Their primary aim throughout is to uplift the Tanzanian people as a whole.

As in all political movements which have, as their goal, the social transformation of a people from a weak to a strong economy, Nyerere's and Tanzania's efforts show clearly the constant pulls between doctrinaire idealism and political pragmatism; between his people's respect for the traditional and their need for the modern; between democracy and authoritarianism. Some observers may characterize these efforts as "Fabian Socialism," others may label them "African Socialism;" but what do these terms really mean in an East African milieu? We can only assume that Nyerere and his lieutenants seek to create in Tanzania a whole people: a nation which is self-sufficient in its economic base, united and democratic in its political life, just in its national and international standards.

For Nyerere, his country's attainment of independence marked only a beginning, not an end. For Nyerere and his colleagues, social experimentation was a necessity which, in lieu of major resources other than labor, represented the only pathway open to even minimal economic independence. For the Tanzanian leaders, too, experimentation in political philosophy and institutions represented an honest effort to supplant ill-fitting foreign ideologies with something more adequately African in character and in aim. In all these efforts, the Tanzanian leaders were driven by the realization that, within a short span of time, they must catch up with the outside world. That world—through a triple-tiered catastrophe of isolation, of slavery, of colonial domination—had left Africa, and especially Tanzania, far behind.

Whether speaking out on public issues, writing for foreign journals, or leading his compatriots into innovative social programs, Nyerere constantly demonstrates his respect for the concepts of human dignity and for traditional African values, including family loyalty and love of the land. He is both classicist and modernist; idealist and pragmatist; a complex mixture of Jeffersonian Democrat and Agrarian Socialist. Nyerere combines within himself, in thought and in action, the nature, the fealties, the contradictory pulls of a modern militant nationalist with a deep respect for his traditional African past. Thus Julius Nyerere's character, his leadership position, his steps to solve his nation's problems—and indeed those problems themselves—inculcate the classic confrontation of past and present, the Bronze Age meeting the Atomic Age in Africa.

It has been the primary aim of this book to make Tanzania's political doctrines and its innovative social schemes, particularly the *Ujamaa* (Family-hood) program more widely understood. President Nyerere's own character and his efforts to build a party into a national movement, thence into nation-hood, are also described and analyzed at length. In seeking to portray in depth Nyerere the leader and Tanzania the nation, the authors have undertaken their tasks on two levels. William Redman Duggan has painted the broad historical, political, and economic setting. Father John Civille has portrayed "*Ujamaa* Socialism" in parameters of philosophy, religion, and social justice. The authors and the publisher hope that the reader will find in this volume a definitive portrait of both subjects—Tanzania and Nyerere.

PART ONE

A STUDY OF
UJAMAA
AND NATIONHOOD

WILLIAM REDMAN DUGGAN

To Bunny, my wife,
who shares with me an abiding affection
for Africa and its peoples

CHAPTER 1

THE LAND AND THE PEOPLE

The United Republic of Tanzania today comprises a land area of 363,708 square miles with a population of 14.5 million (1975 estimate). That populace includes more than 14 million Africans stemming from 120 diverse tribal backgrounds. There are more than 100,000 Asians (including 86,000 Indo-Pakistanis and 15,000 Chinese). There are 85,000 Arabs and some 15,000 whites (Europeans).[1]

Dar es Salaam, the nation's capital, today has a population in excess of 300,000. It is located on the western shore of the Indian Ocean at a latitude of 6° south and 39° east. Being the largest city of the country, it is the seat of both political and economic power.

Mainland Tanzania lies between the Indian Ocean on the east and the great lakes of Central Africa (Lakes Victoria, Tanganyika, and Malawi/Nyasa) on the west. It is bounded on the north by Kenya and Uganda; on the west by Rwanda, Burundi, and Zaire; on the south and southwest by Mozambique, Malawi, and Zambia. The country lies wholly in the southern hemisphere, resting between 1° and 11° 45′ south. Longitudinally it rests between 29° 21′ and 40° 25′ east.

Climatically and topographically the country can be divided into four principal areas: (1) the hot and humid coastal lowlands of the 550-mile-long Indian Ocean shoreline; (2) the hot and arid zone of the broad central plateau; (3) the high inland mountain and lake region of the northern border, this containing the famed Mount Kilimanjaro, highest peak in Africa—19,340 feet; and (4) the temperate highlands of the northeast and southwest. The country is subject to two important and distinct monsoon-ruled seasons. The northeast monsoon runs from October to February, while the southwest monsoon

9

brings the major rains of February to May with cooler temperatures in their wake.[2]

The most fertile and heavily populated areas of the country lie in a gigantic broken circle, its circumference resting virtually along the nation's borders. More than two-thirds of Tanzania's populace lives in this circumferential area. Over one-half of the country's land is nonproductive, owing to lack of water and to continuing infestation of tsetse flies. The most arable land lies in the northern and southwestern highlands.

Though now relatively unified politically, the peoples of Tanzania include racial, ethnic, and tribal strains as diverse as any to be found in the world. There are black Africans of divergent hues, customs, and economic, political, and geographic backgrounds. There are Asians who range from Indo-Pakistani and Goan to Chinese. There are Arab and Afro-Shirazi who emanated from the Persian Gulf and the Arabian peninsula by means of a series of sea-treks covering a thousand years. There are whites, known as Europeans, who include such diverse nationalities as British, German, Greek, and American.

Most reputable surveys of Tanzania claim the existence of 120 different, more or less indigenous, black African tribes. It is preferable not to set a precise figure because of difficulties in defining true tribes. Today certain of these so-called tribes are actually clustered into larger groupings. Given the effects of urbanization, modernization, and politicization, some of the smallest tribal groups are disappearing.

Most anthropologists define a tribe as a group of people who, because of social, cultural, familial, political, and linguistic similarities, develop a sense of unity associating them with one another, apart from other groups. Such tribal groupings in Tanzania vary from the Sukuma, numbering in excess of 1 million persons, to the small but highly distinct Sonjo, numbering less than 4,000. Other large and important tribes include Wanyamwezi, concentrated in the west-central region, numbering 500,000; the Hehe and Bahaya, each numbering more than 250,000, these located in the southern highlands and northwest corner respectively; and Wachagga of the Kilimanjaro region, numbering more than 400,000. (Wachagga illustrate the kind of grouping which originated with smaller tribal units eventually banding together and changing composition as a result of educational, political, and religious motivations.)

Other important tribes include the Masai, numbering above 125,000, who live in the north-central area of the country, and the Makonde, numbering above 350,000, living in the southeastern Mtwara-Ruvuma region. Both these tribes are split by national borders—the Masai having a like number of their tribe living in Kenya; the Makonde having a similar number of relatives living south of the Tanzania-Mozambique border. (This last-named tribe has provided the base for the nationalist "Freedom Fighter" actions in northern

Mozambique, a subject discussed in greater detail in chapter 13 of this book.)

The Zaramo, a highly diluted and urbanized tribal composite, numbering above 250,000, constitute another important "tribal" unit in numbers and influence. These cluster about the environs of Dar es Salaam and the adjacent coastline. One of the smallest yet significant tribes is the Zanaki, numbering 30,000, grouped near Musoma in the Lake Victoria region. From this tribe, as detailed elsewhere, came the nation's founder-leader, President Julius K. Nyerere, whose father was chief of the Zanaki.

In their ethnologic origins, the hundred and more tribes of present-day Tanzania stem from five main sources: the Aboriginal Bushmen, the Nilotic, the Hamitic, the Nilo-Hamitic, and the loose-knit conglomerate known as Bantu. The differing ethnic strains show mainly in physical characteristics, language, customs, mores, and special lifestyles such as agricultural or pastoral economies, or a combination thereof. Certain of their chieftaincy arrangements, linguistic forms, and familial relationships, for example, are useful in denoting their distinctiveness and probable ethnic origins.[3]

The Aboriginal Bushmen, perhaps the earliest inhabitants of Africa still extant, carry on hunting and fishing American Indian-style, exporting their culture northward from South Africa and the Kalahari Desert. The Bushmen group retains its linguistic clicks reminiscent of the Xhosa dialect of South Africa. Among the Bushmen derivatives in Tanzania are the Kindiga, numbering 1,000, living near Lake Eyasi, and the Sandawe, numbering 35,000 living in the Kondoa district.

The Nilotic grouping is claimed to be true Negroid and probably had its origins in the upper Nile Valley and in West Africa. Again, the linguistic traits are highly distinctive. These are largely pastoral people. Examples of this group in the present-day tribal structure of Tanzania are the Luo tribe of northwest Tanzania (and southwest Kenya), numbering more than 75,000 in Tanzania alone.

The Hamitic group, who probably originated in early Egypt, are ordinarily a brown-skinned and fine-featured type. These tribes developed the art of chieftainship and government to a high degree. Hamitic stock has come in from Ethiopia and Sudan to dominate many of the tribes of west and northwest Tanzania. Some of these are now merged with the larger Bantu tribal stocks such as the Sukuma. Examples of the Hamitic strain in Tanzania, numbering almost 2 million, include as well the Hima (75,000) and Watutsi (100,000).

Representative of the Nilo-Hamitic blood combination are the Masai of north-central Tanzania (numbering 125,000), and the Tatog-Barabaig groups of the Mbulu district (numbering 30,000). These have highly developed age-sex platoon systems.

Peoples of Bantu origin represent the preponderance of the tribal groups of Tanzania. They are reported to have originated from roots in southern Africa, providing a bloodline from the Zulu, Mashona, and Matebele. Though the question seems not yet resolved by anthropologists it should be noted that the "Bantu" of South, Central, and East Africa were originally said to have come from a loose combination of Hamitic and Negroid blood-lines which has common linguistic attributes. Today the term "Bantu" is used by social scientists to designate and to cover the numerous tribal categories of these areas with common linguistic roots. Furthermore, and somewhat inexactly, the term "Bantu," as now used in southern and eastern Africa, denotes a general grouping of black Africans regardless of tribal origin.[4]

So diverse are their blood-lines today, and so different their customs or tribal practices, that their linguistic roots appear to be the only remaining common denominator. (Even this, of course, is now diluted by the overlay of Swahili, a dialectical combination of Bantu, Arabic, and English, which has become the *lingua franca* of the region.) Bantu tribes are mainly subsistence agriculturalists and pastoralists in Tanzania, as are their cousins to the south. Tribal examples of Bantu origin in Tanzania are the Hamitic-dominated Lacustrine tribes of the lake region; the Meru and Chagga of the northern region; Wagogo and Wanyamwezi of the central plateau; the Hehe of the southern highlands; the Makonde of the eastern coastal lowlands; and the southern-intrusive Nguni.

One other African grouping requires special mention and definition. This is the combination which has resulted from intermarriage on Zanzibar and Pemba of mainland Africans with "Shirazi," or people of Persian stock. Since 1964 this group, known as Afro-Shirazi, has dominated Zanzibar's politics and economy.

Tanzania contains non-African tribes as well—Asian, Arab, and white. From medieval times East Indian merchants and businessmen accompanied the Arab *dhows* on their rounds of the Indian Ocean littoral and probably took up residence on Zanzibar or on the mainland as early as the eleventh century.[5] By 1811 there were records of settlements of Indians (known as *banyans* or *dukawallahs*) on Zanzibar and the mainland.[6]

When the British decided to build the Kenya-Uganda Railway line from Mombasa (Kenya) to Lake Victoria in the late nineteenth century, they imported from India some 32,000 Indian "coolies" to construct the project. Though some of them returned to India and several thousand died during completion of the hazardous task, many of these laborers and their descendants later came into Tanzania to settle.

East Indian movement into Tanzania increased again after World War I when certain of the British Indian soldiery was demobilized in East Africa. During the period from 1920 to 1940 some recruitment of Indians for the civil service of Tanganyika Territory also occurred. Following World War II, however, East Indian migration to Tanganyika was limited to 3,000 yearly. After Tanganyika's attainment of independence in 1961 that immigration virtually ceased. Some 20,000 Indo-Pakistanis have departed Tanzania (and

Zanzibar) since independence, leaving about 86,000 still in the country. The Indo-Pakistanis have been mainly engaged in the commercial life of Tanzania, serving as businessmen, shopkeepers, and artisans. A high proportion of the Tanzanian Indo-Pakistanis are of the Ismaili Muslim sect of the Aga Khan, while others are Hindu, Sikhs, Parsees, or Muslims of other sects.

As described in later chapters of this book, there are to be found in Tanzania's coastal ruins traces of Chinese merchandising, such as porcelain and money. However, no long-term settlement in the region by the Chinese seems to have occurred. A new and expansive association with the Chinese has developed today. This association involves participation by Chinese engineers and laborers (numbering about 15,000) in the construction of the Tanzanian-Zambian (Tan-Zam) railway line.

The Arabs, now numbering 85,000, have been present for centuries on the islands of Zanzibar and Pemba, along the eastern coastline from Tanga to Kilwa, and along the central rail route from Dar es Salaam to Kigoma-Ujiji on Lake Tanganyika. Trading in slaves and ivory, Arabs from the Arabian peninsula and Persian Gulf colonized and dominated enclaves along the Indian Ocean littoral from northern Kenya to Mozambique. They probably visited East Africa prior to the time of Christ and certainly established settlements in that area shortly after the birth of Islam. Their suzerainty declined quickly after European colonization of the region and virtually disappeared with the rise of black African nationalism. Their settlements now represent only the minor remnants of Arab power and influence detailed in the historical chapters of this book.

The whites, now numbering less than 15,000, represent the remainder of colonial influence and of American/European religious, commercial, and educational associations. Whites hold specialized technical posts in shipping and in educational and missionary activities. They are also in a few residual agricultural ventures. The whites may be said to have a continuing important managerial-educational-technical influence, but politically they are of no real consequence. In addition to some long-time British and German settlers remaining in Tanzania today, there are a few Italians, Greeks, Americans, Canadians, Dutch, Comorians, and French.

NOTES

1. *Background Notes*, U.S. State Department, on United Republic of Tanzania (U.S. GPO).

2. J.P. Moffett, ed., *Handbook of Tanganyika* (Dar es Salaam: Government Printer, 1958). This work contains, in its first chapter, an excellent, highly detailed description of the country's topography and climate.

3. Ibid., pp. 283ff.

4. Monica Wilson and Leonard Thompson, eds., *Oxford History of South Africa*, vol. 1 (London: Oxford University Press, 1969), p. xi.

5. R. Coupland, *East Africa and Its Invaders*, 1st ed. (Oxford: Clarendon Press, 1938), p. 27.

6. Ibid., pp. 182–83.

CHAPTER 2

HISTORICAL BACKGROUND

Tanzania has several important archeological sites attesting to prehistoric cultures. By far the most famous of these is the Olduvai Gorge in the north-west section of the country near Ngorongoro Crater. Although this region became world renowned in 1959 as a result of findings of the late Dr. Louis S. B. Leakey, noted student of prehistory, the Olduvai area had actually been the scene of other earlier archeological exploits. The gorge was discovered by European scientists in 1911 and became the site of archeological excavations led by the German Professor Hans Reck. His group found much fossilized animal life as well as unverified traces of Stone Age man. During the 1930s British archeologists continued excavations in this area and these scientists found and verified several Stone Age cultures.

Dr. Leakey's most valuable archeological find brought to light in 1959 the "Tanganyika Man" (*Zinjanthropus*). This was the near-perfect skull of a man who had lived in the Olduvai area more than one and one-half million years ago. The anthropological and historical questions which this find aroused are still creating worldwide debate.

The forbidding environment of East Africa has left most of the early history of its indigenous peoples shrouded in mist and tribal legend. Unlike other continental masses, there were few harbors, no navigable rivers, a narrow maritime plain, humid, infertile, beset by mosquito and tsetse fly. It is clear, however, that in the prehistory of this region there came onto the uplands of East Africa wave after wave of migrants from both the Nile Valley in the north and the plateau lands of the south. Thus it was clear that, for some millennia before the invasions from other continents, there was a commingling of the pastoral Bantu peoples of the south with the dominant Hamitic blood of the north. These mergers created the hybrid tribal mosaic which we see in East

14

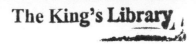

Africa today (described briefly in chapter 1). Even today, however, despite much anthropological study, the real history of these merging indigenous African peoples remains more or less unknown. Thus it is that most of the history of East Africa begins only with the recorded actions of its foreign invaders.

Available evidence from other recent archeological sites and historical records attest to the existence of seven major waves of foreign intrusions onto the Tanzanian littoral over two millennia. These included (1) the Greco-Roman-Phoenician exploits, possibly ranging from the fifth century B.C. to the first century A.D.; (2) the early Arab "trading" era of the ninth century A.D. to the fourteenth century A.D.; (3) the inconclusive Chinese trading influences, possibly covering from A.D. 900 to A.D. 1500; (4) intrusions from Southern Asia, from India and Persia, these spanning the period from A.D. 1000 to A.D. 1900; (5) Portuguese intrusions ranging the entire coastline from the late fifteenth century through the middle eighteenth century; (6) a second wave of colonization from the Arabian principalities of Muscat and Oman, this intrusion resulting in Arab domination of Zanzibar and certain East African coastal enclaves spanning the eighteenth to the twentieth centuries A.D.; (7) the period of European colonialism beginning with the great explorers of the mid-nineteenth century and ending with African independence in the 1960s.

The successive cultures of the East African coast from Somalia to Mozambique appear to have been closely associated with contemporaneous cultures of the Arabian peninsula and the Red Sea. These ranged over at least six different periods from 500 B.C. to A.D. 1850. A sequence of layers of pottery, coins, and artifacts can be reconstructed at many points along the Tanzanian coast to correlate with these distinct periods. These studies of available antiquities are still in preliminary stages in sites such as Bagamoyo, Kilwa, Pangani, Mafia, and Pemba.

Some historians record that Solomon provided the Phoenicians with a port on the Red Sea in order that they might develop trade along the Indian Ocean periphery. It is believed that the Phoenicians touched in at Zanzibar and Sofala about 500 B.C. and that they may have proceeded around the Cape of Good Hope during those voyages. Even in the pre-Christian era, the Greeks and Romans are thought to have carried on trade along the eastern shores of Africa. It is also conjectured that Arab merchants and mariners may have piloted or directed exploits into this area for the Mediterranean peoples.

One of the earliest recorded accounts of East African coastal exploration is that of Herodotus (written about 445 B.C.). He described circumnavigations of Africa made by the Egyptians. Along with the writings of Herodotus and of Heraclitus regarding African exploration, there appear references to such exploits among the Carthaginians. Ptolemy, Aristotle, and Alexander the Great also make reference to African journeys. All these, however, are fragmentary and unsupported by African sources. A manuscript, known as the

Periplus of the Erythraean Sea (the Greek name for the Indian Ocean) was written about A.D. 80 by a Greek merchant seaman. This work appears to have been a pilot's guide to the Indian Ocean and many of the locations thereon can be specifically determined.[1]

The first recorded Arab associations with the East African coast came soon after the death of the prophet Mohammed in A.D. 632. Muslim history records that partisans of the Prophet emigrated from the Yemen to the Banadir coast (the East African coast) in about 639. To support the belief in the association of Arab and Phoenician, Sir Richard Burton, the noted nineteenth-century British explorer, contended that the *dhow*, the specially designed sailing craft common to the monsoon seas of the Indian Ocean for centuries past, was actually, in origin, a Phoenician craft. (This vessel has two masts, a high poopdeck, and forecastle.)

From remotest times, the prevalence of trade winds and their effective utilization even by the most primitive of sailing vessels provided an open door to East Africa from Arabia and India. The northeast monsoon blows consistently from November through February, thus providing steady power for the voyage of sailors southwestward from Asia to Africa. The southwest monsoon, blowing with similar consistency from April to September, furnishes a fairly easy voyage for the Asian and Arab trader homeward bound.

The early Phoenician as well as later Arab and Persian settlements on the east coast of Africa appeared to have been fortified towns on the mainland or nearby islands which were relatively free from attack and easily defended. Among these were the present-day towns of Lamu, Mombasa, Zanzibar, Kilwa, Sofala, Wete, and Chaka Chaka. All these were advantageously situated to the needs of the ancient colonial traders.

The result of these intrusions was settlements and cultural interweaving—African, Arab, and Asian. The oldest known of the permanent settlements appears to have been Kilwa (located ninety miles south of present-day Dar es Salaam), a town still inhabited and containing many partially excavated ruins. Kilwa is mentioned in Arab chronicles in the middle of the tenth century and its existence is consistently noted through the arrival of the Portuguese in the late fifteenth century. The early Arab *Chronicles of Kilwa* also records the arrival of Arab and Persian (Shiraz) traders in Kilwa during the tenth century A.D.[2] The same chronicles indicate Persian settlement on the nearby island of Mafia.

Historians of East Africa differ as to the earliest dates of direct trade between that area and China. Certain Arab geographers recorded exchange of African ivory for Chinese pottery and porcelain. The Chinese did not appear to have traded directly with the East Africans before the thirteenth century. Prior to that date, however, there is some indication that African ivory and animals were taken to China via India, and celadon porcelain of the Ming period appeared in East Africa via the same route. Between 1417 and 1431, as

Chinese records show, Chinese sailors in their junks appeared at both Malindi (Kenya) and Mogadiscio (Somalia) with probable stops at other East African ports. Further attesting to the existence of Chinese trade with the peoples of medieval Tanzania are the Chinese coins and bits of porcelain to be found today in ruins of ancient Arab towns ranging from Bagamoyo to Kilwa.[3]

A recent scholarly study of Chinese association with the East African coast has been produced by Teobaldo Filesi, director of the Italian Institute for Africa. Titled *China and Africa in the Middle Ages*, it appeared in English in 1972. Filesi's book contains the thesis that the Chinese were not at that time interested in settlement or conquest of the East African littoral. Instead they seem to have appeared in East Africa only as navigators and as merchants.

In 1497–98 the most famous of Portuguese explorers, Vasco da Gama, made his first voyage along the South and East African coasts. Early in 1498 he visited Mozambique and Mombasa, but bad weather forced him to bypass Kilwa.[4] The Portuguese discoverer of Brazil, Pedro Alvarez Cabral, arrived along the Tanzanian coast and anchored at Kilwa with six ships in July 1500. Portuguese records indicate that neither group met any enemy action on these visits. However, in 1502 Vasco da Gama landed at Kilwa and made the Arab emir of the city his temporary prisoner. Again in 1505 Portuguese records indicate that tribute was levied upon the city by Portuguese voyagers returning from India. Thereafter a Portuguese garrison occupied Kilwa from 1506 to 1513, at which time the Portuguese viceroy of India, the Duke of Albuquerque, ordered the garrison withdrawn.[5]

During the last half of the sixteenth century the Portuguese extended their control over the East African coast from Mombasa in the north to Lindi in the south and onward to Mozambique. They also held suzerainty over Zanzibar and Pemba. In the early part of the seventeenth century the various Arab sultanates rose in rebellion against the Portuguese occupiers and gradually overthrew the Portuguese rule. Virtually all settlements on the Tanzanian coast came into rebellion during this century, and in 1652 the Arabs of Oman succeeded in taking control of Zanzibar from the Portuguese. Then, during the final ten years of the seventeenth century, the existing settlements near the present site of Dar es Salaam were wrested from Portuguese control. Only in Mombasa and Kilwa did Portuguese rule survive long into the eighteenth century.

During the early part of the nineteenth century, Zanzibar assumed international repute as a market for both ivory and black African slaves. The coast of East Africa now saw frequent visits by American clipper ships and British privateers putting into port for trade, water, and supplies. Until now this trade had been the main concession of the Portuguese and the Dutch. As early as 1833 the sultan of Muscat and Zanzibar, Seyyid Said, concluded a treaty of "Amity and Commerce" with an American ship's officer, Captain Edmund Roberts.[6] By terms of this treaty Americans were guaranteed freedom of trade in any of the East African ports under Arab control in exchange for a duty of 5 percent charged for goods landed from American ships. Appointment of the first American consul (Richard Palmer) on Zanzibar was also provided under the treaty.

While the number of United States ships traversing this great distance was not large, the Yankee merchantmen did leave one important trading imprint on East Africa. The cotton cloth, product of the New England textile mills which provided the bulk of their input, became known as "merikani." This import successfully displaced British and Indian textiles for some time. This cloth even became a form of currency along Arab trade routes into the African interior.[7]

Existing records attest to the fact of constant movement of Arab trading caravans into the interior of Africa from the coast at least as early as 1769. These intrusions continued for the next century. Prime purposes of these expeditions were to obtain indigenous slaves and ivory. For some years the sultanates managed to maintain treaties of friendship and commerce with the interior tribes, particularly the powerful Wanyamwezi of the Tabora area. With Arab guarantees of safe conduct, European explorers and missionaries now began their movement into the interior. It was under such guarantees and guidance that both David Livingstone and H. M. Stanley were to travel.

Meantime, in 1866, the sultan of Zanzibar, Majid, sailed into the harbor of Dar es Salaam, named it "Haven of Peace," and decided to establish it as both his new capital and his new *entrepôt* for interior trade and control. Majid died in 1870 before he was able to complete plans for this capital city. His brother and successor, Sultan Barghash, continued the effort. Soon, however, these Arab efforts dwindled away and the buildings fell into disrepair.

In 1877 there was a spurt of renewed interest in the building up of Dar es Salaam as a city and port when two Britons, Sir William Mackinnon and Thomas Buxton, began construction of a road between Dar es Salaam and Lake Nyasa. In 1881 work was abandoned on this effort and Dar es Salaam again relapsed into quiescence.

Arab hegemony over the interior of Tanzania was not always undisputed. During the last half of the nineteenth century Arab suzerainty was challenged by powerful tribal chieftains. Notable among these were the military genius Mirambo of Urambo and Fundikira, the ruler of Unyamwezi. These two chiefs were especially successful in imposing customs duties on the Arab traders as they passed through their domains. Mirambo effectively closed the trade routes between the towns of Tabora and Ujiji for two years (1871–73). It was necessary for the sultan of Zanzibar to send a force of 3,000 men from the island to reopen this trade route.

As the sultans of Zanzibar sought to conclude treaties of commerce with tribal leaders of the African hinterland, they also sought to conclude extensive trade agreements with outside nations. As noted, the first of these was concluded with the Americans (1833). Others were concluded with France (1839) and with the Hanseatic League (1849); at later stages protectorate arrangements were made with Germany and Britain.

The islands of Zanzibar as well as mainland Tanzania (then called Tanganyika) during most of the nineteenth century held special fascination for famous European explorers seeking new knowledge of the African continent. Early among these were the Germans Johann Rebmann and Ludwig Krapf, who laid claim to being the first Europeans to lay eyes on Mount Kilimanjaro.[8] The redoubtable Sir Richard Burton records his entry on the East African scene (1857) in his *First Footsteps in East Africa*. Burton and his explorer-companion John Speke visited Zanzibar as well as Bagamoyo and crossed Tanzania in their search for the source of the Nile. Still later (1858 and 1862) Livingstone and Stanley were separately to follow the same trails across Tanzania. And in 1871 Livingstone and Stanley were to have their famous meeting ("Dr. Livingstone, I presume. . . ") on the shores of Lake Tanganyika at the small Arab village of Ujiji. This was an important period in the history of East Africa, since it sparked European curiosity about the area and provided the basis for later colonial settlement by European powers.

Interest in the area was also heightened by the efforts of Europeans (especially David Livingstone) to abolish the barbaric slave trade. This, of course, was mainly under Arab control but involved slave transport by ships of many flags. Even today there are no clear indications of the numbers of Africans taken into bondage from the East African coast by slavers during the many centuries of that inhuman activity. Though slavery was abolished by British law within the Protectorate of Zanzibar in 1897, slavery on the mainland (then under German rule) was not finally eradicated until 1922. This action was formally and finally taken by the British administration of Tanganyika under its League of Nations mandate.[9]

By 1880 the highly irresponsible and long troublesome European colonial scramble for Africa had begun. By 1884, in terms of the Treaty of Berlin, various "franchise areas" of Africa were allocated to certain major European powers. Partition of these areas was effected by creation of artificial boundaries, thus breaking up major tribal groupings. Many such boundaries and tribal divisions still exist.

By 1870 East Africa had been visited by a few German explorers and merchants who established connections on Zanzibar. In that year the German consul resident there reported to Bismarck's government that the ruling sultan of Zanzibar, Barghash, had asked to be placed under German protection. No response from the German government was made to the sultan's presumed request. Up to this time there had been little German interest in East African colonization, as Germany was too preoccupied with its European problems. Not until 1876, when Leopold II of Belgium initiated his famous geographic conference (which resulted in eventual partition of Africa and creation of the

Belgian Congo), did the German government, under pressure from its own nationals, become interested in East Africa.[10]

It was not until February 1885 that Germany issued to the German Colonization Society of East Africa a charter of protection, declaring the "Territory of German East Africa" to be under the kaiser's suzerainty. Thus was granted to the Society the management of the territory subject to jurisdiction of the German government. Terms of this agreement were later communicated to the sultan of Zanzibar, who in 1885 sent a telegram protesting the intrusion of the emperor of Germany. To force the sultan's submission to German hegemony several German naval vessels were sent to Zanzibar. Soon thereafter the Germans took title to specified areas of the hinterland.[11] Almost at once conflict arose between British, French, and German land-delimitation commissioners over territorial borders.

Finally in 1886, by terms of agreement reached between Germany and Britain—an agreement literally forced upon the sultan and taking no consideration of the wishes of the indigenous peoples—the following determinations were made: (1) The sultan's basic sovereignty over Zanzibar, Pemba, and Mafia was recognized; (2) Germany was given control over the ports of Dar es Salaam and Pangani; (3) Germany's sphere of influence was extended southward to the Ruvuma River; (4) Germany was awarded the Kilimanjaro area; (5) Britain recognized German title to lands in northwest Tanzania as far as Lake Victoria; (6) the Kenya strip (200 miles long and 10 miles wide) was reasserted as a nominal fief of the sultan of Zanzibar.[12]

In 1888 a fifty-year lease was concluded between the German East African Company and the sultan's government. Two years later the imperial German government officially took over administration of the territory as a colony. This territory embraced what is now mainland Tanzania plus what are now the independent nations of Rwanda and Burundi. The Germans retained colonial authority over all this region until World War I when, as a result of their defeat and the subsequent provisions of the Versailles Treaty, Tanganyika was awarded as a mandate to Britain under the League of Nations. At that time Belgium took similar League mandate authority over Ruanda-Urundi (now Rwanda and Burundi).

The Germans were zealous in their efforts to develop their East African colony economically but, in so doing, they were insensitive to the religious, political, and social feelings of the indigenous inhabitants. One serious uprising against the German occupiers occurred in August 1888. This incident was inspired by Arab and African peoples resident at Bagamoyo and Pangani. The German government sent in troops to bring the uprising under control.

During the period 1888–1907 the Germans came into conflict and open warfare with various of the Tanganyikan tribes, including Wachagga, Wanyamwezi, Wagogo, and Wahehe. The Wahehe proved especially determined to resist and under their chief, Makwaia, waged serious guerrilla warfare against the Germans, which lasted on and off for fifteen years.

The most important of the indigenous uprisings against the ruthless colonization efforts of the Germans was the Maji-Maji rebellion of 1905–07.[13] This uprising, led by African chiefs and medicine men, broke out in the hills near Kilwa. The name of the rebellion, Maji-Maji, apparently derived from the concoction of water, maize, and sorghum which the African witch doctors prescribed as a magic protection against the weapons of the German soldiery. This uprising probably resulted from the rigorous administrative strictures, including forced labor, which the German colonial system imposed on the Africans. African casualties are said to have exceeded 50,000.

The German economic exploitation of the territory left its mark on Tanzania long after German rule was gone. Lack of communications had restricted the German colonists to the coastal regions during early years of their occupation and the climate restricted the nature of their crops. However, they were successful in establishing primary plantation crops in the area—sisal, cotton, coffee, and tea. These remain the country's major staple products today. In implementing colonial legislation, the needs of the local Africans were seldom considered. Demands of German administrators and plantation-owners which conflicted with indigenous interests were always resolved in favor of the Europeans.

As the German interest in the territory was primarily economic, there was an understanding that European settlers would be necessary but that the goals of these would not be primarily political. The German occupation of the territory thus brought on some beginnings in economic, vocational, and religious—but not political—fields. This situation differed materially from that of British settlers in Kenya, who sought major political goals, including home rule, in protection of their economic interests.

Thus in their efforts at empire in Africa, the Germans kept four goals in mind. They created sources of raw materials which the fatherland required; they created new outlets for German goods and thereby a certain dependence on Germany; they created *lebensraum* for those Germans wishing to find new homes overseas; they sought to counter the far-flung British empire. By 1910 in German East Africa the kaiser's government had achieved only the first of these goals.

To support plantation economies and exports, the Germans built two rail lines—one through central Tanzania, the second running from Tanga to Moshi/Arusha parallel to the northern border. Ports, telephone lines, roads, administrative headquarters (or *bomas*) were built in support of the German colonial effort.

Following the Maji-Maji uprising and before the outbreak of World War I, the German government finally realized that it was essential to seek better rapport with the local inhabitants than had been achieved in the past. There were efforts to improve the colonial administration as well as to expand education and missionary activities. There were efforts to improve infrastructure and the plantation economy. However, there was little time left before the Treaty of Versailles excluded the German administration from the territory.

The legacy which the Germans left to Tanzania remains important to this day. It includes the beginnings of economic infrastructure—evident in the railroads, the harbors, civic buildings and, most of all, the tropical plantation economy—and a certain residue of discipline which inspired some of the larger tribal groups. The German ruthlessness of rule was mixed with a clarity of purpose which the Africans appeared to comprehend.

With the onset of World War I the Germans had two advantages, namely, the capability of their commander, General Paul von Lettow-Vorbeck, and the assessment which the German command had made in forecasting the eventual extension of the war in East Africa.[14] It was Lettow-Vorbeck's thesis that Britain, with its mighty navy, would soon control the seas, but would not be willing to engage the Germans on the land in areas outside Europe. Thus, concluded Lettow-Vorbeck, it was to the kaiser's advantage to engage Britain on land in Africa and elsewhere in order to dissipate its military-economic strength. Lettow-Vorbeck thereupon decided to engage the British in their own Kenya colony from his relatively strong situation at the foot of Mount Kilimanjaro. The British administration in Kenya and Uganda moved to protect their southern borders. They brought additional troops from India and received support from British naval units in the Indian Ocean.

The German troops took little initiative, preferring to keep themselves in a compact mobile unit rather than trying to defend the entire territory of German East Africa. When British military reinforcements arrived from India it was decided to try to capture the port of Tanga, the railhead for Lettow-Vorbeck's supply line. From there the British hoped to move in on Lettow-Vorbeck's position near Mount Kilimanjaro. The action against Tanga by the British, in early November 1914, was a disastrous failure. The genius of Lettow-Vorbeck showed up in his reconnaissance and superior military planning. For the next year and more both Germans and British carried on guerrilla action along the entire northern border from Tanga to Uganda, but these were inconsequential in effect.

Quick conclusion of fighting against the Germans in South-West Africa gave the British an opportunity to move reinforcements from that area into East Africa. Joint command of British, Indian, and South African troops had been placed in the hands of the South African general (and later prime minister) Jan Christiaan Smuts. Because of the hatred engendered by the Boer War, the appointment of Smuts was not wholeheartedly accepted by the British. Smuts thus faced political as well as military problems. His military strategy was only partially successful. The Germans were driven back into central Tanzania but their forces remained intact. Meanwhile, Belgian forces occupied Ruanda-Urundi. The British moved into German East Africa from the northwest and the southwest.

Lettow-Vorbeck refused to be engaged in any major battles, making only brief stands and then escaping to regroup again. Smuts constantly pressed on to harass Lettow-Vorbeck and seek his capture. By January 1917, however, Smuts had not yet succeeded in engaging the Germans when he handed over command of his troops to General Arthur Hoskins. At the time of his departure, Smuts incorrectly concluded that the East African campaign was at an end. The British never succeeded in capturing Lettow-Vorbeck or in demolishing his force. Taking his troops into Northern Rhodesia (presently Zambia) via Mozambique, Lettow-Vorbeck was there at the time of the armistice.

Under terms of German surrender, Lettow-Vorbeck's force was dismissed at Tabora. Thus he achieved his original aim of pinning down large numbers of British forces in East Africa. Lettow-Vorbeck's great military genius, coupled with his ability to have his forces "live on the land" in guerrilla fashion, remains a monument in military annals.

As a result of this long conflict it was the determination of British settlers and military that, under no circumstance, should German East Africa revert to German rule in the postwar era. Britain even approached Italy informally to discuss an Italian takeover of the territory. Similar discussion was undertaken with American authorities who, under President Woodrow Wilson, refused to add further colonial territories to the American flag. It was South Africa's Smuts who successfully urged that the administration of German East Africa be taken over by Great Britain.[15] It was also he who suggested that the territory be administered as a League of Nations' "mandate" rather than as a Crown Colony. In expectation of this move British civil and military headquarters were set up in Dar es Salaam.

NOTES

1. R. Coupland, *East Africa and Its Invaders*, 1st ed. (Oxford: Clarendon Press, 1938), pp. 16ff.
2. Ibid., p. 23.
3. J.P. Moffett, ed., *Handbook of Tanganyika* (Dar es Salaam: Government Printer, 1958), p. 28.
4. Charles D. Ley, ed., *Portuguese Voyages—1498–1663* (New York: E.P. Dutton, 1947), pp. 19ff.
5. Moffett, *Handbook of Tanganyika*, pp. 29ff.
6. Coupland, *East Africa and Its Invaders*, pp. 368ff.
7. Ibid., p. 379.
8. Ibid., p. 384.
9. Moffett, *Handbook of Tanganyika*, pp. 79ff.
10. Ibid., pp. 48ff.
11. Ibid., pp. 51ff.
12. Ibid., pp. 55ff.
13. Ibid., p. 71.
14. A comprehensive study of World War I in East Africa, and especially of Von Lettow-Vorbeck's exploits, is to be found in Brian Gardner, *German East* (London: Cassell, 1963).
15. Judith Listowel, *The Making of Tanganyika* (London: Chatto & Windus, 1965), pp. 66ff.

CHAPTER 3

MANDATE AND TRUSTEESHIP: FIRST FOOTSTEPS IN POLITICAL DEVELOPMENT

In 1920 there appeared, in the language of the Treaty of Versailles, a new name—Tanganyika Territory—replacing the name German East Africa. Apparently the creation of a British civil servant, Sir Cosmo Parkinson, "Tanganyika" comes from the Swahili words *tanga* (meaning "sail") and *nyika* (meaning "bright arid plain").[1] The newly christened Tanganyika Territory became a mandate administered by the British under authority of the League of Nations.

To both the new British administrators and the African inhabitants the significance of the change from German to British rule was unclear. The British were unfamiliar with any kind of colonial rule other than direct supervision. They had no guidelines for associations with a third party such as the League of Nations. The Africans could only imperceptibly see prospects for improvement over their earlier German-dominated colonial status.

The concept of a "mandate," as finally set forth in Article 22 of the League Covenant, was originally envisaged by Prime Minister Jan Smuts of South Africa.[2] Smuts's idea was that former German colonies should not become the possessions of the conquerors but, rather, should be administered under impartial mandates associated with the League of Nations. These territories, as envisioned by Smuts, were to be led toward self-determination and eventual independence by the administering authorities. The League Covenant clause which eventually established this concept represented a compromise between the divergent views of President Wilson and those of European leaders. The

24

League's new mandate system divided the former German dependencies into three distinct classes—A, B, and C mandates grouped according to the political advancement of the individual colonies.

A Class B mandate status was assigned to the newly christened Tanganyika Territory. This mandate provided for freedom of religion; prohibited such international abuses as traffic in arms, liquor, and slaves; prohibited establishment of fortifications and naval bases; and prohibited military conscription of the indigenous inhabitants. It also sought to guarantee equal opportunity for trade and commerce in the area for all members of the League of Nations.

Article 22 also provided that the unique status of the territory could not be unilaterally altered either by the League of Nations or by the Mandatory Power. Furthermore, the inhabitants of the territory were to be trained and supervised by the Mandatory Power until they could stand on their own socially, economically, and politically. Further, the Mandatory Power agreed to submit to overall supervision by the League of Nations and to report annually to that body's Permanent Mandate Commission resident in Geneva.

Probably as a balance to his own wishes concerning the future administration of South-West Africa by South Africa, General Smuts pleaded persuasively that mandatory supervision over German East Africa be awarded to the British to permit linkup of British holdings in Africa from Cape to Cairo.[3] When the Belgians protested, they were pacified by receiving mandates over the amputated northwesterly segments of Tanganyika—known as Ruanda-Urundi (now the independent nations of Rwanda and Burundi). This action sheared away some 20,000 square miles and 3 million people from the former German East Africa.

At the end of World War I, Tanganyika Territory was being ruled by the victorious Allied powers, represented by the British civil servant Sir Horace Byatt. In 1920 his rule over the territory was formalized within the mandate system when Byatt was designated as Tanganyika's first governor and commander-in-chief.[4]

Byatt had to build up his new British administrative structure from scratch, and he had the twin tasks of repatriating German settlers and disposing of their properties. When their large plantations were put on sale many went to Greek and Asian buyers, relatively few going to British settlers. This fact became important in later years, since, unlike the neighboring British colony of Kenya, it meant that there was never a large claque of British white settlers demanding political autonomy and white control of Tanganyika.

During Byatt's rule one other important legacy was set up for the Tanzania of the future. This involved the breakup of certain German-owned estates—particularly the cotton and the coffee farms in the northwestern highlands—with assumption of fragmented leaseholds on those lands by Africans. This presaged the large African-owned-and-operated cotton and coffee cooperatives, of which more will be detailed elsewhere. Here then the Africans became cash-economy farmers of consequence. In part, it was the existence of this group which, in later years, gave the British administrators of Tanganyika justification to dispute and quell numerous efforts by London and Nairobi to unite Tanganyika with Kenya and Uganda.

Byatt's rule is perhaps significant for one other political innovation—the creation of an Executive Council, or governing board, headed by a chief secretary who functioned as the head of the civil service and as the governor's chief-of-staff. The five-man Council was created in 1920. Not until 1926 was an incipient parliamentary group, known as the Legislative Council, introduced. That Legislative Council, though presumably only an advisory body, eventually became the lawmaking body of the territory, subject, of course, to possible veto by the Colonial Office, the British Parliament and Privy Council, and the less direct, but still effective, Mandate Commission of the League of Nations.

It should be noted here that the Protectorate of Zanzibar, which included the fiefdom of the Kenya strip (the coastal strip of Kenya 200 miles long and 10 miles wide, including the city of Mombasa), continued under British "protection" and direct colonial rule as it had prior to World War I. This protectorate was administered by the British Colonial Office without recourse to, or association with, the League mandate of the Tanganyika mainland. This protectorate status was continued through the era of the League as well as through the Trusteeship era of the United Nations. The protectorate was not given up by Britain until December 1963, when Zanzibar became independent and the Kenya strip was merged into the newly independent nation of Kenya.

One of the most effective and important of Tanganyika's governors was Sir Donald Cameron, who succeeded Byatt in 1925. Cameron had previously served under Lord Lugard in Nigeria where he absorbed Lugard's concept of indirect rule, or utilization of native chiefdoms on a local basis in fields of customary law and local security. Indirect rule thus sought to make the remaining chiefdoms loyal local working allies and functionaries of the colonial administrator rather than his enemies. Cameron introduced and effectively utilized in Tanganyika this concept of indirect rule.[5]

During Cameron's administration an important change in British theories of colonialism took place. During the century or so preceding, British colonial philosophy had espoused the concept of "paramountcy" of native interests. This philosophy of "paramountcy" embodied the thesis that Britain served as custodian of the well-being and future of indigenous peoples. In essence it meant that Britain's colonial rule was a Kiplingesque "white man's burden" aimed at safeguarding and advancing indigenous interests to the point of eventual self-determination.

By 1925, however, under pressures of such white settler blocs as the highly vocal Kenyans and Southern Rhodesians, the "paramountcy" theory was overthrown for one of "coordination of native interests." This theory, in actuality, meant total subordination of native interests to European interests. In the face of this change and in the face of opposition from Kenya and his London superiors, Cameron extended a spur of the central rail line northwest from Tabora to Mwanza on Lake Victoria.[6] Opposition to that effort had been inspired, in large part, by continuing pressures of white settlers in Kenya and Uganda to subordinate Tanganyika economically and to amalgamate the territory into a single East African colonial state. It was Cameron who kept insisting that Tanganyika was a League mandate and not a British colonial possession.

As governor Cameron was also effective in giving central administrative direction to his far-flung staff and in pressing for expansion and diversification of Tanganyika's economy. He particularly sought infusion of new capital and expansion of education. His successful rule as governor extended from 1925 to 1931.

Two of Cameron's most important political accomplishments were the introduction of the Legislative Council (previously noted) and his establishment of the Tanganyika African Association.[7] This was a multiracial socio-political forum of civil servants designed to debate and discuss public issues. It had branches in several urban centers and sought to bring together Africans and whites on equal terms. Here then was the seedbed of the African nationalist movement, later culminating in the Tanganyika African National Union (TANU), which, under Julius Nyerere's brilliant leadership, successfully brought independence to the country in 1961. It is probable that Cameron's early efforts to inspire these nonracial associations and constructive political discussions helped to preclude violence and bloodshed in Tanganyika's movement toward nationhood.

It was unfortunate that the world depression of the 1930s coincided with the end of Cameron's tour as governor of Tanganyika. Both events had a depressing effect on Tanganyika's economy and stunted its growth. Prices of its prime products—sisal, coffee, and cotton—declined sharply, and it was not until after World War II that they recovered. Thus, during the entire decade of the 1930s, Tanganyika Territory failed to progress and instead drifted into the shadow of its neighbors and into the shadow of greater events in Europe and North Africa.

The hostilities of World War II brought little change in Tanganyika's drifting. There was some association of Tanganyikans, black and white, with the East African Allied campaign to free Ethiopia from Mussolini's invading armies. At the same time most German residents of the territory were repatriated or interned.

The really important effect of World War II on Tanganyika was that which came at the end of hostilities. Under the dying League of Nations the old

Tanganyika mandate had fallen into obsolescence and disrepute. The change in the status of Tanganyika from a mandate to a trust territory resulted from the demise of the League of Nations and the birth of the United Nations in 1945.

The alternative to continuation of the mandate as a trust was, of course, British assumption of Tanganyika as a colony. The British government recognized that this would have constituted a betrayal of its original contract with the League. However, there were many in East Africa and in Britain who urged British officials, including Arthur Creech-Jones (Colonial Office representative to the United Nations founding meeting in San Francisco), to recommend transfer of Tanganyika to true colonial status. The postwar Labour government of Britain resisted these pressures and instead moved for establishment of the trusteeship under United Nations auspices.[8] With the inception of the United Nations, Britain placed under the new trusteeship system the three former German territories of Africa it was then administering, namely, British Togo, British Cameroons, and Tanganyika.

The basic principles of both mandate and trust were essentially the same. Both insisted on protection and advancement of the interests of the indigenous peoples. Both provided that the administering authority could not be unilaterally abolished. Both declared the objective that the administering power's tutelage should eventually enable backward peoples to stand on their own feet. However, the United Nations Charter went on to lay out, far more specifically, requirements on the administering authority.

The erection of the new trusteeship system under the United Nations Charter gave an unexpected fillip of vitality and mobility to Tanganyika's internal and external situation. As the old Class B mandate faded into the new trusteeship status, there was new and increasing pressure on Britain (as the ruling authority) to provide self-rule for this and other colonial dominions. This pressure was inspired by newer members of the United Nations, themselves so recently independent. As a result of these pressures, far sooner than expected Britain would be forced to give this trust protégé full independence and nationhood.

The trusts encouraged human rights and fundamental freedoms for all without distinction as to race, sex, or religion. Unlike the mandates, the peoples of the trust territories had to be consulted by the administering authority and the United Nations whenever basic interests were affected. Internal political and economic requirements took priority over those of outsiders, including the administering power. Under the League the mandatory power had been forbidden to exploit the military potential of the territories administered. Under the United Nations, however, the administering authority was encouraged to develop and make use of volunteer forces in furtherance of international peace and internal security.

The greatest difference, however, lay in the international supervision by the

United Nations as contrasted with the League. Individual members of the Permanent Mandates Commission of the League had sat in Geneva, unconcerned with the real political development of the various mandates. Members of the new United Nations Trusteeship Council, on the other hand, representing all of the great powers as well as the various administering authorities, took active, direct, and daily interest in the development of their trust protégés. Thus did the Trusteeship Council accurately reflect the new international climate of postwar concern for anticolonialism and self-determination. Furthermore, under the mandate, representatives of indigenous groupings residing thereunder could only launch complaints through the mandatory power. Under the trusteeship system, however, complainants could appear before the Trusteeship Council as petitioners. (Thus in 1955 Julius Nyerere was permitted to appear before the United Nations Trusteeship Council as a petitioner and was to influence materially the future course of his country's history.)

In Tanganyika, oddly enough, no official word had been given concerning a new trust status. First public and official announcement of the change of status came from Ernest Bevin (then United Kingdom foreign secretary) speaking to the point in January 1946 in a House of Commons debate:

We welcome the Trusteeship Council . . . and we are ready to accept the obligations which will rest upon us as administering authority under the new system. The peoples of the territories themselves and the world at large should be left in no doubt that the continuity of administration will be maintained, until the ultimate object of the Trusteeship system, self-government or independence, is attained.[9]

Following upon this statement by bureaucratic action, there was published in July 1946 a so-called Command Paper 6840 entitled "Trusteeship Territories in Africa under United Kingdom Mandate." Tanganyika's Executive Council member, Sir Charles Phillips, in Dar es Salaam, issued a paper indicating approval of the trusteeship status for Tanganyika under an Executive Council order. This resolution appeared as an annex to the Command Paper.[10]

These actions were taken without prior consultation with the indigenous inhabitants of Tanganyika. Britain had no presumable obligation to consult with the inhabitants and the very task of informing them (then over 90 percent illiterate) would have been formidable. Thus Britain took no direct action to formalize its new status as administering authority. Instead, the mandate seemed simply to float into the trust with tacit acceptance.

Some Europeans and Asians of the territory considered these actions arbitrary on the part of a British government, especially one of Labour complexion. In any event, Tanganyika's trust status under British administration was accepted by the General Assembly of the United Nations in December 1946. It would be only fifteen years from that date—December 1961—when Tanganyika would accede to full independence.

There should now be recorded an event occurring in Tanganyika which was of considerable importance. This was the so-called Groundnut Scheme of 1946–50,[11] a plan that sought to achieve a unique and swift development of Tanganyika's resources by costly means. It caught the world's fancy but ended in financial and agricultural failure.

The Groundnut Scheme sought production of 600,000 tons of groundnuts (peanuts) yearly in Tanganyika—this where none had grown before. The project was located on 5,000 square miles of territory in central and southern Tanganyika. The scheme required massive logistics, settlement, and clearance efforts. It was to be solely governmental, rather than private. The eventual aim was to give over the 3 million acres of cleared and planted lands to the indigenous Africans of the territory. This in turn was to be developed into a massive cooperative enterprise for production and marketing of groundnuts as a means of alleviating then existing world shortages of vegetable oils.

By 1950 the British government was publicly to acknowledge its complete failure. In hindsight the scheme failed to comprehend such problems as the heavy seasonal rains which made developmental activities immobile. There was also insufficient expertise employed in soils study and labor utilization. Finally, the world shortages of fats and oils which had originally propelled this scheme into being had now been alleviated. In the short three years of its life, the Groundnut Scheme had reportedly cost the British taxpayer (and, indirectly, the Tanganyikans on whom the money might have been more wisely spent) the sum of 30 million pounds. Eventually the assets of the Groundnut Scheme were given over to the Tanganyika Agricultural Corporation, which operated somewhat more successfully though far less spectacularly.[12]

Tanganyika's political and economic development immediately following World War II and until 1950 had been exceptionally slow. The lag was especially noticeable when compared with Britain's other major African colonial ventures. In West Africa both Ghana and Nigeria were speeding toward self-rule. Their economies were expanding and outside capital was beginning to flow into both countries. In East Africa the economy of Kenya was burgeoning. Southern Rhodesia, for some years past, had enjoyed internal autonomy and was now, under Britain's aegis, federating with Northern Rhodesia (now Zambia) and with Nyasaland (now Malawi). In Tanganyika, on the other hand, movement toward self-rule had been almost imperceptible. The economy, too, was lagging, despite the costly injection of the Groundnut Scheme.

It had now become apparent to officials in Whitehall, and to certain more far-sighted members of the United Nations Trusteeship Council, that Britain would be required to pursue more sagacious and far-reaching economic and political paths if Tanganyika were ever to attain the self-government and independence envisaged for such trusts. The British wish to improve the situation in Tanganyika resulted in the selection of a new and more dynamic governor, Sir Edward Twining, to replace the wholly ineffective governor, Sir William Battersill. In some ways Twining proved to be a useful leader, yet his imperiousness and nineteenth-century colonial mentality proved highly controversial and retrograde.

Twining had been governor of the Windward Islands and of North Borneo. Thus he had a background of senior colonial responsibility. It is understood that, on his appointment to Tanganyika, Twining was instructed by his British superior to prepare the territory for eventual self-rule and independence. In anticipation of those goals, Twining was instructed to strengthen the economy and to bring the indigenous population into active association with the government. To Twining's credit, it must be admitted that he gave a certain new energy to the British civil servants administering the trust. He likewise gave new life to the territorial economy by encouraging expansion of sisal, cotton, coffee, and tea production. He also placed the territory's financial situation on a sounder footing. This latter was accomplished by placing an export levy (or cess) on certain primary products, particularly sisal, the price of which had increased markedly as a result of the Korean War. During his regime, too, Twining, by strong security methods, successfully protected Tanganyika against Mau Mau invaders who had infiltrated from Kenya.[13]

Results of Twining's administration in the political arena were largely on the debit side, though he gave some new life to the territory's Executive and Legislative Councils. In the Legislative Council he initiated a system of racial "parity," including therein whites, Asians, and black Africans. (The ratio he established was, however, unfair to the heavily preponderant black African population.) Furthermore, rather than remaining aloof from party politics as an impartial governor of a trust territory, Twining insisted on active participation in and dominance over the presumably multiracial (but white-dominated) so-called Government Party, the United Tanganyika Party. As a result, this party became a personal political tool of Governor Twining and certain of the more influential white settlers. This fact plus the formula of the 1-1-1 "parity" only served to inflame the racial issue and to provide extra catalytic action for growth of African nationalism in the territory. The debate over these and related issues coincided with the return to Tanganyika of a young African, Julius Nyerere, who had just completed political studies at Edinburgh University. Nyerere provided immediate and inspired leadership for the few young African nationalists in the territory, and from then on he furnished the central focus of their activities.

It should be noted that, almost as an accident and in possible hope of making him a political conformist, Twining, in May 1954, appointed Nyerere a "temporary" member of the territory's Legislative Council. Nyerere held that post only a short time, substituting for a regular member, David Makwaia, who was then serving on an interim Royal Commission. This legislative exposure redoubled Nyerere's determination to create a political role for himself.

At once Nyerere and his associates began to build an African nationalist group (not yet a movement) which utilized the African Association format inspired two decades earlier by Sir Donald Cameron. At the outset the efforts of African politicians were weak, financially frustrating, and so frail as to fail to arouse the interest or suspicion of Governor Twining. Allied with this failure on the part of Twining was his even greater failure, as governor of a trust territory, to comprehend the great waves of nationalism which were then sweeping over Africa from Senegal to Kenya and from Algeria to the Cape of Good Hope. In retrospect it seems clear that Twining's major failure to recognize the strength and breadth of African nationalism—as well as its epitomization in Tanganyika in the persons of Nyerere and his colleagues —gave the real opening for realization of Nyerere's political potentials and goals. As Nyerere himself has stated to the author, "Twining, by his failure to recognize our existence, gave us our real opportunity."

NOTES

1. J.P. Moffett, *Handbook of Tanganyika* (Dar es Salaam: Government Printer, 1958), p. 89.
2. W.K. Hancock, *Smuts*, vol. 1: *The Sanguine Years (1870–1919)* (London: Cambridge University Press, 1962), pp. 502ff.
3. Ibid., pp. 539ff.
4. Judith Listowel, *The Making of Tanganyika* (London: Chatto & Windus, 1965), p. 67.
5. Moffett, *Handbook of Tanganyika*, pp. 318ff.
6. M.F. Hill, *Permanent Way*, Story of the Tanganyika Railways, vol. 2 (Nairobi: East African Railways & Harbours, 1957), pp. 213ff.
7. Listowel, *Making of Tanganyika*, p. 82.
8. Ibid., pp. 123ff.
9. Ibid., p. 125.
10. Ibid., pp. 125–26.
11. Moffett, *Handbook of Tanganyika*, pp. 133ff.
12. Ibid., p. 143.
13. Listowel, *Making of Tanganyika*, p. 162.

CHAPTER 4

POLITICAL DEVELOPMENT: PRELUDE TO INDEPENDENCE

On July 7, 1954, Julius Nyerere with a few of his compatriots founded the Tanganyika African National Union (TANU). The day is still commemorated in Tanzania as *Saba Saba* Day—meaning the seventh day of the seventh month. On that day in 1954 Nyerere brought himself and his followers forcefully to Governor Twining's attention by adopting a resolution challenging the authority of the British queen, Elizabeth II, as sovereign over Tanganyika.[1]

At that moment a personal and bitter struggle between Twining and Nyerere began. Until then Twining had failed to take Nyerere seriously. Twining contended that Nyerere's manifesto condemning the sovereignty of the queen and creating the Tanganyika African National Union insisted on "Africa for the Africans" and Tanganyika only for its black African inhabitants. Thus it held out no place for either the white and Asian settlers or the British administrators. Twining had failed to recognize the validity of Nyerere's thesis of majority rule, given the preponderance of the African population of the territory. Certainly, in terms of the demands of other African leaders of the time, these demands of Nyerere, set within the context of the aims of the United Nations Trusteeship, were neither racial nor radical. Twining failed to recognize the nature of African nationalism both inside and outside Tanganyika. He failed to appreciate that Tanganyika was a United Nations trust and not a British Crown Colony. These failures of judgment on Twining's part made Nyerere a national figure, assured success to TANU as a political movement, and hastened Tanganyika's independence.

The arrival in Tanganyika in August 1954 of a United Nations Visiting

33

Mission, just one month after the formation of TANU, broadened Nyerere's strength and political opportunities. The United Nations group included the late Mason Sears, United States Permanent Representative on the United Nations Trusteeship Council. Sears was a volatile man of strong liberal conviction and highly motivated idealism. The immediate association of views of Sears with Nyerere's basic aims further infuriated and isolated Twining from the realities of the situation. Twining, unfortunately, claimed that Nyerere and his group did not represent nationwide African views and that the Africans, in fact, had no recognized national spokespeople or leaders. This contention inflamed Nyerere. He and his group placed their thoughts in writing before the United Nations Visiting Mission. They also talked at length privately with individual members of that mission. They asked, too, for permission to appear before the United Nations as petitioners seeking independence for Tanganyika.

The report of the 1954 United Nations Visiting Mission proved to be a time bomb for Twining and the British government. Sears, highly impressed with Nyerere and with his aims, insisted that the British plan independence for Tanganyika in the shortest possible time. This target, Sears contended, should be set for no later than twenty years. (Actually Tanganyika attained independence within seven years.)

The British government refused to accept the recommendations of the Visiting Mission. The recommendations likewise failed to obtain the approval of the United Nations Trusteeship Council. Mason Sears was forced to retract certain of his own conclusions concerning a target date for Tanganyika's independence. In explanation of his part in the affair Sears has reported to the author (in a letter dated March 10, 1973) that Secretary of State John Foster Dulles said that " . . . as a member of the Mission I [Sears] had a perfect right to make any recommendation I saw right but as a representative of the United States he [Dulles] required me to disavow my strong belief in target dates, etc."

Sears goes on to say: ". . . The Belgians and the British were irate about target dates but it was the British who kicked up the biggest fuss. So in the end it was the Americans who caved in. . . . [In] a short statement [made before the Trusteeship Council] I said I differed with my own government but that I did not represent government policy."

In March 1955 Nyerere appeared for the first time before the Trusteeship Council of the United Nations. In an atmosphere of considerable heat, the report of the Visiting Mission was still being debated. The United States and the Soviet Union were leading the attack against Britain as the administering authority. In their own defense, the British (whose delegation included the attorney general of Tanganyika, A.J. Gratten-Ballew), contended that to fix a target date for Tanganyikan independence (as Sears had suggested) would be to cut economic input and to create political insecurity in the territory. The argument was made, too, that the Africans of Tanganyika were not yet ready to govern themselves, in fact that the preponderance of Africans in the territory were apolitical and against independence for Tanganyika.

In Nyerere's countering statement to the Trusteeship Council, he indicated that his main purpose in coming to New York was to shatter the thesis that the Africans of Tanganyika were opposed to the recommendations of the recent Visiting Mission. Nyerere then elaborated upon TANU's main goal—that of preparing the people of Tanganyika for self-rule and independence. He asked United Nations help in establishing the democratic elective system in Tanganyika, and he sought the elimination of the artificial barriers imposed by the "parity" elective system. He asked that the Africans of Tanganyika be given assurances that they would eventually attain to majority rule in the territory.

Nyerere was praised for his tolerance in stating that "TANU sought not discrimination but brotherhood" and that he believed the United Kingdom, as administering authority, held the same view. In all his comments he played down any criticism of Governor Twining and, in fact, sought to create the illusion that Twining, like Nyerere, was seeking to strive toward eventual self-government for all the races of Tanganyika. Nyerere's statement is also remarkable for the clarity with which it sets forth his party's aims for Tanganyika's peaceful, but determined, movement toward independence. The most important elements of that statement are quoted below:

This is the first time since Tanganyika became a Trust Territory that an African from there has been sent here by a territorial organization to express his people's hopes and fears. . . . My people are very grateful for this historic opportunity. . . . The outrageous assertion was made that the vast majority of the Territory's inhabitants were against the major political recommendations of [the] report [of the last Visiting Mission]. I have been sent here to tell the Council that that claim is unfounded. . . . The recommendations of the last Visiting Mission have given us great hope and fresh confidence. . . .

What does my organization [TANU] stand for? Politically, its major object, as declared in its constitution, is to prepare the people of Tanganyika for self-government and independence. As a first step towards that goal, my organization seeks to see the elective principle established, and the African securing a majority on all representative bodies of a public nature. This, we believe, is in accordance with the terms of the Trusteeship Agreement and Article 76 of the United Nations Charter.

When, therefore, the United Nations Visiting Mission made the recommendation that Tanganyika should become self-governing in a period of twenty or twenty-five years, we did not expect that either this Council or the Administering Authority would express violent opposition to that proposal, for, although we have never stated a date when we should be self-governing, we had expected that, with your help and with the help of the Administering Authority, we would be governing ourselves long before twenty or twenty-five years. For how can we be left behind when our neighbours are forging ahead?

I think that it is somewhat unrealistic to estimate the ability of a community to govern itself by looking at its least progressive members. If that were the case, I doubt whether any country in the world would be self-governing. . . . In our view, the best way of estimating our ability to govern ourselves in twenty or twenty-five years is to ask whether, in that period, we can have local men—Africans, Asians, and Europeans—sufficiently trained and sufficiently experienced to run the government of the country. . . .

I come now to the important question of constitutional development. The foundation on which we want to see all constitutional development built is the firm belief that although Tanganyika is multi-racial in population, it is primarily African. We have accepted the principle of parity of representation on our Legislative Council, but we have accepted it on the understanding that it is a transitional state towards a more democratic form of representation. . . . We want an assurance that future forms of representation will be in the direction of giving the Africans a majority on all representative bodies of a public nature. . . . What will satisfy my people is a categorical statement, both by this Council and by the Administering Authority, that although Tanganyika is multi-racial in population, its future government shall be primarily African. . . .

Our major objective, politically, is the preparation of the people of Tanganyika for self-government and independence. . . . We mean to work towards self-government in a constitutional manner.[2]

From this time on, Nyerere had as his most influential foreign friends a majority of the United Nations Trusteeship Council. The activities of individual members of that Council in the years to follow before Tanganyika attained independence were in sharp contrast to the excessive timidity and fear of certain British administrators in London and Dar es Salaam. In reaction to Nyerere's foregoing statement the British asked that the United States restrict Nyerere to the United Nations headquarters area of New York. As noted previously the British also insisted on a retraction by Mason Sears and they excluded Sears from Tanganyika for several years. This ban on Sears disappeared only after Twining's departure as governor. (When Sears revisited Tanganyika for the first time thereafter, in 1959, the new governor, Sir Richard Turnbull, not only rescinded the earlier Twining ban but invited Sears to be his personal house guest.)

Unfortunately, Twining, after the 1954 mission experience, took one more vengeful action. He asked the U.S. State Department, through the British Colonial and Foreign Offices, to remove the then U.S. consul in Dar es Salaam. That consul, Robert MacKinnon, a knowledgeable and liberal foreign service career officer, now deceased, was recalled to Washington in deference to Twining. A "more conservative" United States representative, Consul Robert Ware, was sent to Tanganyika in MacKinnon's stead. Twining's sole justification for requesting MacKinnon's removal appeared to be that MacKinnon had been too friendly with Nyerere and with members of the "Sears" Visiting Mission.

The next United Nations Visiting Mission (1957) did not prove as bombastic and controversial as had the preceding mission of 1954. In the light of events elsewhere in Africa (such as Ghana's independence) it became self-evident, however, that Twining with his nineteenth-century colonial mentality would soon need to be replaced.

During the early part of 1957 Governor Twining imposed a ban on Nyerere's public speaking activities. However the ban was soon lifted, Twining presumably being under pressure from both London and New York. In July 1957 Nyerere was nominated as a representative member of the Legislative Council. He resigned from that post in December 1957, utilizing his party's broadsheet *Sauti ya Tanu* (Voice of TANU) to explain his departure. He indicated that he had accepted the post in the belief that Twining's government had a "change of heart." In a ten-point memorandum Nyerere specified his disillusion with the government's constitutional actions designed to block movement toward majority rule.[3] Nyerere stressed throughout that he could no longer compromise with Twining or with his own conscience on such matters.

In permitting himself to become a foil and a *bête noire* for Nyerere's African nationalists, Twining made other blunders as well. He instituted a libel suit against Nyerere for allegedly defaming two British district officers, thus building up Nyerere's national eminence among his fellow Africans. The libel suit arose out of an angry editorial written by Nyerere which appeared in *Sauti ya Tanu*, on May 27, 1958. That editorial warned against incendiary activities by "bush governors who think they are above the law." Nyerere went on to insist that his followers wage their war against colonialism only by nonviolent means.[4]

On July 9, 1958, hearings began on the libel case against Nyerere. (Twining had departed the territory for retirement after the case had been instituted but before the trial.) The case was badly mishandled from beginning to end by government prosecutors, the territory's attorney general even being cited for contempt of court in the process.[5]

On August 11, 1958, the court's judgment was rendered, Nyerere being fined 150 pounds or, in lieu, six months in prison. With TANU funds he paid the fine. In retrospect it seems clear that, had Nyerere gone to jail and had Twining remained on the scene, the road toward Tanganyika's independence would have been far more rocky. Nyerere later jokingly told the author that he regretted he had not gone to jail over the affair at that time. Thereby he claimed he would have joined an internationally distinguished group of British colonial "prison graduates," which included Gandhi, Nehru, Kenyatta, Nkrumah, Banda, and others.

Between the dates of hearings on the government's libel suit against Nyerere and the date of sentence, Tanganyika's new governor, Sir Richard Turnbull, was sworn into office. In the later view of many, including Nyerere, Turnbull was to become Tanganyika's greatest governor. He was a man of exceptional administrative skill and political know-how. Turnbull was to have an immediate and electric effect on Tanganyika's drive toward independence and nationhood. In fact, his influence in helping Tanganyika to achieve nationhood was, in historical terms, second only to that of Nyerere.

Sir Richard Turnbull had come to Tanganyika after more than twenty-five years of colonial service in nearby Kenya. He was accepted in Dar es Salaam with some mistrust at first. He had attained to the post of Kenya's chief secretary—a post he held during the Mau Mau rebellion. He had acquired an undeserved reputation in Kenya for being heavy-handed with Africans. It was conceded, however, that his work in quashing the Mau Mau outbreak in Kenya had been brilliant. Thus, as a newcomer to Tanganyika, Turnbull was expected to be nothing less than a tyrant. It was surprising to the local populace to find instead that Turnbull had at heart the interests of all the populace, but especially those of the Africans. Even in his acceptance speech of July 15, 1958, delivered in fluent Swahili, Turnbull evidenced his willingness to aid the territory in its quest for independence. From the outset he emphasized that traditional chiefs and the new nationalist TANU leaders needed to work together with his British administration.

In his letter of farewell, dated December 4, 1962, to Sir Richard Turnbull (by then an independent Tanganyika's governor general), Nyerere warmheartedly and humorously described their first meeting of July 24, 1958. In part, Nyerere wrote:

Then you came. I expected that you would want to meet me, but I imagined you would wait until I had been sentenced (for the libel affair). To my surprise you did not; but called me to Government House while the case was still undecided. . . . I remember your first words to me: "I am glad to meet you, Mr. Nyerere. You and I have a great responsibility in this country."

Then we got down to business . . . during which I explained our demands for Responsible Government. By that we meant a majority of Elected Members of Legco, and a majority of Elected Ministers in the Government. These, you thought, were "reasonable" demands. . . . It had not occurred to me that the Bad Sir Richard would be of the same mind. . . . In spite of my original contention that all colonial Governors were the same to me, my first meeting with you had persuaded me that *one* Governor, at least, deserved to be given a chance. My going to prison would have given you no chance at all. It would have meant certain trouble. I chose to pay the fine . . . and . . . I cannot honestly say I have ever regretted my decision. . . . If my reputation as an agitator is slightly dimmed by my inability to add the letters "P.G." after my name, you must accept the blame for that. For, however inapproapriate the term "reasonable" may be for an agitator, a "reasonable" Governor is sufficiently rare a phenomenon to unsettle even the most orthodox of nationalists.[6]

In September 1958 Nyerere was elected a member of the territorial legislature representing the Eastern Province, including Dar es Salaam. TANU-sponsored candidates won all the elective seats which they had contested. After assuming his seat Nyerere was unanimously elected leader of the Tanganyika Elected Members Organization (TEMO). Thus, in effect, he became Leader of the Opposition in the Legislative Council. Immediately thereafter, Nyerere made one of his more sagacious political moves. Speaking in the Legislative Council on October 15, 1958, Nyerere publicly stretched out a welcoming hand to the new governor, Sir Richard Turnbull. In his address Nyerere said:

I . . . have the most pleasant duty . . . in welcoming the Governor and Lady Turnbull to Tanganyika. . . . It is not . . . very easy for a Colonial country like Tanganyika struggling for its freedom, to welcome the appointment of any Governor, unless of course, the Governor has specific instructions to end the Colonial status of that Country. But I think it is agreed, Sir, by all sections of the community . . . that, during the very short period his Excellency has been in this country, he has earned the respect of all sections of the community.

His Excellency said there has been some misunderstanding, misapprehension, in this country as to the multi-racial policy and His Excellency said that he would prefer to use the word "non-racial" . . . and this misapprehension has been a very sound misapprehension. . . . When there was an emphasis in this country on multi-racial policies, we felt, with great justification, that there was something sinister about this multi-racial policy in Tanganyika. . . . I do not even like the word "non-racial" to be used in any policy in Tanganyika. . . . What we do want . . . is that every citizen of Tanganyika, irrespective of his race, as long as he owes allegiance to Tanganyika, is a complete and equal citizen with anyone else. . . .

I was very pleased . . . when His Excellency [said], "It is intended . . . that when self-government is eventually attained, both the Legislature and the Government are likely to be predominantly African [and this] should in no way affect the security of the rights and interests of those minority communities who have made their homes in Tanganyika." We have always waited for a Governor of this country, even to indicate that it was Government's policy that when self-government is eventually attained in this country that the Africans will have a predominant say in the affairs of the country. . . . Once you have made that statement you have removed the fears of the Africans.[7]

Thus, through the foregoing statement, Nyerere made three important moves: He publicly extended the hand of friendship to the new governor; he pressed his views for a "non-racial" society in Tanganyika; he pushed the Colonial Office and the British government into recognition that any future government of the country was bound to be African.

In March 1959 Governor Turnbull announced proposals for constitutional advance for the territory. A new Council of Ministers was established with five of these drawn from the recently elected TANU legislative membership. Three of the five were African, one Asian, and one white. On March 19 Nyerere's nationalist members accepted the proposal on the basis that the offer showed movement toward what he characterized as "semi-responsible government." Nyerere himself refused to accept a ministerial portfolio though it was offered to him. Sagaciously, as he informed the author at the time, he preferred instead to push for independence from outside the government.

On December 16, 1959, Governor Turnbull announced that Tanganyika would be granted responsible self-government in 1960 after new general elections. In those elections Nyerere and his TANU supporters won all but one of the elective seats in the Legislative Council. Following this electoral sweep in March 1961, Tanganyika was granted full internal self-government by Britain. Nyerere became prime minister. On December 9, 1961, the country acceded to full independence.

In building their political movement, Nyerere and his lieutenants concentrated on three major objectives—independence, unity, and equality. In seeking to make these relevant to the daily life of Tanganyika's workmen, herdsmen, and farmers, Nyerere and colleagues emphasized the necessity of seeking freedom from poverty, ignorance, and disease. He did so in a parliamentary address, delivered December 16, 1959, answering Governor Turnbull's announcement that responsible self-government would be introduced in 1960.

His precise words were: "Our greatest task must be to win the war against the three chief enemies of our people—disease, poverty and ignorance. . . ."[8] Thus it seems to have been Nyerere who, among world leaders, first used this now-famous phraseology.

It is a fact of Tanzania's political history that Nyerere and his confreres were able to establish TANU as a political party in July 1954 and, in the short space of seven years, were to make of it a unified national movement which peacefully achieved the country's independence. In his writings and speeches Nyerere, quite properly, insists that this was not "out of thin air." Nor does he attribute any exceptional political sense to his people. Instead, he points out, the movement and the main objectives of nationhood were attained by conjunction and an admixture of a series of favorable political circumstances, internal and external.

Among the most important of the favorable internal circumstances were (1) Tanganyika was a United Nations Trust Territory; (2) the experience of the chieftaincies of the many tribal groups provided valuable leadership on which TANU could quickly build; (3) the country was so undeveloped that there existed in Tanganyika no vocal and politically restive special-interest groups such as existed among the white settlers of Kenya and Rhodesia; (4) Swahili provided a link among the various tribes as *lingua franca*; (5) no single tribe dominated all others in the territory, in size, wealth, education, or monopoly of leadership. All these factors combined to provide fertile soil for a quickly unifying movement toward self-government.

Among the favorable external factors were the pressures of nationalism throughout the Afro-Asian world, led by India and Pakistan in the late 1940s and projected into Africa by Ghana and Algeria in the late 1950s. These pressures turned attention upon such territories as Tanganyika and upon its upcoming nationalist leaders—in the world press, in church and educational circles, in the United Nations corridors—and finally upon Britain as the administering authority for Tanganyika.

It is now time for a closer look at Nyerere and for an examination of TANU, the political movement which brought independence to Tanganyika.

NOTES

1. Judith Listowel, *The Making of Tanganyika* (London: Chatto & Windus, 1965), p. 244.
2. Julius K. Nyerere, *Freedom and Unity* (London: Oxford University Press, 1966), pp. 35ff.
3. Ibid., pp. 48ff.
4. Ibid., p. 59.
5. Listowel, *Making of Tanganyika*, pp. 328ff.
6. Ibid., pp. 424–25.
7. Tanganyika Legislative Council Notes (Hansard), October 15, 1958.
8. Nyerere, *Freedom and Unity*, p. 80.

CHAPTER 5

JULIUS K. NYERERE: FOUNDER-PRESIDENT

What manner of man is Nyerere? It has been the author's privilege to have been well-acquainted with President Nyerere for the past twenty years and during that time to have held more than a hundred private conversations with him. Over that period the author has also heard Nyerere's ringing perorations in public forums varying from political rallies in an open field to the sanctimonious chambers of the United Nations. As a result of these associations the author has often been asked by Europeans, Americans, and Africans of many nationalities to characterize Nyerere.

Nyerere is slight in stature, fine-featured, dapper, with curly hair that was once black and is now gray. He sports a small Chaplinesque mustache. Invariably and jauntily he carries a walking stick. In dress, in his early years, he preferred flashy Western-type sport shirts and dinner jacket. In recent years he has favored a variation of the Chinese-style peasant suit.

Nyerere has a personality which can best be described as incandescent. He can turn the charm off and on at will. In conversation he can be scintillating but seldom hard, pedantic but never boring. He lacks most of the vanities and conceits of the world's great. He is able to laugh at his own mistakes. He is never arrogant. His face reflects his many moods. He has a bright, lively face with sparkling brown eyes. He has an infectious, yet sometimes mischievous, smile. On occasion he can be morose and impenetrable, then assuming an obtuse "African mask."

Nyerere is highly intelligent and loves debate. His is inclined to philosophize in conversation but not to the point of loquaciousness. Nyerere speaks and writes eloquently. His writings and speeches are invariably his own and he is likely to seclude himself if working on an important statement. This is in sharp contrast to many other statesmen of his age who are so dependent on speechwriters or their own verbosity.

Nyerere is intensely human, affectionate toward family and friends, earthy rather than pompous. He has made caustic criticism of "pomposity" as shown in an instruction issued to his ministers on July 13, 1963. That letter outlined the dangers inherent in confusing dignity with pomposity.[1]

Nyerere is intensely loyal to friends, as attested by his long friendship with Prime Minister Rashidi Kawawa and other of his ministerial colleagues. This selfless loyalty sometimes tends to interfere with his administrative clout. It took a long time for Nyerere to react to the widely recognized disloyalties of certain of his lieutenants (described later in this book). Nyerere appears slow to anger but slow to forgive humiliation, falsehood, and treachery. He is consistently honest, reliable, and sincere.

In sum, Nyerere is a man of great charm, poise, intelligence, attractive alike to the elite and to the masses. If one could make a simple comparative capsule characterization it would be that he is like Adlai Stevenson, though with greater political flair, finesse, and success. Like Stevenson, too, he is an idealist but, unlike Stevenson, he has gained pragmatism with political responsibility. He has the charisma of John Kennedy, the friendly cheerfulness of Gerald Ford, the gentility of George McGovern, the elan of Winston Churchill. He has the political acumen of Robert Kennedy and, like Kennedy, cannot ignore the agony of others.

Nyerere is a practicing and devout Catholic. This cloak of his faith Nyerere wears gracefully in a country predominantly animist and Muslim. At no time, however, has he permitted his religious convictions to sway him in his efforts in behalf of his countrymen.

Nyerere is 100 percent African, but for Tanzania he seeks a useful mix of the modern and the traditional, the industrial and the agricultural societies blended. Holding firmly to the thesis that Africa belongs to the Africans, he contends that his people have the right to shape their country, their economy, their political and social systems, according to their needs. He is anti-colonialist, anti-imperialist, antiracist, and innately democratic. He believes these attitudes are essential if Tanzania is not to have a "paper independence."

Nyerere's concept of the state is strongly rooted in the African tradition of the clan, the extended family, and the consensus of palaver. Here everyone works for the benefit of the clan, the tribe, the nation, and all are responsible for the security of each member, young or old. The nationalization of land and property which Nyerere has effected in Tanzania is construed by him to support his humanistic social thought and the needs of the community. This idea is best exemplified in Nyerere's famous Arusha Declaration (see chapter 9).

Certain astute observers of Nyerere's government have pointed to the fact that, without taking brutish dictatorial actions, Nyerere's regime has lasted more than a decade—this despite great economic odds and several periods of internal traumas. There do not yet seem to be major signs that Nyerere has outlived his political popularity or outlasted his role as his country's founder-leader. In part this success may stem from the fact that Nyerere accepts unquestioningly for himself the burdens which he asks others to take up. Illustrative is the fact that he formally requested the Tanzania Parliament to reduce his salary (along with those of his ministers) by one-third. Furthermore, he does not like the stateliness of the Government House (the country's preindependence colonial "White House"). Instead, he lives quietly with his family in a secure but much less pretentious dwelling in the northern environs of Dar es Salaam. He has commented to the author that he prefers not to live in Government House, since it reminds him and his people too much of "earlier colonial times." He desires few of the usual trappings of the modern chief of state.

Finally, as indicative of Nyerere's democratic aspirations for his nation (and in sharp contrast to other African leaders such as Kwame Nkrumah and Haile Selassie), Nyerere has refused to be named president for life. He insists that the selection of a president should take place at regular (now five-year) intervals. (The next presidential election is scheduled for 1980.) Both friends and acidulous critics judge President Nyerere to be one of the best among the present leaders of Africa.

Julius Kambarage Nyerere was born at Butiama, a village near Musoma in northwestern Tanzania. The year was 1922, the precise date unknown. His father was chief of the small Zanaki tribe numbering 40,000 persons. Nyerere's father died in 1943 at the age of eighty-two, reportedly having sired twenty-six children from eighteen wives. Nyerere's mother, Mugaya, who bore her husband six children, remains close to her famed son. The name Nyerere in the Zanaki language means "caterpillar." This name was apparently given Nyerere's father to denote the fact that, in the year of the latter's birth (1860), the countryside was infested with these creatures.

Nyerere's childhood was much like that of other African children in a rural tribal environment. As a small boy he shepherded the family livestock. A precocious child, Nyerere pressed his family to permit him to attend school. He was allowed to attend boarding school in Musoma (on the eastern shore of Lake Victoria), where he soon led his class. There he developed an interest in the Catholic religion and there he prepared for entry into the Tabora Government Secondary School in 1937. He was baptized into the Catholic faith in 1943. Nyerere entered Makerere University in Kampala, Uganda, in the same year, remaining there until 1945.

During his two years at Makerere, Nyerere became acquainted with a number of other young black African scholars. These were later destined to be political leaders, some of them his own lieutenants. Among them were Abdulla Fundikira and Ibrahim Sapi, both sons of famous Tanganyika chieftains. This group of young African aristocrats composed an intellectual nucleus for nationalistic thought and discussion. In that atmosphere Nyerere developed his debating techniques, his brilliant discursive talents, and his political idealism. There too he took particular interest in the history of activities and political potential of the Tanganyika African Association which, many years before, Sir Donald Cameron had founded as an African social study group. In this weak and primarily social organization Nyerere foresaw a vehicle of eventual political utility in his own land. He and several of his Makerere associates decided that, when they returned to their native Tanganyika, they would reactivate and broaden the Tanganyika African Association into a nationwide political organization.

After the years at Makerere, Nyerere returned to Tabora. There he accepted a teaching post at St. Mary's Catholic Boys' School, operated by the White Fathers. At St. Mary's he came under the tutelage of Father Richard Walsh, a man who, along with various Catholic Maryknoll missionaries of the Musoma area (particularly Father William J. Collins) had considerable influence on Nyerere's life and thought. At St. Mary's College in Tabora Nyerere taught history and biology. Reports of those years from fellow instructors and from students give clear indication of Nyerere's popularity, imagination, and talents. At Tabora, too, Nyerere continued his interest in resuscitating the Tanganyika African Association and he became an officer of the Tabora branch. Nyerere remained at Tabora until 1949, when he entered Edinburgh University. From Edinburgh he received a Master of Arts degree in 1952. It was Father Walsh who had assisted Nyerere in obtaining his Edinburgh University entry and financial backing.

Prior to entering Edinburgh University Nyerere had determined on the girl whom he wished to make his wife, Maria Gabriel Magige of the Msinditi tribe of North Mara district near Musoma. She too had been baptized a Catholic and received her schooling from the White Sisters convent near Mwanza. She was to become the first woman teacher of her tribe. Julius and Maria were engaged in December 1948, just before Nyerere's departure for Edinburgh. For his fiancée, Nyerere paid the traditional bride-price with six head of cattle. Nyerere's good friend and early mentor, Father Collins of the Maryknoll Mission, Musoma, assisted with these formalities. During his absence in Britain the bursary which Nyerere received also provided some financial help to his widowed mother and his fiancée.

At Edinburgh, Nyerere concentrated on history, politics, and English. He entered into student discussion and did extensive outside reading. He claims that he evolved most of his political philosophy while at Edinburgh. There, too, he sought to clarify and set to paper his views on politics and racialism in

East Africa. In an unpublished handwritten manuscript entitled "The Race Problems of East Africa"[2] (which had certain application to southern Africa as well), he made eight major theses, as follows:

1. He saw the problem of combating racial tensions in East (and southern) Africa as one of harmonizing and of learning to live together.

2. He contended that the blacks do not question the right of whites to live in Africa, but rather that the blacks have the need to govern themselves in those territories in which they make up the majority of the population.

3. He condemned the domination of one race by another.

4. He contended that the root of the problem is racial hatred on both sides of the color line, this requiring mutual effort at finding solutions, and he saw these causes as political and economic rather than cultural.

5. He stated the problem then faced by East (and southern) Africans as ultimately dependent on the redistribution of political and economic control and on the acceptance by all communities concerned of the principles of social, economic, and, above all, political equality.

6. He pointed up the disparity in numbers between black and white inhabitants of East (and southern) Africa and pleaded for a democratic political voice of the majority, restoring to blacks their hereditary rights on the African continent.

7. He contended that violence might be necessary to achieve restoration of these black African rights to equality and political control, stating that "a day comes when the people will prefer death to insult and woe to the people who will see that day!"

8. He envisaged, optimistically, the establishment of a harmonious, non-racial society in Tanganyika and in East Africa.

It is especially noteworthy that this dissertation by Nyerere contained a phrase which, in a later African milieu and from an American source, proved highly controversial. Nyerere's quotation was: "Africa is for the Africans, and the other races cannot be more than respected minorities. . . ." It will be recalled that an analogous quotation, "Africa for the Africans," was made by the American Assistant Secretary of State G. Mennen Williams, speaking at a Nairobi airport news conference in a politically overheated Kenya in 1961. That quotation brought down on Williams's head the opprobrium of many conservative world statesmen, among them Prime Ministers Harold Macmillan and H.F. Verwoerd. It also brought from President John Kennedy the personal gentle reproof to Williams to remember that Africa was indeed for the Africans, this in response to Williams's offer to resign over the tempestuous affair.

Nyerere concluded his studies at Edinburgh in mid-1952 and returned to Tanganyika. He married his youthful sweetheart, Maria, in January 1953 and today they have seven children. He took a teaching position at the Catholic secondary school of St. Francis at Pugu, a few miles inland from Dar es

Salaam. There, in 1955, he made his decision to enter a life of politics. An American Catholic priest, who taught at Pugu with Nyerere, had told the author with embarrassed good humor that he tried to talk Nyerere out of a life in politics, believing that he would make a better teacher than politician. (Nyerere's present Swahili sobriquet—*Mwalimu* or "Respected Teacher"—is a continuing indication of his pedagogical capabilities.)

Nyerere was appointed a temporary member of the Tanganyika Legislative Council in 1954, retaining that post only until formation of TANU and his resulting conflicts with Governor Twining. He was elected a full member of the Legislative Assembly in 1958, remaining therein until assumption of the presidency of the republic in 1962.

Nyerere's personal and political philosophy is clearly set forth in various writings and public pronouncements made over the years from 1951 to date. As detailed elsewhere in this book, Nyerere appeared as a petitioner for his country's independence before various United Nations bodies between 1955 and 1957. One of his most significant preindependence statements was contained in his speech to the United Nations General Assembly's Fourth (Trusteeship) Committee on December 21, 1956.[3] There he pointed out that between 1885 and 1900 indigenous tribes of his country fought desperately to keep the German invaders out. He emphasized that that desperate fight was carried on because the Tanganyikans did not believe in the right of the whites to civilize and dominate the blacks. He said:

The Mandatory system . . . could have given our people fresh hope. But promises of the mandate were not explained to the people, and with the exception of one administration under Sir Donald Cameron, all British Governors administered the country as if it were a British colony. . . .

After World War II came the Trusteeship system. Under the Mandatory system it was recognized that the interests of the indigenous inhabitants of Tanganyika were paramount, and Sir Donald Cameron had made this abundantly clear. . . . But the Tanganyika [white] settler . . . saw to it that this paramountcy of native interests should not . . . be a specific principle of the Trusteeship Agreement. . . . There was a significant omission . . . about the Paramountcy of Native Interests.

Throughout this and later statements in the United Nations and elsewhere, Nyerere emphasized TANU's moderation, nonviolent aims, nonracialism, and political realism, to wit:

We in Tanganyika are determined to move gradually toward our goal of self-government. We are determined to see that those Asians and Europeans who have chosen to live permanently in Tanganyika shall enjoy the same political rights as everybody else. We shall oppose discrimination on grounds of race, colour or creed. But we are not prepared to see any section of our people treated as second-rate citizens in our own country. I therefore plead with you . . . to prevail upon the Administering

Authority to grant the things we have asked for, namely: (a) To declare that Tanganyika shall be developed to become eventually a Democratic State; and since 98 percent of the population is African, this means that Tanganyika shall eventually become a self-governing African State. (b) To change the constitution so as to give equal representation as between the Africans and non-Africans. This is not a Democracy, but we ask it as a symbol of the intention to develop the country as a Democratic State. (c) To introduce elections on common roll for all representative members on universal adult franchise.

On December 22, 1956, still appearing before the United Nations Fourth Committee, Nyerere indicated that he was strongly in favor of fixing a target date for his country's independence. He admitted the difficulty of specifying a date, but he then expressed the belief that Tanganyika should become independent in about ten years' time. He was to gain that independence for his country by peaceful means within five years.

One of Nyerere's most notable pre-independence pronouncements reflecting his political aspirations is his speech known as "A Candle on Kilimanjaro."[4] On October 22, 1959, speaking in the Tanganyika Legislative Assembly, Nyerere elaborated on his people's goal of independence for Tanganyika. He emphasized that his people's patience was running out. He said that TANU now demanded an elective reponsible government with elimination of the colonial civil service overlords. He continued to press for early constitutional changes in that direction and applauded the government's announcement that new elections would be held the following years. He stated:

I have said before elsewhere that we, the people of Tanganyika, would like to light a candle and put it on top of Mount Kilimanjaro which would shine beyond our borders giving hope where there was despair, love where there was hate and dignity where before there was only humiliation. We sincerely pray the people of Britain and our neighbors . . . to look upon us, to look upon Tanganyika and what we are trying to do not as an embarrassment but as a ray of hope. We cannot, unlike other countries, send rockets to the moon, but we can send rockets of love and hope to all our fellow men.

Six weeks after his country attained sovereignty, Nyerere resigned his prime ministerial post. He did so in order to be free to help bridge the gap between his people's aspirations and his government's attainments. His efforts, he said, would be aimed at coordinating his national movement with the economic needs and the political aspirations of the peoples of his country.

Late in 1962, when the government of Tanganyika was changed to a republic, Nyerere was elected its first president. In choosing Nyerere, the Tanganyika electorate gave him 96 percent of all votes cast. He was sworn in as president of the new republic on December 9, 1962, the first anniversary of the country's independence.

In April 1964, when the nations of Tanganyika and Zanzibar united to form the Republic of Tanzania, Nyerere was chosen to head the new union. On September 3, 1965, he was chosen president for a second term of five years, again with an overwhelming majority vote. On October 30, 1970 Nyerere was re-elected without opposition for a third time as president of Tanzania. And on October 26, 1975, he was reelected for a fourth term, receiving over 90 percent of his electorate's approval.

Who have been the chief influences in Nyerere's life? He would probably place the American Catholic missionaries, Fathers Collins and Walsh at the top of his list. These men were obviously greatly influential in his formative years. The former Catholic archbishop of Dar es Salaam, Edgar Maranta, and the Anglican bishop of Masasi, Trevor Huddleston, also have provided important inspiration to him. Nyerere was certainly influenced by the actions and philosophies of the major African nationalists of the 1950s—the early Nkrumah, Kenyatta, and Luthuli. Among world statesmen he appears to have been influenced by Abraham Lincoln, by Mahatma Gandhi, by Franklin D. Roosevelt, by Dag Hammarskjöld. (Nyerere gave a particularly impressive tribute to Hammarskjöld in the traumatic days following Hammarskjöld's tragic death.) He would admit to having taken some political meanings and lessons both from President John Kennedy and from Chairman Mao Tse-tung—probably in equal parts.

Those who so often like to characterize Nyerere as "a communist" will be surprised to learn that among his philosophical heroes are not Marx and Engels but Pope John XXIII and Pierre Teilhard de Chardin. The principles of human dignity, equality, and respect, regardless of race, which Pope John so brilliantly set forth in his famous encyclical *Pacem in Terris*, are too well known to require repetition here. It will suffice to say that they surely gave great impetus and guidance to those principles which had long inspired Nyerere in thought and active political life (see also Part Two below).

As the ideas of French Jesuit Teilhard de Chardin are less well known, they require specific reference and relationship to Nyerere. Perhaps the most important philosophical and spiritual statements produced by Teilhard were *The Phenomenon of Man* and *The Divine Milieu*. In a conversation with the author in May 1968, Nyerere said that he considered Teilhard's works just named to be two of the most important books he has ever read. These deep statements of faith, of the supernatural side of humanity, of human universality, of eventual heavenly afterlife were written in Tientsin, China, during the 1920s and published only in 1955 after Teilhard's death. Teilhard de Chardin was then serving in China as a missionary-teacher-anthropologist and had a major role in the discovery of the "Peking Man." His works reflect his efforts to reconcile theology and evolution, human nature and divine nature. They express the totality of God's relationship with humankind and the constant evolutionary uplifting of the human race. It is obvious that in Teilhard's thoughts Nyerere has found much to support his own concepts of human dignity and the unity of humankind.

In sum, to build his philosophical background Nyerere has taken a distillation of thought from the world's great thinkers and writers ranging from Aristotle through Shakespeare (Nyerere is fond of translating Shakespeare into Swahili) and from Lincoln to Teilhard de Chardin. From that synthesis Nyerere apparently has sought to create and instill into the Tanzanian way of life a government partly democratic and partly socialistic but essentially egalitarian.

Nyerere's personal charismatic aura is built upon the twin foundations of his political role as the country's founding father and his presidential leadership role of *Mwalimu* (Respected Teacher). However, his authority as leader of the party, as distinguished from his philosophical role, contains an element of democratic sanction and control by the party which is not found in authoritarian states. Nyerere cannot, for example, dictate the entire membership of his National Assembly or of the TANU Party Executive. He cannot unilaterally impose legislative decisions upon the National Assembly of the TANU Executive without prior party discussion and consensus or compromise. These combined roles thus make it imperative that Nyerere judge correctly the moods, the resilience, and the strengths or weaknesses of his people, his party elite, and his legislative position.

Moving toward his national goals and objectives, Nyerere has thus far successfully utilized several techniques. He has played off the radical elements of his party against its conservative wing. He has swallowed into his national movement opposing forces, parties, and potential opponents. He has provided jobs and political indoctrination for those potential opponents (the Zanzibaris, the Asians, certain African chiefs). He has even sought to maintain his personal and political security by balancing the police wing against the military arm of the nation. He has achieved, thus far, a delicate but effective balance between proponent and opponent.

NOTES

1. Julius K. Nyerere, *Freedom and Unity* (London: Oxford University Press, 1966) pp. 233ff.
2. Ibid., pp. 23ff.
3. Ibid., pp. 40ff.
4. Ibid., pp. 72ff.

CHAPTER 6

TANU: PARTY PLATFORM AND LEADERSHIP

Political momentum in Tanganyika followed World War II, sparked first by the independence of India and Pakistan and later by the revolutionary anti-colonial seething throughout Africa. The Tanganyika African Association, founded by Sir Donald Cameron in 1929, established first as a social and debating forum for Africans, later developed political goals as the country's first true nationalist organization in embryo. By 1940 it had only one hundred members, but in 1948 it managed to give support to the first nationwide petition from Tanganyika to the Trusteeship Council of the United Nations.

In 1952 Nyerere returned to his native land from his university study in Edinburgh, the second indigenous Tanganyikan to earn a university degree outside Africa. He began campaigning for a truly African political party on grounds that the country must eventually become self-governing as promised by its trust status under the United Nations.

With several of his present associates, Nyerere set out to revitalize and reconstitute the Tanganyika African Association as a full-fledged political grouping in 1954. Formal organization of the group known as the Tanganyika African National Union (TANU) took place on July 7, now a national holiday.

Lack of funds, lack of widespread literacy, and lack of national media for communications provided extraordinary difficulties for Nyerere and his TANU lieutenants in their early days. The generosity of friends who provided several Land-Rovers, which enabled TANU representatives to criss-cross the country in drives for membership and funds, was one important means of assistance rendered the movement. The dedicated efforts of lieutenants and family members, including Nyerere's wife, Maria (who operated a small shop to support her husband's political activities), were also an important element. The support which was provided TANU in the early days from the various African trade unions, particularly the Tanganyika African Government Servants Association (TAGSA) and later the Tanganyika Federation of Labour (TFL) provided other means of support—physical, financial, and psychological. Financial assistance which came from friendly European and Asian settlers also proved a valuable means for Nyerere and TANU to survive the lean years from 1954 to 1960.

By 1956 TANU was becoming sure-footed and increasingly powerful as a political force in the country. By this time Governor Twining and various other white leaders of Tanganyika finally began to sense the strength and potential of this new African nationalism. They realized the need of developing a white-oriented political body to counteract Nyerere's black-oriented TANU. They saw, too, that their grouping should be multiracial in theory if not in fact. Under Twining's aegis, this first European-led political party, the United Tanganyika Party (UTP), appeared in 1956. In the first territorial election for the Legislative Council, which took place in 1958, the UTP was overwhelmingly defeated by TANU. Never thereafter was a white-dominated political grouping able to challenge TANU's supremacy.

Furthermore, an Asian Association, which had been established in 1950, sought now to bridge the politico-social gap between the Indo-Pakistani community and the Africans of Tanganyika. After 1958 both membership and leadership of the Asian Association were swallowed by TANU, which was never again challenged as a major political force in the country.

The implication that Tanzania never was, or is no longer, a democracy has always been resented by its leaders. Nyerere and his colleagues contend that Tanzania satisfies the definition of a democratic state so long as its people and its leaders show respect for the rule of law; so long as there is an independent judiciary; so long as the electorate is given a choice in periodic democratic and free elections; so long as there is political participation by the civil service; so long as there is broad national consensus and unity of purpose. TANU officials insist, quite properly, that the number of parties in a nation is no proper measurement of democracy but rather indicates that nation's inclination toward factionalism and disunity.

Between 1954, the date of the foundation of TANU, and 1958, Nyerere appeared to hold the view that he could develop his country along the lines of a British-type parliamentary system with a multiparty democracy. Realizing that he lacked trained leadership to staff a complex parliamentary system with a viable economy, he and his lieutenants moved to rule out what they sensed as the luxury and divisiveness of a multiparty state. They adopted instead the one-party format, announcing that they would ensure democratic principles by evolving a constitutional system which gives the whole populace effective representation.

Speaking to this point at Wellesley College, Massachusetts, in February 1960, Nyerere said:

Democracy has been described as a "government of the people, by the people and for the people." . . . Surely, if a government is freely elected by the people, there can be nothing undemocratic about it just because nearly all the people, rather than only some of them, . . . voted it into power. . . . Young nations which emerge as a result of a nationalist movement, having united their people, will be governed at first by a nationalist government as distinct from a party government. No one should therefore jump to the conclusion that such a country is not democratic.[1]

Nyerere and TANU built their case for equality by indirection, condemning outright the denial of equality which occurred in all colonial societies and in governmentally inspired racist situations. It was thus possible to show that Tanganyika, as a colonized country, was not exempt from this inequality.

Nyerere and his principal lieutenants had always conceded that one of their major problems was to prevent TANU from becoming racist, and thus antiwhite or anti-Asian. At the outset, however, the TANU leaders considered it essential to keep the membership of their organization to Africans alone, with a few exceptions. (This ban on non-African membership in TANU continued until early 1963, nine years after TANU's foundation and two years after the country's attainment to nationhood.)

In attempting to comprehend the rationale for this apparent inconsistency, it should be recalled first that TANU was created in 1954, a period of strong colonialist domination by the Twining administration, a period when segregation was the mode. Therefore, it would have been self-defeating for TANU to adopt a full multiracial membership at the outset. However, following its initial successes and especially after independence, Nyerere and a few of his more liberal supporters fought for removal of the ban on TANU membership for non-Africans.

Nyerere contends that most of the antagonism to opening TANU roles to whites and Asians stemmed from a real lack of self-confidence among the Africans. They feared, in fact, that the presence of whites and Asians within TANU might presage "takeover" and domination of the party by non-Africans. Thus the Africans had first to prove their political capacities and their leadership before they could come into open competition with other races. This attitude may be better understood when one recalls the long period of subjugation and humiliation that the Africans have borne. Colonial subjection had left a malaise and a feeling of political inferiority that had first to be overcome.

In this connection, Nyerere has often discussed with the author his personal thesis that the greatest scar which the colonial conquerors left on the African body politic was the great loss of confidence and personal humiliation. Thus one of the greatest challenges for the builders of any political movement in

Africa and especially in Tanzania has been to seek to restore and restructure that self-confidence and self-respect. According to Nyerere the originial exclusivity of TANU was essential to the restoration of the Tanganyikans' confidence in themselves and their capabilities. Nyerere pointed out, however, that this situation did not derogate from his movement's basic endeavors toward the goal of equality of race in general. (The rules established for waging the various postindependence election campaigns in Tanzania have borne out this contention. Here racial equality was generally accepted and was demonstrated by parliamentary results.)

Within Tanzania today, TANU is politically all-powerful and as such is expected to be a principal agent of change. Its militancy, its direction, its goals—all are controlled completely by Nyerere and his principal lieutenants operating through their combined guidance of National Executive and National Assembly. Furthermore, an interlocking directorate operating at national, regional, and local levels makes National Assembly action and implementation a concomitant of party action. Since it is now recognized constitutionally as the only legal political party on the mainland, TANU becomes also the primary instigator of governmental policy in social, economic, and political fields. TANU also serves as what Nyerere chooses to call a "two-way street" encouraging free flow of ideas to and fro between bureaucracy and public.

TANU today is considered to be one of the best-organized, as well as most powerful, political parties in all Africa. There are four categories of party allegiance—members, supporters, electors, and militants. Although national membership has been claimed to be as high as 1.5 million Tanzanians, perhaps 500,000 are active, dues-paying members of the organization. The remaining million might better be considered only as nominal members. Perhaps 80 percent of the country's entire adult population (estimated at 8 million) can be considered electors. However, in the 1970 elections only 3.7 million persons voted.

The militants, leaders and subleaders, constitute the nucleus of party direction. These are estimated to number about 2,000, ranging from cabinet ministers to regional officials to TANU youth directors. This group of militants forming the core of the party leadership is organized in pyramidal form.

At the apex of this leadership pyramid is Nyerere, holding two posts as president of the nation and head of his party. Nyerere must be re-elected to the party presidency annually and to the presidency of Tanzania every five years.

With Nyerere at the apex of the leadership pyramid and on a power level just below him are a few intimates and long-time party lieutenants who form the core of TANU's contingency policy grouping, the party's Central Committee. Within this top echelon of party leadership are several individuals who are deserving of special mention. One or more of them could be a potential heir-apparent to Nyerere. Foremost among these is Rashidi M. Kawawa, now holding the posts of prime minister and second vice president of the country. As a preindependence labor leader, Kawawa was one of those who early developed an astonishing capacity for political popularity, for party organization, and for unswerving loyalty to Nyerere and his cause. It was in Kawawa's hands that Nyerere left control of the country during the year 1962 when, immediately after it attained independence, Nyerere unexpectedly vacated his office. At this writing, Kawawa stands *primus inter pares* as a likely successor to Nyerere's presidential chair. His succession to that position, however, presumes his ability to obtain the backing of TANU.

Other important long-time disciples of Nyerere include Paul Bomani, former cabinet minister and present ambassador to the United States; Solomon Eliufoo, former minister of education and present leader of the Chagga tribe; Job Lusinde, former minister of communications and transport; Saidi Maswanya, recent minister of home affairs; Wilbert Chagula, present minister for economic affairs and development planning; Amir Jamal, present minister of commerce and industry; and Derek Bryceson, former minister of agriculture and now director of Tanzania's national parks. Jamal is an Asian; Bryceson is white; the others are indigenous Africans. All the foregoing were supporters of TANU before independence and all have held steady allegiance to President Nyerere.

Two men, by nature of their actions vis-à-vis TANU and Nyerere, now require more and contrasting attention. After Nyerere these men have figured most prominently in party and country history thus far. One man has proved to be constructive and loyal, the other man destructive and disloyal. First of these is the country's prime minister, Rashidi Kawawa, mentioned as a possible successor to Nyerere. The second, now in political exile, is Oscar Kambona, former cabinet minister and secretary-general of the party.

In his relationships to Nyerere, Prime Minister Kawawa (age about forty-seven) is the exemplary, self-effacing, capable, and loyal chief-of-staff. To Nyerere he has proved himself a devoted friend, administrative right arm, and even (as in 1962) an *alter ego*. His loyalties to party and to country have been unquestioned.

On the other hand, Kambona (age about forty-nine), who at first proved of importance to Nyerere in founding the party and helping to obtain independence, through personal jealousy became a political rival to Nyerere. As secretary-general of the party both before and after attainment of independence in 1961 and until the abortive coup of 1964, Kambona showed himself to be an astute organizer and a deft bureaucrat. In addition he successively held important ministerial portfolios of Education, of Home Affairs, of Defense, of Foreign Affairs and, finally, of Regional Affairs. However, his part in the 1964 coup attempt was never made clear. From that time onward, Nyerere and Kawawa evidently distrusted Kambona. In fact, Kawawa and Kambona were openly antagonistic to one another. Thus, by 1965 Kambona's power had waned and his enmity toward the Nyerere regime was so pronounced that he was forced into exile to avoid arrest on several charges, political and financial. From that exile, mainly in Britain and the Netherlands, Kambona has since tried, always unsuccessfully, to mount disturbances against the Tanzanian government. (Kambona's activities antagonistic to Nyerere and Tanzania are described in detail in chapter 9.)

The next lower leadership tier comprises the remainder of the National Executive, composed of sixty national leaders, which is the prime policy-making body. This body has recently attained new status and power, its membership receiving the same privileges as do members of the National Assembly.

On the fourth level of the leadership pyramid is the annual Delegates' Conference, which is composed of approximately one-hundred members including regional and local officials as well as members of certain central bodies such as the Central Committee. In this group are regional commissioners who provide a bridge between central party thinking and local administration. To cement the decentralized political and bureaucratic responsibility the various regional and district commissioners serve concurrently as regional and local secretaries of the party.

Tribal affiliations remain important in obtaining local support for candidates to national office whether for governmental or for party positions. However, only a few of the traditional chieftaincies are represented at top level, since Nyerere has sought consistently to subordinate tribal affiliation to national sovereignty and citizenship.

Party decisions are transmitted through both public and private channels. Government officials must take full cognizance of party demands. Cabinet members must belong both to the TANU National Executive and to the Central Committee. Almost all important party members are also members of the National Assembly. TANU fully controls leadership of trade union, youth, and women's groups as well as the news media.

Nyerere does not usually cross with the party executive when that body's views are counter to his own. For example, it took Nyerere five years to win TANU approval to bring non-African members into TANU. It was the TANU hierarchy that first put the brakes on Nyerere's ideas of East African Federation. It was the TANU executive, too, acting upon recommendations of a presidential commission, which brought on, in 1965, constitutional acceptance of the one-party state.

Nyerere and his political lieutenants have always considered their organization as a national movement rather than a national party. Before independence, their aim was for freedom from colonial rule, which was to be achieved, if possible, without force. After independence, the objectives of the party have been shifted to creation of a true nation by unification of the diverse populace; to give policy guidance to the government; to Africanize the leadership and civil service; to effect agricultural and industrial modernization; and to achieve social reform with egalitarianism.

TANU has sought to gain its objectives by a specific program in four principal areas: (1) strengthening national unity by centralized party control over institutions which could breed opposition, this including direction of trade unions, women's groups, and the civil service; (2) strengthening the party mechanism by coordinating party machinery with governmental administrative structure at national, regional, and local levels, thus making of the party an initiator and stimulator; (3) emphasizing self-help factors in economic development by creation of social programs broadening community development, villagization, literacy campaigns ("each one teach one") with a foreign aid program operating on the principle of accepting aid from any friendly donor who recognizes Tanzania's sovereignty and nonalignment; (4) creating a Tanzanian concept of "African socialism"—combining racial equality, positive neutrality, regional association, equality of economic opportunity, and an enhancement of human dignity.

Utilizing a number of mass demonstration techniques, Nyerere and his colleagues have been able to develop party authority and broad popular appeal. TANU has also developed real charisma for its leadership, particularly for Nyerere. They have made use of such symbolic unifying devices as TANU-green (aspen green) shirts for their members. They have made extravagant use of popular mottoes such as *Uhuru* (Freedom), *Uhuru na umoja* (Freedom and unity), *Ujamaa* (Familyhood and communal cooperation). They have successfully redirected their people's attention from an attack on the "devil" of colonial rule to an attack on the "devils of poverty, ignorance, and disease."

Seeking to face up to its economic dilemmas in novel and imaginative ways, TANU, under Nyerere's leadership, issued the famed Arusha Declaration in February 1967. This called for governmental control over all principal fields of production and distribution and emphasized the need for broader developmental planning. It also called for a code of ethics for the country's political leaders. The Declaration emphasized that the only means of ensuring adequate production for the nation was through self-reliance.

These proposals were followed by legislation that nationalized some industries and provided major governmental control over others, including the country's commercial banks, food processing plants, trading firms, and certain of the country's largest sisal estates.

As to the new code of conduct, government and party leaders were given one year to meet the standards. These prohibited double salaries; condemned profit from wage-labor employees; prohibited ownership of rental houses and realty; proscribed ownership of stock in private enterprises. (Some ministers and National Executive members resigned rather than give up their business directorates and ventures.)

On the third anniversary of the Arusha Declaration, the country's largest privately owned newspaper, *The Tanganyika Standard*, was nationalized. At the same time, most of the nation's remaining private import-export firms and wholesale ventures were also nationalized. Finally, in 1971 the government, under party direction and following parliamentary action, nationalized all rental properties valued at more than $14,000 (U.S.).

The legislation backing the Arusha Declaration called for adequate compensation in exchange for the nationalization of industry, certain commercial ventures, and the banks. However, that compensation process has been relatively slow. In some cases, the Tanzanian government has accepted management contracts from existing or previous owners as a means of helping with the liquidation effort and to permit continued operation of the businesses. Government and party leaders continue to give great stress to the terms of the Arusha Declaration, and party emphasis has been upon the theme of self-help rather than dependence on foreign aid. It is clear that TANU has been the principal originating and motivating force behind all these socio-economic objectives, actions, and attainments.

In both 1970 and 1975 general elections Nyerere and his TANU party leaders continued to insist that the principles of the Arusha Declaration be maintained; that rural candidates for office represent the new *ujamaa* villages; that cooperative expansion be reflected in the new parliamentary membership; and that public participation in the electoral process be continually expanded.

In the 1970 election all but six of the 120 constituencies for the newly-enlarged National Assembly (up from 107) were contested by two TANU candidates. These had been selected by the TANU National Executive following recommendations first made by TANU district meetings. One-third of the membership of the previous National Assembly were defeated, including two cabinet ministers and one junior minister. President Nyerere was reelected without opposition, endorsed by 95 percent of the 3.7 million voters.

In the last presidential election held October 26, 1975, Nyerere received the backing of 93 percent of the country's constituency. Now beginning his fourth term as President, he has led his country for more that fourteen years. (In celebration of his latest political victory, Nyerere gave clemency to more than 7,000 prisoners and reduced jail terms for some 3,500 others. The amnesty did not cover cattle rustlers, political detainees, or those who had served in government at the time of their conviction.)

In postelection statements President Nyerere warned his fellow Tanzanians that he is neither infallible nor immortal and that he intends to retire at the end of his present term. In the author's opinion, his most likely successor could be one or the other of the country's two vice presidents, Rashidi M. Kawawa and Aboud M. Jumbe. The latter is also leader of Zanzibar's Revolutionary Council and the Afro-Shirazi Party and is becoming increasingly influential on the mainland.

The 1964 unification of Tanganyika with Zanzibar into the United Republic of Tanzania left a political residue outside TANU. This residue took the form of the Zanzibar Revolutionary Council, which was the nucleus of the original Afro-Shirazi Party of Zanzibar. Of the 204 seats in Tanzania's National Assembly, thirty-one seats were allocated on an interim basis to entice the Zanzibaris into acceptance of unification. A certain number of nominated seats are also awarded to Zanzibaris as are one or two cabinet portfolios. In addition, the first vice presidency of the United Republic is held by the current chairperson of the Revolutionary Council. Thus, as yet, TANU holds no monopolistic position on Zanzibar. However, eventual constitutional changes could provide for that monopoly.

Thus, Zanzibar's own political leaders retain considerable local autonomy. In point of fact, apart from voting for the office of president of Tanzania (in which Zanzibaris supported Nyerere in 1965, 1970, and 1975 elections) the Zanzibaris have held no local elections since their 1964 revolution. However, Zanzibar has been able to maintain an interlocking governmental *cum* political party hierarchy and structure similar to that of TANU on the mainland. Thereby, the president of the Zanzibar executive operation is simultaneously the chairperson of the Zanzibar Revolutionary Council, the islands' controlling (and self-appointed) legislative-executive body.

The president of the Afro-Shirazi Party (who is also leader of the Revolutionary Council) serves concurrently as first vice president of Tanzania. That post was first held by Sheikh Abeid Karume from mid-1964 until April 1972 when he was assassinated. Today, as noted earlier, the post is held by Aboud Jumbe.

NOTE

1. *Africa Report*, December 1961, p. 5.

CHAPTER 7

THE GOVERNMENT: NATIONAL, REGIONAL, AND LOCAL

The government of the United Republic of Tanzania is based on a strong central executive similar to the central government of France. Heading the executive is the president, who is chief-of-state and commander-in-chief of the armed forces. With the approval of the party executive the president has the right to appoint two vice presidents. The first vice president serves also as head of government and political leader on Zanzibar. The second vice president, who also carries the title of prime minister, is concurrently administrative head of the Tanzanian bureaucracy, leader of government political action in the National Assembly, and deputy to the president. The first vice presidency is currently held by Aboud M. Jumbe, chairman of the Zanzibar Revolutionary Council. The second vice president and prime minister is Rashidi M. Kawawa, long-time confidant and political protégé of President Nyerere.

The country has a unicameral legislature and a constitutional one-party system. Executive direction is supported by a cabinet, presently composed of seventeen ministers. These ministers, as well as first and second vice presidents, must be chosen from the membership of the National Assembly, or parliament.

The present "interim" constitution was adopted in 1965. Under it the president and members of the National Assembly are elected concurrently by direct popular vote for five-year terms. Should the president dissolve the Assembly he, too, must stand for election. The president obtains nomination through the formal action of the TANU National Executive and is confirmed by the parliament after his election by a majority of the voters. That nomination of a single presidential candidate constitutes the sole mechanism for presidential succession in effect today.

The unicameral National Assembly presently provides for a total of 217 members of whom 120 are elected by universal suffrage from single-member constituencies. The president is empowered to nominate up to ten additional members. Fifteen additional members, chosen from the mainland and Zanzibar, are selected by the National Assembly from such special-interest groups as trade unions, the cooperative movement, and the university. In order to achieve more thorough amalgamation of the party's National Executive with the electorate's choices, and thus to accomplish party *cum* government integration in the National Assembly, members of the National Executive not already elected or appointed are also given seats in the parliament.

The National Assembly also includes up to thirty-two members of the Zanzibar Revolutionary Council, these given nominal appointment by the president. The president also has the right to appoint up to twenty additional members of the National Assembly from Zanzibar/Pemba. The various regional commissioners from the mainland, numbering eighteen, and from Zanzibar/Pemba, numbering four, are entitled to ex officio membership in the National Assembly.

The constitution gives much political power to TANU, the sole recognized political party on the mainland. TANU has the power to nominate the president, to approve of the vice presidential selections, and to choose the elective candidates for each National Assembly seat. (It should be kept in mind that the Zanzibar Revolutionary Council, as distinct from TANU National Executive, continues to control political affairs and National Assembly representation from Zanzibar/Pemba. Furthermore, the Zanzibar representational block in the Assembly appears to be only nominally part of the TANU-dominated Assembly membership; thus it is not necessarily subject to the TANU voting whip.)

The original postindependence structure of Tanzania's (then Tanganyika's) government was British in tone and in pattern, with the parliament, or National Assembly, as its foundation stone. Both constitution and parliamentary forms left as legacy of the United Kingdom administration presumed the existence of a multiparty, Westminster-model state.

The first parliament of the immediate preindependence and postindependence phases contained eighty-one members—seventy-one elected and ten nominated. Of the seventy-one elected members all but one supported TANU. The single exception, an Independent, was an ex-TANU member. Thus, TANU completely dominated the government from its semi-autonomous inception and into independence.

Nyerere has always considered that his multiple role as founding father, as president of his country, and as leader of his party must be used not only to unify, but to innovate and modernize, politically and socially, for the public benefit. These beliefs of Nyerere can best be demonstrated by the fact that, only six weeks after his country's independence and his own assumption of its premiership Nyerere unexpectedly (and at first inexplicably) resigned his post. He left that post in the hands of his trusted lieutenant, now Second Vice President/Prime Minister Rashidi Kawawa. In taking this step, it afterward became evident that Nyerere sought dramatically to revitalize and to regenerate both citizenry and party from the grassroots upward.

Late in 1962 Nyerere again returned to public life as Tanganyika's first president when the country assumed republic status. Thereby, Nyerere supplanted the British sovereign as chief-of-state of his nation. In this post he has since sought to create and activate a spirit of national compromise, coordinating the objectives and activities of presidential office, the cabinet, the parliament, and the TANU National Executive.

Early in 1965, by constitutional change, the country formally became a one-party state. After the adoption of the 1965 constitution (still in force) elections were held for the office of president and for the National Assembly elective seats. Nyerere was renominated by TANU's Executive Committee, and two candidates were designated to run against each other in 101 of the 107 electoral districts on the mainland. About 75 percent of the electorate (3.5 million) cast ballots. In the 1965 elections Nyerere received the uncontested approval of 96 percent of both mainland and Zanzibar voters.

In order to give the nation's voters a choice of candidates, during the 1965 election the National Executive devised a system whereby two nominees for the National Assembly, both chosen from a nominated group of four or five, were put up by petition process with local and central party approval. They ran against each other in ninety-eight constituencies. Even in those constituencies where cabinet ministers ran, such contests took place. Five non-Africans won by large margins. As a result of these intramural political contests, only 20 percent of the membership of the new Assembly was carried over from the old body. One cabinet minister and six junior ministers were defeated. Thus a certain inner "cleansing" of party and parliamentary leadership was achieved.

In the October 1970 general elections, the second since Tanzania's independence, all but six of the 120 elective constituencies for the newly enlarged National Assembly were contested by two designated TANU candidates. These candidates were selected by the party's National Executive on the basis of recommendations made by the local TANU district councils. One-third of the seventy-one incumbents of the previous 107-member Assembly who ran for re-election in 1970 were defeated, including two cabinet ministers and one junior minister. President Nyerere, the party's only presidential candidate, was endorsed by 95 percent of the 3.7 million voters. Zanzibar participated in the presidential voting, giving Nyerere approximately the same heavy majority as he received on the mainland. Once again, however, as in 1965, the Zanzibaris did not hold elections for their own Assembly representatives.

Nyerere, his ministers, and his party lieutenants have usually favored extended debate in Parliament to provide constructive criticism for all major governmental action. In the electoral runoffs of 1965, 1970, and 1975 debate on certain issues, foreign and domestic, was circumscribed. Debate on issues of race, tribe, and religion was strictly prohibited. Local issues were uppermost.

Through recent and extensive governmental reorganization (1972) Nyerere stressed the importance of governmental decentralization, the continuing emphasis on tandem development of agricultural and industrial needs, and the shifting of power from the bureaucracy to the TANU Executive Committee. It was at this time that the title and administrative functions of prime minister were added to the title and office of second vice president.

One element of the decentralization scheme provides for the Ministry of Finance to continue to hold responsibility for raising taxes and controlling revenues, but each regional administration will control distribution of those revenues. Thus it is hoped to facilitate decision-making and implementation of government services at local levels.

The various cabinet ministers are appointed by the president from among membership, elective or nominative, of the National Assembly. At present there are seventeen cabinet positions. These include ministries of Agriculture; Capital Development; Commerce and Industry; Communications and Transport; Defense and National Service; Economic Affairs and Development Planning; Finances; Foreign Affairs; Health; Home Affairs; Information and Broadcasting; Labour and Social Welfare; Land, Housing and Urban Development; National Culture and Youth; National Education; Natural Resources and Tourism; Water Development and Power; and a minister assisting in the first vice president's office.

The Bill of Rights section of Tanzania's constitution sets forth the goal that the operations and institutions of the one-party state must not encroach on the freedom of the individual. Protection of civil liberties by the courts has always been a major aim of Nyerere and his more liberal lieutenants. However, it has been recognized that individual rights must give way when the national interest is paramount or is endangered. Nyerere has contended that an independent judiciary is the foundation and the guarantor of the rule of law in a one-party state, just as it is within a multiparty state. However, preventive detention legislation remains on Tanzania's statute books and trial by jury is not yet accepted.

Tanzania began its national life with courts and rules of jurisprudence based on the British model. Tanzania accepted this heritage with great difficulty. On attaining independence, Tanganyika possessed only two black Africans with law degrees, though it did have a few resident-citizen lawyers of Asian and

European extraction. Zanzibar, at independence, had no African lawyers who could serve as judges, though it, like Tanganyika, had a few Asian lawyers. It devolved upon expatriates, therefore, to continue in service in the Tanzanian courts. Despite pressure to overcome these shortages by instituting the law faculty of the University of Dar es Salaam as its first priority action, dependence on expatriate justices has continued to this day.

Recently the situation of the courts, their power and their efficacy, has become somewhat murky. When Tanzania modified its constitution in 1965, efforts were made to institute trial by jury. Those efforts proved unsuccessful. Instead, as before, the courts operated with judges associated with assessors.

The situation of the courts was brought into even sharper focus recently when a number of Tanzanian (and Zanzibari) officials were arrested for alleged complicity in plotting coups against Nyerere and the now deceased First Vice President Karume. The summary detention in Tanzania of those accused and the subsequent removal of some of them to Zanzibar for imprisonment and execution brought considerable criticism from international jurists. The International Commission of Jurists in particular has come out strongly against these legal deviations, contending that they represent an erosion of the rule of law. The Commission has also contended that a double standard of justice cannot be employed by countries such as Tanzania. The 1969 edition of the Commission's journal, *The Review*, gave special attention to the situation on Zanzibar where "for some considerable time it has been obvious that there is arbitrary rule . . . exercised by a small clique."

The Commission was referring to the trial of fourteen people and the reported execution of four of them. Mystery surrounded the executions, but they were reported to have included Kassim Hanga, former vice president of Zanzibar and former minister in Tanzania's cabinet, and Othman Sharif, former Tanzanian ambassador to the United States. According to the Commission: "The court which tried Sharif, Hanga and others was not a court of law in the accepted sense. . . . It was no more than an extension of the will of the Zanzibar Revolutionary Council. . . . It must have been clear to President Nyerere for some time that justice which he, himself, has hitherto upheld, is not being practiced in Zanzibar. . . . "

The Tanzanian mainland today operates a judicial structure which seeks to compress together the juridical trio of tribal, Islamic, and British common law. Appeals are permitted from local through district to High or Supreme Court. The president has the right to appoint all magistrates, appeals court judges, and justices of the High Court. Until 1970 Zanzibar maintained a similar juridical system. However, at that time primary and district courts were replaced by a dozen so-called People's Courts. These consist of a chairperson and two members (or assessors) appointed by the president of Zanzibar (the first vice president of Tanzania). Procedures of these Zanzibar People's

Courts make no provision for defense counsels, for juries, or for appeals to higher courts.

At the time of independence in 1961, two-thirds of the civil service were British expatriates. Thus the first task which the new government faced was to "Africanize" this group. The second task was to achieve a successful meld of the civil service with the party machinery and thus to develop popular support for formerly unpopular colonial administrators. Civil servants are today permitted to take an active role in politics. There is now a constant interchange between civil service and party positions. Thus party militants on the local level are able to gain a greater sense of participation in, and responsibility for, policy formulation and execution.

The administrative bureaucracy divides Tanzania into twenty-four regions, or political subdivisions, twenty on the mainland and four on Zanzibar. Each region is headed by a regional commissioner appointed by the central government. These officials have considerable local autonomy, their administrative work being closely integrated with local party activity. All regional commissioners are ex officio members of the National Assembly. These regions are subdivided into some sixty districts on the mainland and nine on Zanzibar.

TANU remains both the local pressure group and the implementer. By controlling both political and administrative mechanisms, Nyerere and his colleagues seek to deflect local criticism while harnessing local enthusiasm. On the surface, this amalgam of political and administrative leadership looks good. However, on the local level, the scarcity of skilled administrative and technical talent remains a major problem for Nyerere and for Tanzania, as it does for most developing nations.

As a means of experimenting and, it is hoped, of improving its local administrative-political structure, Tanzania in 1965 introduced the so-called cell system into its governmental structure. A cell is designated as a group of approximately ten houses, grouped together as a basic organizational unit. Each cell is headed by a volunteer leader, chosen by his fellow cell members. The leader is usually a long-time TANU stalwart.

Organization of the cells clearly represents a continuing effort of the government to extend its political authority into the "grassroots." Likewise, it is considered a means of diffusing orders and background information down to the local scene while, at the same time, serving as a conduit for passing local petitions or demands upward to regional and national bureaucracy. The system is considered by outside observers to be relatively effective in passing orders downward, but not so effective in passing demands upward.[1]

On the political level just above the cell structure, there are TANU branch offices which combine a number of cells together in a geographic unit. This is usually in a group of some 25,000 population. These branch areas are coterminous with the administrative subregional districts of the governmental structure. These administrative divisions, or districts, are headed by divisional executive officers (D.E.O.) and village executives (V.E.O.).

Part of the rationale for the cell system has been to enhance the local developmental planning process and the villagization schemes. Thus in addition to being a communications channel between central government and the rural populace, it also gives impetus for communal enterprise and initiative, provides local barometers of real progress or lack thereof, and mobilizes feedback.

The cell leaders are generally said to be activists, but not innovators. They have some advisory and adjudicative responsibilities, settling disputes at local levels, similar in many respects to the work of the earlier tribal chiefs or village elders. They are helpful in linking government and party. In areas of low literacy, they serve an important function, making oral presentations and implementing such complex programs as the Arusha Declaration and *Ujamaa*. (The term *ujamaa*, meaning "familyhood," designates the nationwide program of collective villagization. It is described in detail in chapter 12 and in Part Two.)

It will be recalled that the Tanzanian capital, Dar es Salaam, was first an Arab, then a German, and later a British administrative center. The Africans have generally resented these colonial facts. They have long desired a capital city of their own making. Despite all his political and economic problems, Nyerere and his TANU lieutenants have not cut back on this hope, namely, the moving of the country's capital from Dar es Salaam to Dodoma, 250 miles to the west. While this new site is a more central location, it is a bleak and underdeveloped area. However, that region has become a center of *Ujamaa* activity. The change will require massive expenditures of public funds for the relocation. Some estimate the total cost of that relocation at $500 million. Canadian, German, and Japanese architects are already at work on the project. It is assumed that Nyerere is under pressure from some of his younger lieutenants to make this move. These contend that as well as centralizing the government, the move will break the last remaining links with the vestiges of German and British colonialism remaining in the buildings and vistas of Dar es Salaam.

NOTE

1. Jean O'Barr, " Cell Leaders in Tanzania," *African Studies Review* (December 1972), pp. 437–65.

CHAPTER 8

TANGANYIKA AND ZANZIBAR
• 1961–1964

Psychologically, the de facto independence of Tanganyika came, not on December 9, 1961, but in March of that year. For it was on March 29, 1961, speaking in Karimjee Hall, Dar es Salaam, that Julius Nyerere and the late United Kingdom Minister of Colonies Iain Macleod announced that Tanganyika was now to have a "responsible government" and the country would attain independence in December of that year. This announcement of internal self-government propelled Tanganyikans into such spontaneous bursts of joyful celebration that the more formal, elaborate de jure celebrations of December 9, 1961, proved to be anticlimactic by comparison.

In the 1958–59 territorial election, TANU had, formally and practically, become the official opposition. In the 1960 elections which followed, TANU had swept the board. By September 1960 Nyerere had formed what might be termed a "semi-responsible government." Nyerere then became chief minister and his cabinet was composed of nine elected ministers and two British civil servants. In a radio broadcast immediately after forming the new government, Nyerere announced to his people that Tanganyika aimed to achieve complete independence within the Commonwealth during 1961.

It appeared to outside observers then in Dar es Salaam that throughout his association with Nyerere, Britain's Minister of Colonies Macleod was bent on proving to the world that, in Tanganyika at least, the British could bring a colonial people to independence without bloodshed and violence. This was predicated on Prime Minister Macmillan's now famous "winds of change" speech of February 3, 1960, delivered in Cape Town, South Africa, which helped set the tone for Tanganyika's swift movement toward sovereignty.

The colonial secretary arrived in Dar es Salaam in March 1961. On March 27 a Constitutional Conference opened. This proved to be the shortest Constitutional Conference in history involving a British colonial territory. It lasted only twenty-four hours. In opening the session, Macleod stated that the meeting had been convened to discuss both internal self-government and eventual independence for Tanganyika. He indicated that the British government welcomed Tanganyika's peaceful movement toward independence. He stated:

In Mr. Julius Nyerere, this country has a leader to whom not only the people of Tanganyika but many others in all parts of the world can look with confidence to guide this emerging nation successfully. . . . The time has come to replace the candle of responsible government first with the lantern of full internal self-government and then with the beacon of independence. That is what we are all here to do.[1]

In an unprecedented step for Britain, Macleod accepted Nyerere as prime minister even before independence. He further agreed that full independence would be granted the country in December 1961. Nyerere asked that Tanganyika be permitted to become a republic on attaining independence, though remaining in the Commonwealth. To this request Macleod did not accede.

Responding to Macleod's public pronouncements at the Conference, Nyerere said: "This is a day of triumph for Tanganyika. . . . It is not a day of triumph over anybody. . . . It is a happy day of victory for a good cause in which all are winners. . . . Uhuru 1961."[2]

At the close of this session, Governor Turnbull was given a standing ovation. Nyerere was then driven in triumphal procession through the streets of Dar es Salaam. Commenting on these events later, Macleod said: "It may be dangerous to give Africans independence too soon, but it is much more dangerous to give it too late. . . . "[3]

To those who witnessed these scenes it appeared that the United Kingdom Colonial Administration and the nationalist leaders had entered into a harmonious partnership designed to bring Tanganyika into nationhood quickly and without major conflict. The authors of this new rapport were, of course, Nyerere and the country's sagacious governor, Sir Richard Turnbull.

This honeymoon period was short-lived. The Tanganyikans made the point that recently independent states of British background, Ghana and Nigeria among them, had been given surprisingly generous independence dowries by Westminster. The Tanganyikans expected the same generosity. In July 1961 talks began between British and Tanganyikans over the terms of the country's "independence dowry" from Britain. The British government became reluctant, equivocal, and surprisingly ungenerous. Officials of the British Treasury and Colonial Office implied that Tanganyika should look not to Britain but to the United Nations for its postindependence financial needs, since Tanganyika was a trust territory.

Tanganyika's astute finance minister, Sir Ernest Vasey, had drawn up a three-year postindependence development plan requiring 24 million pounds. The plan included costs of separation payments to British colonial servants departing the territory. It requested Britain to provide those funds, one-third in grants, two-thirds in an interest-free loan.

When Nyerere and his colleagues consulted with British officials in London in the summer of 1961, Macleod informed the Tanganyikans that, owing to current British government austerity requirements, the Tanganyikan request for 24 million pounds must be halved. Nyerere and his colleagues were not impressed by British pleas of "poverty" in comparison to the dire needs of Tanganyika's far more afflicted populace. The Tanganyikan outrage at British officialdom was highly emotional. The financial conference was broken off. In a press conference in London on July 21, Nyerere sorrowed over Britain's penuriousness and lack of financial support to his countrymen. He emphasized his country's immediate needs and indicated that he would be required to approach other countries for help, including the U.S.S.R.[4]

Nyerere and his colleagues, bitterly disappointed, decided to reject the British offer. On July 28, realizing the desperation and incipient tragedy of the situation, Governor Turnbull flew to London. The governor convinced his British colleagues of the dangers of the situation and was reported to have offered his resignation in protest. He emphasized that Tanganyika's political moderation and friendship toward Britain could be sacrificed by London's failure to provide a mere 12 million pounds additional aid. The British cabinet reconsidered and the full loan/grant of 24 million pounds was provided.

The long-sought date of Tanganyika's actual and legal independence, December 9, 1961, was now fast approaching. To prepare for that day, the country's young leaders had not only to plan a celebration. There were problems of Africanization of the administrative structure; of establishing diplomatic relationships and embassies abroad; of burgeoning new financial, economic, and commercial relations. There were plans to be devised for the takeover of police and military functions. Finally, there was the all-important factor of welding together the diverse tribal, religious, and racial groupings into a unified citizenry and nation.

In certain of these areas, Nyerere and his lieutenants encountered sluggishness on the part of colonial officials. Problems of Africanizing the civil service, police, and military mounted and defied solution. These shortages were to become more evident and more tortured in less than three years, when the country faced revolutionary situations.

Like so many other African statesmen of the time, Nyerere was forced to dig into the thin ranks of doctors, lawyers, public servants, and chiefs to support the new and upcoming demands for qualified governmental personnel to serve as diplomats, judges, engineers, financial advisers, and senior administrators. Old friends of Nyerere from the Makerere intellectual group were soon to become diplomats. Labor leaders like Rashidi Kawawa were now required to take over ministerial portfolios. Tribal chiefs of all political and religious persuasions had been drafted into government. Yet the demand for qualified personnel at top levels was still unsatisfied. Even so it would be necessary for Tanganyika to rely on expatriate advisers from the United Kingdom and elsewhere for some years to come. Nowhere was the shortage more evident than in the military-security field.

The independence celebrations of December 9, 1961, were well executed—inspired by British planning and correctness, by the Tanganyikan's affability and natural friendliness, by the surprising number of world-renowned figures who attended, and by lack of untoward incidents. Chief among the participants were Prince Philip, representing the Royal Family, and Duncan Sandys, representing the British government. Philip flew his own plane across Africa to attend the celebrations, a feat which gave to his arrival and departure special zest.

Among the African nationalists (now chiefs-of-state) present were Jomo Kenyatta of Kenya, Kenneth Kaunda of Zambia, Hastings Banda of Malawi. The brilliant, suave, and ill-starred Sylvanus Olympio of Togo was also present.

The United States delegation to the celebrations was led by Franklin D. Roosevelt, Jr., a personal choice of President John Kennedy. The United States delegation also included Rhode Island's Senator Claiborne Pell and now deceased Illinois Representative Barrett O'Hara.

His Highness Prince Karim, the Aga Khan, was present. So, too, was Cardinal Rugambwa, first Catholic cardinal in black Africa, who represented Pope John XXIII. Present also was the late United Nations Under-Secretary Ralph Bunche.

The midnight flag ceremony, betokening the official birth of Tanganyika as a nation, has been described in the introduction to this book. On the following day, December 9, there took place the Presentation of Instruments of Government and the opening of Tanganyika's Parliament by Prince Philip. In his speech, upon receiving the Instruments of Independence, Nyerere said:

These Instruments . . . are the embodiment of my country's independence. . . . This is the day for which we have looked so long, the day when every Tanganyikan can say, "I'm a citizen of a sovereign, independent State." . . . This is a moment heavy with responsibility. . . . In addition we have wider duties . . . towards all those other African states, . . . duties towards all the nations upon earth and opportunities to influence by example the policies even of the most powerful. [5]

There then followed days of recognition and of planned diplomatic exchange between Tanganyika and various governments of the outside world. On December 9 the United States government presented letters of recognition and the author was appointed chargé d'affaires of his country's newly elevated embassy. At the same time, Prime Minister Nyerere was given a letter from President Kennedy announcing the American intent to make $10 million in development and technical aid available to the new nation.

Some twenty other countries immediately recognized Tanganyika. Soon there were to be thirty-six diplomatic establishments in the Tanganyikan capital. The Tanganyikan authorities set up diplomatic establishments in London, the United Nations, Washington, Bonn, Paris, New Delhi, and Moscow—and others followed.

One of the most important events of the country's first postnatal days was appointment of the popular governor, Sir Richard Turnbull, as Tanganyika's first governor-general. His wise guidance undoubtedly provided an important stabilizing influence during the crucial year 1962, when Nyerere was not at the helm.

A few days after the independence celebrations Nyerere proceeded to the United Nations General Assembly in New York, leading his country into that body as its ninety-ninth member. Nyerere's brilliant statement of his country's foreign policy, as set forth on that occasion, is recorded in chapter 13 of this book. From the outset Nyerere began to exert an independence of spirit in foreign affairs that has characterized his country's actions to this day. When the United States delegation, then led by the late Ambassador Adlai Stevenson, approached him to seek support on exclusion of Communist China from United Nations membership, Nyerere was straightforward in rejecting the request. He contended then, as he does today, that membership in the world body must be universal and should therefore include mainland China. (Recent changes in United States policy fully justify his stand.)

The year 1962 brought two singular events of note for Tanganyika. One of these caused international sensation and bewilderment. That event was Nyerere's abdication from power as prime minister, leaving that post in the "caretaker" hands of his trusted lieutenant, Rashidi Kawawa. The second event, less baffling to outside observers, was Tanganyika's declaration of a republic, with Nyerere's return as its president.

By 1962 TANU as a political force and mass movement was weakening. Certain of the tribal groupings were beginning to show friction and new independence of spirit; so too were the trade unionists. Problems of Africanization of the civil service, problems of education, problems of agricultural and economic development—the usual problems faced by a poverty-ridden new nation—were now facing Nyerere and his TANU lieutenants. Having obtained independence, and presumably unity and equality, the populace was impatient for political and economic miracles.

In order to speed the unifying process and to cement his party's hold over the whole country, Nyerere decided to free himself from central governmental tasks. He saw that only by going to the grassroots would he be able to inspire his people into a sense of national unity, of realization of the responsibilities as well as the gifts of freedom. A highly sensitive political philosopher, Nyerere by this action believed he could reinvigorate and reconstitute his party and assuage the impatience of his people for postindependence miracles. Like Gandhi, he sought to get closer to his people once more and thereby better to assess their demands.

On January 22, 1962, the following press statement was issued by Prime Minister Nyerere's office:

Today I relinquished my position as Prime Minister of Tanganyika. Before doing this, I myself selected a new team of Ministers with Mr. Rashidi Kawawa at its head. . . . I myself shall not be a member of this Government, but will support it from my position as a Member of Parliament, and President of TANU.

I have taken this action, and have won support of my colleagues for it after a long debate. . . because of our firm belief that this is the best way of achieving our new objective—the creation of a country in which the people take a full and active part in the fight against poverty, ignorance and disease.

To achieve this purpose it is necessary to have an able elected Government which has the full support [and co-operation] of the people. . . . It is also necessary to have a strong political organization active in every village . . . along which [road] the purposes, plans and problems of the Government can travel to the people, at the same time as the ideas, desires and misunderstandings of the people can travel direct to the Government. This is the job of the new TANU.

. . . I myself [will] devote full time to the work of TANU. . . . I know that this will come to many of you as a shock, but this is because of habit. . . . We know that it is unusual for a Prime Minister to step down . . . to undertake leadership in the country of the Party which supports the new Government. But we do not believe that it is necessary for us to copy the institutions of other countries; we do believe that we must work out our own pattern of democracy and that the step I have announced today is the best way for us to proceed at the present moment.

It is, therefore, with the fullest confidence in the new Government and in the people of Tanganyika that I now undertake my new task—that of taking part in the building up of the new TANU, . . . reshaped to meet the circumstances of independent Tanganyika. I call upon every Tanganyikan citizen to join in this next phase of our struggle for a better life, . . . and I ask our friends abroad to understand these changes and not to try to read into them a different significance than they have. The changes mean one thing . . . only; a determination to build a really democratic society in which the people can take the fullest part in the development of their country. We go forward, as before, in unity, with good humor, and with great joy at the opportunity we now have before us. *Uhuru na kazi!*[6]

During the months to follow Nyerere traversed Tanganyika's highways, back roads, and game trails. He talked to his people now of *Uhuru na kazi* (Freedom and work), of *Uhuru na umoja* (Freedom and oneness). He sought to develop a feeling not alone of nationhood but of self-help. In these efforts he had success, both personally and in the task of nation-building, enhancing his own prestige and his affinity with his people. That enhanced respect accorded him was, during this period, clearly demonstrated in the name then given him by the public—*Mwalimu* (Respected Teacher).

On the international front, Nyerere's reputation took a sudden nosedive. His motivations in leaving Tanganyika's helm so precipitately were caustically questioned. Foreign private venture capital which had been exploring prospects of investment in Tanganyika took a new and quizzical look. It was necessary for TANU to send parliamentary spokespersons abroad to explain just what Nyerere's real motivations were. They served as apologists and interpreters for this latest twist.

It took some time for Tanganyika's—and Nyerere's—international reputations to be reestablished. The practical idealism and basic good sense of Nyerere's actions were long misjudged and, to this day, a few international figures unfairly consider Nyerere to have shown himself, by this action, somewhat erratic. In the author's opinion, those critics failed completely to measure the problems, psychological and physical, of building Tanganyika into a nation.

During Nyerere's absence from the helm, Rashidi Kawawa, as the country's prime minister *pro tem*, proved singularly loyal to Nyerere and to his task, keeping Tanganyika's ship of state on an even, peaceful keel. During this period old and new-found friends, Communist and non-Communist—some bearing questionable gifts—appeared on governmental doorsteps in Dar es Salaam. Soviets and satellites began a broad program of informational activities, of student exchanges and official visits. Chinese Communists established themselves in a luxurious compound on the ocean shores in Dar es Salaam and began to talk of trade and aid. Western nations set up their diplomatic establishments in Tanganyika's capital, bringing in cultural exchanges, trade, and aid programs. Notable among these were West Germany, Israel, and the United States.

During that period of 1962 when he was out of office as prime minister, Nyerere devoted much of his time to writing and to synthesizing his views of government and of African unity. One of his more important works was a paper called *Ujamaa—The Basis for African Socialism* (*Ujamaa* means "familyhood and communal cooperation.") This document was to become of major significance later, since it apparently served as the philosophical basis for Nyerere's Arusha Declaration of 1967. The paper examined the premise that "socialism, like democracy, is an attitude of mind." The paper condemned the uneven distribution of wealth, acquisitiveness, and parasitism. It stressed the prime elements of production—land, tools, and human energy. It set forth the need of all societies to work—emphasizing the hospitality of Tanganyika in the Swahili proverb that guests should be treated as guests for two days and on the third day given a hoe. Nyerere rejected capitalist methods and attitudes of mind, contending that the traditional African way of life must, in certain phases, be re-established in his country. His paper emphasized the need of reintroduction of traditional African forms of land ownership, respect for age, concepts of service, brotherhood, and unity. He described *ujamaa* and the extended family as being both essence and objective of African socialism. This he contrasted with capitalism, which he defined as exploitation of man by man, and with doctrinaire socialism, which he saw as justifying inevitable conflict of man with man (see chapter 12 and Part Two).

Britain had given to Tanganyika a Westminster-model constitution, with the two nations standing in relationship to one another under preindependent "responsible government" in the manner of London and Belfast. After December 9, 1961, and full independence the similarity was more akin to the relationship between London and Ottawa. Setting forth its demands for a republic, Tanganyika now sought to emulate the model of India or of Pakistan, in which the country would remain within the Commonwealth but would replace the British monarch as head of state with a strong elected president.

Accordingly it was decided that, on the first anniversary date of independence, the Tanganyikans would constitute themselves a republic. First formal discussion of Tanganyika's becoming a republic occurred during June 1962 in parliamentary debate between Tanganyika's leaders. Nyerere, speaking as a "back-bencher," defended retention of Commonwealth membership. In the same month, Nyerere wrote an article for the *London Observer*, spelling out his concept of the type of constitutional government essential in Tanganyika. This concept embodied the idea of republic with the president as a strong executive.

In August 1962 Nyerere was unanimously chosen TANU's candidate for president. Standing against him was a longtime political foe, Zuberi Mtemvu, who was head of a tiny opposition party, the African National Congress (ANC). At the polls Nyerere swamped his opponent, winning some 1.1 million votes against Mtemvu's 21,000. Thus on December 9, 1962, Julius K. Nyerere became Tanganyika's first president. Rashidi M. Kawawa became the vice president. At that time Tanganyikans bade farewell to their long-time friend and mentor, the British governor-general Sir Richard Turnbull.

In his inaugural address of December 10, 1962, Nyerere first spelled out his controversial "villagization" program. This idea sought to bring rural people together into small villages, providing for their communal education, agricultural and social needs, and thus to speed development for that 90 percent of all Tanganyikans who live on the land. He also stressed the need for unity; for continuance of war on poverty, ignorance, and disease; and he appealed for racial tolerance.

By contrast with the innovative year 1962 and the far more sensational year of 1964 to follow, 1963 proved relatively calm. Chief among the events of 1963 were (1) the decision of TANU that the country must become, in constitutional terms, a one-party state; (2) the increasingly rapid Africanization of the civil service; (3) the creation of the Organization of African Unity (OAU), in which Nyerere played a major part; (4) the visit of Nyerere to the United States as a guest of President Kennedy; and (5) the independence of the nearby islands of Zanzibar/Pemba.

On January 14, 1963, at a TANU meeting, the party's National Executive determined to make the country a one-party state. At that meeting, under Nyerere's guidance, plans were laid for required constitutional changes. Considerable discussion was undertaken as to the means whereby creation of such a state would still provide electoral choices of candidates for voters. As noted elsewhere, results of this discussion were seen in the 1965, 1970, and 1975 national elections.

The problems of swift Africanization of national, regional, and local civil service staffs had been vexing. In June 1963 the Tanganyikan government issued a relatively optimistic report on the progress made in Africanizing the civil service. At that time Prime Minister Kawawa announced that there had been a rise of 40 percent, in one year, of Africans holding senior and middle-level government positions. Furthermore, of the more than 32,000 posts of all types in the civil service some 27,000 were now filled by Africans, or 88.8 percent. About 1 percent of civil service personnel were non-African citizens and 10 percent expatriates. The successful inauguration of the OAU in Addis Ababa in May of 1963 was a particularly happy occasion for Tanganyikans. Creation of that body symbolized for Nyerere and his TANU colleagues, as did no other institution yet devised, visible movement toward the goal of continental African unity. A full discussion of Nyerere's and Tanzania's part in setting up the OAU is given in Chapter 13 of this book. Nyerere characterized the birth of the OAU as the most important event of 1963 for his country.

In July 1963 Nyerere visited Washington as a guest of President Kennedy. The two men had met briefly in 1960 prior to Tanganyika's becoming independent, neither man yet chief-of-state.

The essentials of the conversation between the two leaders were, of course, highly classified. Press reports indicated that they discussed the inception of the OAU, problems of southern Africa, global race problems, and matters of aid. Nyerere later told the author that in these conversations with Kennedy he questioned the American president closely as to the rationale behind American foreign-aid generosity. Nyerere said the president responded that such aid was not primarily for altruistic motives but for reasons of national self-interest. When Nyerere asked the president to elucidate this point, President Kennedy is reported by Nyerere as saying that the self-interest lay principally in building a national and international defense against the encroachments of Communism. As a postscript, Nyerere informed the author that he much appreciated this candor on the part of the American president.

With Tanganyika now nearly two years free from colonial rule and with Kenya's independence set for December 1963, the British colonial administrators were hard put as to what to do about the independence of the Zanzibar Protectorate. These neighboring offshore islands had been in a state of political ferment since their first "representative" elections of 1957. The troubled islands were also beginning to throw shadows across the faces of the political leaders on Tanganyika's mainland.

Illustrative of this mood was a conversation which the author held with President Nyerere in Washington in July 1963, at the time of Nyerere's state visit described earlier. The author then questioned Nyerere as to what he foresaw for Zanzibar. To this query Nyerere was noncommittal. The author then bluntly stated that he foresaw Zanzibar as becoming "Tanganyika's Cuba." Nyerere obviously appreciated the characterization. More than a year later, in Dar es Salaam, Nyerere recalled this conversation to the author, saying that he had, on more than one occasion, used that "Cuba" characterization in discussing the Zanzibar problems with his cabinet.

A word on Zanzibar's recent political history is now in order. The brief German suzerainty over the islands of Zanzibar/Pemba in the late 1800s was superseded by the long period of British colonial rule beginning in 1895. From 1911 until 1960 the islands had slumbered peacefully under the popular "rule" of an Arab sultan, His Highness Seyyid Sir Khalifa bin Harub.

The old sultan died October 9, 1960, and was succeeded, for only a short time, by his son Abdulla. The latter, a religious recluse, passed away the following year and he, in turn, was succeeded by his son, Jamshid. At the side of these various Arab "rulers" Britain had placed a local resident (or Governor) who, in fact, ruled the island protectorate on behalf of the British Colonial Office.

Growth of the various African nationalist movements on the mainland, particularly in Kenya and Tanganyika, propelled Arabs, Africans, and Asians on Zanzibar/Pemba into political thought and action. By 1956 there was considerable pressure on the colonial authorities to grant popular elections and eventual independence. Early in 1956 the Zanzibar Nationalist Party (ZNP) was created to protect the Arab minority. The next year the African majority merged its two political associations into the Afro-Shirazi Party. Thus the fatal lines between African and Arab political groups on Zanzibar were drawn. (As an interesting sidelight, Nyerere attended the founding meeting of the Afro-Shirazi group simply as an observer.) Among the founders of the Afro-Shirazi Party were Sheik Abeid Karume, Othman Sharif, and Kassim Hanga. The latter two were executed at Karume's order in 1969 and Karume himself was assassinated in 1971.

The 1957 elections to the Legislative Council were contested by the Afro-Shirazis, led by Karume; the Arab dominated ZNP, led by Ali Muhsin; and the Muslim Association (mainly Asians). The results were Afro-Shirazis, five; the Muslim Association, one; and the ZNP, none. The British administration then proceeded to appoint to the Legislative Council the Arab, Ali Muhsin, who, with his ZNP, had lost the elections. Furthermore, the British authorities rejected Abeid Karume, leader of the Afro-Shirazis, whose group had won the elections.

The sultan's household and coterie, not ordinarily associated in politics till then, now sought to combine certain of the Arab and African political elements into a new party, the Zanzibar and Pemba Peoples' Party (ZPPP), led by Sheik Mohammed Shamte. This effort, on the part of the sultan, with tacit approval of British administration, was aimed at dividing the black African Afro-Shirazis and strengthening the Arab cause.

Zanzibar's second general election was held in January 1961. It pitted the Afro-Shirazis against the ZNP and the ZPPP. The Afro-Shirazis again won, with ten seats to nine for the ZNP and three for the ZPPP. The Afro-Shirazis thought they had won the election but the other two parties combined against them and the British resident (governor) refused to allow the Afro-Shirazis to form a minority government. A "caretaker government," with a civil servant as chief minister, was then instituted with new elections promised within six months.

In those new elections, held in June 1961, twenty-three constituencies were contested. That election resulted in the Afro-Shirazis winning ten seats. The ZNP won ten seats as well. The ZPPP won three seats. The latter two parties then combined against the Afro-Shirazis and an Arab-dominated coalition government resulted. Shamte was named chief minister. On the day of the election there were serious disturbances in Zanzibar and vicinity with several hundred people reported killed. British forces were brought in to restore order.

In July 1963 new elections were held, with a total of thirty-one contested seats. The Afro-Shirazis won thirteen seats with 87,000 votes; the ZNP/ZPPP combination won eighteen seats with a total of 73,000 votes. Again the Arab-oriented minority coalition formed the government.

In September 1963 a Constitutional Conference was held in London. The British promised the islands independence on December 10, 1963. Under terms of this agreement, the Arab sultan's position as hereditary and nominal chief-of-state was to be safeguarded. Thus the seeds of revolution were laid—a minority, feudal government installed against the obvious wishes of the predominant African majority in an uneconomic, one-crop (cloves), impoverished state.

At 2:00 A.M. on January 12, 1964, a revolution broke out in Zanzibar. Within forty-eight hours all security forces on the islands had surrendered. American and British nationals were soon evacuated and a Revolutionary Council, led by Abeid Karume, leader of the Afro-Shirazi Party, assumed full control. Meanwhile, according to reliable estimates, some 4,000 persons had been killed and 15,000 (mainly Arabs and Asians) exiled. Within a few days the revolutionary situation spread also to mainland Tanganyika and Kenya.

Initial leadership of the revolutionary coup forces in Zanzibar was in the hands of an audacious, twenty-seven-year-old Ugandan, John Okello. Late on the night of January 11–12 he and about three dozen African followers attacked and took over several police stations and ammunition stores in Zanzibar City and environs. Okello and his fellow conspirators were given impetus by a larger group of Afro-Shirazi supporters. They found that both remaining British civil servants and the Arab colony lacked any defenses. The control of Zanzibar/Pemba passed completely into African nationalist hands within a week. Within the first forty-eight hours the islands were virtually sealed off from the outside world; members of the sultan's family had fled to Mombasa. Provisions were soon made for evacuation of some 300 British nationals and sixty Americans, including the sixteen-man staff of NASA's tracking station located on Zanzibar.

Within a few hours of the first attack the rebel-held radio stations proclaimed Zanzibar a republic under the so-called Revolutionary Council. It was Okello who announced by radio the dissolution of the government and confiscation of Arab and Asian properties. On January 15 the Revolutionary Cabinet was announced. Abeid Karume, head of the Afro-Shirazi Party, was proclaimed president. Kassim Hanga, a labor leader, was named prime minister. Sheik Abdull Rahman Mohammed (better known as Babu) and long time leftist "firebrand" of Zanzibar political life, was named as minister of external affairs and defense. Othman Sharif, a long-time Afro-Shirazi leader, was made minister of education. All of these have since disappeared from the political scene, dead or imprisoned.

Very shortly after his successful coup on Zanzibar, Okello visited mainland Tanganyika, apparently determined on making trouble there as well. Very quickly he became anathema to Zanzibari and mainland leaders, including Nyerere and Kenyatta of Kenya. Thereafter, excluded from both Tanganyika and Kenya, Okello returned to his native Uganda. There he presumably still lives in obscurity.

It is now clear beyond doubt that the Zanzibar revolution was wholly the work of the black nationalist groups, the Afro-Shirazis and dissidents from the Arab-led ZNP. It is also clear that intense racial enmity between Africans and Arabs, plus the inept administration and favoritism of the British administration toward the feudal Arab regime, plus sluggishness of the island's economy provided the tinder and the fuel which fired the revolution.

The Zanzibar revolt appeared to be a classic coup—that is, it was staged in an area where political, economic, and social conditions favored its institution and guaranteed its success. At the outset no major external Communist influence was openly in evidence. That influence came onto the islands in the wake of the revolt.

The uprising had caught the British off-guard in both Zanzibar and London. Though certain British and Arab administrators on the islands requested the intervention of British troops, that request was turned down by London. As the island's administrators (British and Arab-dominated) had obviously lost control of the situation, the British apparently did not feel inclined to challenge the postrevolution status quo. The British later sent into Zanzibar harbor a small hydrographic survey ship for protection and later evacuation of British and American nationals.

At the time of the islands' independence (December 1963) and just a few weeks before the coup, the American government had upgraded its consulate on Zanzibar to embassy status. Unfortunately American policy appeared to be following the British lead too closely in supporting a minority and racist Arab-dominated government. Furthermore, in retrospect, it appears that the American government had paid too little attention to the incipient African nationalist leadership. No important Afro-Shirazis had been to America, either as exchange visitors or as VIPs, whereas a number of young African militants had visited and presumably received training and funds from Cuba, the Soviet Union, and China. American aid to Zanzibar was virtually nonexistent and British economic planning for the islands' after independence had been unimaginative. Finally, when the coup did occur, there was a definite sense of panic among Americans and British on the island. These fears were later proved largely unfounded, since no whites were injured or killed.

Both London and Washington withheld recognition of the new government for many weeks after the coup. These delays in recognition were undoubtedly instrumental in strengthening pro-Communist elements on the islands. The Soviets, Communist Chinese, and East Germans quickly recognized the new Revolutionary Council. Both Soviet and Chinese projections of influence on the islands bear out the belief that, by withholding recognition, American and British governments made serious miscalculations.

The Tanganyika uprising which followed that on Zanzibar began in the early hours of January 20, 1964. The coup attempt on the mainland did not appear to have a direct connection with the Zanzibar uprising other than being designed to take full advantage of the unsettled situation in the area. The Tanganyika disturbance appeared to center about a group of some thirty noncommissioned African officers of the Tanganyika African Rifles, an army group stationed at Colito barracks near Dar es Salaam. A number of British commissioned officers were arrested by the insurgents and the British commander of the troops in Dar es Salaam went into hiding. It was later ascertained that the coup leaders had been dissatisfied over promotion procedures for Africans and continuing British leadership of the military. Within the next forty-eight hours there were other concerted or parallel uprisings of soldiery in Tabora and Nachingwea barracks.

During the same period a group of dissident labor leaders and anti-TANU subchiefs gathered in Morogoro and planned to associate themselves with the military insurgents. Word of the meeting quickly spread to Dar es Salaam and the leaders of this cabal were shortly thereafter jailed. A number of cabinet members were also temporarily held by the instigators of the coup. About twenty persons were killed and several hundred injured in the skirmishing.

It has never been made clear where Nyerere was at the time of the attempted coup. With a few trusted lieutenants, so the story goes, he is said to have fled first to a small offshore island and later to a Catholic convent, where he remained in hiding for about thirty-six hours. Nyerere's actions at this time were undoubtedly influenced by the fate of his great friend, Sylvanus Olympio, who had been assassinated in Togo on January 13, 1963, this too by army revolt. He may also have been influenced by the memory of the Congo's (now Zaire) martyred Patrice Lumumba.

During the time of Nyerere's disappearance Oscar Kambona, long-time TANU leader, who then held the portfolio of minister of home affairs, "dickered" with the revolutionaries. Kambona appeared to have considerable control of the situation. The first night after the coup Kambona went on the air over Radio Tanganyika to reassure the populace, to contend that peace had been restored, and to attest to his own pre-eminence in allegedly restoring order. In that broadcast he announced himself as minister of foreign affairs, a post he had not previously held. Not once during the broadcast did he mention President Nyerere's name.

On January 21 Nyerere made his first postcoup broadcast to his people. There remains some question as to whether this broadcast was live or recorded. The announcer introduced him as "the Father of the Nation, *Mwalimu* Julius Nyerere." Nyerere said:

My countrymen: Yesterday a slight crisis occurred here in Dar es Salaam. The causes for this crisis have been explained to you more than once, as has the fact that it ended the same day. It is not my aim to repeat the reasons why that crisis occurred. My aim first is to dispel your anxiety. . . . Fabricators allege that my whereabouts were unknown, that Ministers' whereabouts were unknown, and that there was no more Government. Such inventions could turn a small event into a bigger one. . . . I want to advise you . . . not to spread alarmist rumors. . . . I am happy that many people were calm throughout the crisis . . . but there were many who became alarmists; . . . there were others who were a disgrace. . . . Yesterday was a day of great disgrace to our nation. I thank all the people who helped [keep] this disgrace from getting out of hand. I hope that our country will not . . . witness any repetition of such a disgrace.[7]

To ensure their own situation in the face of rising violence throughout East Africa, Prime Ministers Obote of Uganda and Kenyatta of Kenya had called for supporting British troops in their respective countries. There was considerable dissension and delay among Tanganyikan cabinet members as to whether or not British troops should be called in to restore order. On January 22 Nyerere appeared in public in Dar es Salaam and thus appeared to reassure the populace. On January 24 Nyerere finally made a request for British help.

At dawn on January 25 sixty commandos were transferred by helicopter from the British aircraft carrier H.M.S. *Centaur* and the destroyer-escort H.M.S. *Cambrian* to the center of coup activity at Colito barracks. These British commandos, with the help of rockets and fireworks, induced some 800 mutineers to surrender within an hour. The naval vessels provided a covering volley of blank shells. Five Tanganyikan soldiers were killed and a number were wounded. Other detachments of British troops moved in to guard strategic locations and government officials. Still other British units disarmed mutineers at Tabora—some 500 miles inland—and at Nachingwea near Tanganyika's southern border. Later the same day, Nyerere announced by radio that he was disbanding the 1,400-man Tanganyika Rifles and said that a new military unit would be replacing it. In the same radio broadcast Nyerere asked for recruits for the new unit from among TANU's Youth League.

On this same day—January 25—Nyerere received a "loyalty" delegation of women at the State House. This delegation was led by Bibi Titi Mohammed, a member of Parliament and first woman member of TANU. (She was subsequently arrested and convicted for her complicity in a September 1969 purported coup attempt against Nyerere.) Other similar loyalty demonstrations took place countrywide.

On January 28, obviously forced ahead by recent events, Nyerere took action to activate a commission empowered to make changes in the national constitution and the TANU constitution and to make Tanganyika "a democratic, one-party state." These actions had belatedly followed upon a January 1963 recommendation by the TANU National Executive.

One event, at first glance seemingly having little to do with the coup, may possibly have been a causative factor in those actions. This was the issuance by Nyerere, on January 7, 1964, of a policy circular having to do with Africanization and citizenship. It will be recalled that Africanization had been proceeding quickly throughout Tanganyika. The policy circular clearly implied a "slowdown" of Africanization. Extracts follow:

On 9 December 1961 the vast mass of the people of this country became citizens of an independent country; Tanganyika citizenship became a legal fact. There were, however, a few people whose legal right to become citizens meant renouncing citizenship of another nation. These people had two years in which to make their choice.

This period of grace has now expired. Since 9 December 1963 we have known exactly who are citizens of this country by right of birth. And from that date everyone has to make an application which can be accepted or rejected by us according to the individual merit of the application. . . . The period of transition is over. It is now up to us to make quite certain that being a citizen of this Republic is a matter of great pride; . . . We must be able . . . to say proudly "I am a Tanganyikan."

. . . There are wide international circles . . . where the name of Tanganyika denotes something worthwhile. This arises out of our constant appeal to certain basic principles, the most important of which has been our appeal to the morality of human equality regardless of colour, race, or country of origin. . . .

Two years ago we introduced a form of racial discrimination into the civil service. For both recruitment and promotion we gave Tanganyika citizens of African descent priority over other Tanganyika citizens. There were good reasons for this action then, which we fully explained. It was necessary to counteract the effects of past discrimination against citizens of African descent so that our civil service could develop a "local look." . . .

The time for this compromise with principles has now passed. The reasons which were valid in 1961 are not valid in 1964. . . . There is no longer any doubt about who is a citizen of . . . Tanganyika. . . . We cannot allow the growth of first and second class citizenship. . . .

The distinction between citizens of African descent and citizens of Non-African descent must now be ended. This means that discrimination in civil service employment . . . must be brought to an end immediately. . . . The only distinction which can in future be accepted is that between citizen and non-citizen. . . . We must use the reservoir of skill and experience which the nation possesses; the skin in which this skill is encased is completely irrelevant.[8]

For Nyerere and his TANU compatriots, the tasks of nation-building were only beginning. During the coming years those tasks would be compounded. One of their major problems, emanating from the successful coup in Zanzibar and the abortive coup in Tanganyika, would be met by union of those two lands.

NOTES

1. Judith Listowel, *The Making of Tanzania* (London: Chatto & Windus, 1965), p. 385.
2. Ibid., p. 389.
3. Ibid., p. 390.
4. Ibid., p. 395.
5. Julius K. Nyerere, *Freedom and Unity* (London: Oxford University Press, 1966), pp. 142ff.
6. Ibid., pp. 157ff.
7. *Tanganyika Standard*, January 22, 1964.
8. Nyerere, *Freedom and Unity*, pp. 258ff.

CHAPTER 9

TANZANIA 1964–1970

By April 1964 the Soviets, Communist Chinese, and East Germans were beginning to cement themselves into Zanzibar and to use those islands for stepping-stones onto the Indian Ocean littoral. By this time there were present on the islands several hundred "diplomats," presumed diplomats, and technicians from Soviet and satellite countries, including about one hundred East Germans. There were also several hundred Chinese.

In a conversation with President Nyerere early in 1964, the author was told by him that he was becoming increasingly worried over the Zanzibar situation. Here he was faced with a major dilemma. He lacked sufficient military-security strength to take definite action to annex Zanzibar or to neutralize it. He also lacked sufficient economic strength to project Tanganyika's beneficent suzerainty into Zanzibar's national life. Either he could let the festering sore develop without action or he could take a calculated risk in seeking political amalgamation with Zanzibar. The latter course would require "swallowing" and "digesting" the islands into the larger Tanganyikan political whole. (He later took the latter course, that of union.)

Mainly with the help of his "number one" lieutenant, Rashidi Kawawa (who had solid trade-union connections on the islands), and Kassim Hanga (also a former trade unionist and then Zanzibar's Prime Minister), Nyerere secretly achieved an agreement for union of Zanzibar with Tanganyika. The two units, combining, were to become one United Republic of Tanzania. At that time a new flag heralded the new union—blue being added to the original tricolor of green, black, and yellow.

On April 23, 1964, President Nyerere and President Karume of Zanzibar signed articles of union under which their countries were to become a single sovereign state. On April 25, 1964, Nyerere called the National Assembly into special session. After brief debate essential legislation was passed unanimously. Union Day is now commemorated each April 26. By terms of the union Nyerere was to remain president while Abeid Karume was to become first vice president of the United Republic of Tanzania. Concurrently, Karume would remain administrative head of Zanzibar/Pemba. Rashidi Kawawa was to become second vice president as well as deputy to Nyerere on the mainland.

Various members of the Zanzibar Revolutionary Council, including Kassim Hanga and Abdulrahman Mohammed Babu, were given cabinet posts in the union government. Though Tanganyika itself was a one-party state, the Afro-Shirazi Party was permitted to continue its political domination over the islands. In addition, thirty-two members of the Zanzibar Revolutionary Council were given seats *en bloc* in the Tanzanian National Assembly.

Shortly after the announcement of union, the Tanzanian Foreign Ministry announced that countries having diplomatic establishments on Zanzibar would be asked to downgrade their establishments to consulates. The United States, the Soviet Union, and China took such action. East Germany made bitter complaint but was finally forced to comply with the downgrading, though it had no embassy on the mainland.

These were some of the steps by which Nyerere and his TANU colleagues sought to "swallow" and thus control the Zanzibar revolutionary polity. Whether that digestive process has been successful remains a moot question, requiring later detailed examination. Forecasting indigestion, the *Economist* (London) of June 13, 1964, carried a pessimistic article on the union titled, "The Perils of Nyerere." The article contended:

Despatches from Dar es Salaam have been . . . disheartening. . . . Dr. Julius Nyerere, President of Tanganyika, managed half the work of a python: he swallowed Zanzibar all right. But he did not crush its fighting force first. The live animal is a long time digesting, and its kicks are being felt hurtfully, and possibly even fatally, deep inside Tanganyika's body politic. Zanzibar's Ministers have largely carried on as if the United Republic had never been heard of. . . . If the battle is to be won, in Dar es Salaam's view it must be won by politics. This means playing along with the Zanzibaris.

President Nyerere's New Year's message of January 2, 1965, attested to the seriousness with which he viewed the Zanzibar dangers to the mainland and the significance of its ameliorative step:

The Union between Tanganyika and Zanzibar is the event which history will record for 1964. . . . It has enormous importance. . . . Because of it there will be less and less possibility for the enemies of Africa even to try and use one of us against the other. And because of this Union we can now work together to exploit our resources, and reinforce each other's efforts. . . . The Revolution itself was a necessary precondition; . . .

had the basic principles of democracy been followed in the independence constitution of Zanzibar the progress which has begun could have begun earlier, . . . without bloodshed. . . . But the attempt to impose on Zanzibar a minority government of privilege inevitably introduced a necessity which the mainland was spared by the fact that independence was achieved by the Party of the masses—TANU.

Visiting Africa in December 1963 and again in June 1964, Chinese Communist Premier Chou En-lai had pressed for worldwide intensification of revolutionary pressures by "have-nots" against "haves"; for pressures from the agrarian East and South against the affluent, metropolitan West; for alliance of Asia, Africa, and Latin America against Europe and North America. News sources at the time quoted Chou En-lai as saying, "An excellent revolutionary situation exists in Africa."

Indeed, in many countries of Africa, that situation was true. This is attested by the difficulties experienced in East Africa during 1964 and by coup situations which arose within other African nations before and since. Between December 1963 and June 1964 the Chinese Communists changed their focus of attention in Africa and readjusted their priorities. Instead of concentrating their attentions on West Africa (notably Mali, Guinea, and Ghana) they shifted attention and priority to East Africa (including Tanganyika, Zanzibar, Kenya, and Somalia). By late 1964 the Communist Chinese had extended to Tanzania trade and aid agreements valued at $30 million. Peking reserved its greatest African effort for the agreement to finance, engineer, and construct the costly Tanzania-Zambia (Tan-Zam) railway. Given the extent of the financial, manpower, and technical energies which had been required of Peking in this venture, the Chinese were clearly gambling long-term for African support and friendship.

In June 1964 Premier Chou En-lai made an official visit to Dar es Salaam. The communiqué that he and President Nyerere released following that visit is of importance as the first indication of Peking's growing association with Tanzania. Both parties noted the international struggle against "colonialism and neocolonialism." They paid high tribute to the Vietnamese people fighting "heroically" against foreign (United States) intervention; they condemned "foreign exploitation in Latin America"; they condemned racial discrimination pursued by the South African and Southern Rhodesian white racist minority governments; they pledged support to indigenous southern Africans in their struggles for independence; they pledged continuing cooperation between the two countries in behalf of Afro-Asian solidarity.

In February 1965 President Nyerere paid his first of several state visits to China. He addressed a mass rally in Peking, where he restated his policy of nonalignment (this in distinct contrast to the highly partisan and anti-Western communiqué mentioned above). The essence of Nyerere's statement was as follows:

Where there are hostile blocs, . . . Tanzania will ignore the threats or blandishments from both sides, and pursue her own interests. . . . We shall seek economic and technical cooperation from wherever we can find them without strings which limit our freedom. We inherited an economy linked and geared to the capitalist world; we are shaking off the restrictions which that implied.

In the thirteenth and fourteenth centuries the East Coast of Africa had trade with China. Now our independent countries are once again having trade with you. We are anxious to build up this trade. . . . Our non-alignment policy means that we wish to be friendly with all nations on the basis of human dignity and equality. . . . Each country must choose for itself its own form of society according to its own objective circumstances. . . . We will never allow our friends to choose our enemies for us. . . . We are told that China was "dangerous," . . . that a few of her technicians could undermine our whole country. . . . I say . . . "nonsense." We offer the hand of friendship to China as to America, Russia, Britain and others. We shall see for ourselves what are China's intentions toward us. We shall not be told by others.[1]

Between the time of Tanganyika's independence and early 1964, relations between Tanganyika and the United States were generally good. During 1964–65, however, the political atmosphere between the two nations had radically altered. Part of the abrasion may have stemmed from the tensions of the Zanzibar revolution and the abortive coup on the mainland. Debate over Cold War issues, including Vietnam, was also a contributory factor. The upsurge of the Congo troubles, especially the "Stanleyville" incident, further muddied the waters. So, too, did the increasing interest of the Tanzanians in Peking. Unjustified accusations against (and expulsions of) American diplomats by the Tanzanian government heightened bad relations between the two nations.

In a far-ranging politico-economic memorandum entitled "Principles and Development," issued in June 1966, Nyerere made caustic reference to the foregoing difficulties with the United States:

We have twice quarreled with the U.S. Government, once when we believed it to be involved in a plot against us, and again when two of its officials misbehaved and were asked to leave Tanzania. Both matters have since been cleared up by agreement and in neither case was any existing aid agreement affected. But the disagreements certainly induced an uncooperative coldness between us, thus suspending and then greatly slowing down further aid discussions. A comparison of American aid to Tanzania and to other African countries supports that contention. . . . Our total policies have led to a lower level of assistance than might otherwise have been granted.

It will be recalled that in 1963 TANU membership had pushed for adoption of a one-party state in Tanganyika and elimination of the British-model multiparty constitution. In recognition of these demands, Nyerere had set up a presidential commission to study the situation in January 1964. The report of that presidential commission recommending establishment of a "democratic one-party state" was published on March 22, 1965. The recommendations of that commission were incorporated into a new "interim" constitution for Tanzania, approved by the National Assembly on July 5, 1965.

In summary, the Commission's study:

1. opened TANU membership to all Tanzanian citizens who adhered to the party's principles and sought to make of the party a truly national movement;

2. rejected the proposed amalgamation of the TANU National Executive and the National Assembly but changed the composition of the National Assembly and the method of its election and thus achieved a closer association between the Executive Council and the National Assembly;

3. recommended that all members of the National Assembly (and candidates for election thereto) be members of TANU;

4. determined that three (later changed to two) candidates for parliamentary seats and local offices be put forward to voters, these candidates chosen by district committees and countersigned by the National Executive;

5. decreed that all members of Parliament be designated ex officio delegates to annual party conventions and that the Central Committee supervise work of both party and Parliament;

6. determined that all ministers and junior ministers be made members of the National Assembly;

7. designated the National Executive of TANU on the mainland and the Afro-Shirazi Party on Zanzibar to put forward one candidate for president and that name would be approved by electorate with "Yes" or "No" vote on the same day that parliamentary elections take place. If the majority voted "No" an alternative name was to be set forth;

8. required presidential as well as parliamentary election to follow upon any dissolution of government;

9. provided for selection of a new president, in event of the death of the incumbent, by the National Assembly sitting as an "electoral college";

10. provided that civil servants be permitted to join TANU and made members of the National Assembly if so nominated by the president;

11. coordinated work and membership of the National Executive and local authorities but made TANU and local authorities separate and distinct bodies;

12. decreed that relations between party and trade unions be coordinated but that trade unions be subordinate to party and government.

Detailed discussion of the 1965 elections in Tanzania is contained in chapter 7 of this book. A brief restatement of the essential results of that election, however, will not be amiss here. Those elections took place during the period September 21–26, 1965 and, despite the operation of a one-party state, they provided an important political innovation. The election, based on universal suffrage, provided choices of candidates in almost all the 107 constituencies on the mainland (voting in Zanzibar took place only for the presidential candidate). The most important result was that 75 percent of the membership of the National Assembly was changed by the election. This two-candidate system gives a certain justification to Nyerere's thesis that one party states can still be "democratic" in nature.

A new and thorny foreign-policy issue now arose for Tanzania. On November 11, 1965, Southern Rhodesia declared itself unilaterally independent of Britain. Nyerere at once recognized the likely failures of British and United Nations sanctions to "bring Smith's Rhodesian regime down." Realizing that Britain did not intend to use force to accomplish that purpose, Nyerere initiated an OAU drive to break diplomatic relations with Whitehall. In the *London Observer* of December 12, 1965, Nyerere stated his views, titled "Why I am Threatening to Break with Britain." Saying that Britain had flaunted both Commonwealth and African advice on the Rhodesian issue, Nyerere contended that his country, despite enormous economic losses, would be obliged to cut its diplomatic ties with Britain unless it took decisive action to end the Rhodesian independence. Nyerere claimed that Tanzania would not leave the Commonwealth, since that was a multinational organization and not primarily British. He insisted that Britain settle the Rhodesian Unilateral Declaration of Independence issue forthwith, by force if necessary. Soon thereafter Tanzania did sever diplomatic ties with Britain (losing 7.5 million pounds of promised aid from London as a result). Those ties remained severed until June 1968.

As a concomitant of the Rhodesian Unilateral Declaration of Independence (UDI), relationships between Zambia and Britain also became complicated. Fallout from that problem in turn directly affected Tanzania. Zambia's main source of power, Rhodesian coal, along with the movement of mined copper (outward) and essential supplies (inward), had been heavily dependent on Rhodesian railways and on the Portuguese ports in Mozambique and Angola. Zambia's leaders decided that they could no longer be so dependent upon these white-dominated, racist, minority governments. Thus it was in their national interest to seek alternative outlets to the sea.

Zambia, in cooperation with Tanzania and with foreign-aid donors including the United States, took decisions to alleviate this situation. First, it was decided to institute an airlift of copper outward and essential supplies inward. This airlift was to utilize the seaports and airports of Dar es Salaam and Mtwara/Lindi in Tanzania. Next, it was essential to increase the all-weather capabilities and truck-carrying capacity of the Great North Road, running from Dar es Salaam southwesterly via Iringa and Mbeya to the Zambian border. Then it was essential to construct an oil pipeline from Tanzanian seaports to Zambia and with this action to shift over a high proportion of

Zambia's smelting needs from Rhodesian coal to Arabian oil. All these efforts were in progress or in full use by 1968 as a result of high-priority action by all governments concerned.

Finally, it was agreed by Zambian and Tanzanian authorities that the so-called Tan-Zam railway from Dar es Salaam to Zambia's copperbelt would need to be constructed. The World Bank and several Western nations (including the United States and Britain) refused to provide funds for engineering and construction of this line (presumably on economic grounds alone); the communist Chinese were then approached by Tanzania and Zambia. The Tan-Zam rail project described in detail in later pages represents Peking's largest aid effort of the African continent to date, matched in size and value only by the Russian-financed Egyptian Aswan Dam and the United States-backed Volta River power project in Ghana.

The year 1966 in Tanzania brought about a period of consolidation and concentration on development planning; on problems of national and international unity; and, as noted above, major assistance to Zambia in the wake of the Rhodesian UDI troubles. Tanzania's Development Plan for the period 1964–69 had set a goal of 246 million pounds. Some 40 percent of this was to come from foreign grants and loans, the remainder to be obtained from internal sources, public and private.

In a paper circulated in Tanzania in 1966, a Canadian economist, G.K. Helleiner, head of the Bureau of Economic Research, University of Dar es Salaam, made the following striking contentions: (a) as of 1966 the developed nations of the world were growing twice as fast as the developing nations; (b) aid from the rich nations to the poor nations had actually shrunk rather than increased during the first half of the First United Nations Development Decade; (c) more public capital funds were now flowing out of the underdeveloped world than were flowing inward, since poor nations were now repaying more on past loans than they were receiving in new loans; (d) "tied" aid cuts away as much as one-half of ordinary foreign aid in terms of value received; (e) prime commodities were falling in value so fast that loss of income derived therefrom was not made up by foreign aid, public and private.[2]

By mid-1966 Nyerere and his financial advisers were coming to realize that Tanzania was a classic illustration of a poor nation suffering from all these economic stresses. It was also becoming evident to them that the current economic development plan was overweighed in several sectors and that new priorities would need to be developed. For example, agricultural development and villagization would need to be rejuvenated and re-energized. Furthermore, in view of the increasing lack of funds for foreign aid as well as the lack of investment capital from internal sources, Nyerere decided that it was essential to revitalize his 1962 *Ujamaa* principle of self-help. In the face of these national needs, the broad and revolutionary concepts of nationalization and of austerity were set forth in the 1967 Arusha Declaration.

In his June 1966 memorandum to TANU's National Executive, entitled "Principles and Development," Nyerere answered external criticism by spelling out his views on *Ujamaa*, on international investment, and on African socialism as applied to Tanzania:

It is suggested that if Tanzania were to adopt a policy of capitalistic economic development our development would be much faster. In particular our progressive taxation, and our emphasis on the need for public enterprise is said to discourage private capitalists themselves, and also to result in a lack of interest in our needs on the part of international institutions.

. . . The truth is that we not only undertake negotiations to attract private investment into certain kinds of industry, but that we have also put on to the Statute Book several pieces of legislation . . . designed to meet the reasonable fears of those who are considering bringing their money into Tanzania from outside. . . . It is probably true, however, that a taxation policy based on the principle that the wealthy should pay a much higher proportion of their income than the poor does discourage some possible investors. Obviously a balance must be maintained . . . but it is important to understand that we want private (foreign and local) investment for a purpose, and only if it fulfills that purpose can we be expected to welcome it.

We want capital investment here so that the amount of wealth which can be produced in Tanzania is increased and our people will therefore become better off in the future. Yet because we are now a poor nation . . . we cannot spend much money on improving our capacity to produce in the future. . . . We have to assess the benefits of foreign investment for both sides. . . .

But there is another side altogether in this question of *Ujamaa.* In a country like ours, development depends primarily on the efforts and hard work of our own people and on their enthusiasm and belief that they and their country will benefit from whatever they do. . . . If the people do not have reason to believe that the object of their government is the well-being of the people as a whole why should they be expected to cooperate with that government in its activities?

In African society in particular this is very important. Traditionally we lived as families, with individuals supporting each other and helping each other on terms of equality. We recognized that each of us had a place in the community, and this place carried with it rights to whatever food and shelter was available in return for the use of whatever abilities and energies we had. . . . But the community was a unit in which every individual was important, and among which the goods available were shared without too great inequality.

This attitude is, basically, what we mean by saying that traditionally African society was a socialist society. And when we say that Tanzania is aiming at building "African Socialism" we mean that we intend to adopt the same attitude in the new circumstances of a nation state which is increasingly using modern techniques of economic production. . . . But the purpose remains the same as in the traditional society. This is, the welfare of every individual in the context of the needs of the society of which he is a member. . . .

If our determination to pursue this objective annoys some people who might otherwise have assisted us in our economic development, what are we supposed to do? Abandon our objective?

On July 13, 1966, speaking at the inauguration of the University of Zambia in Lusaka, Nyerere made several important points on major African issues.[3] He stressed the need for movement toward Pan-African unity. He spoke to the need of developing a "national outlook" among students and that a true feeling of nationhood be encouraged. He spoke of the need to overcome tribalism, separatism, and fragmentation. He spoke of the fears of new foreign domination which could come in the wake of such disunity. He spoke of the need for regional cooperation which could offset such dangers. He forewarned that Africa, in another century, may be disunited and weak like Latin America, rather than united and strong and wealthy like the United States of America.

In the same speech, Nyerere admitted that the two components of his own republic—mainland Tanzania and Zanzibar—"are not yet fully integrated but . . . there is no question about their being much more integrated than they would have been had two separate governments merely tried to cooperate. . . . "

The establishment in 1947 of the East African High Commission, later to become the East African Common Services Organization, had been the work of Arthur Creech-Jones, then colonial secretary of the United Kingdom. He believed that to unite the three East African territories into a common market would not only benefit Kenya, Uganda, and Tanganyika economically, but eventually would build racial and political cooperation between them. At that time and subsequently both Tanganyikans and Ugandans resisted these moves toward economic or political unity because they much feared Kenya's eventual white-settler domination.

The East African Community, including Tanzania, Kenya, and Uganda, was formed by a treaty of cooperation concluded at Kampala on June 6, 1967. This treaty provided for a regional common market; a common investment policy; continuation, on a decentralized basis, of existing common services including railways, harbors, airways, customs, posts and telegraphs. It also provided for convertibility of the existing individual national currencies. The treaty further sought to harmonize investment policies and to establish an East African Development Bank. The governing body of the East African Community is comprised of the three heads of state of the partner countries. These are assisted by ministerial councils as well as economic planning and consultative bodies.

The East African Authority Secretariat and Legislative Assembly is located at Arusha, Tanzania. Headquarters of the Development Bank and Posts and Telegraphs are located in Kampala, Uganda. Airways and Railways headquarters are located at Nairobi, Kenya. Harbors headquarters are located at Dar es Salaam with inland marine services centered at Mwanza, Tanzania.

A broader but still tentative regional economic association is being sought by the East African partners with a membership of nations including Zambia, Malawi, Ethiopia, Somalia, Rwanda, Burundi, Mauritius, and Madagascar. Establishment of this community was proposed at a meeting, sponsored by the Ethiopian-based United Nations Economic Commission for Africa (UNECA), in Lusaka, in November 1965. When a follow-up meeting was held in Addis Ababa, in May 1966, seven countries signed up as associates of the group with three more joining later. The major function of this regional community is to carry out cooperative economic programs; to aid industrial and economic development; to coordinate transportation, agricultural and scientific research; and to support the reorganization of the East African Community.

The most outstanding events of Tanzania's national life in 1967–68 occurred during the early months of that year and included (1) the Arusha Declaration, (2) the various acts of nationalization, (3) the political "passing" of Oscar Kambona.

Preliminary to the drafting of the Arusha Declaration late in January 1967, two other related events had occurred. On January 2 the National Union of Tanganyika Workers meeting in Dar es Salaam had passed a resolution calling for appointment of a presidential commission to define socialism as it applied to Tanzania. Three weeks later, addressing the country's regional commissioners in Arusha, Nyerere set forth a code of ethics for members of TANU. Among other things, he said leaders of TANU must live by the sweat of their brow and not by the labor of others; they must constitute the vanguard of socialist construction in Tanzania; they must have only one house and none other to rent; they must have no shares or directorates in capitalist companies; and they must receive no more than one salary.

During the period January 26–29, 1967, meeting in Arusha, the TANU National Executive drew up the so-called Arusha Declaration.[4] Details of this Declaration were made public by Nyerere on February 5 when the president addressed a mass rally in Dar es Salaam. The Declaration defines African socialism as requiring the absence of exploitation; the control and ownership of major means of production by workers (including lands, forests, minerals, water, oil, communications, banks, insurance, industry, various forms of trade, etc.); an elective democracy; and a firm dedication to socialism as an ideology. A composite of presidential and party thought, it embodies the country's basic political and social philosophy.

On February 10, 1967, addressing the diplomatic corps in Dar es Salaam, (as reported by American Embassy sources), Nyerere reiterated the theme of self-reliance for Tanzania's citizens:

No other nation is, or should be responsible for Tanzania's development. This policy of self-reliance is essential to us. But it does not mean that we wish to isolate ourselves from the world, or that we have become less appreciative of assistance and co-operation from other countries. A man who recognizes that he must build his own house is not ungrateful to those whose assistance enables him to make faster progress. . . . Although Tanzania has adopted this policy of self-reliance, its future is still bound up with the world economy.

The following day, February 11, 1967, Nyerere issued a statement summarizing the various actions taken by the government of Tanzania to nationalize major areas of production within the terms of the Arusha Declaration. The principal areas of nationalization were (1) all foreign banks in the country, excepting only the cooperative banks; (2) all firms engaged in food processing, larger industrial plants, and some sisal plantations; (3) insurance, for which a national insurance company was set up to take over all new private life insurance activities; and (4) import-export and wholesale trade, accomplished by the government's taking over all major import and export houses and using them to form a new State Trading Corporation. Nyerere also announced that the government would assume controlling interest in breweries, shoe manufacture, tobacco, container plants, and eventually all sisal plantations. He announced that full and fair compensation would eventually be paid for nationalization actions.

The Arusha Declaration and allied nationalization actions had clearly reestablished earlier (1962–63) national priorities for *Ujamaa* villagization and peasant farming. It took the current emphasis off development of industry and back into agriculture. Concentration on urban development and a private capital economy was now to be downgraded in favor of rural development and state "socialism."

First reactions to the nationalization acts were confused. Import-export business came to a virtual standstill. Banking services temporarily shriveled up. First estimates of the compensation bill ranged from $75 million to $200 million. (Nyerere's actions to nationalize have not been alone on the African continent. Similar actions have been taken in Ghana, Zaire, Sierra Leone, Sudan, Zambia and, most recently, Uganda.)

Many Western economists and businessmen construed such actions as speculative gambles, self-defeating and administratively impractical. Many construed such nationalization steps as, in fact, compounding Tanzania's economic ills by frightening off both public and private foreign capital. To Nyerere it may have appeared that, facing the economic stagnation and deepening gloom of his nation's economy, lacking internal capital and confronted with the drying up of external aid, there was no alternative. It now appears that some of Nyerere's top foreign advisers, including Canadians and Americans, may have advocated such an economic route—including revitalization of the themes of self-reliance and massive re-emphasis on agriculture.

Musing to a friend in July 1967, Nyerere said: "I am a democrat and I could not be a Stalin. I would not regiment my people. Democracy in the African context is not the sophisticated and many faceted thing which it is in places where democracy works at every level such as Britain and the United States. We need less sophisticated [political and economic] models in our present phase."

The year 1967 was also notable for the disappearance from Tanzania's political scene of Oscar Kambona. As previously noted he had been one of the founders of TANU and the party's secretary-general for thirteen years. He had held portfolios of Foreign Affairs, Defense, Home Affairs, Education, and Regional Affairs.

A constant political associate of Nyerere over the period from 1954 to 1967, Kambona was a man of many faces. He was considered a ruthless, highly pragmatic politician and one of the two men most likely to succeed Nyerere (the other being Rashidi Kawawa). Though Kambona never, until 1967, showed himself in clear-cut opposition to Nyerere, his antagonisms to Nyerere and to Kawawa were long suspected by many Tanzanians and outsiders. Only Nyerere's intense loyalty to his long-time associate had kept Kambona in power till then.

Kambona had been associated with the most militant of Tanzania's foreign affairs activities. He had been chairman of the OAU African Liberation Committee planning and activating the Freedom Fighters program aimed at liberating southern Africa from white rule. It is the opinion of this author, who has known him for some years, that Kambona has always held extremist racial views and sensitivities. He played both sides of the political fence—Communist and anti-Communist, pro-Western and anti-Western. He was often virulent in his condemnation of the West, particularly Britain and the United States. He might even have been implicated in the Zanzibar coup of January 1964. The extent of his association with the subsequent Tanzanian mainland coup attempt was never clarified. He probably avoided challenging Nyerere openly because of the great affection in which Nyerere was held by the mass of the Tanzanians and because other principal lieutenants proved loyal to Nyerere.

In June of 1967 Kambona resigned from the cabinet after a reshuffle had presumably demoted him from regional affairs minister to minister of local government and rural development. At the same time he gave up his post as TANU's secretary-general. The long-standing quarrels with Kambona had been pushed into the open by his demotion and by the "austerity" measures directed at ministers in the wake of the Arusha Declaration. Subsequently, Kambona fled to Europe after being accused of complicity in a plot to overthrow Nyerere. Certain of his henchmen (including Kassim Hanga, former Zanzibar coup leader and later minister in the Tanzanian cabinet) were arrested. It now appears that, in the belief that, even in jail, Kambona would prove to be a dangerous political force, Nyerere deliberately let him escape.

From his places of exile in Europe, Kambona has continued to rail against Nyerere's regime.

On January 11, 1968, Vice President Kawawa, speaking in the National Assembly, gave evidence that Kambona had deposited unexplained sums in his Dar es Salaam bank account, had managed to purchase five houses during 1965 and 1966 and, in December 1966, received a large sum from an "undetermined" source in London. At a subsequent public rally, Nyerere characterized Kambona as a "thief and a prostitute," charging that he had robbed Africa.

In 1969 the political ghost of Oscar Kambona reappeared in Tanzania. A group of Kambona's henchmen were arrested, accused of planning a coup against Nyerere. The group, numbering seven, included Michael Kamaliza, former labor leader and protégé of Vice President Kawawa; and Bibi Titi Mohammed, first woman member of TANU and long-time' member of Parliament. The prosecution claimed that Kambona had masterminded the plot and that four of the seven accused were members of Kambona's tribal tree.[5] After a lengthy trial, the accused were convicted and imprisoned.

An *Atlantic* report on Tanzania (May 1973) attests that these supporters of Kambona have now been quietly released from prison. The same *Atlantic* reportage intimates that Kambona has recently been actively associating himself with Nyerere's enemies in Portugal, South Africa, and Uganda. These efforts appear still to be aimed at enlisting support and financing for Nyerere's overthrow.

Well aware of Kambona's vitriolic influences, Nyerere often warned publicly against the dangers of divisiveness of racialism and tribalism. In a signed editorial in the newspaper *The Nationalist*, appearing on February 14, 1968, he urged Tanzanians not to interject racialism and xenophobia into the current drive toward socialism: "Otherwise socialism will become ruthless Fascism and will lose the belief in the oneness of man. Neither is it sensible for socialists to talk as if all capitalists are devils. . . . To divide up people working for our nation into groups of good and bad according to their skin colour or their national origin, or their tribal origin, is to sabotage the work we have just embarked upon. . . . "

In a nationwide broadcast, December 9, 1968 (the seventh anniversary of his country's independence), Nyerere again warned all Tanzanians against the dangers of tribalism and racialism. He said people "should be treated according to their actions as individuals and not according to their colour." Stating that he had heard more and more whispers of tribalism and racialism, he said he wished to bring these dangers into the open as it "was absolutely taboo for a socialist country to divide and persecute people on account of their colour."

The years 1968–69 in Tanzania brought continuing concentration on nationalization and its aftereffects; continuing emphasis on *Ujamaa;* and renewed attention by Nyerere to international problems including African unity, Nigeria/Biafra, Zambia/Rhodesia, and the white redoubt of southern Africa.

During May 1968 heads of the fourteen associated East and Central African states met in Dar es Salaam. Tackling the problem of Rhodesia, the "summit" group decried the failure of sanctions and advocated stronger action by the United Nations and by Britain. On the Nigerian issue, Nyerere pushed for recognition of Biafra (a step concurred in only by Gabon, Zambia, and the Ivory Coast). The conference also gave voice to the need for reality as opposed to theory in African unity.

In his book *Freedom and Socialism*, published in 1969, Nyerere admitted that efforts to build a modern-traditionalist socialist state in Tanzania divided his people into three main groups: (1) those who subscribed wholeheartedly to Nyerere's policies, including complete support of the Arusha Declaration; (2) those who considered it wrong for the country to have abandoned its traditional ways before Tanzania's economy was stronger; and (3) those who considered that Tanzania's socialism was halfhearted and should become more communistic. Nyerere in this work continues to emphasize *Ujamaa*, communal cooperation, selflessness and self-denial. His domestic opponents construed much of this as idealist, too anemic, insufficiently militant, and insufficiently ruthless. Nyerere, however, continued to be optimistic and tolerant of his politico-economic opponents. He continued to emphasize the need of closing the gap between urbanized elite and rural masses, combining theories of democracy with theories of socialism. In the wake of rising prices and inflationary pressures, some Tanzanian politicians pressed for more nationalization, though Nyerere had earlier promised that it would cease.

An editorial, attributed to Nyerere, appearing in *The Nationalist* newspaper of Dar es Salaam on February 6, 1969 (the second anniversary of the Arusha Declaration), spoke somewhat glumly of the country's progress in socialization. The editorial emphasized that Tanzania needed more "socialists" who understood problems of building a nation. It added: "It is not enough that our traditional life should have been based on socialist principles; that is good, but it is necessary that the leaders in modernization should also accept those principles and be able to apply them in the very different psychological and international conditions of the 20th Century."

Another summit conference of fourteen East and Central African heads-of-state convened in Lusaka in April 1969. The most important action taken by the conference was the issuance of the so-called Lusaka Manifesto on Southern Africa. This manifesto was reportedly drafted by Presidents Nyerere and Kaunda. The document reaffirmed the equality of all men; condemned domination of a majority by a minority; acknowledged the need of progress toward goals of tolerance and equality in all nations; expressed hostility toward the colonialist governments of southern Africa and appealed to other members of the human race for support (against these racist regimes) and their denial of human equality; emphasized that the conference's hostility was not toward these states because they were white-ruled but because they avoided self-determination and equality.

At the same time the Lusaka conferees promised that they would seek no alteration of present boundaries of the states of southern Africa; advocated dialogue and negotiation rather than violence to achieve emancipation of the southern African majorities; regretted that, while peaceful progress toward self-determination was blocked, it had no choice but to give support in the struggle to existing liberation movements; insisted on withdrawal of Portugal from Africa; insisted that Britain reassert its authority over Rhodesia and provide majority rule for that territory before granting its independence; reemphasized that a political settlement in South-West Africa, based on majority rule, remained a United Nations responsibility; emphasized that treatment of peoples within South Africa is ordinarily an internal responsibility, but that the outside world must intervene to overthrow apartheid and restore principles of humanity; stated that action must follow words and South Africa must be ostracized and isolated by the world community if it rejects principles of human equality; reaffirmed the commitment to principles of human equality, human dignity, self-determination, and nonracialism.

The Lusaka Manifesto elicited much favorable reaction in the United Nations, London, and Washington. However, it provoked little comment, and no official reaction, in Pretoria, Salisbury, or Lisbon. Though Prime Minister John Vorster of South Africa has since made certain economic and political overtures to some neighboring black states (particularly Malawi and Zambia), it has now become obvious that prospects of any real dialogue between black states and white states emanating from the Lusaka proposals are more remote than ever.

In the October 1970 general election President Nyerere, running unopposed for a third term, received 95 percent of the popular vote. As in 1965 TANU again chose two candidates in each of the 120 constituencies. Again, as in 1965, a large number of former parliamentarians and several ministers were defeated. While the Zanzibar/Pemba constituencies voted for the office of president, they did not re-elect their representatives in the National Assembly. These stood over from 1964–65 Revolutionary Council leadership which had originally been included in the parliamentary body.

NOTES

1. Julius K. Nyerere, *Freedom and Unity* (London: Oxford University Press, 1966), pp. 323ff.
2. See *Washington Post*, February 26, 1967.
3. *The Nationalist* (Dar es Salaam), July 13, 1966.
4. Text in Julius K. Nyerere, *Freedom and Socialism* (London: Oxford University Press, 1970), pp. 231ff.
5. *Africa Report*, December 1970), p. 5.

CHAPTER 10

TANZANIA:
THE SECOND DECADE

At the height of the Congo troubles in the early 1960s, United States Secretary of State Dean Rusk was quoted as saying that many newly independent countries became states before they became nations. This wise observation was all the more apt since, between 1943 and the present day, more than seventy-seven new states have joined the world community. Of these, forty-seven (including Tanzania) are in Africa.

By attaining statehood in 1961, Tanganyika met one of its three prime goals—freedom. There remained to be met the goals of unity and of equality, the latter including major social and economic advances for its people. In Tanzania's first ten years, President Nyerere and his government struggled constantly, against great odds, to reach these goals.

By the time Tanzania celebrated its first decade of existence, December 9, 1971, it appeared that Tanzanians were nearing the second of their major goals—unity. Thus they now met Secretary Rusk's implicit concept of nationhood—being now both state and nation. They still struggle mightily, however, under programs of *Ujamaa* and self-reliance to meet their third goal—social and economic equality.

During the years 1971–75, four recurrent themes dominated Tanzania's national and international life. First among these was the running conflict with the Uganda military regime of General Idi Amin. Second was the pressure for completion of the Tan-Zam railway and related transport facilities. Third was the ubiquitous problem of Zanzibar, re-energized by the April 1972 assassination of the island's leader, Abeid Karume. Fourth was the continuing emphasis on self-reliance, which was aimed at improving the economic lot of the ordinary Tanzanian. Each of these situations requires detailed consideration.

In their early postindependence years, the governments and peoples of Uganda and Tanzania appeared to become increasingly friendly. They had found natural grounds for alliance in their mutual antagonisms toward purported or attempted domination by Kenya of East African politics and commerce. They had built useful intellectual associations as well through development of sectors of the new East African University, of which institution Nyerere had become chancellor. Even the reserve which Nyerere and Ugandan President Obote had shown toward one another in early years had apparently disappeared. The only real abrasions in the Tanzanian-Ugandan relationships lay in the peculiar geographic-economic dependence of the far northwest region of Tanzania (the Bukoba area) which, by its very location, was oriented toward Uganda.

A military coup on January 24, 1971, was mounted against Obote's regime while he was absent from the country. General Idi Amin supplanted Obote as Uganda's leader. That military takeover was to shake the positions and confidence of other constitutional East African leaders, including Nyerere. The change was to worsen materially Ugandan-Tanzanian relationships. The new frictions resulted in part from the fact that the deposed Obote and some of his followers found political refuge in Tanzania. From there Obote has sought means to overthrow Amin's regime, so far unsuccessfully. Thus leaders and people of Uganda and Tanzania became sworn enemies. Both nations have indulged in constant verbal barrage and occasional halfhearted military forays across one another's borders.

Amin, until his takeover of the Ugandan government, had been second in command of the country's armed forces. He had found bases for his action in tribalism, in discontent with Obote's treatment of the military, and in the fact that, since Obote had come to power at independence, Uganda had held no elections for nine years. The deposed Obote mounted diplomatic efforts against Amin, seeking to prevent other African nations, including the Organization of African Unity (OAU), from recognizing the Amin regime. These efforts, however, were unsuccessful and only Nyerere's Tanzanian government, hosting Obote, held out against recognition. (The OAU recognized Amin's regime on June 11, 1971.)

In the months thereafter, sporadic air raids and ground attacks were made by military forces of both sides. These attacks took place in the contiguous border area of the northwestern region of Tanzania and southeastern region of Uganda. Despite these difficulties, it appeared in October 1971 that the two countries had partially reconciled their differences. At that time they were able to agree on continuation of their association in the East African Community (EAC) and Ugandan officials thereof were permitted to pursue their work at EAC headquarters in Arusha, Tanzania.

In September 1972 Amin again came into the international spotlight with his expulsion of some 70,000 of the 75,000 Asians resident in Uganda. Many of these were British subjects, others were Ugandan nationals. Some of the exiles were admitted to the United Kingdom. Others found new homes in Canada, Western Europe, India, the United States, and Tanzania. All of them were driven from Uganda virtually penniless, the Ugandan government confiscating their assets and terrorizing them in the departure process.[1]

These expulsions precipitated new efforts to invade Uganda from Tanzania by Obote and his followers. The foray parties included some newly exiled Asians. These invasion efforts, which took place in September 1972, failed. Their only result appeared to be a strengthening of Amin's internal position, especially among tribes antagonistic to Obote.

The innate distrust of Africans toward Asians extended to Kenya and Tanzania as well as Uganda. However, there were in Tanzania no overt moves against the Asian population. Nyerere condemned the expulsion of the Asians from Uganda, terming the action "clearly racialism. . . . Either Asians are citizens or they are not, . . . and once they are, you are enjoined to accord them the same treatment that you accord all the others."[2] Under Nyerere's socialism programs which followed upon the Arusha Declaration, some economic pressures have been mounted against the Asians in Tanzania as a result of nationalization of sisal plantations. However, there were a few private, but no officially inspired governmental efforts to exile the Asians from Tanzania. Although some 20,000 Asians are reported to have left mainland Tanzania in the wake of the Uganda troubles and unrelated difficulties in Zanzibar, some 86,000 Asians still remain. Most of these hold Tanzanian citizenship.

In October 1972, through mediation inspired by Somalia, Sudan, and other OAU members, Tanzania and Uganda finally agreed to a cease-fire and a demilitarized zone along the troubled borders. They also agreed to admit temporarily an observer force from Somalia, to cease their antagonistic propaganda barrages, and to refrain from subversive action against one another. Thus they sought to restrict activities by Obote and his followers, who were still sheltered in Tanzania. Both countries also agreed to free hostages held by each.[3]

Despite this 1972 accord and subsequent conciliatory statements made by both sides, hostile attitudes continued to bedevil relationships between Tanzania and Uganda. On March 25, 1973, Ugandan authorities contended that a small military force from Tanzania attempted invasion of Uganda. The accusation was made from Kampala that this invasion was the work of Nyerere and Obote.[4] Dar es Salaam disagreed, insisting that the "so-called invasion was complete nonsense." More recent press reports indicate that Uganda was seeking additional arms and planes.

The Economist of June 2, 1973, reported that, at the tenth anniversary meeting of the OAU in Addis Ababa, efforts were made to bring the Tanzanian and Ugandan presidents together. They are said to have shaken hands and "signed an agreement to restore friendly relations." However, bad blood continues between the two leaders to this day, and there has been much sabre-rattling on both sides of their joint border.

As early as 1963, Tanzanian officialdom had looked with favor on the prospects of building a railway between Dar es Salaam and the Zambian copper belt. This venture was expected to tap large, undeveloped deposits of iron and coal in southern Tanzania as well as relieve transport pressures on landlocked Zambia. The Unilateral Declaration of Independence by Rhodesia in November 1965 gave impetus to the railway idea. That action by a white minority government provided new political and economic abrasions between Rhodesia and its northern neighbor, Zambia.

Presidents Nyerere and Kaunda looked in turn to Britain, the United States, West Germany, Japan, the Soviet Union, and the World Bank for financial backing for the railway project. Most of these political donors, on the basis of dated and dusty surveys, had claimed the project was uneconomic and unlikely to provide sufficient traffic to support itself until or after 1999. These generally recommended instead the use of an all-weather highway. None of these possible financial sources took political account of the value of the project, nor indeed of the peculiar relationship of Zambia to the project. Nyerere and Kaunda were unsuccessful in these approaches, although they gained financial support from the United States, Sweden, and the World Bank in rebuilding the road between Dar es Salaam and the Zambian border. They also obtained assistance from Italian sources in building an oil pipeline from Tanzania to Zambia. Thus deflected from finding financial support in the West for their main project they turned to the People's Republic of China for help.[5]

China first formally offered help on the Tanzania/Zambia railway (Tan-Zam) project on the occasion of Nyerere's state visit to Peking in 1965. Final agreements were signed in 1970. China then agreed to a thirty-year interest-free loan of $400 million. The loan was to be financed by purchase of goods from China by Tanzania and Zambia. China's aid was to cover engineering, construction, and supplying of railway stock for a 1,150-mile, single-track line with an annual carrying capacity of 1.75 million tons of freight each way. Construction was officially begun in Dar es Salaam in October 1970. According to various press reports, some 15,000 Chinese were engaged in building the line with the help of some 30,000 Africans. Completion of the project was originally set for 1977, but it was inaugurated in October 1975, two years ahead of schedule.

The *Journal of Commerce* (December 1, 1972) reported that preliminary work had begun on the Dar es Salaam port involving construction of three new deep-water berths. These cost some $22 million and were slated to be completed by 1975 to coincide with completion of the railway.

It is of special interest to note Tanzania's obvious reluctance to take additional Chinese aid until the railway project was completed. This reaction was officially confirmed to the London *Times* (October 18, 1972) when Nyerere said: "China is not a rich country, and the railway is a huge undertaking, and there are other projects in the country which operate through Chinese aid. So really I think we are required to see the railway out of the way before we discuss anything else with China." This attitude is, of course, a reassertion of a prime thesis of the Arusha Declaration, namely, that "independence means self-reliance. Independence cannot be real if a nation depends upon gifts and loans from another for its development."

Numerous and conflicting reasons have been given for Chinese aid of this magnitude in Africa. It seems clear that these boil down to (1) desire for recognition by African nations that China is indeed a world power; (2) geopolitical and strategic advantages for Chinese access to the Western littoral of the Indian Ocean; (3) successful usurpation by China of friendships in the Third World which might otherwise accrue to the Soviet Union or to the United States; (4) desire for extended trade and new markets.

During recent years the islands of Zanzibar and Pemba continued to be a millstone around the neck of the Tanzanian government. *Africa Report* (December 1970) characterized the situation thus: " . . . The haste with which the match was made left Nyerere with a house which he did not control. During the past six and one-half years he has fought a continual and often fruitless battle with Zanzibar's 32-man Revolutionary Council in attempts to persuade them to adopt a more democratic as well as socialist path. . . . " Most observers continue to believe, however, that to break the union would not help the situation within Zanzibar.

Throughout the eight-year period of Tanzania's union during which Abeid Karume ruled the islands, he exercised personal autonomy and internal domination, paying little heed to the mainland government. Though Zanzibar's leaders have followed the Tanzanian central government's foreign policy direction, they have resisted administrative control from the mainland. Understandably, in the wake of the 1961 and 1963 preindependence elections, when minority governments were installed by the British overlords in spite of Karume's majority party victories at the polls, Karume and his followers remained suspicious of elections as being a measurement of real democracy. Thus the union cannot be construed as yet a happy one. Though Nyerere has reportedly been much troubled by the situation, he was unable to intervene because of the provisions of the Tanzanian interim constitution.

In March 1972 relations between the islands and the mainland reached a nadir. At that time the *Washington Post* (March 24, 1972) reported that the Tanzanian union was "crumbling." Karume's personal willfulness and his lieutenants' belief that the Nyerere administration was not sufficiently "radical" appeared to be at the heart of the troubles. The better economic situation of Zanzibar vis-à-vis the mainland also appeared to be of importance. Zanzibar had been able to pile up its own foreign reserve surpluses as a result of the high cost of cloves ($2,860 per ton) on world markets. Early in 1972, Zanzibar was reported to hold foreign reserves of $74 million, half again as much as did the union government. These reserves Karume refused to share. Karume had also ceased purchasing Zanzibar's imports through Tanzania's State Trading Corporation, preferring to make such purchases through his own buyers. Finally, the Zanzibaris continued to hold a disproportionate share of seats in the Tanzanian Parliament. Given all these factors, it was clear that Nyerere's influence over Zanzibar had, thus far, not been effective.

An entirely new chapter in Tanzania-Zanzibar relations opened up on April 7, 1972, when Karume was assassinated. The Revolutionary Council, now led by Aboud Jumbe, announced that it remained in control and would continue Karume's "leftist policies."[6] The killing was carried out by four young army officers as an act of personal vengeance but it had obvious political implications. The assassins, apparently Arabs, were killed by Karume's guards in a subsequent gunfight. However, in the wake of Karume's killing, as many as 1,000 persons were picked up and jailed as possible accomplices. The most important of these was Abdul Rahman Babu, a former Tanzanian cabinet minister who had long been a political associate of Karume on Zanzibar.[7]

Aboud Jumbe, Zanzibar's new leader, is a considerably different personality from Karume. About fifty-five years of age, somewhat taciturn, a former schoolteacher, Jumbe is definitely an intellectual. He possesses a university degree from Makerere, Nyerere's own alma mater. Jumbe had long been a confidant of Karume and was his minister of state on Zanzibar.

Jumbe, as president of Zanzibar's Afro-Shirazi Party and chairman of the Revolutionary Council, has also assumed the first vice presidency of the Tanzanian Union. Thus he has inherited a large degree of Karume's autonomy. However, Jumbe is considered to be more moderate and less racist than his predecessor. As an intellectual he is working in closer harmony with Nyerere. He has already sought some decentralization of power on Zanzibar to ensure greater "grassroots" support—an obvious goal of Nyerere's own philosophy.

A week-long conference of the Afro-Shirazi Party which opened on Pemba on December 1, 1972, seems indicative of Jumbe's new attitudes. This meeting, the first such political conclave since the 1964 revolutionary period, apparently had the aim of democratizing the government on the islands by transferring more power to the people through the party. As *The Economist* noted (December 9, 1972) the conference seemed to be a landmark in opening Zanzibar's window to the world at least "an inch." This attitude Jumbe is said to favor. The press was welcomed at the conclave and saw features of local life, for some of which, newsmen reported, "the Afro-Shirazis can be proud."

There remains some debate among observers of the Zanzibar scene as to whether the majority of the islands' inhabitants are better off now than in British colonial times. Certain it is that the redistribution of large plantation holdings into three-acre plots for African farmers has improved subsistence farming. With clove prices at a record 1,000 pounds per ton and a foreign exchange balance of 40 million pounds, which the islanders refuse to share with the mainland, there are ongoing efforts to develop a true welfare state. This includes free housing and hospitalization, but the per capita income is still about $100 yearly and some foodstuffs continue in short supply. It is agreed, however, that extension of free primary schooling, formerly given only Arab and Asian elites, has helped the African populace. Furthermore, they are now accorded practical and technical education at secondary levels, previously unavailable. Housing in the form of large apartment blocks to replace mud huts has been a matter of major concentration for the authorities, but much of this effort is tied to high-interest foreign-aid loans, chiefly East German. Diversification of food crops (under mainland China's help) and re-establishment of tourism have high governmental priority.

As noted at the outset of this chapter, the program of *Ujamaa* has represented one of the four major themes pervading Tanzania's life in its second decade. For a fuller understanding of this innovative program in both economic and social consequences, it is first essential for the reader to have some knowledge of the basic economic and social structures of Tanzania today. Accordingly the next two chapters discuss these matters in some detail. Both in the "Cooperative and *Ujamaa* Villages" section of chapter 12 and in Part Two, the reader will find intensive discussions of all facets of the *Ujamaa* program.

NOTES

1. *The Economist* (London), November 11, 1972, pp. 49–50.
2. *Washington Post*, August 22, 1972.
3. *The Oregonian* (Portland), AP Wire Series, October 8, 1972.
4. *Washington Post*, March 25, 1973.
5. *Africa Report*, January 1972, pp. 10ff.
6. *The Oregonian* (Portland), April 9, 1972.
7. Ibid.

CHAPTER 11

THE ECONOMY

Tanzania's economy can best be described as one of evolving, experimental socialism. The country has been classed by United Nations agencies as one of the twenty-five least developed and poorest nations on earth. Tanzania's economy is basically agricultural and virtually dependent on export of only a few major crops. Its economic growth has been accomplished only by a massive mobilization of internal resources and by some foreign aid. It is unlikely, however, that foreign aid input or internal capital formation at present rates can continue to provide the necessary funds for Tanzania's developmental needs. Given inflationary pressures, uncertain world markets and prices for its goods as well as its steady population growth and basic poverty, the economic odds are against it. For some time to come, therefore, Tanzania will be required to maintain strict austerity and to make increasing demands on its people for imaginative and cooperative effort. In sum, the country's economy is rigorous but sound; its growth potential is distinctly limited. Perhaps its best potential lies in fields of agricultural diversification and in tourism.

Tanzania, with few natural resources, possesses an extraordinarily harsh climate, much arid land, and an inadequate transportation network. It is mainly dependent for foreign exchange and for capital development on a few price-volatile agricultural products—sisal, coffee, cotton, cashews, and cloves. As yet the country has a scarcity of skilled manpower, only a small educated elite, and no real middle class.

Since independence, with the exception of the extraordinary financial backing ($400 million) given by Peking for the Tanzania/Zambia railway, the country has been unable to obtain sufficient foreign aid or adequate public or private investment capital to meet its developmental needs. Thus it has not been able to move forward from a basic subsistence status, through the various stages of agricultural diversification and industrial growth, to the stage of economic "take-off."

These fundamental lacks in Tanzania's economy have forced the leaders of Tanzania into formulating economic alternatives and finding capital substitutes. These alternatives have at their core the concepts of self-reliance, collective farming, familyhood (*ujamaa*), and nationalization of many private ventures into state or so-called parastatal organisms. These alternative courses and bodies, their philosophical bases, their strategy and tactics, have been mentioned in earlier chapters of this book. In this and subsequent chapters on the nation's social institutions we will examine these alternatives in greater detail.

Tanzania's 1974 estimated per capita income was $113.[1] This figure is only half the average for the African continent as a whole and is less than one-third of the current per capita income of more prosperous black African lands such as Ghana, Gabon, and Ivory Coast. Agriculture, including subsistence production, accounts for about 40 percent of Tanzania's gross domestic product (GDP) of $1.6 billion.[2] In recent years the country's rate of economic growth has been sustained in real terms at 4 percent. However, given inflationary pressures, a fast-increasing population (2.9 percent annually), and unstable world markets for Tanzania's prime products, this economic growth figure is insufficient and unlikely to be maintained. With a population of 14.5 million (1975 estimate),[3] most of whom are subsistence farmers, Tanzania seems unlikely, by itself, to be able to generate adequate capital for replacement, diversification, and expansion of both industry and agriculture.

Over 90 percent of the country's work force is occupied with farming, either subsistence or cash crop. In 1973 there were only 402,000 workers in the cash wage sector.[4] This figure, which excludes 45,000 workers engaged on the Tan-Zam project, represents only one-twelfth of the available work force. Available statistics also indicate a total of 60 percent of the wage earners operating in the private sector and nearly 40 percent employed in the public sector. More than 30 percent of the cash wage group was itself employed in agricultural-related pursuits. Some 30 percent were in industry; some 39 percent in services. These low cash wage employment figures reflect the usual problems which have faced most emergent nations—namely, the difficulty of moving from a subsistence to a cash economy plus growing unemployment resulting from urbanization and the lack of skilled labor.

Parastatals

In comprehending Tanzania's economy and social system, it is essential to understand the nature and scope of the so-called parastatals. These are defined as enterprises established and owned by the government or having majority governmental participation and control. They are run along general commercial-cooperative lines. In activity they range from agriculture and mining to manufacturing and commerce. They may involve both import and export, production and distribution, wholesale and retail trade. They even include such diverse activities as construction, banking, insurance, and electrical power.

The accounts of the parastatals are not directly related to the ordinary governmental budget. It is understood that at the beginning of 1972 parastatal corporations in Tanzania numbered nearly one hundred. Total investment in parastatal corporations amounted to more than TSh 1.4 billion in 1971 (U.S. $1.00 equals Tanzanian Shilling (TSh) 7.85 as of 1976). The tax on parastatal surpluses is 40 percent. These taxes amounted to TSh 187 million in 1971, an increase of 23 percent over 1970. Beyond this, however, from profits the parastatal sector is able to carry on certain fixed capital investments which are highly important to an economy so constricted for funds as Tanzania's. Retained and reinvested profits from the parastatals amounted to TSh 216 million in 1971, 65 percent over the preceding year.[5] (Later figures are unavailable at this writing.)

Agriculture

As noted previously, the country's primary agricultural exports include sisal, coffee, cotton, cashews, and cloves. (Other important agricultural products, mainly consumed domestically, include sugar, maize, rice, wheat, tea, and tobacco.) In 1972 domestic production of these five commodities—coffee (TSh 231 million); cotton (TSh 221 million); sisal (TSh 142 million); cashews (TSh 115 million); cloves (Tsh 25 million)—represented more than 85 percent of all agricultural production. In foreign-exchange terms the same commodities represented 47 percent of the worth of all exports.[6]

Tanzania has long been the world's largest producer of sisal and has been seriously challenged in this field only by Brazil and the Philippines. Production and export of sisal, historically the principal export from the country, was miniscule until World War II, when production of sisal trebled. The price of sisal reached an all-time high of $700 per ton during the Korean War. Severe declines in world prices occurred thereafter, owing to shrinking markets and competition of substitute natural and synthetic fibers. By February 1973, however, the price of sisal had again increased to about $500 per ton because of worldwide shortages. Owing to both nationalization of many estates and shrinking world markets and prices, many private sisal growers in Tanzania had stopped producing sisal.

In October 1967 the Tanzanian government nationalized nearly 60 percent of the privately owned sisal plantations. Simultaneously it created the Tanzania Sisal Corporation (TSC) as an operating and holding agency. The TSC is currently engaged in encouraging shifts from sisal to alternate crops in order to increase employment and to utilize sisal lands. Among commodities introduced into these areas have been citrus fruits, cattle, coconuts, rice, sorghum, and cocoa. Furthermore, Tanzania has sponsored experimentation in production of pulp and paper from the sisal plants. These experiments have not yet proved successful.

In 1972 Tanzania produced only 156,800 metric tons of sisal, compared to 181,000 metric tons in 1971 and 202,000 metric tons in 1970. Total sisal exports from the country in 1972 were valued at $20 million.[7] Principal buyers were the United Kingdom and the United States. Sisal now accounts for about 11 percent of the country's agricultural earnings, ranking behind coffee and cotton as a major export crop. Unless recent efforts by the United Nations Food and Agriculture Organization (FAO) to improve world sisal markets are successful, it is expected that Tanzania's production of sisal will have declined to a level of about 160,000 tons in 1976 and after.

In 1970 coffee became Tanzania's biggest foreign exchange earner, with exports valued at $36 million and production reaching 48,680 metric tons.[8] Exports in 1971 were valued at $32 million from production of 45,800 metric tons.[9] Coffee production increased to 51,600 metric tons in 1972 with exports earning $39 million. Both *arabica* and *robusta* are grown in Tanzania. Processing of the *arabica* is handled by the Tanganyika Coffee Growers' Association and the Kilimanjaro Native Cooperative Union. Marketing of all the coffee crop is handled by the Coffee Board, a governmental entity.

Production of coffee of the high quality *arabica* variety was originally encouraged by early German settlers. This, in turn, provided a steady market in Germany for the coffee so produced. Continental Europe is still Tanzania's best market for the high-quality coffee, although the *robusta* (soluble) has found an increasing market in the United States. In light of the vagaries of international marketing and the accumulation of coffee inventories in Tanzania (now said to be more than 1 million bags), the government is determined to reduce dependence on coffee by diversifying into other crops and by restriction of coffee production to areas best suited for intensive cultivation.

Since the decline of sisal production and world market prices thereof, cotton and coffee have jockeyed constantly for first place in value of production and of export in Tanzania. Since 1950 production of cotton has tripled. In 1972 production reached 79,800 metric tons valued at TSh 260.6 million.[10] Though drought affected the cotton crop and foreign exchange earnings therefrom in 1973, Tanzania had set for itself a production goal of 600,000 bales by 1975, concentrating attention of many *Ujamaa* villages on new or expanded cotton planting.

Cooperative organizations own and operate most of the ginning facilities in the country. A governmental entity, the Lint and Seed Marketing Board, has responsibility for purchase and sale of all cotton lint and seed produced nationwide. In recent years, Japan, West Germany, Hong Kong, United Kingdom, and China have been among the country's best customers. The establishment of several local textile factories within the country (under a Communist Chinese aid project) has permitted practical domestic industrial development.

Tanzania is the world's second largest producer of cashew nuts, following Mozambique. In 1972 production of cashews was valued at $17.1 million, comprising 137,700 metric tons.[11] More than 75 percent of the crop was exported to India's State Trading Corporation for processing, most of the finished product finding its way to the United States. The remainder of the crop is processed within Tanzania and then re-exported, again principally to the United States. Marketing is handled by the National Agriculture Production Board (NAPB). Production of cashews has been increasing steadily and is likely to rise.

The islands of Zanzibar and Pemba are the world's largest producers of cloves. Zanzibar's principal customer for these is Indonesia (which mixes the cloves with tobacco to flavor cigarettes). The United States and United Kingdom import some cloves and clove oil. The price of cloves on world markets is highly volatile, partially as a result of a natural cycle of crops, one year good, the next bad. Thus it is necessary to maintain large stocks in order not to depress world prices. Total production of cloves in 1971 was estimated at 7,500 tons, with export values reaching $25 million. Cloves, clove oil, and coconuts comprise more than four-fifths of Zanzibar/Pemba's export trade. Production of cloves alone represents more than one-third of the island's GDP.

Mainland Tanzania is largely self-sufficient in foodstuffs. Zanzibar, however, is required to import a number of staple food items. With the help of the People's Republic of China and East German aid projects, the Zanzibar government has been seeking diversification of its agricultural base to lessen dependence on imported foodstuffs.

Tea and sugar are important staples of the Tanzanian's diet. Tea accounts for about 9 percent of Tanzania's foreign exchange earnings, with production at 10,500 metric tons valued at TSh 61.6 million in 1971. Some sugar is locally produced, but production has not been able to meet domestic demands, which are increasing at a rate of some 15 percent annually. Domestic production in 1971 was about 95,800 metric tons valued at TSh 383 million.[12]

Tanzania produces other important commercial crops such as tobacco, timber, pyrethrum, and oilseeds (including groundnuts, castor, sesame, and sunflower). Growing of pyrethrum (an increasingly valuable export item) is being encouraged in the *Ujamaa* villages. Production of livestock, rice, cassava, maize, and wheat is also being stimulated to diversify domestic food supplies.

Cattle-herding represents an important element of many tribes, some still nomadic. Major efforts are being made to improve standards of cattle-raising and marketing. Efforts are also being made to increase production of milk.

While increased emphasis is being placed upon development of the entire livestock industry, there continues to be a traditional reluctance among herdsmen to sell their cattle. Another major problem continues to be elimination of the tsetse fly which infests cattle-raising areas.

It has previously been stressed that the *Ujamaa* concept seeks to marry environmental potential to economic potential through use of the country's widely dispersed and basically rural unskilled human resources. It is planned, therefore, that such *Ujamaa* villages will, if the environment permits, practice either intensive or extensive agriculture. If population and skills warrant, the villages may enter into small-scale industrial as well as agricultural activities. It is expected, for example, that geographic areas of heavy population such as Kilimanjaro and Tukuyu will need to combine industrial activities with intensive farming. More arid regions like Tabora will concentrate on extensive farming such as livestock-raising. Agriculture is bound to continue to represent the mainstay of the country's economy.

The so-called Iringa Declaration, issued by the TANU National Executive in May 1972, emphasized dependence on agriculture and the necessity of modernizing that sector. In line with the foregoing aims, Agricultural Development Authorities have been established in various fields, ranging from cotton and maize through sisal and cashew production. These authorities are designed to control all phases from planting to export marketing. The authorities will be on a vertically integrated crop-by-crop basis. They replace earlier efforts to integrate domestic production, marketing, and export on a composite horizontal basis. Authorities will be parastatals, generally receiving governmental funds only for technical and research services.

Natural Resources

Tanzania is the largest fish producer in East Africa, using rivers, inland lakes, and seacoasts for its take. In 1971 fisheries production amounted to 185,000 metric tons, valued at $17 million. Fish exports have been increasing in recent years, and in 1970 were valued at about $4 million.[13]

Tanzania possesses a few minerals and much flora and fauna. With the exception of diamonds and salt, overall mineral production has been declining in recent years. In 1970 proceeds from mining and quarrying amounted to some $26 million or 1.7 percent of the country's GDP. This income is concentrated in extraction of diamonds, tin, gold, and gemstones. Smaller amounts of salt, mica, magnesite, coal, and meerschaum are also produced. Diamonds, however, in 1970 represented 87 percent of all mineral values and ranked fourth among the country's exports, earning $15.1 million.[14]

The diamonds come from the famous Williamson mine, located at Mwadui near Lake Victoria. The mine bears the name of its Canadian geologist-discoverer and was brought into operation during World War II. It has consistently held an important place in the national economic picture. Until 1974 direction and profits were shared between the Tanzanian government (through its National Development Corporation) and the mine operators, the South African firm of Anglo-American (De Beers). Today this mine is wholly owned and operated by the Tanzanian government.

The country also has unproven, but apparently large, reserves of low-grade iron and coal. These may now prove economically valuable as a concomitant of the opening of the Tan-Zam railway. The deposits are in the southern area of Tanzania near the site of the railway line. The Tanzanian government is today also actively encouraging exploration for other minerals, including petroleum, copper, and soda ash.

The country possesses some of the world's most beautiful scenery, ranging from Indian Ocean beaches to Mount Kilimanjaro and several world-famous wild game reserves. National game parks, which include the famous Serengeti Plains and Ngorongoro Crater, cover more than 11,000 square miles. Herein lies an expanding potential for tourism. That potential has been only partially tapped as Tanzania in 1972 welcomed 100,000 foreign tourists. (This number was only one-fifth the number visiting neighboring Kenya.) Gross foreign exchange earnings from these 100,000 visitors were estimated at $25 million. Tanzania's second and third five-year development plans have hoped to double the number of its foreign visitors, but recent figures have actually shown declines.

Foreign Trade

Tanzania's foreign trade figures have been relatively steady in recent years, although patterns of both imports and exports have been changing. Tanzania had favorable trading balances in 1968 and 1969 but an unfavorable trading balance in 1970. In both 1970 and 1971 trading deficits resulted, in part, from extensive capital imports for the Tan-Zam railway and for the new Kilimanjaro airport. In 1973 there was an unfavorable trade balance of $126 million, exports amounting to $361 million and imports reaching $487 million.[15] This imbalance reflected declines in prices of agricultural prices, drought conditions, and resulting required imports of foodstuffs.

The country's major suppliers are the United Kingdom (24 percent), Western Europe (20 percent), Kenya (14 percent), the United States (7 percent). Its major imports include machinery and transport equipment, manufactured goods, fuels, and foodstuffs. Imports from the United States include machinery, cereals, and dairy products. In 1973 the United States provided $11.3 million of Tanzania's imports.[16]

Tanzania's principal customers include the United Kingdom (29 percent), the United States (9 percent), Zambia (8 percent), Hong Kong (7 percent), India (6 percent), West Germany (5 percent). Other prime customers are Japan and Indonesia. Principal items of export are sisal, cotton, coffee, diamonds, petroleum products, and cashew nuts. To the United States it exports coffee, pyrethrum, cordage, cloves, cashews, and tea. In 1973 the United States purchased from Tanzania $26.6 million of that country's exports.[17]

Industry and Commerce

Although Tanzania's manufacturing sector has grown remarkably since independence, that portion of the economy still produces less than 10 percent of the country's GDP. As of 1970 there were 450 separate manufacturing plants, employing some 49,000 persons.[18] Among industries now in operation in the country are those processing agricultural commodities, including canneries; cordage plants; flour mills; textile, tobacco, chemical, and furniture factories. There is a single oil refinery (dependent on imported crude), a tire factory (American-participant), a shoe factory, a cement plant, aluminum and steel rolling mills, several breweries, etc. Growth in these various fields has averaged 10 percent annually in recent years. This rapid growth is largely accounted for by expansion of agricultural processing and by establishment of import substitute factories in secondary and consumer fields. Tanzania hopes to double its manufacturing capacity between now and 1985.

Two of the most important parastatals have been the National Development Corporation (NDC) and the State Trading Corporation (STC). Impetus for and direction of industrial development has been largely provided by the parastatal NDC. This is a large, publicly owned conglomerate, which until recently covered both manufacturing and extractive mining. (In 1972 mining control was transferred to a new parastatal—the Tanzania State Mining Corporation.) Manufacturing can be separated into three categories: (1) state-owned; (2) state and private participant with government in majority control; (3) wholly private enterprises. While NDC is engaged in all three categories, it is presently wholly engaged in operation of forty companies, covering nearly one-half of all industrial output and employment. It is understood that the NDC plans expansion of its activities in a number of fields, including breweries, cement, farm implements, and intermediate goods. Shortage of skilled technical and administrative manpower, lack of finances, inflationary cost over-runs, and price squeezes on capital imports, however, are delaying many of these expansion activities. Given existing lack of capital for the many pressing developmental needs in Tanzania, there is likely to be concentration on consolidation and greater efficiency of existing facilities.

The National Small Industries Corporation (NSIC) a subsidiary of NDC, handles development of small-scale industries. It is expected that the government (in line with its decentralization and *Ujamaa* concepts) will broaden this organization into a full-scale parastatal entity.

In the commercial field the State Trading Corporation (STC), established in

1967, has been dominant till now. In that year it took over the activities of those private firms engaged in external trade and domestic wholesale. The STC handles most imports of consumer goods and has been increasingly concerned with exports as well. It has been estimated by foreign sources that the STC in 1972 handled more than 30 percent of all imports and 10 percent of all exports. In addition to the work of the STC in these areas, however, there are a number of other governmental or quasi-governmental bodies which handle both imports and domestic distribution of some goods, as well as some exports. These groups include cooperatives, district development corporations, and the National Food Distributors Body.

As the government has found that the STC is now too unwieldy to carry out its operations efficiently, failing in both sales and financial areas, it is now in process of phased decentralization. It is expected that the STC will be broken into three specialized companies (pharmaceuticals, construction, and agricultural supplies), three national central companies (handling foodstuffs, household supplies, and other consumables), and eighteen regional trading companies. The last-named would handle wholesale distribution and would be accountable to regional authorities. The central bodies would be responsible to appropriate ministries. The export functions of the STC will be transferred to the proper ministries (agriculture, etc.) or to new parastatal bodies (such as shipping).

Transport, Communications, and Power

The problem of transport is complex in a country as large and as impoverished as Tanzania, especially since the main centers of population are scattered around the nation's periphery. There are now 21,000 miles of roads, of which only 4,000 miles are hard-surfaced. The 1,000-mile hard-surfaced Tanzania/Zambia highway connecting Dar es Salaam with Lusaka is the most important highway construction now underway. This project has been financed by the United States, the World Bank, and various European aid donors.

There are some 1,638 miles of railroad trackage, excluding the 1,150 miles of recently completed railway line as Tanzania's portion of the Tan-Zam railway. Other facilities are single track 1-meter gauge. The new Tan-Zam line, also single-track, is slighty wider, 1.067 meters. Other facilities comprise three main lines: Dar es Salaam to Tabora and onward to Lake Tanganyika at Kigoma; a branch line from Tabora to Mwanza on Lake Victoria; and a line from Dar es Salaam northward to Tanga, Moshi, and Arusha. (An important adjunct to the existing rail transport network is the 1,050-mile-long pipeline connecting Dar es Salaam with Ndola. This is used for carrying refined petroleum products into Zambia.) Kenya, Uganda, and Tanzania rail systems are joined on Tanzania's northern border at Voi. Direction of railways, lake shipping, and inland trucking in the three countries of East Africa is merged into the East African Railways Corporation, an adjunct of the East African Community (EAC).

Tanzania's four major seaports are Dar es Salaam, Tanga, Mtwara, and Zanzibar. The regional port system is handled by East African Harbours Corporation, a subsidiary of the EAC. The port of Dar es Salaam is currently being expanded, a result of the Tan-Zam development.

Air transport helps to alleviate the country's shortage of ground transport. Internal air service is provided to a number of Tanzanian cities by the East African Airways Corporation, an adjunct of EAC. In addition there are international air services to Dar es Salaam, provided by East African Airways, Pan American, Alitalia, KLM, and BA. A new international-standard airport has recently been opened near Moshi-Arusha. This airport is designed to facilitate entry of international air tourists to the nearby, world-renowned Serengeti game park and Ngorongoro Crater Conservation Area, as well as other tourist havens.

Hydroelectric installations generate most of the power in East Africa, including Tanzania. Development and distribution of that power is handled in the country by yet another parastatal, the Tanzania Electric Supply Co. Ltd. (TANESCO). Here, too, output is expanding, reaching a figure of 343 million kilowatts in 1970, up 19 percent over 1969. Industrial users take more than 60 percent of power sales. The country's second five-year development plan accentuated expansion of existing power facilities as well as development of new facilities.

Fiscal Matters

Tanzania's currency is based on the shilling (TSh), divided into 100 cents. Present value of the TSh is 13 cents U.S. or TSh 7.85 to U.S. $1.00. Currency controls are in operation and currency is noninterchangeable even in neighboring Kenya and Uganda. A Central Bank of Tanzania serves as fiscal agent, comptroller of credit and coinage. The only commercial bank in Tanzania is the state-owned National Bank of Commerce with eighty-five branches. This entity replaced the seven groups of private banks which were nationalized in 1967. Insurance facilities are also centralized in the parastatal National Insurance Company, which replaced all private insurance companies nationalized in 1967. On Zanzibar the government-operated People's Bank, established in 1966, conducts all banking business.

With Tanzania's fiscal year running from July 1 to June 30, its financial system calls for both recurrent and developmental budgets. Tanzania's budget in recent years has been one of rapid growth, some surpluses on current account, and increasing deficits overall as a result of heavy expenditures in the capital sector. These deficits have brought about increasing reliance on foreign financial sources.

For the fiscal year 1971–72 current revenues totaled TSh 1.86 billion; current expenditures were TSh 1.73 billion. Development expenditures were TSh 889 million and the overall deficit was TSh 763 million.[19] The share of Tanzania's dependence on foreign sources for its deficit financing doubled from one-third in 1968 to two-thirds in 1972. This increase represents the massive insertions of outside capital for such specific development projects as the Tan-Zam railway and the Kilimanjaro airport. Illustrative of the diversity of financial sources is the fact that the financial assistance for the railway came from mainland China; help for the airport came mainly from Italy; aid funds and engineering support for the Dar es Salaam-Tunduma road came from the United States and the World Bank; money for the new Tanga jetty came from West Germany and the Netherlands. In the year 1971 alone, unofficial United States sources report receipts by Tanzania of $230 million from Peking; $24 million from Sweden; $18 million from West Germany; $15 million from Canada; $10 million from the U.S.; $10 million from Japan; $7.5 million from Norway; $7.2 million from the Netherlands; $4 million from Finland. (Total economic aid from the U.S. between 1960 and 1975 exceeded $86 million with an additional $25 million projected for fiscal 1976.)

Governmental revenues come mainly from income taxes, taxes on rental properties, export and import duties. The government's total debt stood at $254 million in 1970. The external debt was then $144 million. Tanzania's balance of payments was in surplus during 1966–69, but in 1970 there was a deficit. Invisible earnings appear to be increasing, but private capital inflow has slowed in recent years owing to nationalization with related compensation payments to foreign investors and reductions in foreign credits. At the beginning of 1971 Tanzania's foreign exchange reserves were valued at TSh 765.6 million, the equivalent of only five months' imports.[20] Overall costs of servicing governmental and parastatal debts are now said to be running in the neighborhood of $13 million annually or about 5 percent of all foreign exchange earnings.

Since 1967 when the Arusha Declaration took effect and the nationalization program was originated, the public sector and international aid have been the main sources of investment in the country. The second five-year development plan sought a goal of TSh 3 billion for new investment. Of this total, governmental and parastatal bodies were to supply two-thirds of capital needs.

External loans and grants during fiscal 1971–72 amounted to TSh 330 million, which comprised 39 percent of all central governmental resources available for investment. In 1972–73 the total of external loans and grants were expected to exceed TSh 541 million, this figure reaching 55 percent of government resources available for investment. During the first two years of the second five-year development plan, foreign aid input fell behind projections. In the third and fourth year of the plan there was considerable improvement. The aid pipeline now seems to hold better promise. Debt servicing, however, continues to be a problem and will remain so unless exports can be increased materially.

It is clear that Tanzania will continue to need more aid, but this must be of a different kind from that of the past. That aid, for too long, has been "tied" aid—linked to procurement of imported equipment for materials for large projects. In the future Tanzania will need a much larger proportion of external aid for its rural development and agricultural projects. In spite of its record of political stability, Tanzania has not succeeded in attracting much foreign private investment. This has been due in part to skittishness of risk capital resulting from the abortive 1964 coup and the nationalization actions of 1967 and after. While official government policy continues to permit private foreign investment in certain sectors, most areas are restricted to public enterprise or governmental partnership with private investors. Approved foreign enterprises continue to be guaranteed rights of repatriation of profits and capital. Certain incentives are given foreign investors, especially in industrial and hotel activities.

There is no clear indication today as to the extent of foreign private investment remaining within the country. Best estimates consider total fixed capital investment at about $150 million, of which approximately one-third may still be foreign-owned—United Kingdom, United States, Italian, Swiss, and German. United States private investment has been limited mainly to petroleum marketing facilities and a joint-venture tire factory located in northern Tanzania. (An investment guarantee for United States firms is in effect on the mainland only.)

The Development Plans

Tanzania has sought to improve its economic structure by creation of several long-range development plans. As noted in foregoing pages, these have been aimed, primarily, at expansion of industry and agriculture, development of power and water resources, and improvement of communications. The plans have concentrated on land resettlement and expansion of secondary industry as a means of curtailing imports. Because of the situation of Dar es Salaam as an *entrepôt* for Zambian copper exports and fuel imports, much of Tanzania's capital development funds from external aid sources have been directed to high-priority improvement of railways, roads, and harbors.

The country's first five-year development plan (1964–69) emphasized industrial and commercial development to balance dependence on agriculture. Its overall objective was to double per capita income by 1980 and to give the country a modicum of industrial self-sufficiency. During the period covered by that development plan the country's GDP increased at an annual rate of 2.7 percent.

President Nyerere announced that his first five-year development plan had achieved 75 percent of its objectives. He added that planning bottlenecks and the drastic fall in the price of sisal (which, till 1964, had been the backbone of the economy) accounted in large measure for the shortfall. Nyerere also emphasized that the first five-year development plan put 65 percent of its cost reliance on foreign sources, a goal not realized.

A second five-year development plan was then projected for 1969–74 calling for total investment of $1.1 billion. This plan aimed at enhancing rural development, diversifying agricultural production, and expanding villagization under the self-reliance schemes of *Ujamaa*. Under this second five-year development plan the government sought to increase GDP at an annual rate of 6.5 percent. Success of this program was dependent on governmental capacity to expand exports, conquer inflationary pressures, and overcome its skilled manpower shortages as well as finding success in public acceptance of the villagization schemes.

In view of the deficiences of the first five-year development plan, Nyerere stressed that his second five-year development plan would rely more heavily on governmental, parastatal, and private sectors of the country for its success. A very few of the goals may have been realized by the "fallout" from the Chinese-financed Tan-Zam project and by increased receipts of foreign aid grants and loans from the United States, Canada, Western Europe, and especially the World Bank.

Although postponed for one year in its implementation, announcement has been made by Tanzanian authorities of the general goals of that country's third five-year development plan. Total costs of the plan, beginning July 1975 and ending 1980, were projected at $2 billion. Four great imponderables—harsh drought with resultant shortages of domestic foodstuffs, general inflation, falling agricultural prices, costs of the oil embargo and energy crisis—have dried up most of the country's currency reserves.

The disastrous drought of 1973–74, combined with the massive agricultural losses resulting from population shifts of some 3 million people in the *Ujamaa* villagization program, necessitated the importation of some $250 million in foreign foodstuffs during 1974 alone. This drain, representing 40 percent of the country's normal food needs, is expected to continue for another year or two before domestic crops bring a return to self-sufficiency. Local costs of the Tan-Zam railroad estimated at $20 million yearly (and in the form of required imports of Chinese goods) is said to represent one-fourth of all Tanzania's normal imports. Banning of luxury imports, curtailing of capital goods imports, and deferring many of the socialization schemes will surely occur. As a result, it is expected that foreign exchange borrowings and foreign aid required to finance this third development plan will come to $700 million or more.

NOTES

1. *Background Notes*, U.S. State Department, on United Republic of Tanzania, December 1974.
2. Ibid.
3. *World Book Atlas*, 1975.
4. Basic statistics on Tanzania supplied by American embassy, Dar es Salaam, February 1973.
5. International Monetary Fund statistics, March 1973.
6. Ibid.
7. *Europa Yearbook*, 1974.
8. *Overseas Business Reports*, U.S. Department of Commerce, June 1972.
9. International Monetary Fund statistics, March 1973.
10. *Africa South of the Sahara* (1974).
11. *Europa Yearbook*, 1974.
12. International Monetary Fund statistics, March 1973.
13. *Washington Post*, March 24, 1972.
14. *Europa Yearbook*, 1974.
15. *Background Notes*, U.S. State Department, on United Republic of Tanzania, December 1974.
16. *Overseas Business Reports*, U.S. Department of Commerce, June 1972.
17. Ibid.
18. International Monetary Fund statistics, March 1973.
19. Ibid.
20. World Bank document, December 13, 1972.

CHAPTER 12

THE SOCIETY

For a fuller understanding of Tanzania as a developing nation, it is essential to give brief attention to certain elements of its society and culture. Accordingly, there follows a brief discussion of language, religion, education, health, women, youth, media, labor, cooperatives, *Ujamaa* villages.

Language

Like the subordination of the hundred and more tribal groups to the country's national unity, the cohesive presence of the indigenous *lingua franca*, Swahili, has also been a help in unification of the nation. Since 1964 this has been the official language of Tanzania. Of secondary importance has been the use of English in education, business, and international communication. Most tribal dialects have now been relegated to regional use.

Swahili, a composite of Bantu dialects and Arabic, had its origin along the East African coast and on Zanzibar. Impelled by nationalistic trends, it is now coming into wider use in Kenya and Uganda as well. It is likewise used and understood in northern Mozambique, in parts of Zaire, Zambia, and the Horn of Africa. It has been estimated that those who know the language fluently, plus those who use it in transitory conversation, may now number in the range of 35 to 50 million persons. Thus Swahili must now be considered as one of the major languages of the world. After French, English, and Arabic, Swahili now holds fourth place on the African continent.

In Tanzania the interrelationship between language and literature is becoming increasingly important. Indigenous drama, poetry, and dance are being utilized as vehicles of political ideology to capture the interest of a far-flung population. For example, Swahili poetry has been used constantly in the press to sing the praises of the Arusha Declaration. Many drama and dance groups have come into being, these sponsored not only by the national government, but by various associations of factory employees, by the university, and by school groups.

Religion

Of mainland Tanzania's population of 14 million there are some 3 million Muslims and 4 million Christians. The remainder are animists or agnostics. Of the Christians about half are Roman Catholic and the other half Protestant. Anglicans, Lutherans, Methodists, and Baptists represent the largest Protestant sects. Of the Asian community about half are Muslim (including Ismailis) and half Hindu with a scattering of other Eastern sects. Islam is heavily dominant on Zanzibar and Pemba.

Among the country's animists there appears to be some unity of belief—nature worship; associations of living and dead; the reality of the soul and other spirits; ancestor worship; use of magic and witchcraft; good and evil influences. Associating both animism and Christianity is the so-called African Independent Church movement. This recent phenomenon represents in part a splintering from some established Christian sects into small communal or family groupings. These seem designed to make religion respond to special African needs: to meld traditional animistic concepts with ceremonial aspects of the established Christian sects of which they are the offshoots. Adherents of these groups do not consider themselves "backsliders" but, rather, members of the universal brotherhood. As such they are slowly becoming tolerated by the older Christian denominations. The African Independent Church movement has come about, in part, from a sense of dissatisifaction with the "European," or "Western," religions. The Africans have considered the mission churches too close to white racism and colonial authority, as failing to comprehend traditional African values and mores, as failing to fit Christian education and dogma into an African mold. These independent "churches" are often centered about a single father-figure or prophet-leader. In southern Africa it has been estimated that there may be as many as 2,000 such sects. In Tanzania foreign observers judge that there may now be several hundred of these.

Among foreign sects, Islam was the first to make itself effectively felt along the East African coast. It was introduced along the routes of the Arab traders and slave caravans. By 1880 there were large numbers of Islamic worshipers on Zanzibar and the mainland coast as well as in the western interior. Islam expanded in these areas, first in the 1920s, and again in the 1950s when heightened Arab nationalism in North Africa brought its influence to bear on the education of many East Africans in Cairo, Algiers, and Beirut. In general Islam was considered a religion of moderation. Africans found Islam to their liking, since it presented them with a basic life-plan rather than a "Sunday go-to-meeting" experience. Africans, too, found that Islam recognized and (unlike Christianity) refused to condemn such established institutions as polygamy. Though statistics on the point are lacking, it appears that Muslim influence is continuing to grow within Tanzania today.

The Christian influence, brought to bear in Tanzania first by the missionary-explorers and antislavery advocates of the nineteenth century, and later by the German and British colonial administrators, reached its apogee in Tanzania about the time of that country's independence. The Germans brought in the Lutherans and the Catholics. The British brought in the Anglicans and the Presbyterians. Additional Roman Catholic groups, Methodists, Pentecostals, and Baptists were influences entering from America. All of these bodies were agencies of transformation and modernization in Africa—especially in the fields of education and medicine. Indirectly, perhaps even unknowingly, they were also agents of political change— introducing the work ethic, concepts of democracy and anticolonialism, the "deification" of advanced education, and the training of many of today's African leaders. Among Roman Catholic mission bands in Tanzania, particularly impressive has been the work of Maryknoll, the Benedictines, the White Sisters, and the Capuchins. Among Protestant groups the Lutherans have been outstanding. The established Christian religions, however, often fell under the control of colonial administrations and, in the face of African nationalism, began to lose their power. There was also much proselytizing and competition among the various Christian faiths. There was racism and lack of charity, concern with structure rather than with faith, hierarchical control by Europeans rather than Africans. Unless there is a massive Christian renaissance, it seems likely that, by the end of this century, established Christian churches and their mission influences will have a far less dominant role in Africa, including Tanzania, than they had prior to 1960. All these factors have contributed to the present-day splintering of old-established bodies into the multitude of African Independent churches.

Education

Problems of education have always held a priority position in President Nyerere's thinking and in Tanzania governmental action. When Nyerere assumed leadership of his country, less than 15 percent of children of school age were reported to be attending school. Primary education has expanded from 120,000 pupils at independence to over 1 million today. However, the total of primary school-age children in the country today is now estimated to be in excess of 2 million. Universal primary education has been given high priority and is now scheduled for attainment by 1977.

By 1971 there were also great advances in secondary and higher education. In that year there were numbered some 33,500 secondary school students,

2,950 students in teacher training; and 3,950 Tanzanian university students in Africa and overseas.

With a target of increasing school attendance by 10 percent annually, special attention is being given to teacher and technical training, to the problem of "drop-outs," to adult literacy courses, and to education of girls (a social situation counter to earlier African tradition). Universal functional literacy is targeted for the mid-1980s, moving up from the present literacy level of 30 percent.

One of the key aims of the country's educational program has been the expansion of university and other tertiary enrollments to the point of general "Tanzanianization" by 1980. This will permit the elimination of most expatriate administrative, technical, and educational positions. These are now said to number in excess of 5,000. University and tertiary specialized enrollment is now said to be in the region of 5,500, with graduates numbering 1,400 annually.

The author recalls from his earliest conversations with Nyerere that he considered educational needs for his country, and especially a university, as matters of highest priority. As early as 1956, Nyerere said his "two major goals for Tanganyika, in order of need, are first a university and second independence." By the end of 1961 he had led his nation to independence. In the same year, even before independence, he dedicated the law school of the University College of East Africa in Dar es Salaam. On August 21, 1964, he dedicated the present campus of the full-scale University College. That institution was operated as an adjunct of the University of East Africa until 1970 when it became fully independent. Speaking at the university dedication ceremonies in 1964, Nyerere emphasized:

None of the work which has been done here would have been possible had it not been for the overall policy of the Government of this country. . . . The cost of keeping a student at this College will be about 1,000 pounds a year. That is to say that it takes the annual per capita income of more than 50 of our people to maintain a single student at this College for one year. . . . It is obvious that this disparity can only be justified, morally or politically, if it can be looked upon as an investment by the poor in their own future. This indeed must be the whole purpose of the economic policies of the Union Government—the uplift of the conditions under which the mass of our people live. Everything else must take second place.[1]

Historically, in Tanzania as elsewhere in Africa, knowledge was passed on, training was given, and social growth was accomplished by oral tradition. Education was thus integrated with all other elements of traditional African family and tribal life forms. Colonial education, however, brought to Tanzania and to other parts of Africa classical forms of teaching in the European pattern. It bruised the indigenous system, created the urban elite from mission school graduates. It fostered rote methods and destroyed pride in everyday indigenous activities such as agricultural work. It substituted for traditional African values the idea that the way to success was via higher-school "certificates."

With its concentration on broadening the primary school base and expansion of adult literacy, the Tanzanians have turned the earlier "colonialist" concept of education around. Instead of creating a small, highly educated group of urban civil servants—elitists—the Tanzanian authorities recognized the needs of their preponderantly rural citizenry. This reinforces the basic *Ujamaa* concept that it is essential to keep the unskilled and unemployed rural worker from migrating to urban areas. It embodies also the idea that there must be a related expansion of work opportunity, of local educational prospects and improved living conditions. In sum, modernization must be effected in rural communities by harnessing together all community services, including the classroom.

With the inception of the Arusha Declaration the country was finally forced to divest itself of the narrow concepts of the colonial past. Schools dropped the "colonial heritage" of the Cambridge Overseas Exam and have replaced both curricula and exams with East African modifications. Schools are being adapted to the needs of the communities within which they operate. Thereby, the political and social consciousness of the rural populace—adult as well as youth—is being activated. Thereby, too, Tanzania's leaders seek to redirect the goals of their people from capitalism back to the traditional egalitarian ideas of the extended family and self-reliance. Nyerere epitomized these goals when he said: "Our education must . . . inculcate a sense of commitment to the total community, and help the people to accept the values appropriate to our kind of future, not those appropriate to our past."[2]

It is generally agreed by observers that it is still too early to judge the success or failures of Tanzania's educational program. Very serious problems still remain, among which are the need of high incentives for university graduates and the need of continuing inspired direction and energetic support of the *Ujamaa* program in this field.

Health

Tanzania has the usual problems of health associated with tropical and underdeveloped countries. Major diseases include malaria, bilharzia, tuberculosis, yaws, leprosy, sleeping sickness, and trachoma. Malnutrition and high infant mortality are the norm. The average life span is 43.5 years. Regional health disparities are great. Physicians and hospitals are in short supply. There is one hospital bed for each 800 persons and one physician for each 34,000 inhabitants. Tanzania's second five-year development plan, in recognition of these deficiencies, aimed at improvement of health services, particularly in rural areas. Basic agencies for attaining better national health are the rural health dispensaries and clinics associated with the new *Ujamaa* villages. Some ninety-five health centers (austerity hospitals), 300 rural health clinics, and 1,400 dispensaries are now in operation. Needs for staffing these facilities have given priority to training medical aides and village midwives. The University of Dar es Salaam has also expanded its medical facilities to train doctors to supplement the mere 160 Tanzanian-citizen physicians now in the country. (The work of these is currently being supplemented by several hundred expatriate physicians, including Chinese.) By 1980 it is hoped that 800 physicians, local and expatriate, will be in the field.

Women

In connection with the government's drive to improve the standard of living of its people, there has been a steady concentration on improving the situation of women. Many ministerial statements have accentuated the need for women to play a more effective role in the life of the nation. Governmental efforts in behalf of women are channeled through the party organization, the *Ujamaa* village program, and *Umoja wa Wanawake wa Tanzania* (United Women of Tanzania). This group has served as a particularly powerful impetus for instituting many of the social programs: nurseries, adult education, health centers, and other social services. Notable leaders in these activities have been the president's wife, Maria Nyerere; Prime Minister Kawawa's wife; and Lucy Lameck, a long-time member of Parliament. Special note must be taken of the work of Bibi Titi Mohammed, former member of the National Assembly and first woman member of TANU. It was she who brought into TANU an exceptionally large number of women members and it was she who led a loyalty demonstration in support of Nyerere following the abortive 1964 coup. (While Bibi Titi was jailed in 1969 on grounds that she was an accomplice in Oscar Kambona's subversive efforts, it is understood that she and others so implicated have since been released.)

Youth

Youth groups have always been an integral part of TANU's nation-building. Thereby the country's leaders have sought to inspire enthusiasm from the grassroots; to unearth incipient leadership; to handle party mechanics such as parades, policing political meetings, and even carrying out protest demonstrations on matters ranging from Vietnam to miniskirts. The youth groups have played a particularly important part in developing enthusiasm and preparatory actions for *Ujamaa* projects.

Tanzania's youth was originally organized into a TANU Youth League (headed by present Prime Minister Rashidi Kawawa). It was later nicknamed the "Green Guard." This group, ranging in age from sixteen to thirty-five, engages in construction of dispensaries, village schools, and clearing of land for cultivation. Though it has never become a paramilitary organization, such as China's Red Guard, it has provided a major vehicle of support for official and party ideology and action on foreign and domestic issues. A junior version of the Youth League is termed the Young Pioneers. This group is similar to Boy Scout and Girl Guide movements in other lands.

The Youth League has also served as the basis for the National Service Program now in operation. This is a nation-building movement concentrating on teaching and rural development. Members give six months' compulsory free service, either civilian or military, plus an additional eighteen months of voluntary effort while serving in their regular jobs at half pay. Associated with this program is the concept that university graduates, sent to school through government bursaries, must pay off those bursaries by agreeing to work at least five years in government service following graduation. Underlying all these youth movements, according to Tanzanian officials, is a dedication to the national ethic of self-reliance and selflessness.

The Media

The independent power of the press in Tanzania has been curbed by TANU leaders and subordinated to the national one-party interest. The preindependence, foreign-owned, daily English-language *Tanganyika Standard* has been nationalized and merged with the English-language party paper, *The Nationalist*. These are now published by the government as the English-language *Daily News*. TANU continues to publish a Swahili-language daily, *Uhuru*. There is also a second, smaller Swahili-language daily, the privately owned *Ngurumo*, and a bi-weekly Catholic Swahili-language paper, *Kiongozi*. Circulation figures on all papers are small. Nyerere occasionally pens editorials in both the *Daily News* and *Uhuru*. Neighboring papers like Nairobi's *Nation* and *East African Standard* were earlier influential but more recently have had rough going in Tanzania. Foreign correspondents, too, have occasionally been adjudged prohibited immigrants, and their articles, in such diverse periodicals as *Time*, *Newsweek*, and the London *Sunday Times*, have sometimes been banned.

The government-operated Radio Tanzania provides countrywide programs in Swahili and English. There are about 135,000 radio receivers in the country. There are no television facilities on the Tanzania mainland but TV has been installed on Zanzibar.

A long-range, shortwave station, broadcasting to southern Africa, was built for Tanzania in 1968 as an aid project from China. This station, costing $1.5 million, is operated jointly by the Tanzanian government and the OAU. It broadcasts some 250 hours monthly, directed to southern Africa in ten different dialects indigenous to that region, ranging from Afrikaans to Zulu and

Ovambo. The service is especially designed to carry into those areas news and propaganda concerning the operations and leadership of the various southern African "liberation movements" sited in Tanzania.

Labor

The working population of Tanzania has been estimated at 5.5 million. Of these only some 4 million are said to be employed. Of that number only 402,000 were in wage-paid employment in 1971. The remainder are in agricultural subsistence activities. Of the cash-wage earners, nearly one-third are in government work, one-third in industry, and one-third in commerce. About 200,000 workers are self-employed. While there is some urban unemployment, those unemployed are either retained or encouraged to return to their home districts to take advantage of *Ujamaa* projects.

Today in Tanzania there are no trade unions. Strikes and lockouts are prohibited. There are, however, provisions for conciliation of disputes between workers and employers. In July 1972 minimum wage rates were set as follows: for industrial workers—TSh 240 per month; for agricultural workers—TSh 140 per month; for government workers—TSh 270 per month. These rates represent an increase of 40 percent over 1967 for lowest paid workers and reflect the government's continuing emphasis on erasing income disparities between vocational categories and population sectors.

In this effort to erase income disparities, a parliamentary law of December 1973 called for a 100 percent tax levy on all income above TSh 4,000 ($600 U.S.) per month. This leveling-down process will affect some 20,000 upper-class Africans, Asian professionals, and expatriate businessmen. The measure may drive some of the latter two categories from the country.

Nyerere has never permitted trade unions to develop challenges to his party's leadership and authority. Before independence, plantation workers, teachers, government employees, railway workers, and dockworkers became powers to be reckoned with and the combined membership of these individual unions was above 200,000. Leaders of these bodies, notably Kawawa (now prime minister), mastered the techniques of political leadership through their schooling in these union groups. Without denigrating the worthy social aims of the trade unions in other venues than Tanzania, however, Nyerere sapped their political potency by siphoning off their leadership into his party and governmental structures. In addition, Tanzania's rulers exiled several trade union leaders who would not fall into line.

Cooperatives *and* Ujamaa *Villages*

An important part of Tanzania's socio-economic scene, cooperatives and the interlocking *Ujamaa* village program deserve special attention. Even before nationalization began in 1967 some 40 percent of all the country's exports were grown and marketed through the cooperative movement. In that year Tanzania had nearly 1,400 cooperative societies of all types with membership in excess of 500,000.[3] By 1970 the number of such societies had increased to 2,000, many of them now in direct association with the parastatal organizations and with *Ujamaa* villages.

Cooperative efforts have been particularly important in production and marketing of coffee, cotton, sisal, tea, and cashews. Cooperatives have also become involved in finance, retail sales, and industrial transport. The cooperative effort is also established in Zanzibar which, even before independence, had known cooperative action in the marketing of cloves. Furthermore, the cooperative producer-consumer thesis is now being applied as the core of operation of the *Ujamaa* villages.

It has already been noted that 90 percent of Tanzania's population is rural and dependent on agriculture. Economic survival of this dispersed and disparate populace is made the more difficult by the fact that only 30 percent of the country's land is arable and only 10 percent is actually under cultivation. In the light of these figures it is understandable that strengthening of the country's rural economy, mainly through development of the *Ujamaa* village concept, has become the central theme in Nyerere's politico-economic philosophy and of his government's developmental programs.

When President Nyerere first announced the "villagization" program for his country before Parliament on December 10, 1962, he said:

The first and absolutely essential thing to do, . . . is to begin living in proper villages. . . . For the next few years Government will be doing all it can to enable the farmers of Tanganyika to come together in village communities. . . . Growth of village life will help us in improving our system of democratic government. . . . The operation of democracy itself is not yet what it should be, nor can it be while the majority of our rural population remains so widely scattered.[4]

In pushing these villagization schemes, Nyerere and his lieutenants appeared to have at least four goals in mind. They sought to illustrate what the rural masses of Tanzania could do for themselves. They sought to give those masses a feeling of actual participation in government and thus to give them a feeling of nationhood as well as familyhood. They sought to avert the major problems of urbanization (lack of housing, unemployment, and social disorder) which have so plagued the world in the twentieth century. Finally, they sought to narrow the economic gap between the rural masses and the urban elite.

Redefining their economic goals to utilize their two principal resources, land and people, the country's leaders have turned away from a strategy of heavy investment in industry to investment in rural agricultural development. They thus seek to achieve a shift from dependence on outside markets and money to domestic self-sufficiency. In the process, they have found it necessary to nationalize and socialize the major means of production and distribution.

Under the *Ujamaa* plan there have been developed several principles of social justice designed to meet the nation's goals of economic freedom (self-sufficiency and social equality). These were incorporated into the concept "familyhood," which extended kinship responsibilities beyond tribe or clan to the nation as a whole. The idea embraces also a kind of devolution of power back to the "grassroots." All this is based on the collective farming plan of *Ujamaa*, which centers on establishment and expansion of villages. These, in turn, would centralize cooperative farming enterprises, production, and marketing with amenities such as schools, water, sanitation, and health centers. This is the Tanzanian version of "African socialism."

Originating in 1962 and given heavy emphasis by the Arusha Declaration of 1967, the government's renewed attention has been directed upon establishment of small new villages associated with cash-crop communal farming. The country's second five-year development plan was also centered upon promising these new villages help in agricultural extension-type programs, in sanitation and health, in school and other community services. In essence, it has been the government's aim to establish small-holder farmers on communal plots, then to integrate them into producer cooperative groupings. Thereafter, when cash-crop production has been attained, the groupings will then be registered formally as cooperatives, and cottage industries will be encouraged.

Later association with established parastatals in marketing and transport is also envisaged. In substance, the *Ujamaa* village can best be described as a combination of the Israeli *kibbutz*, the Chinese-type communal farm, and the traditional African extended family. Thus the *Ujamaa* village is designed to merge both ideology and economic needs, traditional and modern.

Press reports indicate that, by 1974, 3 million Tanzanians were residing in more than 5,600 *Ujamaa* villages.[5] Many of these, however, were said to have not yet reached economic viability. Lack of funds and technical support as well as lack of fertilizers, seeds, tools, and water facilities are said to be the main limiting factors. Better planning, infrastructure, rainfall, and cooperation are now vital to the program's success.

Like all Fourth World countries, Tanzania has suffered immeasurably in recent years from falling prices for its few prime crops combined with rising prices for manufactured and capital-goods imports. Thus a part of the rationale for the *Ujamaa* effort is to offset Tanzania's previous heavy dependence on a few primary commodities which were highly volatile in price and in demand. Sisal, cotton, and coffee are examples. To rescue crop production from such narrow dependence on external trade factors, the new *Ujamaa* villages are being diversified. The goals of the second five-year development plan were heavily concentrated on financing these ventures. However, inflation and foreign exchange losses resulting from necessary importation of foodstuffs to offset losses and poor population-readjustment planning of *Ujamaa* have delayed or diluted expected success of the program.

Given such a radical and extensive program, imposed mainly by persuasion rather than by force (as in the collective farms of China and Russia), results thus far appear spotty and indecisive. Some small landholders, who were marginal producers until now, appear to have taken well to the idea, continuing to work their *shambas*, or personal farm plots, but associating actively with the cash-crop commune. Yet other villagization schemes appear to have been poorly conceived, poorly directed, and poorly supported. Some of these have involved urban rejects and economic misfits. Still other *Ujamaa* villages have come into direct and unpopular competition with larger, already successful, cooperative operators such as the coffee-growers of Kilimanjaro, the tobacco farmers of the Iringa district, and the cotton-growers of Sukumaland. Here the *Ujamaa* villages have had their roughest going.

As to urban benefits from the nationalization and *Ujamaa* programs, the situation is not clear. There seems to be considerable loss of initiative and incentive among the middle class, including merchants, civil servants, and university graduates. Many thousands of Asian shopkeepers and landlords, being affected, have departed the country. Though all retail trade and professional activity is not yet nationalized, the nationalization accomplished thus far has created many problems. The governmental takeover of rental properties has caused a real housing shortage, since nationalization resulted in inadequate compensation for new builders. There has been a consistent shortage of goods and services. As a result of all this there has been mounting criticism of both policies and politicians.

The country has so little in the way of resources that it does not have much to lose in trying to broaden its agricultural and general economic bases. The paucity of resources and skills together with the poverty of his people and land severely restricted President Nyerere's options. The question remains whether Nyerere's initiatives can continue to give sufficient inspiration and impetus to his people. Nyerere alluded to the social dislocations of his country when he said: "A man who has inherited a tumbledown cottage has to live in even worse conditions while he is rebuilding it."[6]

(For the authors' personal assessment of the value of the *Ujamaa* program in its political, economic, philosophical, and moral aspects, see chapter 14 and Part Two.)

NOTES

1. Julius K. Nyerere, *Freedom and Unity* (London: Oxford University Press, 1966), pp. 306–7.
2. *Africa Report*, January 1971, p. 27.
3. *Africa Report*, December 1970, pp. 12ff.
4. Nyerere, *Freedom and Unity*, pp. 183–84.
5. *National Geographic*, April 1975.
6. *Washington Post*, April 2, 1973.

CHAPTER 13

FOREIGN AFFAIRS

In the field of foreign affairs, the Tanzanians seem to have compartmentalized their efforts, giving certain of these priority. Uppermost have been their associations with the United Nations and its specialized agencies; the Organization of African Unity; and the shifting relationships with its neighbors, particularly Zambia, Kenya, and Uganda. On the negative side, prolonged and hostile, there has been priority attention to the "white supremacy" regimes of southern Africa. Of lesser priority have been those relationships with the Commonwealth, the United States, and the Communist world (particularly Peking). Each of these major external relationships receives attention in pages following.

Tanzania and the United Nations

In his first postindependence address to the United Nations at the time of his country's admission to that organization, December 14, 1961, then Prime Minister Julius Nyerere outlined his country's foreign policy priorities. He stressed the country's debt to the United Nations, the need of world peace, a recognition of human rights, and the importance of African unity. He said in part:

The fact that we have been a Trust Territory . . . has greatly helped us to achieve our independence in the way in which we have achieved it. . . . When we welcome our admission to the United Nations, we are acknowledging our inter-dependence with all other peoples. . . . We know that we cannot sit unaffected by the great controversies and conflicts which send their reverberations through every corner of the world. . . .

The basis of our actions, internal and external, will be an attempt, an honest attempt

130

to honor the dignity of man. . . . We believe that it is evil for any people to ill-treat others on grounds of race. . . . We shall try to use the Universal Declaration of Human Rights as a basis for both our external and our internal policies. . . .

We are all concerned, first and foremost, with the establishment of world peace. . . . We believe that, . . . ultimately, the problem of world peace depends upon the achievement of a state in the world where you have a world government. But that state of affairs does not exist at present. We realize that the United Nations itself is not a world government, but it is a practical acknowledgement of the need for world peace.

The first principle of a Government's foreign policy is, therefore, a recognition of the fundamental importance of the United Nations. . . . This international Organization has great purpose and still greater potentiality. . . . Within this Assembly every nation is an equal, and we believe that in this lies the unique character of the United Nations and its greatest asset. . . . The importance of the United Nations can and will grow, dependent only upon the determination of all of us to make it work. . . . Tanganyika will look at every one of its policy decisions in the light of its recognition of the fundamental importance of the United Nations.[1]

Nyerere added that it is the small and weak nations which most need the United Nations. Therefore, countries like Tanganyika must put in the extra effort to make the United Nations succeed.

Links between the Tanzanians and various United Nations agencies have always been close. Before independence the Trusteeship Council and after independence the General Assembly have furnished special protective canopies and practical political platforms to this new nation. Furthermore, the specialized agencies such as the Food and Agriculture Organization (FAO) and the World Health Organization (WHO) have been of considerable help in improving the living conditions of the peoples of Tanzania, islands and mainland.

Of paramount importance in any analysis of Tanzania's foreign policy is an understanding of the underlying philosophical view which Nyerere and his confreres have always held toward the United Nations. The author recalls several conversations with Nyerere and his lieutenants on the subject of the United Nations immediately after independence. Recognizing the high costs of maintaining diplomatic missions abroad, Tanzanian leaders have espoused the notion that the small nations of the world should utilize the United Nations as a forum for carrying on their bilateral as well as their multilateral diplomacy. They realized the need of keeping their few educated and experienced people at home for essential internal administration. At the outset, therefore, the Tanganyikans established diplomatic missions in only a few capitals —London, Washington, Bonn, New Delhi, Nairobi, Kampala, Moscow, and Ottawa as well as the United Nations.

In contrast, Tanzania being the first independent nation of East Africa, the establishment of a large number of diplomatic missions in the country was almost precipitate. By 1963 more than thirty foreign diplomatic missions had been established in Dar es Salaam. The 1964 troubles on Zanzibar and on the mainland propelled various Communist nations into the Dar es Salaam diplomatic arena. Tanzania early established a ceiling on the number of incoming diplomats accredited to each resident mission. These ceilings have been maintained. There are now some thirty-six resident missions in Tanzania. Faced with the incursions of these many embassies, with their resultant multifaceted associations, the Tanzanians were forced to undertake broader bilateral diplomatic tasks. They came to realize, too, that the United Nations diplomatic milieu required a different kind of focus. Yet another cause of the shift was the realization that a great proportion of Tanzania's United Nations representation must necessarily concern itself with the external problems of Africa rather than the internal problems of Tanzania. Thus the Tanzanians utilized both Security Council and General Assembly for distinct African purposes, namely, as an aid in welding together the Afro-Asian bloc, to keep both spotlight and external pressure on the apartheid regimes of southern Africa, and as a training ground for budding diplomats. The success of Nyerere and others in molding the highly effective Afro-Asian voting bloc, which now numbers seventy-one among the total United Nations membership of 143, is self-evident. The power of that group has materially changed the complexion of the United Nations itself.

Tanzania has been a special force in pushing for strong resolutions against the various apartheid regimes of southern Africa. As an adjunct to these activities, Tanzania has afforded safe haven and funds to exiled African nationalists from southern Africa and has thus furnished both a political platform and a petitioning venue for United Nations committee hearings on these issues.

Tanzania and the Organization of African Unity

After World War II, while the drive for independence of colonial territories gathered strength, there grew up in Africa an embryonic spirit of Pan-African unity. In the decades of the 1950s and 1960s pressures for freedom of the colonial territories in Africa took understandable priority. After independence was attained, the founding fathers of these new nations turned again to the concept.

Regional groupings of these new states, economic and technical, gave impetus to that concept of African unity. This pressure culminated in a meeting of the heads of independent African states (excepting South Africa), which commenced in Addis Ababa, Ethiopia, in May 1963. From that meeting came the Organization of African Unity (OAU) with representatives of thirty African nations signing the charter. Since that inauguration eleven additional nations of Africa have become members.

Main purposes of the OAU, a regional offshoot of the United Nations, include: support of Pan-African goals for political independence and economic betterment; support of the United Nations Charter and the Declaration of Human Rights; eradication of colonialism; recognition of individual sovereignties; peaceful settlement of disputes; nonalignment on great-power issues. The late Haile Selassie, then emperor of Ethiopia, characterized the grouping as the one African organization through which Africa's single voice may be heard and within which Africa's problems may be studied and resolved.

The OAU operates through four main bodies and a number of ad hoc commissions. Chief among these is the Assembly of Heads of State which convenes annually. A second major group, the Council of Ministers, comprising foreign ministers of member nations, handles fiscal and emergency problems. The third group is the General Secretariat, located in Addis Ababa, responsible for general administration and liaison. A fourth sector is the Commission of Mediation, Conciliation and Arbitration, which seeks to reconcile disputes between OAU member states. Other ad hoc and specialized commissions operate in economic, social, educational, scientific, cultural, health, and defense fields.

The most controversial of the ad hoc groupings set up within the OAU has been the eleven-member African Liberation Committee (ALC). This group is given responsibility for "harmonizing assistance from African States to national liberation movements in the dependent territories of Africa." The Committee, headquartered in Dar es Salaam, operates with levies on individual members for military and propaganda purposes, but its administrative costs are borne within the OAU normal budget.

At the founding meeting of the OAU, President Julius Nyerere, stressing the tasks of liberation and unity which lay ahead, said:

The whole of Africa speaks with one voice; . . . our desire is to see Africa completely free from colonialism. . . . We came here . . . to find out what we should all do now in order to bring about the final liberation of Africa. . . . We came here to find out our common denominator in our approach to African unity. . . .

In order then to complete this picture of unanimity let me add Tanganyika's voice. . . . Because of that proximity to non-independent Africa, we are already making a humble contribution to the liberation of southern Africa, but we are prepared to do more. In particular we are prepared to support the proposal . . . that one percent of our national budget should be set aside for the purpose of liberating non-free Africa. . . . We in Tanganyika are prepared to die a little for the final removal of the humiliation of colonialism from the face of Africa.

Africa is not free; . . . it is Africa which should take the necessary collective measures to free Africa. This is the clear and serious message that should go from this conference to the Security Council of the United Nations. . . . Let us all unanimously accept the Charter as our first step. . . . [2]

Following the Zanzibar-Tanganyika mutinies of January 1964, Nyerere called for a special meeting of OAU foreign ministers. He opened that conference in Dar es Salaam on February 12 by describing the outbreak and saying that its ultimate effect was not easy to gauge. Continuing, he said:

To disarm the Tanganyika Rifles I therefore asked for . . . [British] troops . . . [which] have remained in Tanganyika to assist in . . . maintaining law. . . . There is no evidence before us to suggest that the mutinies in Tanganyika were inspired by outside forces—either communist or imperialist. . . . The Government of Tanganyika has drawn constant strength from the evident loyalty of the masses of the people of this country. . . . It is therefore not for internal political reasons that we wanted an opportunity for discussion with our brother African states. Our national humiliation arises from the necessity of having non-Tanganyikan troops to do our work for us; . . . [this] has serious implications in the context of African nationalism, and . . . non-alignment. . . .

At Addis Ababa last year, Tanganyika joined with all the other independent countries of our continent in asserting that Africa must unite, and through unity determine her own policies and deal with her own problems. . . . It is because of that commitment that my Government decided to call for this Emergency Meeting.

. . . Tanganyika is a "border state." By virtue of that fact the headquarters of the Liberation Committee of the OAU is situated in our capital. In addition, we have many Freedom Fighters from Mozambique and South Africa organizing their affairs in this country. These matters are not only the concern of Tanganyika. . . . A state of affairs in Tanganyika which might interfere with the effectiveness . . . of these Freedom Movements is the concern of the whole of Africa. . . . The enemies of African liberation will continue to mock at Africa while any African State relies on outside troops to safeguard its citizens.[3]

As a postscript to the foregoing, shortly thereafter Nigerian troops were sent to Tanganyika to assist in establishing order. A little later Canadian military advisers supplanted the British and Nigerian military presence and remained in the country until late 1969. These in turn were supplanted by Communist Chinese military advisers who remain in the country today.

During the next several years, Nyerere constantly returned to the need of African nations uniting. Speaking at a state banquet in Bamako, Mali, in April 1965, he made reference to the fact that "thirty-six sticks of wood might each break under the weight of a heavy burden; but what if those thirty-six sticks of wood are bound together? Then the burden can be carried safely. . . . We have to bind ourselves together."[4]

As an adjunct to OAU activities, brief mention should be made of the various exile groups located in Dar es Salaam and of the work which the African Liberation Committee (ALC) has attempted. Among these exile groups have been South African black nationalists: the African National Congress (ANC) and the Pan-African Congress (PAC). South-West African exile groups include South-West African Peoples' Organization (SWAPO) and South-West Africa National Union (SWANU). There are the Rhodesian African exiles, including wings of Zimbabwe African Nationalist Union (ZANU) and Zimbabwe African People's Union (ZAPU). Also, there are exiles from Malawi, dissident former members of Dr. Hastings Banda's cabinet. Most important and numerous have been the representatives of the now victorious Mozambique Liberation Front, or *Frente de Libertação de Mozambique* (FRELIMO). Recent arrivals include the remnants of ex-President Milton Obote's "high command" from Uganda.

These and other exile representations now located in Dar es Salaam attest to Tanzania's dedication to the liberation of remaining "colonial" territories of southern Africa and to the end of "white supremacy" throughout Africa. The essential functions of the ALC have been to engage openly in that struggle and to channel financial, strategic, moral, and diplomatic support from the OAU to "Freedom Fighters."

When the ALC was approved by the OAU in 1965, it was reported that a combination of militarily capable African states had promised to raise a fighting force of some 500,000 men. To begin with, financial support of about $4 million plus training and logistical facilities were requested by ALC proponents. Most OAU members have since shown considerable reluctance to supply funds, and even fewer to supply troops. While there have been particular shortages of funds and war material from black nations of sub-Saharan Africa, it is understood that arms are now being supplied from Algerian and Libyan sources. Several years ago it was understood that non-African support of ALC activities was coming from Moscow and Belgrade. Today, however, it is believed that the Soviets have lost interest in the ALC and that most external help is now coming from Peking. The ALC has been tight-lipped about its finances, training, and sources of help. Yet the ALC has been openly critical of the support it receives from most members of the OAU.

Leadership of certain of the exile groups has been badly divided, weakening both effectiveness and goals. There have been open enmities among many leaders, especially within FRELIMO and the southern African groups. Insofar as actual military activity is concerned, FRELIMO received the preponderance of ALC funding and training. Much of that training has been given within Tanzania and Zambia. Several thousand "graduates" of those Freedom Fighter camps are said to have entered the fighting in Mozambique. Furthermore, the Tanzanian government has sometimes found the competing rebel groups embarrassing. Likewise, it has found the care of refugees and rebels costly and long-drawn. Yet Nyerere and his government continue their commitment to the cause of liberation of southern Africa.

Analyzing political developments at the end of the OAU's first decade, the *Baltimore Sun* (May 20, 1973) pointed out that when OAU was founded in 1963 only two military regimes (Sudan and Egypt) were admitted to membership. Togo's new military junta was temporarily rejected. Today, a decade later, some seventeen military regimes are members. Military men, dictators, and monarchs are becoming respectable. Multiparty polities survive in only eight countries. President Nyerere, in a 1973 interview, says Africans "should thank the imperialists" for having Pan-Africanized 2,000 African nations into fifty.[5] He sees the last ten years as having been spent "consolidating that achievement."

It is still too early to appraise the regional, continental or worldwide effectiveness of the OAU. Until recently that organization's influence was growing solidly, especially within the United Nations. In various bilateral African disputes, such as the Algerian-Moroccan controversies, the Ethiopian border troubles, etc., the OAU proved itself relatively successful as an arbiter. OAU pressures against Portugal in its former African possessions were also impressive. Less successful, however, were the OAU's early post-independence conciliation efforts in the former Belgian Congo and in the Biafran-Nigerian conflict. Unsuccessful, too, has been full attainment of OAU objectives in white-ruled southern Africa. Black majority rule in Rhodesia, in Namibia, and in the Republic of South Africa is still far from realization. The issue of the Angolan civil war and of foreign intervention (Soviet, Cuban, South African, American) therein has proved especially troubling to the organization. In fact, during a special session on that issue held in Addis Ababa early in 1976, the OAU deadlocked. In that meeting even such stalwart friends as Nyerere of Tanzania and Kaunda of Zambia divided over recognition versus reconciliation options of the Angolan question.

Major problems still confront the organization. Most thinking Africans, while wanting to preserve and strengthen the OAU, admit that its first priority remains the need of solving the problems of southern Africa. In all OAU activities, Nyerere and the government of Tanzania have taken a leading part—both by reason of geography and by reason of aspiration toward African unity.

Tanzania and Its Neighbors

By all odds, the most important of Tanzania's neighbors is the Republic of Zambia, which shares with it a spectrum of associations. Of lesser consequence, though still important, are Tanzania's ties (and conflicts) with its East African Community partners, Kenya and Uganda. Less important still are its relationships with Burundi, Rwanda, and Zaire. Openly abrasive are its relationships with Malawi. Openly hostile were its relationships with Portuguese controlled Mozambique until Portugal relinquished its claim, and pervasively antagonistic are its attitudes to white-ruled Rhodesia and the apartheid Republic of South Africa.

Tanzania's associations with Zambia are based upon the long-time friendship and intellectual affinity of the founder-presidents Nyerere and Kaunda and the geo-political relationship between landlocked Zambia and sea-girt Tanzania. In the wake of Rhodesian UDI and the resulting crises between Rhodesia and Zambia, the roads, rail routes, and seaports of Tanzania have become highly important to Zambia as channels for Zambia's copper, petroleum, and other essentials. The Tanzania-Zambia railway, built with Peking's aid, ties these countries even more closely, for Zambia's heavy dependence on white-ruled Rhodesia and war-ravaged Mozambique and Angola for rail transport is at an end. A new highway and oil pipeline also link the two nations.

Tanzania's associations with Kenya and Uganda have been of long duration. In the economic sphere they were developed by British colonial overlords through the East African High Commission (now the East African Community, EAC). As noted in previous chapters, this body maintains a common-market relationship in the fields of posts and telegraphs, airways, rail and harbor facilities, etc. Though sometimes turbulent in its postindependence application, the concept has given a certain cohesion to these three East African nations.

In this connection it is important to recall that, as far back as 1960, Nyerere offered to slow down the pace of Tanganyika's movement toward independence if he received firm assurances from the British government that Kenya and Uganda might be allowed to attain independence at the same time. Nyerere's hope in seeking this guarantee from Britain was to give strength to the prospect that the three nations might thereby move forward toward full-scale economic association and political federation. When Nyerere failed to receive such an assurance from the United Kingdom he pushed for early independence for Tanganyika alone. Nyerere still believes the British failed in this regard to realize a golden opportunity for East Africa's unification. After independence, associations between these three states have depended in large part upon the personal relationships, written and oral, between the various founding fathers—Nyerere of Tanzania, Kenyatta of Kenya, Obote of Uganda (and subsequently the abrasive Amin).

In his association with Kenya, President Nyerere, in the traditional African sense, pays deference to the elder statesman, Jomo Kenyatta, affectionately called *Mzee* (Honored Elder). However, this personal deference toward the Kenyan president was earlier diluted by Nyerere's close personal friendship with Kenya's young, brilliant national leader, Tom Mboya, assassinated in 1969. That Mboya had been a Luo tribesman, and therefore suspect to Kenyatta and the latter's Kikuyu lieutenants, tempered somewhat the depth of Nyerere's private friendship with Kenyatta. Even so, the two leaders Kenyatta and Nyerere have clear-cut respect for one another and a shared determination to work for broader "African" goals.

One peculiar impediment to a balanced working relationship between Tanzania and Kenya has been what is known as the "Nairobi syndrome." This results from the heavy concentration of commercial, financial, transportation, and communications headquarters in or near Nairobi—with these in turn overshadowing such activity in both Tanzania and Uganda. Out of this concentration has grown the tendency for Kenyans in both public and private sectors to dominate or even look down upon their neighbors as supposedly subordinate politicians and "submanagers." This tendency toward superciliousness has rankled Nyerere, his ministers, and the person-in-the-street. Even Western diplomats and businessmen resident in East African capitals have not been immune to the "Nairobi syndrome" and its troubling effects. In turn, this attitude has caused tensions in the workings of the East African Community. These have been alleviated only in part by the decentralization of EAC and the transfer of its headquarters to Arusha, Tanzania. In the face of such abrasions, the salving personal relationships of Kenyatta and Nyerere have proved efficacious.

From the time of Tanganyika's independence in 1961, the relationships between Tanzania and Uganda have been difficult to assess. Though never openly hostile, the associations between Nyerere and Uganda's first president, Milton Obote, were somewhat reserved until Obote was deposed by General Amin.

In 1971, following General Amin's successful coup against Obote, President Nyerere, reportedly somewhat unhappily, offered refuge to the deposed Obote. Nyerere probably offered that refuge because of his own innate hatred of unconstitutional coups and militaristic regimes. Partly because of this "welcome" to Obote and partly as a result of friction (described elsewhere in this book), hostility between the two nations broke into small-scale warfare. Subsequently there were unsuccessful covert efforts to reinstate Obote with Tanzanian aid. At this writing, Nyerere continues to withhold formal recognition of Amin's regime. Given their economic and geographic associations, including such important factors as the riparian benefits of Lake Victoria, the two countries share national interests complementary rather than inimical.

Tanzania's relationships with the former Belgian trust territory, Burundi, also hinge on a great lake—Tanganyika. Across this lake, from Kigoma to Bujumbura, move goods to and from Burundi: coffee outward, petroleum and general supplies inward. Thus Tanzania stands as *entrepôt* to Burundi. There is also a compatible relationship between Tanzania and Rwanda, though the latter is not so dependent on Tanzania geographically.

Like the adjoining countries of Zaire and Uganda, Tanzania has been affected by the long-standing feud of Bahutu and Watutsi tribesmen in both Burundi and Rwanda. Tanzania has provided refuge for members of both tribes forced to flee their homelands. It has been reported that some 15,000 Watutsi refugees from Rwanda have been relocated in northwest Tanzania during recent years. Latest press stories from the area indicate that some 20,000 Bahutu from Burundi are also being accommodated.

Tanzania's attitude toward its larger western neighbor, Zaire (the former Belgian Congo), has been contradictory. Nyerere had rapport with that country's founding father, Patrice Lumumba, and grieved when he was assassinated. Nyerere, like most other African militants, openly disliked Moise Tshombe, Lumumba's controversial successor, considering him to be a stooge of Belgian mining interests. Tanzanian relations with Zaire's present leader, President Mobutu, have varied from early antagonism (especially over the Stanleyville troubles and the more recent kidnapping of American university students from Tanzanian soil by Zairian "rebels") to present amicable reserve. There might very well have been more conflict between these two nations—Tanzania and Zaire—had not their basic national backgrounds been so divergent and the geographic distances between their capitals so great.

Relations between Tanzania and its southern neighbor, Malawi, have also varied considerably over the past decade. Shortly after Tanzania's independence, anticipating breakup of the Central African Federation, Tanzanian leaders gave some political and financial support to Malawi's founder-president, Dr. Hastings Banda. Subsequent to Malawi's breakaway from British colonialism, personal relationships between Nyerere and Banda deteriorated. That situation was compounded by Rhodesian UDI, by Zambia's related troubles, and by heightened Tanzanian support of Mozambique's Freedom Fighters. On these matters, in Tanzania's eyes, Banda appeared to react less like a militant African nationalist than a kind of Uncle Tom. This impression was given further substance by Banda's movement closer to Prime Minister John Vorster of apartheid South Africa. This situation was given a final fillip by Dr. Banda's exchange of diplomats with South Africa, by Banda's acceptance of South African financial aid, and by Banda's unqualified espousal of so-called "dialogue" between the white regimes of southern Africa and black African regimes to the north. These events brought on mutual recriminations from leaders of both Tanzania and Malawi, even including territorial claims against one another's lands. At this writing, relations between Nyerere and Banda appear to be less than harmonious, though relations between ordinary Malawian and Tanzanian citizens seem somewhat less antagonistic.

Tanzania and the "White Redoubt"

The author recalls a number of conversations with President Nyerere in the period 1960–68 concerning the White Redoubt (the minority governments of southern Africa, including Rhodesia, the Portuguese provinces of Mozambique/Angola, and the Republic of South Africa). In those conversations Nyerere consistently contended that these last bastions of white supremacy in Africa must be overcome by black African nationalism in stages—first Rhodesia, then the Portuguese provinces, and finally the hard-core venue of apartheid, South Africa.

Tanzania's leaders have long been critical of British handling of Rhodesia. In fact, Nyerere and his lieutenants condemned the makeup of the Central African Federation (created in 1953), which associated the now separate nations of Southern Rhodesia (now Rhodesia), Northern Rhodesia (now Zambia), and Nyasaland (now Malawi). This ill-fated merger was long ago characterized by some Tanzanians as the equivalent of a "shotgun" wedding which neither partner really wanted. As early as 1961, when Africans elsewhere were attaining independence, the principal Rhodesian African politicians, like Nbadaningi Sithole, leader of the Zimbabwe African National Union (ZANU) and Joshua Nkomo, leader of the Zimbabwe African People's Union (ZAPU), obtained TANU support for Rhodesian independence under a black majority government. Even at that time the situation was worsened by the imposition and subsequent suspension of an unsatisfactory London-drafted constitution. Nyerere and other East and Central African leaders then correctly forecast the breakup of the Central African Federation. They foretold, too, a Rhodesian orientation toward South Africa and white supremacy.

Thus in 1965, when Prime Minister Ian Smith led Rhodesia into the Unilateral Declaration of Independence, the Tanzanians were not surprised. At once they came to Zambia's aid. Nyerere was in the vanguard of the fight to push Britain into using force to solve the Rhodesian crisis quickly. Failing that, Tanzania pushed Commonwealth and other African nations to break diplomatic ties with Britain. With a few exceptions, the Tanzanians were unsuccessful, though for several years (1965–68) Tanzania and Britain did sever relations. Meanwhile, in the United Nations Tanzania stood out among the more militant states asking concerted action—economic, political, psychological, or military—against the Smith regime. In these activities Tanzania was in constant accord with Zambia. Other East and Central African states, notably Kenya, Uganda, and Zaire, were far more conservative in their demands of Britain. Tanzania and its United Nations allies did succeed, however, in pushing Britain and the United States into sanctions action under Chapter VII of the United Nations charter ("a grave threat to world peace") against Rhodesia. On these grounds economic sanctions were mounted against the Rhodesians by a United Nations majority. Both Tanzanian and Zambian leaders have since become wholly disillusioned with the efficacy of the sanctions program, especially in the face of open violation thereof by South Africa, Portugal, and the United States. It can be assumed that if Rhodesia and Zambia come into full-scale conflict, Nyerere would surely ally his country on the side of Zambia's president, Kenneth Kaunda.

Tanzania's successful help to Mozambique Freedom Fighters in their effort to rid Portuguese Africa of Lisbon's rule is well known. In addition to exerting pressures against Portugal in world forums, the Tanzanians have supplied Mozambique rebels with funds, logistical support, a venue for political exiles, and military training. Furthermore, the first major Mozambique nationalist, Eduardo Mondlane, leader of *Frente de Libertação de Mozambique* (FRELIMO), maintained headquarters in Dar es Salaam until his assassination there in 1968. Nyerere, his close friend, both directly and through the African Liberation Committee of the OAU, gave Mondlane and his Mozambique Freedom Fighters sanctuary and financial and psychological support. After Mondlane's death FRELIMO continued to operate from Dar es Salaam.

A major reason for this support by Tanzania is the fact that one of its important tribes, the Makonde of the southeastern area, was split by the conflict. This tribe, numbering approximately 250,000, had been cut in half by the political geography of the region and by the struggle itself. Thus the Mozambique uprising resulted in part from the artificialities of the nineteenth-century German-Portuguese border demarcation and in part by Tanzania's independence, a movement which infected the Makonde on both sides of the border with nationalist spirit.

At the height of Portugal's military involvement in Mozambique (1973) there were some 60,000 Portuguese and local soldiery in the field. Pinning them down were only 5,000 guerrilla-type Freedom Fighters. These in turn were backed by an additional 10,000 men in training in camps in Tanzania. At the apogee of the conflict, northern Mozambique was a no-man's land. At that time one-half of Portugal's national budget was being drained off by the fighting in Portuguese Africa (Mozambique, Angola, and Guinea-Bissau). Clearly this was Portugal's "Vietnam." The innate poverty in money and human resources of metropolitan Portugal could no longer stand the strain. This situation, therefore, combined with hatred of the long authoritarian rule in the homeland, forced the widely discussed military coup against the Salazar-Caetano regime in Lisbon. This situation in metropolitan Portugal, in turn, hastened the new government's decision to give up the fight to retain Angola, Mozambique, and Guinea-Bissau. Today independence has been gained by both Mozambique (June 1975) and Angola (November 1975) though the latter is torn by civil war. Mozambique's independence represents a decided victory for the FRELIMO forces and for their faithful allies, the Tanzanians. There is no doubt that Nyerere's political philosophy as well as his economic ideas will have a profound influence on the new black African rulers of Mozambique. That nation's new leader, Samora Machel, has been clearly impressed by Nyerere and his *Ujamaa* concept.

Tanzania's relationship with the Republic of South Africa during recent years has been consistently hostile. TANU leaders constantly condemn and advocate elimination (by violence if necessary) of the white-dominated apartheid regime of South Africa. It was Nyerere who, early in 1961, initiated a coalition of Commonwealth prime ministers to remove South Africa from membership in the Commonwealth. Since that time there has been a continuing and widespread belief in Tanzania, as elsewhere in black Africa, that returning exiles as saboteurs and Freedom Fighters to South Africa would provide the fuse for revolutionary activism within that country. This cadre of returning exiles could in turn arouse the indigenous nonwhite communities to overthrow the Afrikaner apartheid regime, thereby bringing about black majority rule in the republic. These beliefs have been supported by willing, though often misguided, liberal thinkers and writers in both Europe and America. These views fail to measure the strength of South Africa's defenses, its internal security apparatus, and its white rulers' determination to maintain their supremacy. The revolutionary concepts have also made martyrs of the few Freedom Fighters who have been able to filter back into their homeland.

Competent military observers believe that South Africa could throw a force of 200,000 men into the field immediately. These would probably be supported by Rhodesians and by Portuguese exiles. They would be supported by small but adequate jet fighter forces, tank groups, radar networks, short-range missiles, armament factories, and excellent communications. The defense action would also be supported by a highly industrialized South African economy, rich in gold and other minerals, self-sufficient in foodstuffs, and lacking only petroleum of its own. In sum, South Africa could surely mount a force in strength sufficient to defeat any African military combination brought to bear against the republic. Only if one of the superpowers intervened on the side of the black Africans (as with the Soviets in Angola) would South African borders be endangered. Broad military action by Moscow, Peking, or Washington—considered unlikely—would necessitate costly invasion and blockade of the South African coastline. Far more likely would be a preemptive attack by South Africa (with Rhodesian and Portuguese-exile help) against Zambia, Tanzania, or an independent black-ruled Mozambique or Angola. South Africa's main problem would be that of keeping its nonwhite populace under control while fending off external attack.

In any such military effort against South Africa, Tanzania's physical and financial contribution would necessarily be marginal, but its psychological influence would be great. For only if that external attack were sucessfully coordinated with a major internal uprising would the present white minority regime be likely to fall. (For a full discussion of South Africa's military and economic capabilities see William Redman Duggan, *Socio-Economic Profile of South Africa* [New York: Praeger, 1973].)

While President Nyerere and his lieutenants undoubtedly comprehend the strength of the South African position, they continue to make militant statements against the Afrikaner leadership in United Nations forums and elsewhere. They prove constant irritants to the South Africans. In response, the South African press and propaganda machines have made Tanzanians, and especially Nyerere, into malevolent "bogey men." This situation has been compounded by South African fears of Chinese Communist intrusions into Africa in the wake of the Zanzibar troubles and the Tanzania/Zambia rail project. It seems certain that mutual recriminations of Tanzania and South Africa will continue, even heighten, in the near future.

Of special importance in the Tanzanian-South African relations have been the efforts of Nyerere and Kaunda to prevent Britain and other Western powers from delivering arms to South Africa in violation of the United Nations arms embargo. President Nyerere, in his address to the United Nations General Assembly in New York on the occasion of the twenty-fifth anniversary celebration of that organization, contended that South Africa did not need the arms but sought through such purchases a "certificate of respectability" from European nations.

Despite continuing pressure by Tanzanian and other African leaders for imposition of more extensive international sanctions against South Africa, some economic links between Tanzania and South Africa still remain. Merchant shipping between the two countries continues to operate under British, American, Scandinavian, German, and other flags. Yet another profitable economic link retained between the two countries was the association, only recently terminated, between Tanzania and the huge South African conglomerate Anglo-American Corporation with its Tanzanian-owned Williamson Diamond Mine in northwest Tanzania.

It will be recalled that in 1969, by terms of the Lusaka Manifesto (see chapter 10), Presidents Nyerere and Kaunda advocated opening a "dialogue" with South African leaders on enfranchisement of the black population in the Republic of South Africa. This idea was advanced in an effort to avert future violence. Pretoria first ignored the proposal but in recent months has undertaken informal talks with these and other black African leaders. Pretoria's belated entry into dialogue was inspired by the deteriorating situation in Rhodesia and the new black rule in Mozambique and Angola. At this writing results of the various dialogues cannot be assessed. Informed observers of the African scene remain pessimistic, believing that violence within Rhodesia and within South Africa itself cannot long be averted.

The determination of black Africa's leaders to move again from unsuccessful dialogue into espoused military conflict—especially in Rhodesia—is pointed up by a speech which President Nyerere delivered at Oxford University on November 19, 1975. Reporting the full text of this speech, the magazine *Southern Africa* of January 1976 quotes Nyerere as follows:

Rhodesia cannot survive without South African backing. . . . Even now Smith is not ready to . . . [accept] the principle of majority rule in Rhodesia. . . . South Africa will [not] use force to bring about majority rule [in Rhodesia]. . . . So we are forced back to the alternative strategy outlined in the Lusaka Declaration of 1969. This said, "But while peaceful progress is blocked by actions of those at present in power in the States of Southern Africa, we have no choice but to give to the peoples of those territories all the support of which we are capable in their struggle against their oppressors." Unfortunately, but inevitably, the armed struggle in Rhodesia will have to be resumed and intensified until conditions are ripe for realistic negotiations. And the Freedom Fighters of Rhodesia, like those in Mozambique, will demand Africa's support.

As a postscript to this volatile situation, it should be emphasized that Nyerere and other black African nationalists will never be content until black African majority rule is attained in Rhodesia and South Africa. Only when the so-called "white redoubt" of the apartheid-oriented regimes of southern Africa has crumbled will the pressures from the north against these countries cease.

Tanzania and the Commonwealth

Tanzania's relations with the various members of the Commonwealth must be considered in several categories. Foremost is Tanzania's long-standing association with its old colonial mentor, the United Kingdom. Next, and already described in detail previously, are Tanzania's relations with its neighbors: Zambia, Kenya, Uganda, and Malawi. Less important are its relations with other black African members of the Commonwealth: Botswana, Lesotho, Swaziland, Ghana, Nigeria, Sierra Leone, and Gambia. In yet a fourth category are its relationships with Asian and Western hemisphere Commonwealth members. Finally, there are special associations which have grown up between Tanzania and Canada.

Tanzania's associations with Great Britain, its colonial ruler from 1920 to 1961, have previously been described. In retrospect, many Tanzanians would now probably admit that the British colonial rule had not been despotic, that British colonial civil servants probably did as much as they could to advance the socio-economic position of the average Tanganyikan within the narrow bureaucratic lines granted them by London. Indicative of this attitude is the great respect accorded by Tanzania to the last British governor, Sir Richard Turnbull, who was an honored guest (with eighty other ex-colonial British civil servants) at the tenth anniversary of the country's independence.

On the other hand, the nation's leaders from Nyerere down resented the primacy of economic and financial attention which Britain gave its other black African territories. The Tanganyikans believed, with justification, that among British African areas of suzerainty Tanganyika, a United Nations Trust Territory, was considered a stepchild by London and the real responsibility of the United Nations. Thus, despite well-intentioned efforts of British colonial administrators on the ground, there was embedded in the attitudes of most Tanzanians toward Britain a resentment of British paternalism and failure to espouse equal aspirations and human dignity. This attitude left a great bruise on Tanzania's national character. That bruise of colonial rule Nyerere has often described as one of deep "humiliation" for his nation and, in fact, for all black Africa. These racialist failures on Britain's part, carried over from the preindependence period, are further demonstrated, in Nyerere's estimation, by more recent British action and inaction in Africa. These have included Britain's failure to resolve the Rhodesian UDI crisis, its failure to castigate South Africa over that nation's apartheid policies, its involvement in the Biafran conflict, and its generally weak-kneed support of human rights and decolonizing resolutions within the United Nations.

Since independence, as a result, there has been a love-hate relationship between the two nations. Illustrative of this attitude, on one side of the coin, were mutual recriminations between leaders of the two countries as to British handling of the Rhodesian issue. Tanzanians constantly pressed Britain to use force for a solution. The Tanzanians were deeply perturbed over Zambian difficulties emanating from UDI, especially when Prime Minister Harold Wilson boasted of a "quick kill" of the Smith regime—with no results. When Rhodesia continued to prosper, despite United Nations sanctions, Nyerere and a few other African leaders broke diplomatic relations with Britain and insisted that all OAU members follow their lead. This effort failed and Nyerere tacitly admitted the failure when he restored diplomatic ties with Britain in 1968. On the obverse side of the schizophrenic coin, constructive relationships still exist between Britain and Tanzania in economic, religious, and educational fields.

British commerce and shipping as well as banking and finance have been of continuing importance to the economic life of Tanzania. While there has been resentment in British circles of Tanzania's nationalization, British business-men continue to play an important part in Tanzania's economy. Even today Britain remains Tanzania's best market and its principal supplier.

The English language remains the principal alternative to Swahili and the major commercial language. English also continues to be used in many radio and press activities. Both pre- and postindependence activities in educational, medical, and religious fields by various British-based sects, particularly the Anglicans and the Presbyterians, have provided an important influence for many of Tanzania's leaders of today. Thus Britain has left its unmistakable mark on the Tanzanian national scene and character.

While such conjecture is purely hypothetical, it may be prudent to speculate on how formal British associations with Tanzania might have been better maintained. It is the writer's personal opinion that these bonds could have been kept solid in at least five ways: (1) by sending in top-grade, African-oriented diplomatic officers at the onset of Tanganyika's independence in 1961 (and thus shore up Governor General Turnbull's almost single-handed efforts); (2) by greater magnanimity on Britain's part in giving economic and technical aid to the struggling new nation; (3) by greater foresight and wisdom on the part of the British in resolving the Rhodesian issue; (4) by British honoring of United Nations sanctions against both Rhodesia and South Africa (arms embargo); and (5) by proper preparation of Zanzibar for independence. The former Labour government of Prime Minister Harold Wilson seemed determined to improve relations between the two countries. With that aim Foreign Minister James Callaghan and Minister of Overseas Development Judith Hart have made official visits to Dar es Salaam where they have promised restoration of Britain's aid program to Tanzania.

Relations between Tanzania and other African Commonwealth members which lie farther afield have varied considerably in nature but have been highly personalized. The coterie of African nationalists who brought their respective nations to sovereign independence formed a close-knit fraternity. Kwame Nkrumah of Ghana, Sir Abubakar Balewa of Nigeria, and the Margai brothers, Milton and Albert, of Sierra Leone shared ideas with their East African nationalist contemporaries. Nkrumah in particular seemed to have a real influence on the thinking of younger Tanzanian leaders during the first years of Tanganyika's and Zanzibar's independence. Even after Nkrumah's downfall, his thoughts, especially on Pan-Africanism, were still quoted by East African intellectuals.

It was not until the death of Balewa and the various stages of Nigeria's internal breakup that associations between the Tanzanians and the federal Nigerian leaders began to wane. As a direct result of the Biafran troubles, official and personal associations between Tanzania and Nigeria virtually ceased. Nyerere espoused Biafra's cause and denounced Britain for furnishing arms to the federal Nigerians. Nyerere spearheaded a drive to obtain his own and other African nations' recognition of Biafra. The drive proved unsuccessful—only Tanzania, Gabon, the Ivory Coast, and Zambia recognized the Biafran "regime." Following the end of the civil war in Nigeria, President Nyerere and General Yakubu Gowon restored diplomatic relations. In a conversation between Nyerere and the author in May 1968, Nyerere justified his nation's actions in behalf of Biafra as being solely humanitarian and seeking to avoid mass genocide. In his contentions in favor of Biafra, Nyerere downgraded the dangers of fragmentation of African nations but did not recall his earlier defense of the sanctity of Africa's national boundaries.

Associations between Tanzania and the various West Indian/Caribbean Commonwealth states have been somewhat limited, principally involving Commonwealth meetings, United Nations activities, and ministerial visits. Relationships between Nyerere's government and Asian Commonwealth members have appeared to run hot and cold. This vacillation has seemed to be particularly true with respect to India. Indira Gandhi visited Dar es Salaam in 1961 and again in 1970. She also attended, as did Nyerere, the 1969 nonaligned summit conference in Lusaka. Nyerere has paid state visits to India. More recently, however, the courses of the two nations appear to diverge, possibly stemming from the increased rapport between Dar es Salaam and Peking. Of even greater importance may be the growing enmity between Indo-Pakistanis and black Africans that has developed throughout East Africa. Despite these political troubles, trade between Tanzania and India has been growing.

Of the so-called "Old Commonwealth" members—Canada, Australia, New Zealand—only Tanzania's relationships with Canada are important as yet. Leaders of these two nations have developed special links out of Nyerere's close friendship with the now-deceased Canadian prime minister, Lester Pearson. These links originated with Nyerere's and Pearson's first acquaintance in United Nations corridors and gained strength from their mutual devotion to United Nations ideals.

Soon after Tanganyika's independence in 1961, Canada announced its readiness to grant economic aid and technical assistance to the new African nation. Diplomatic exchanges were arranged. In addition to developmental assistance, Canada offered military aid to the new nation. This offer was accepted in 1965 when British military aid was withdrawn. Thereafter, Canadian military specialists concentrated on building up a small defensive air force for the Tanzanians as well as expanding ground-troop training. Not until late 1969 was this form of aid from the Canadians finally stopped. This withdrawal may have come from the presumption on the part of both countries that Canadians, as members of NATO, would not engage in expansion of Tanzanian military activities specifically directed against Portugal (another NATO partner) in Mozambique. The Canadian withdrawal left the field open to increased military aid on the part of the Chinese Communists, who were not so inhibited.

Ottawa's help to Dar es Salaam, civil and military, has been Canada's biggest single venture into the foreign-assistance field in Africa. It has been estimated by international authorities that such aid ranged from $2.5 million to $5 million annually over the past ten years. A recent Canadian effort (reported by the *Washington Post*, February 21, 1973) involved a loan of $13 million for a hydroelectric project. Members of the Peace Corps-type organization, the Canadian University Service Overseas (CUSO), have been very active in Tanzania. This is a nongovernmental group with costs split between the Canadian government and the host country.

Of special interest in the continuing story of Tanzanian-Canadian relations was the 1969 visit of President Nyerere to Prime Minister Pierre E. Trudeau. At that time, Nyerere is reported to have asked Trudeau to seek the takeover by Canada of Commonwealth leadership—political, financial, and military —from Britain. Trudeau, according to press reports, is said to have refused, probably basing his reaction in part upon the fact of his nation's own internal stresses with French nationalism. In this connection it is interesting to note, however, that the London Secretariat of the Commonwealth is headed by a

Canadian and the 1973 meeting of Commonwealth prime ministers was held in Ottawa. Implicit in Nyerere's reported approach to Trudeau, however, is Tanzania's acceptance of Canada as a leader among the middle group of nations and Canada's avowed commitments to United Nations peacekeeping functions. It would appear that, in making such an approach to Canada, Nyerere continues with his own commitments to the ideal of a nonaligned "third force" and to the validity of Commonwealth membership.

Tanzania and the United States

Relations between Tanzania and the United States have been complex and vacillating, sometimes placid, sometimes turbulent. At this writing the associations between the two nations seem essentially calm. Links between the two lands are best measured in historical terms, as well as on several planes —political, social/cultural, and economic.

On the political plane, divergences appear at once—ranging from a variance of views on Cold War matters to outright cleavage on the Vietnam issue, Rhodesia, and South Africa. Many of these divergences are based on opinions of leaders rather than on collision of national interests. There is in the divergence, too, something of the attitude of Tanzania defending the poor nation against the rich nation, the underdog against the superpower, the anticolonial socialist against the capitalist-imperialist.

When Tanganyika attained independence in 1961 its relations with the United States were amicable. At independence the United States delegation, as noted earlier, presented to Nyerere a letter of intent from President John F. Kennedy promising the new nation $10 million in economic aid. Elements of the newly formed Peace Corps were either in place or on their way to Dar es Salaam. Tanganyika was also benefiting from regional United States AID activities in education and agriculture. Total United States economic aid since 1960 has been $86 million.

On the social/cultural side there was a heavy American religious input. This was reflected in medicine and teaching through the work of American missions, including Roman Catholics, Lutherans, Methodists, Baptists, Adventists, and other sects. Private philanthropies of the United States, notably the Ford Foundation and the African-American Institute, were seeking means of helping the new nation educationally and culturally. Under United Nations aegis, with heavy United States financing, important WHO and FAO projects are underway in Tanganyika.

Of importance culturally and economically has been the work of the Peace Corps in Tanzania. Covering a period of eight years, it ranged from road surveying to medical aid and involved some 500 volunteers. Nyerere had been the first of the black African leaders to accept a group of Peace Corps people in 1961. However, by 1969, bowing to political pressures for Africanization and in the face of criticism that a few volunteers had sometimes interfered unwisely in internal affairs, Nyerere asked that they all be withdrawn.

Despite their political difficulties, Tanzania's economic ties with the United States have been steady, though not extensive. No more than $10 million of Tanzania's foreign private investments of $150 million is today United States-owned, this in the face of post-1967 nationalization. The United States capitalization includes participation in the General Tire plant in Arusha (some $3 million), certain petroleum outlets, a few farmlands still in United States citizens' hands, and small capital involvements of United States airline and shipping interests. The nationalization actions of 1967 and after resulted in takeover of certain United States banking interests and curtailed or quashed more extensive American investment in the country. In trade, the United States has consistently been Tanzania's fifth best customer. United States imports from that country totaled $19.6 million in 1971, the main purchases including coffee, sisal, cashews, and clove oil. The United States share of Tanzanian imports amounted to $13.2 million in 1971, principally heavy-duty goods.

President Kennedy's reception of President Nyerere in Washington in July 1963 probably represented the high-water mark of good relations between the two nations. Before and since, however, there has been some question and puzzlement in the minds of the United States press and public as to Nyerere's basic philosophy and his country's political orientation. Erroneously, many Americans had assumed Nyerere to be a "moderate" rather than a "militant nationalist." His unexpected departure from office in 1962 and his return thereto later that year contributed to American puzzlement about the man and his motives. So, too, did his government's early flirtations with Moscow and Peking.

During 1964 relations between the United States and Tanzania cooled visibly. There were several underlying reasons for the increasing tensions. One of these was the continuing United States involvement in the Congo. There, Tanzanian authorities openly supported the rebels in opposition to United Nations and United States efforts to preserve Congo unity. This situation became more taut with the Stanleyville airlift evacuation (late in 1964) of United States nationals by United States military planes. It was only partially alleviated by Tanzania's eventual recognition of the government of Congo-Kinshasa (now Zaire).

Various irritants likewise appeared between Americans and Zanzibaris in the period before the islands' union with Tanzania. A NASA satellite tracking station had been established on Zanzibar in the early 1960s, an installation inexplicable to Zanzibaris. Both American and British officials failed to convince Zanzibaris, African and Arab, of the peaceful nature of this Project Mercury installation. The Zanzibaris, believing that their island was about to become a pawn in the Cold War and that the installation was actually a secret missile-launching base, reacted with agitation. There had been no adequate advance explanation of its purposes to either political leaders or populace. This failure to explain was followed by certain unfortunate revelations by NASA contract employees as to the real nature of the project. All this reinforced Zanzibari concern and gave the Communists an easy opening to develop propaganda pitches against American "war-mongers." Radio Moscow and Radio Peking made the most of these opportunities. Until its removal late in 1964, the NASA project remained suspect to most Zanzibaris.

Personal relations had deteriorated markedly between resident American officials and the African revolutionary government as evidenced by the much publicized conflict between the African nationalist leader, Abeid Karume, and the allegedly pro-Arab American chargé, Frederick Picard. This situation was brought to a climax by Picard's assistance to several newsmen who had smuggled themselves onto Zanzibar in efforts to obtain the story of developments there. In reaction, Karume confronted Picard with a gun in the lobby of a Zanzibar hotel and demanded he leave the island at once. Picard did so. In a subsequent press conference, Secretary of State Dean Rusk objected to this highly unorthodox method of declaring a U.S. diplomat *persona non grata.*

One major deficiency on the United States side was the failure to move expeditiously and wisely in the matter of the Zanzibar revolution. The precipitous withdrawal of American diplomatic and NASA personnel from Zanzibar in the face of the revolutionary activity may have been, in part, responsible for the successful entry into that power vacuum by various Communist groups. The long delay in American and British recognition of the revolutionary regime also proved harmful. American AID efforts subsequent to the coup were both meager and dilatory. As early as 1964 a technical school (Mbweni Technical College), valued at $1 million, was planned. It was not until June 1972, however, that the school graduated its first class of mechanics.

Late in 1964 Tanzania's foreign minister, Oscar Kambona proffered to the Tanzania cabinet certain documents purportedly implicating the United States and Portugal in a plot to overthrow Nyerere's regime. These documents were obvious forgeries and the Tanzanian government was officially so informed by Washington. This situation appeared to have been ineptly handled by Kambona's office. Rather than privately querying the American ambassador on the source and authenticity of these documents, Kambona called a news conference and openly accused the United States government of subversion. Although Nyerere later implied that he believed these documents to have been forgeries, neither he nor any minister of his government ever directly apologized for the mistaken accusations.

Early in 1965 bad relations between the two countries came to a head with the declaration by the Tanzania government that two United States diplomats, Robert Gordon (now American consul general in Florence) and Frank Carlucci (now American ambassador to Portugal), assigned respectively to

Dar es Salaam and Zanzibar, were considered *persona non grata*. The full bill of complaints by the Tanzanian government against these two men was never set forth. Charges, however, seemed to relate to several innocuous telephone conversations (filled with "bureaucratic gobbledygook") between the two men. These conversations were obviously tapped by the Tanzanians.

Given these multifaceted abrasions, American diplomats in Tanzania were hard put to maintain even a modicum of cordial relations between Dar es Salaam and Washington. The situation between the two nations might have been considerably worse had it not been that the embassy in Dar es Salaam was then in the charge of one of America's most capable career diplomats, Ambassador William Leonhart, a cool, imaginative intellectual able to preserve both mutual respect and some rapport with another intellectual, Nyerere. Unfortunately for the two nations, Leonhart departed soon after to become ambassador to Yugoslavia. He was followed in Dar es Salaam by two successive less able and less empathic American ambassadors. Only in 1973 was that situation ameliorated, when the vivacious and friendly Ambassador Beverly Carter was appointed. Unfortunately Carter, himself a black, was recently withdrawn (on extremely flimsy grounds) from Dar es Salaam by Secretary of State Kissinger. Both Tanzanians and the American congressional black caucus protested mightily, but to no avail.

One other major difficulty which undoubtedly influenced the climate between Tanzania and the United States involved the search for financial backing and engineering of the Tanzania/Zambia rail route. Nyerere and Kaunda of Zambia had unsuccessfully wooed Britain and America in their search for that backing. The two African leaders then turned to the World Bank. It may be safely presumed that when the World Bank declined to undertake this venture, on economic grounds alone, the Africans blamed the influential United States. It was only after these rebuffs that Tanzania and Zambia turned to Peking. The help which the United States and other Western nations belatedly gave in shoring up Zambia with the recently completed oil pipeline and highway between Dar es Salaam and Zambia were, in their eyes, only halfhearted efforts to keep a foot in the door, economically and politically.

Associated with these antagonisms between the two nations may be added at least four other points of friction. One was the long delay attendant upon the beginnings of the various early American AID projects. (It has been claimed that not a shovelful of dirt was dug to initiate the first major aid project for at least thirty months following Tanganyikan independence.) The complexities of the United States AID program, including the tied-loan concept, were frustrating and misunderstood by the novice administrators of this new land. The second matter, even more hazy, was the widespread belief on the part of Tanzanians that officials of the CIA were out to remove Nyerere on the presumption that he and his government were pro-Communist. (This attitude had developed in the wake of the Congo, Cuba, Dominican Republic, Chile, and Vietnam situations.) The third was the increasing tendency of the United States to side with Britain or to be hypocritical on southern African issues. Fourth was the long-drawn series of determined actions taken by the United States to keep Peking out of the United Nations, contravening the desires of the Afro-Asian bloc.

The nadir of relationships between the two countries was probably reached in October 1970. At that time Nyerere, along with many of his fellow African chiefs-of-state, visited New York to help celebrate the twenty-fifth birthday of the United Nations. For them, dedicated as they were to United Nations ideals, it was a most important moment. Unexpectedly they ran into a "cold shoulder" on the part of high American officials. President Nixon was then in the midst of a heated congressional election campaign. He refused to see several African leaders, Nyerere and Kaunda included, at a mutually convenient time. Furthermore, in direct competition with the United Nations celebration in New York, Nixon held a party of his own for a few favored visiting heads of state at the White House in Washington. The Africans were understandably offended. Returning home they put a new chill on diplomatic associations with American embassy officials.

Yet one more important and pervasive factor influencing United States-Tanzanian relationships is the United States civil rights issue. It would be inevitable that Tanzanians would find a natural alignment on the side of American blacks. Tanzanians (and other black African states) have demanded that United States action match U.S. words and constitutional principles. It could not be expected, unless expressly outlined to them, that Tanzanians would be able to appreciate the complexities of the American civil rights struggle and the many advances which have been made in recent years.

In general, however, one might summarize the current official American attitude toward Tanzania as one of "benign neglect."

Tanzania and the Communist World

Tanzania's associations with the principal Communist nations—in particular the U.S.S.R., China, and Yugoslavia—have been of considerable importance. Diplomatic, commercial, cultural, and aid relationships with all these began almost at once following Tanganyika's independence. From the onset of that independence, Nyerere sought to have his people maintain an attitude of "nonalignment" in the Cold War conflict.

When diplomatic/economic relations were first established between the Soviets and the Tanzanians, they were structured along classic Soviet aid lines. There came first the grant of a $20-million line of credit from Moscow coupled with excessive, but temporary, purchases of Tanzania's primary commodities. Then came expanded Soviet cultural exchanges including student scholarships. Parallel with these came Soviet intrusions into informational media. There was a Tanzanian-Soviet accord providing for Soviet geological mapping of southern Tanzania. Along with these have been a number of high-level state visits to and fro including Nyerere's state visit to Moscow in 1969.

It is yet too early to make an adequate assessment of the success of Soviet efforts to influence Tanzanian leaders and policies. It is clear, however, that the Soviets suffered a sharp setback in those efforts as a result of the Moscow-Peking split and the upsurge of Chinese aid activity in Tanzania. There appears to be no doubt, however, that, of the two major Communist powers, the Tanzanians favor Peking. It also appears that for the past several years the Soviets have given much higher priority to their aid programs in Arab Africa than in black Africa. Interestingly, as some Soviet diplomats have claimed in conversations with the author, the Russians are considered by the Africans as white and therefore racist, antiblack, even capitalistic. This is in ironic contrast to the African's presumed acceptance of the historically racist Chinese as their nonwhite brothers.

Immediately following Tanganyikan independence in 1961, Nyerere took up the cudgels in the United Nations for seating Peking. These efforts were sharply opposed by the United States and at once involved Nyerere in diplomatic altercations with Washington. Not for another decade were Nyerere's (and other Afro-Asian) diplomatic tactics in this matter to be successful. It seems sure, however, that these early and prolonged efforts by Nyerere in behalf of China were not lost on the Peking people.

From the moment of their establishment on Tanzanian shores, the attitudes of the Peking diplomats to their new African tasks differed considerably from their Soviet (and Western) counterparts. While Chinese diplomats in Dar es Salaam were at first extraordinarily careful not to make their contacts with local African leaders too broad, the Chinese in Peking feted many Tanzanians and consistently put Dar es Salaam and Zanzibar on their African itineraries.

From the outset, the Chinese seemed determined to tailor their aid efforts specifically to prime Tanzanian needs. One of their first aid projects was a $4 million textile mill designed to utilize Tanzanian cotton. A new brewery and police training programs followed. So, too, did a high-powered long-range radio transmitter designed to beam broadcasts to southern Africa. Next followed the Chinese takeover of military training programs previously supervised by the Canadians. (The extent of this Chinese military aid effort, including the supply of arms, has never been clear.) Finally, and most important of all, has been the Chinese financing, engineering, and building of the railway between Tanzania and Zambia. Associated with this effort have been Chinese-directed programs training Tanzanian rail workers and related health facilities for workers and populace along the railroad right-of-way. Given all these, it is evident that the Chinese aid of $450 million plus to Tanzania has been by all odds the largest aid program for a black African state from a Communist nation.

Relations between the major Communist nations and Zanzibar/Pemba deserve a special word. When the revolution of January 1964 took place on the islands, the Soviets, Chinese, and East Germans took quick advantage of the situation. At once all three nations established embassies. Considering the small local populace (no more than 350,000), all three Communist nations produced large numbers of pseudodiplomats and aid technicians. As late as 1970 there were reported to be some 100 Soviet nationals, 500 Chinese, and 50 East Germans living and working on Zanzibar and Pemba. These figures were in stark contrast to the ten Americans and twenty-five British nationals then stationed on the islands in similar diplomatic and technical-aid capacities. Latest news sources indicate that 400 Chinese but only six Russians remain, while all East Germans have departed.

It is important to note the range of activities which the Communists, especially the Chinese, have undertaken in Zanzibar. Certain of the Chinese are working as financial and economic advisers as well as engaging in police training. The Chinese are also reported to have provided training for a 3,000-person army. In other fields of expertise they have provided the islands with a sugar refinery, a cigarette factory, a shoe factory, a printing plant, a waterworks, and a sports stadium. Total aid from Peking for Zanzibar is estimated to have reached $12 million, with more technical assistance still promised. In addition the Chinese have engaged in agricultural diversification, notably the growing of rice for local consumption. Both Soviets and Chinese have been involved in Zanzibar educational work. A few Soviets still work as seaport and airport advisers. A major question remains as to the nature and size of Chinese missile-tracking facilities on the islands. There are rumored to be three of these.

Another major question mark has been the extent of Chinese and Soviet activities in the military-police sphere. It is reported that new cantonments and training accommodations have been built on both Zanzibar and Pemba with Communist help. With the expanding interest of Soviet naval authorities in the Indian Ocean, it seems obvious that they would make use of the islands as a watering and provision station.

As to Tanzania's relationships with the various Communist satellite states, such contacts have been generally harmonious but neither extensive nor important. Of these the only tie which has developed into one of consequence is that between Tanzania and Yugoslavia. This link is based largely on the personal friendship of Presidents Nyerere and Tito and on mutual interest in developing a "Third Force" of nonaligned states.

The estimable journal *West Africa*, of January 15, 1973, reports that Soviet military aid to developing lands in the past eighteen years was more than twenty times that provided by China during the same period. Moscow reportedly gave $8 billion in military aid to these countries while Peking gave $350 million. Most Chinese military aid is reported to have gone to Pakistan, Tanzania, and Congo-Brazzaville. Over the same period the U.S.S.R. gave $3.6 billion in economic aid, while China gave $2.2 billion. Tanzania has been the largest recipient of Chinese economic aid—about $450 million—in the developing world excepting only North Vietnam.

The Chinese have concentrated on projects involving rapid local employment with Chinese technicians living on the land and remaining in the country as short a time as possible. This eliminates the albatross of tied loans and long stays enjoyed by aid technicians of other lands. There is clear indication that Chinese efforts in Africa are also designed to expand their foreign trade in this area and to pre-empt Soviet influence therein. However, the question of China's permanent penetration of Africa remains a moot point.

Tanzania and Nonalignment

Some critics contend that Tanzania has shown itself to be more closely associated with Communism than the term "nonalignment" would presume. Yet it cannot be proved that the Tanzanians have ever been wholly either pro-East or pro-West. In addition to its many criticisms of Britain, Tanzania has been openly critical of American involvements in Indochina, Latin America, the Congo (now Zaire), and South Africa. Tanzania was also sharply critical of Soviet actions in Czechoslovakia and of alleged Chinese Communist efforts to intervene in internal situations on the Tanzania mainland. Nyerere has specifically referred to the determination of his people to emulate the spirit of the Chinese in successful self-development, but he has pointed out that Tanzania would brook no interference from Chinese or other foreigners with its national affairs or sovereignty. Thus Nyerere has constantly insisted that his nation would be determined by no external force and was not about to exchange one colonial master for another.

Addressing a TANU conference at Mwanza, October 16, 1967, President Nyerere spelled out his country's attitude on nonalignment:

We have no desire to be, "anti-West" in our foreign policies. We shall deal with each problem . . . on its own merits. . . . We wish to live in friendship with all states and all peoples. . . . We shall not allow any of our friendships to be exclusive; we shall not allow anyone to choose any of our friends or enemies for us. . . . We shall not allow anyone, whether they be from East or West, . . . to try to use our friendship for their own purposes. . . . We should always try to limit the effect of differences which occur, and to settle them by negotiation. Only in the case of South Africa, the racialist colonialism of Portugal, and the Smith regime of Southern Rhodesia, does such settlement of differences seem inherently impossible. With those countries we can never negotiate until they abandon their present rejection of . . . the equality of man.

But in all other cases we believe that differences can be settled without compromising the principles of our society.[6]

The *Nationalist* newspaper editorial attributed to Nyerere, appearing in Dar es Salaam on August 15, 1968, pointed up Tanzania's nonalignment and gave specific warning to the Eastern bloc, to wit:

Some people have tried to suggest that . . . [our quarrels with the West] show that we are anti-West and pro-East. . . . This is not so. . . . We are pro-Tanzania. . . . We want to be friends with all nations, but we insist that our friendships should be on the basis of mutual respect. . . . We shall not allow Eastern Bloc nations to interfere in Tanzania just because our relations with some Western Bloc countries are strained. . . . We quarrel with any and every country which tries to interfere with our internal affairs. . . . We did not fight against the Western colonialists . . . to become the plaything of any Eastern country. . . . Let those Eastern Bloc countries who think they can do as they like in Tanzania take note . . . that this is a free and independent nation. . . . The policies of Tanzania are for Tanzanians to determine. To everyone else we say "Hands off!"

In the nonaligned sphere, it is important to note Tanzania's effort to make the Indian Ocean a Zone of Peace. The Indian Ocean problem has resulted from the fact of Britain's withdrawal from naval control of this ocean and its littorals, leaving the entire region a military-political vacuum. Both the United States and the Soviet Union are now seeking to establish hegemony over the area. The Russians have concentrated their efforts in Somalia, Yemen, and India. The United States, lacking firm alliances with all nations of the region save Pakistan, has established, with British help, an "austerity" naval and air base on the island of Diego Garcia in the Mauritian archipelago. Many nonaligned nations bordering on the Indian Ocean have become upset by these actions of the superpowers and fear a confrontation. Tanzania and other littoral nations have introduced resolutions in the United Nations, the O.A.U., and nonalignment conferences seeking to prohibit military-naval activity by either the United States or the Soviets in this region. There has also been consideration of taking the problem to the World Court, but a ruling by the court would be difficult to enforce. There remains a distinct possibility of further intrusions on the part of the superpowers which could result in an undeclared war in this highly neutralist region of the world.

Concluding this chapter on the country's foreign policy, the reader will have judged that Tanzania has engaged in debate and diplomacy on international issues to a far greater extent than its military or economic power would dictate. In all these efforts, the Tanzanian policy-makers have used moral suasion to the utmost. Through the O.A.U., through their Commonwealth membership, through the Afro-Asian bloc in the United Nations, the Tanzanian diplomats have succeeded in playing a role out of all proportion to their size. Sometimes, as in their efforts to seat Communist China in the United Nations, results exceeded their most optimistic expectations. (It was the Tanzanian delegate who performed the dance of glee in the aisles of the General Assembly when China was at long last readmitted to United Nations membership.) Sometimes, however, as in the ill-fated support of Biafra or in their efforts to restore Obote to the Ugandan presidency, Tanzanian diplomacy has gone awry. It is safe to say, however, that Tanzania's diplomatic voice will continue to be heard in international forums, usually speaking on the side of justice and against the oppressor, whoever that oppressor may be.

NOTES

1. Julius K. Nyerere, *Freedom and Unity* (London: Oxford University Press, 1966), pp. 144ff.
2. Ibid., pp. 215ff.
3. Ibid., pp. 287ff.
4. Ibid., p. 326.
5. *Baltimore Sun*, May 20, 1973.
6. Julius K. Nyerere, *Freedom and Socialism* (London: Oxford University Press, 1968), pp. 368ff.

CHAPTER 14

CONCLUSION:
TANZANIA TODAY
AND TOMORROW

In their preindependence drive for nationhood, Julius Nyerere and his TANU colleagues set three major goals for their people: freedom, unity, equality. As counterpoints to these, they set out to eliminate poverty, ignorance, and disease throughout their land. The goal of political freedom was at least partially attained in 1961 when the country shed its colonial yoke and national sovereignty came into being. Once independence was reached, it became the main task of the political leadership to relate that newly attained political freedom to ordinary people's lives and their everyday problems. The leaders then went on to press for interdependence of their peoples, thereby merging their aims of unity and equality. These elusive goals were brought into sight by creation of the grand design of *Ujamaa* (Familyhood).

Throughout his years of leadership, President Nyerere has insisted that his party's goals and his people's goals must be determined by the social, economic, and political needs and conditions which are to be found in Tanzania and on the African continent. These may or may not be consistent with situations to be found in other lands on other continents. Nyerere has emphasized constantly that his people must trudge upward out of the sloughs of isolation, slavery, and colonialism which fettered black Africa for so long. By word and by deed he has insisted that the Tanzanians must seek the grail of human dignity and of true freedom, personal and national, along the only road available to them.

Nyerere's political philosophy has stressed that flag, nation, even the wor-

158

ship of God are properly and primarily for the benefit of the person and of society. He insists that production for the state is not the main purpose of society. Rather, the prime purpose of society is the service of the person and, in turn, the service of God. He decries those who claim that goals of freedom, unity, and equality are too idealistic. He admits, however, that these goals are difficult to attain and to maintain, even in the most advanced nations. Yet he contends they remain valid goals for either small or large societies, for rich lands and poor lands.

In the fifteen years since constitutional independence was reached, Tanzania's goals of freedom, unity, and equality remained the foundation stones of its national interests. Yet their definition and dimension, even their priority positions, differ materially today from placement and definition envisaged in the independence year of 1961.

In global terms, the goal of political independence is now fully realized for Tanzania. In international forums and in chanceries throughout the world, Tanzania's independence of thought and action, its determined philosophy of nonalignment, its championing of those not yet free, are demonstrated again and again. This is an independence which brooks no domination by external power, Western or Eastern, capitalist or communist.

There has always been a tendency in Tanzania to exhort the citizenry to become concerned, aroused, even militant, against all sorts of enemies, foreign and domestic. That tendency has provoked agonies over the Congo, Biafra, Czechoslovakia, Indochina, and especially the white supremacy regimes of southern Africa. Many of these agonies over international affairs have been inspired, even enhanced, by the presence within Tanzania of political exiles from many lands, and by the fact that Tanzania has been the mobilization point for Freedom Fighters massing against the "white redoubt" of southern Africa. In some years past, this tendency to agonize over foreign affairs sapped the country's energies to the point that inadequate attention was given to domestic problems. That tendency to misdirect its energies seems now to have been overcome.

The same deep concern over Tanzania's internal enemies of poverty, ignorance, and disease has been demonstrated by exhortatory slogans such as *Uhuru na kazi* (freedom and work) and *Uhuru na umoja* (freedom and unity). The latest and greatest such effort stresses individual self-reliance, national self-sufficiency, and the familyhood of *Ujamaa*. These slogans and their resulting drives are predicated on the concept of grassroots support harnessed to bureaucracy and party, designed to achieve both individual and national goals.

In carrying out these exhortatory programs, Nyerere and his colleagues have consistently stressed that without unity none of the national goals, major or minor, can be reached and maintained. In their thinking, tribal, racial, religious, and political differences, even economic and educational disparities, must ever be made subordinate to the national interest and to the fundamental concept of nationhood. The fact that such cleavages did not become disruptive influences or barriers to nationhood was because the political, religious, and tribal leaders of this country were far-sighted and "nationalistic" in the best sense. In effect, they brought to bear, in pre- and postindependence drives, a national movement rather than a party rendered weak by factional disputes.

As to the goal of unity, several major hurdles yet remain for Tanzania. Prime among these is the completion of the unification process of the mainland with the islands of Zanzibar and Pemba. Both the reality and the vitality of this union, so-called, are still in question.

Allied thereto are the larger questions of regional and continental unity. The decades of effort which have gone into making the East African Community of Tanzania, Kenya, and Uganda appear, today, to hang precariously on a slim thread. There is constant bickering between the members despite the obvious economic advantages for each. In fact, till now, the three-nation community has been kept together only by dint of the strong personal rapport between President Nyerere and Kenya's President Kenyatta. The recent highly erratic and egocentric leadership of Uganda's General Amin has only created new cracks in the community's foundations. Continuance of this tenuous relationship between the three nations will depend entirely on the wisdom and mutual cooperation of future leaders of the partner countries.

Tenuous, too, are the relations, sometimes fractious, between the conservative, moderate, and militant leaders of the various nations, now numbering more than forty-six, comprising the continentwide Organization of African Unity. While considerable progress has ben made by this organization in its dozen years of life, there remain immense and frustrating problems on its agenda throughout Africa. Not among the least of these are the vexing problems of racial conflict in southern Africa, civilian versus military rule, internecine tribal conflict, problems of flood and famine, and the deep economic traumas of the Third and Fourth Worlds.

As to attainment of its goal of economic independence, Tanzania has yet a very long way to go. It remains heavily dependent on fluctuating world markets for returns from sales of a few prime commodities. With prices on these dropping steadily in recent years, foreign exchange reserves have dried up. During those same years, the country has been badly hurt by general inflationary trends, excessive costs for capital needs, the energy crunch, flood, and drought. Till recently, the country was virtually self-sufficient in foodstuffs, but weather and other conditions have now forced it to make massive importation of staples. There is no doubt that in all but the worst of the drought years Tanzanians can produce their own foodstuffs. Even though theirs may be an austerity diet, there should and must be encouraged sufficient production of maize, livestock, fruits, vegetables, coffee, tea, and sugar. Barter trades of goods in excess must be better accomplished—cloves and cotton exchanged for Asian rice; coffee exchanged for European canned goods and pharmaceuticals; tea exchanged for Australian wheat or meats. There are availabilities in this economy that must be husbanded for the good of all.

As a result of all its economic difficulties and developmental demands, Tanzania has been in great need of outside capital. With the exception of the massive Chinese help on the Tan-Zam railway, and some help from the World Bank and Western aid donors, the country's capital needs have not been satisfied. It is precisely because of these expanding needs and these unexpected financial drains that Nyerere and his colleagues devised the only program which they saw open to them, namely, *Ujamaa* (Familyhood), which, through rural resettlement, villagization, and cooperative expansion seeks to make use of the two abundant resources Tanzania possesses—the arid land and the agrarian people. It is a concept based wholly on scarcity rather than riches—a concept which is labor-intensive rather than capital-intensive. It seeks as well to capitalize on rejuvenation of the social insurance provided by the traditional African extended family system. This concept, associated with various nationalization programs covering governmental control of major facets of commerce and industry, comprises Tanzania's chief weapons—in fact, its only weapons—against the evils of poverty, ignorance, and disease.

Given his country's scarcity of natural resources and capital, the lack of fixed markets and prices, the paucity of its infrastructure, the shortage of an educated elite and skilled manpower, Nyerere's efforts to lead a poverty-stricken people into a viable modern life have proved exceedingly difficult. In a land where one-quarter of all children die before the age of five, where half the children never see the inside of a school, where longevity is only forty-five years (compared to sixty-nine years in the United States), and where per capita income today is only $100 yearly (compared to nearly $4,000 yearly in the United States), Nyerere has had few options. He has sought evolutionary rather than revolutionary means; sought deurbanization rather than further urbanization (with its attendant unemployment). He has sought, as well, an economic system which will enrich the many rather than the few. He and his countrymen realize they can no longer rely on cumbersome foreign aid with its later burdens of interest and principal repayment. They realize the uncertainties of foreign trade involving sales of a few highly volatile cash crops. Now they have determined first to feed themselves and then to diversify their cash crops and expand their cooperatives. Only thereafter will they again turn to expansion of their industries. This reverses the currently fashionable economic theories of First World intellectuals, which hold that all new nations need to industrialize quickly. The Tanzanians have sought to do all this under the African concept of *Ujamaa*—extending that kinship responsibility idea to the nation as a whole.

In short, Nyerere is seeking a middle road between the ideology of capitalism, which builds on exploitation of one class by another, and doctrinaire socialism, which builds on class warfare. To Nyerere and the leaders of Tanzania, both these ideas are anathema. He has taken the middle road.

As Nyerere constantly stresses, conditions of life are harsh in Tanzania. For the poverty-stricken majority of his people, the smaller family unit cannot provide adequate economic safeguards against these conditions—whether ecological or human-made. The vicious circles of destitution, disease, illiteracy, and climate all militate against the smaller-core family group. Thus Tanzania's leaders have come to believe that both modern economy and modern ecology require larger social units for insurance of family, society, and nation. Indeed, the Tanzanian leaders insist that maintenance and strengthening of these extended family units provide the only means whereby poverty-ridden societies in developing states of Africa can survive. They concede, however, that in this process, some personal freedoms must be given up in the national interest and some individual rights sacrificed for the good of the larger brotherhood.

Nyerere has recognized that the traditional African society does not provide the ideal system in the Atomic Age. He has sought, therefore, to blend the best of both traditional and modern institutions. In Tanzania's domestic life today, the concepts emanating from the Arusha Declaration and *Ujamaa* pervade the national body politic. Some have characterized this social experimentation as the most revolutionary in Africa. These efforts have clearly begun to change the country's polity from the roots up, bringing on both psychological trauma and physical change.

Tanzania still has a long way to go before its people enjoy the fruits of an equitable society. Yet the spadework for building such a society is slowly being accomplished. That fact alone makes Tanzania unique in Africa. If it proves successful, Tanzania could well become a model for development in the Fourth World.

Thus far it is difficult to assess the results of the *Ujamaa* communal farm program, especially in the face of the recent compounding problems of drought, inflation, bad planning, and resistance to change. It is certain that the country's collective farming program has been massively harmed by these events. Their success or failure now hangs delicately in the balance. The collectivization element of the program (as was true in China in recent years) seems to encounter continuing resistance from a peasantry long used to the personal independence and satisfactions of subsistence farming. The eventual success of *Ujamaa* may now depend on wise leadership, better planning, and modifications where necessary. Most essential will be the renewed sense of real cooperation and understanding between the rural populace and the bureaucracy, the grassroots and the leaders. In the opinion of the author, Tanzania's goal of self-reliance in the modern sense cannot be realized through forced collectivization. Instead it seems likely that, for a majority of the populace, there will result an amalgam of personalized subsistence farming combined with growing of cash crops for commune and cooperative. All this is making a profound and final test of Nyerere's own leadership. Even more, it will become a test of the soundness of his philosophical-social programs and a test of the leadership of those who are soon bound to follow him into power.

In the past decade the African continent has become renowned—even notorious—for the numbers and bloodiness of its military coups. Many of these have resulted from corruption, tribal conflict, or simply bad leadership. Despite all its problems, Tanzania has remained in essence a civilian democracy. In fact it is one of the few countries on the African continent which still has an elected Parliament. Before independence, Tanzanians were advised that they needed to have several parties in the country. This theory was tested and found wanting. Not a single one of the two opposing parties won seats in the first two elections. As a result the Tanzanians moved to a single-party system with opposing candidates within that political entity. The leaders realized that they had to follow the verdict of the electorate—that Tanzanians wanted only one party. They have sought the use of checks and balances within that system to avoid misuses of power. Thus far they have done very well. Within the party there is leeway for opposition, for debate and discussion. The ballot box still provides ample opportunity for change of legislators and national leaders. By innovation, by experimentation, by parliamentary adaptation, there is no doubt that Nyerere and his colleagues have devised variants of political organizations and political institutions well fitted to Tanzania's needs and capacities. There is still a good deal of political freedom in Tanzania.

Nyerere's personal prestige at home and abroad continues high. The power of his internal political apparatus also remains effective and respected. Yet, as in all movements which have as their prime objective the transformation of the politico-economic order along with the creation of a new nation, Nyerere's regime shows the constant pulls between doctrinaire idealism and political pragmatism, between economic attainments and economic frustrations.

Yet Nyerere and his lieutenants must surely be aware that history has not always been kind to authors of collectivization and nationalization. Caution must temper zeal if the social integration of mass and elite are to accomplish real and permanent ends. The combination of political innovation and social experimentation represents a real gamble for TANU and Tanzanians. If these are successful and self-reliance is reached, then both the second and the third of national goals—unity and equality—may be fully realized.

Fortunately there is in the Tanzanian character the determination, the integrity, the spirit of the poor but proud person. There is in the Tanzanians an abiding, good-natured patience. They have had so little for so long that their expectations from life have never been great. It has been on this solid foundation of fortitude, good nature, and limited expectations that Nyerere's imaginative politico-social programs have been superimposed. In this way Tanzanians have determined to re-create and revitalize their human dignity.

All this has created an intense loyalty, trust, and popularity for Tanzania's national "Chief"—and Teacher (*Mwalimu*)—Julius K. Nyerere. He, in turn, gives his people his utmost dedication. This unusual kinship between nation and leader is the essence of Nyerere's political power, the essence of the country's highly personalized familyhood.

There remains a question as to whether, given existing institutions and drives, Tanzania's political successors to Nyerere might eventually become authoritarian. Will there be a flowering of the existing highly democratic atmosphere? Or, instead, will there be a trend toward despotism? In effect, can Nyerere and his present government devise democratic institutions and safeguards so strong that they can last in what is ordinarily a highly paternalistic and potentially totalitarian African milieu?

Nyerere's highly personalized role and rule, with its intensity of dedication and corresponding loyalty, constitute both foundation and girders for Tanzania's experiments in politics and in society. Whether out of these Tanzania is indeed able to build a viable and lasting economy, polity, and nation may not be fully evident until Nyerere passes from the scene. What is already evident, however, is that thus far Tanzania has been saved from much of the corruption, instability, elitist disruptions, and tribal wars which have beset so many other newly independent nations of the world. Sincerity and dedication of both leaders and masses will be sorely tested if promised progress is not achieved. While Nyerere's political popularity may now protect him, it may not protect any successor who lacks his charisma and his sagacity.

One astute American journalist, perceptively analyzing the problems and potentials of Africa, says that when considering the future of Tanzania (and of Africa) it is necessary "to think like a pessimist and to behave like an optimist." The pessimism over Tanzania must be self-evident through any analysis of its economic prospects, its lack of skilled manpower, its problems of unification with Zanzibar and the rest of Africa. Its optimistic elements can be seen in the extraordinarily wise and innovative nature of Nyerere's leadership; in the country's ability to correct its own mistakes; in the Tanzanian people's determination to adjust to trying situations with fortitude, good humor, and spirit.

In the last private conversation which the author was privileged to hold with Nyerere in Tanzania, the president was asked pointedly how he felt about the future of his nation. Nyerere replied succinctly: "We have problems but we remain cheerful." Thus do Nyerere and Tanzania characterize the stresses and hopes of modern Africa, the sage melding of the old with the new. Thus does Nyerere aptly epitomize both pessimistic and optimistic attributes of his beloved country—Tanzania.

PART TWO

UJAMAA SOCIALISM

An Analysis of the Socialism of Julius K. Nyerere in the Light of Catholic Church Teaching

JOHN R. CIVILLE

To my mother and father

INTRODUCTION

Tanzania is one of the twenty-five poorest countries in the world. But to improve the quality of life of the people it has rejected the capitalist economic system inherited from British colonialism and returned to the ancient tribal system of socialism called *Ujamaa* or Familyhood. While there has been much written of the practicality of this unique experiment, the following study is an analysis of the *Ujamaa* approach to a just society in light of the Roman Catholic tradition on social justice. In this light the ultimate criterion will be on how well *Ujamaa* upholds the dignity of the person.

The method used to analyze *Ujamaa* is taken from Pope Paul's Apostolic Letter *Octogesima Adveniens*. Here the Holy Father upholds the Church's duty "to give an answer, in its own sphere, to men's expectations."[1] But the Church does not intend to put forward a solution to social problems that has universal applicability.

Such is not our ambition, nor is it our mission. It is up to the Christian communities to analyze with objectivity the situation which is proper to their own country, to shed on it the light of the Gospel's unalterable words and to draw principles of reflection, norms of judgment and directives for action from the social teaching of the Church.[2]

Pope Paul is saying that, while the Church upholds and teaches the basic principles of the Gospels, the application of these principles in concrete cases is a matter for the local community. This idea of distinct areas of responsibility was again stressed by the 1971 Roman Synod of Bishops, who said that the Church is not alone responsible for justice in the world, nor does it offer concrete solutions in the social, economic, and political spheres for justice in the world. While the Church has the duty to proclaim justice and to denounce instances of injustice, it is the members of society who must implement the demands of justice.[3]

President Nyerere, in a question period following his Maryknoll address in

New York in 1970, used the same criterion for implementing social reform. In an informal reply Nyerere said:

The church, sometimes because of the language we are using . . . wants to be on the careful side and watch us. So first of all let me say the church is a local church for us. . . . The church has methods of judging whether this is right or wrong. If you find, you know, that what they are doing is establishing a system whereby they sacrifice men, they kill men, you know it's wrong. But if these fellows are talking about building cooperatives, building a new kind of society where people can live together for their own good, I think the church can always say "It sounds all right."[4]

This distinction between principles and action was also underlined by Bishop Christopher Mwoleka of Rulenge, Tanzania. "But these principles [of the Church] do nothing more than point to the directions where ACTIONS must be directed. But actions themselves must be forthcoming, otherwise these principles remain without effect. Principles become effective *only* when they are applied by deliberate actions to concrete existing situations."[5]

In accord with this distinction between principle and practice, this study will do two things: show the correlation between *Ujamaa* socialism and Church social teaching on the level of theory, and examine how *Ujamaa* implements justice in practice. In its implementation of just policies as the people see appropriate to their situation, Tanzania is making a contribution to our understanding of justice. This is especially helpful today in understanding what a 1974 Roman Synod document called our growing awareness of interdependence from living locked together on a limited globe.[6]

NOTES

    1. *Octogesima Adveniens*, no. 42; text included in *The Gospel of Peace and Justice: Catholic Social Teaching since Pope John*, presented by Joseph Gremillion (Maryknoll, New York: Orbis Books, 1976).

    2. Ibid., no. 4.

    3. Synod of Bishops (1971), *Justice in the World;* text included in *Gospel of Peace and Justice*.

    4. "Question and Answer Period following the Maryknoll Address in New York," October 16, 1970 (mimeographed).

    5. Christopher Mwoleka, "Nation-Building in Vatican II as Applied to Tanzania" (Rulenge, Tanzania: Bishop's House, September 1970), p. 12 (mimeographed).

    6. Joseph Bernardin, "Social Justice, Interdependence and Evangelization," written intervention in the 1974 Roman Synod (Washington, D.C.: USCC Publications, 1975), p. 53.

CHAPTER 15

THE MEANING OF
UJAMAA SOCIALISM

Historical Basis

Unlike European socialism, which was born from the class conflict follow-ing the agrarian and industrial revolutions, Tanzanian socialism is a continua-tion of ancient tribal socialism.[1] In traditional society, Nyerere maintains, the individual and the families were rich or poor according to whether the whole tribe was rich or poor.[2] "Nobody starved, either of food or of human dignity, because he lacked personal wealth; he could depend on the wealth possessed by the community of which he was a member. That was socialism. That *is* socialism."[3]

It was from the cultural heritage that Tanzanian socialism developed.

We are not importing a foreign ideology into Tanzania and trying to smother out distinct social patterns with it. We have deliberately decided to grow, as a society, out of our own roots, but in a particular direction and towards a particular kind of objective. We are doing this by emphasizing certain characteristics of our traditional organization, and extending them so that they can embrace the possibilities of modern technology and enable us to meet the challenge of life in the twentieth century world.[4]

In stressing the traditional roots, Nyerere is showing that Africa is con-tributing to the "march of mankind."[5] Furthermore, he is recalling to mind the good qualities of the past in order to regain the former attitude of mind which was weakened by colonial domination.[6] For example, everyone was a worker;[7] there was a sense of security and hospitality;[8] all were expected to share

171

what they had;[9] there was no capitalist or landed exploitation, no loiterers or idlers;[10] and no one amassed wealth for his own benefit.[11]

"Ujamaa," then, or "Familyhood," describes our socialism. It is opposed to capitalism, which seeks to build a happy society on the basis of the exploitation of man by man; and it is equally opposed to doctrinaire socialism which seeks to build its happy society on a philosophy of inevitable conflict between man and man.[12]

Defining Ujamaa

"The foundation, and objective, of African socialism is the extended family."[13] True African socialists will see all people as their brethren, as members of their ever widening family.[14] "By using the word 'ujamaa,' therefore, we state that for us socialism involves building on the foundation of our past."[15]

The Swahili word *ujamaa* was chosen by Nyerere to describe his socialism because it "emphasizes the Africanness of the policies we intend to follow," and because its literal meaning—familyhood—"brings to the mind of our people the idea of mutual involvement in the family as we know it."[16]

In tracing the history of the political use of the word *ujamaa*,[17] Fred Burke says that *ujamaa* is essentially a metaphysical statement of humanistic values which is sufficiently imprecise and flexible to provide justification for almost any government policy.[18]

For Nyerere, *Ujamaa* socialism is an attitude of mind needed to ensure that the people care for each other's welfare.[19] "A socialist society can only be built by those who believe in, and who themselves practice, the principles of socialism."[20] It is not the wealth persons possess but their attitude of mind that makes them socialists. A poor person could be a potential capitalist, an exploiter of others, while a millionaire, in theory, could be a socialist.[21] Whoever tries to "exploit" another is not a true socialist.[22]

On the other hand, as an attitude of mind, *Ujamaa* socialism is equally opposed to scientific or doctrinaire socialism, which is inflexible in its application and rooted in historical inevitableness by class conflict.[23]

That *Ujamaa* as an attitude of mind does not mean that institutions and organizations are irrelevant. "It means that without correct attitudes institutions can be diverted from their true purpose."[24] The implication of stressing the importance of an attitude of mind is that socialist structures will arise out of socialist ideals, not the reverse.[25]

Because *Ujamaa* is the concept of the extended family, there is no place for racialism, tribalism, religious intolerance, or discrimination.[26] Such practices are absolutely opposed to the first precept of socialism—the equality of all people.[27]

The human equality implied by the extended family goes beyond the tribe, the community, and the nation. "For no true African socialist can look at a line on a map and say, 'The people on this side of that line are my brothers, but those who happen to live on the other side have no claim on me'; every individual on this continent is his brother."[28] The extended family must go even further and embrace the whole of humankind.[29]

Ujamaa's stress on human equality also means Tanzania is trying to build a classless society.

> We aim at building a classless society for one reason. In no state is there enough wealth to satisfy the desire of a single individual for power and prestige. Consequently, the moment wealth is divorced from its purpose, which is the banishment of poverty, there develops a ruthless competition between the individuals; each person tries to get more wealth, simply so that he will have more power, and more prestige, than his fellows. Wealth becomes an instrument of domination, a means of humiliating other people.[30]

This emphasis on a classless society means that society, like the extended family, makes no distinction among its members who use their own talents and skills to promote the well-being of the national community.[31]

Nyerere has taken a gradualist approach in implementing his policies. First of all, gradualism means Nyerere has denied the claim of scientific socialism that "class war" is necessary for socialism. Those who insist on the necessity of violence "are almost certainly not socialist in their own attitude. For violence cannot be welcomed by those who care about people."[32] While violence can be a shortcut to the destruction of institutions and power groups of the old society, it is not a shortcut to building the new. In fact violence makes more difficult the development of the socialist attitudes which give life to these institutions.[33]

Tanzania has chosen a nonviolent, gradualist approach to socialism.

> The Arusha Declaration lays down a policy of revolution by evolution; we shall become a socialist, self-reliant society through our growth. We cannot afford the destruction of the economic instruments we now have nor a reduction in our present output. . . . Our change will, therefore, be effected almost entirely by the emphasis of our new development and by the gradual conversion of existing institutions into others more in accordance with our philosophy.[34]

This acceptance of the nonviolent gradualist approach to socialism means that many nonsocialist features of society will continue to remain for some time. The solutions to these problems are slow, depending on the growth of socialist understanding and socialist atttitudes among the people.[35] This is why Tanzania is not yet a socialist society.[36]

Because Nyerere has adopted a gradualist approach to socialism does not mean he is categorically opposed to violence. Sometimes it is the only way "to break the power of those who prevent progress toward socialism."[37] This is the case of southern Africa (Mozambique, Rhodesia, Angola, and South Africa).

Tanzania cannot deny support, for to do so would be to deny the validity of African freedom and African dignity. We are naturally and inevitably allies of the freedom fighters. We may decide, as we have decided, that no Tanzanian will take part in these wars; we may recognize the fact that we cannot arm the freedom fighters. But we cannot call for freedom in Southern Africa, and at the same time deny all assistance to those who are fighting for it, when we know, as well as they do, that every other means of achieving freedom has been excluded by those now in power.[38]

Because it is rooted in traditional values rather than historical necessity, *Ujamaa* is pragmatic. "There is no magic formula, and no short cut to socialism. We can only grope our way forward, doing our best to think clearly—and scientifically—about our own conditions in relation to our objectives."[39]

Specifically this means that democracy in Tanzania does not have to be patterned on the "Westminster model" as if Tanzania needed Western approval of its political system.[40] Nor does socialism in Tanzania have to copy the socialism of another country as if Africa had nothing to contribute to the world.[41] It certainly does not have to believe there is only one road to socialism.[42] "Our task is to look first at our own position and our own needs, and then to consider other experiences and other suggestions in the light of our requirements."[43]

Tanzania is committed to pragmatism because its social change grows from its own roots and not by grafting onto an alien philosophy. "Our social change will be determined by our own needs as we see them, and in the direction that we feel to be appropriate for us at any particular time."[44]

Evaluation of Ujamaa

Nyerere is the first to admit that there were shortcomings in traditional African life apart from the failure of people to live up to the ideals. The first shortcoming was the inferior position of women, who did most of the work; the second was the extreme poverty, even though everyone shared the poverty equally.[45]

Others are harsher in their criticism of the historical values in which *Ujamaa* is rooted. Some call traditional socialism a myth to be manipulated by political leaders to implement their policies.[46] Kwame Nkrumah, who favors scientific socialism, thinks it is a fetish to express nostalgia for the spirit of humanism in traditional African society. Colonialism deserves to be blamed for many evils in Africa, but surely it was not preceded by an "African Golden Age or paradise."[47]

William Friedland attacks any glorification of work in traditional society: "The traditional view of work was probably closer to that of the Greeks, who looked upon work as an evil necessary for survival but not as a social obligation."[48] Ahmed Mohiddin challenges the historical reality of a classless

African traditional society, a notion that he considers based on an emotional nostalgia to overcome the alien influences of colonialism.[49] He evaluates Nyerere's position: "Granted the need for this strong emotional basis, Nyerere's concept of classless society proves to be grounded in his ideas for a new and positive future as much as in a nostalgic past."[50]

Comparison with Scientific Socialism

Nyerere has been criticized, on the one hand, for not following scientific socialism and, on the other, for leaning toward communism—two extremes he has denied.[51] By showing how *Ujamaa* socialism differs from scientific socialism, the meaning of Nyerere's philosophy becomes clearer. For reasons of simplicity, *Ujamaa* will be compared with Soviet Marxism-Leninism as representative of scientific socialism.

The theory of Marxism-Leninism is rooted in the theory of dialectical materialism which, when applied to the sphere of social development in history, is called historical materialism.[52] This philosophy is applied concretely in the doctrines on economic, social, and political life.

Historical materialism teaches that all social and economic relationships are rooted in the relationship of people to the means of production. The means of production follow a determined order from primitive society, to feudalism, capitalism, socialism, and finally communism. This inevitable process of history has been scientifically proven. We can do nothing to change this historical process; we can only promote or hinder it.[53]

The step from the capitalist stage to the socialist stage will necessarily involve violence of a class struggle because of the capitalists' concentration of the wealth. Once the socialist stage is established, the proletariat will set up a dictatorship to ensure the final stage of the dialectical process—communism.[54]

Nyerere has rejected the dogmatism of the Marxists' "scientifically proven" stages of economic development with the necessary class wars.[55] He claims that the scientific approach for Tanzanians is to accept the historical conditions of Tanzania and return to the socialist structure of former times.[56] Because, then, *Ujamaa* is not built on the same foundation as scientific socialism, Nyerere rejects scientific socialism's concept of uniformity in both belief and practice. "It is my contention that socialist societies in different parts of the world will differ in many respects. . . . The differences between these societies will reflect both the manner of their development, and their historical tradition."[57]

Nyerere severely criticizes the rigidity of Marxism-Leninism, which declares itself the sole guide to socialism.[58]

There is, however, an apparent tendency among certain socialists to try and establish a new religion—a religion of socialism itself. This is usually called "scientific socialism" and the works of Marx and Lenin are regarded as the holy writ in the light of which all other thoughts and actions of socialists have to be judged.[59]

While admitting the works of Marx and Lenin are useful for their method of analysis and ideas, Nyerere warns of the dangers of being consumed by Marxism-Leninism.[60]

We are groping our way forward towards socialism, and we are in danger of being bemused by this new theology, and therefore of trying to solve our problems according to what the priests of Marxism say is what Marx said or meant. If we do this we shall fail. Africa's conditions are very different from those of the Europe in which Marx and Lenin wrote and worked. To talk as if these thinkers provided all the answers to our problems, or as if Marx invented socialism, is to reject both the humanity of Africa and the universality of socialism.[61]

I.I. Potekhin, the leading Soviet Africanist, declares Nyerere's pragmatic socialism to be a victim of American imperialist propaganda.[62] Maintaining the rigidity of the Soviet position, Potekhin argues: "Countries which have won their freedom will proceed to socialism along tried and tested paths. . . . There are no grounds therefore for counterposing 'African Socialism' to scientific socialism, if by 'African Socialism' we mean the specific ways and means of the transition to socialism in keeping with African reality."[63]

Democracy. Nyerere is also very critical of the dogmatism of "proletariat democracy," which ensures the uniformity of Soviet ideology at the expense of denying individual freedom.[64]

Once you deal in dogma you cannot allow freedom of opinion. . . . This, I believe is not unlike what has befallen our friends the Communists. They have made their policies a creed and are finding that dogmatism and freedom of discussion do not easily go together. They are as much afraid of the "other party" as any government in a two-party democracy. In their case the "other party" is only a phantom, but a phantom can be even more frightening than a living rival! And their fear of this phantom has blinded them to the truth that, in a one-party system, party membership must be open to everybody and freedom of expression allowed to every individual. No party which limits its membership to a clique can ever free itself from fear of overthrow by those it has excluded.[65]

For Nyerere, then, the people's equality must be reflected in the political organization of the country. All the members of society must equally be sovereign; they must be free to change peacefully the laws that rule them and the personnel in the positions of leadership.[66]

Religion. The Soviet theory of historical materialism denies the existence of any reality that cannot be verified by the senses. Historical materialism explains the phenomenon of God as an idea that evolves at a definite stage of history and likewise will disappear as a childish practice.[67] Moreover, in

Soviet theory religion today is not a harmless eccentricity to answer primitive humanity's questions about the forces of nature, but it is a tool of the bourgeois oppressors to keep the masses ignorant and subservient.[68] In most cases there is an irreconcilable conflict between the principle of communist tactics and the commandments of religion.[69]

While officially the Soviet Union tolerates religion,[70] there are countless numbers of modern martyrs who have apparently died for religion alone.[71]

As explained above, Nyerere's position on the state's relation to religion is that religion is a private matter. The state is secular. It has no authority to interfere with religious freedom unless some people, in the name of religion, infringe on the rights of others, for example, human sacrifice.[72] He sees in this question of religion a great distinction between *Ujamaa* socialism and communism and has stated recently:

> The other aspect, perhaps a more important aspect where I feel there's a difference, is that the Marxist, the Communist, is an atheist. He has to be an atheist. You can't be both a Communist, a Socialist in that sense, and a believer in God. You have to declare yourself on religion. We don't. In our party we have atheists, we have Moslems, we have Christians, we have, if you like, Pagans. We regard religion as basically metaphysical, and we don't see why we should involve our members in the question: Is there a God?[73]

Individual and the Collectivity. Soviet Marxism looks forward to a future and final stage of economic development called communism. This will end the dialectical process; humankind will live in a classless society in liberty and peace; the state will wither away. Bookkeeping offices and statistics bureaus will direct the workers. The principle of distribution will no longer be based on the utility of the individual to society but "from each according to his ability; to each according to his need."[74] There will be no prisons, police, or laws because after a few generations of education all "relics of the past, such as sloth, slackness, criminality, and pride will be stamped out."[75]

To achieve this future perfect society Soviet Marxism in theory and in practice has regarded humanity as expendable. "Having read Marx and Engels, most of their disciples concluded that violence is good, that the end justifies the means, that socialists should aim at total power; and they acted accordingly."[76] Herbert Marcuse explains how Soviet theory justifies this instrumentalistic character of Soviet ethics which suppresses the individual into the collectivity:

> These standards of the future are then related to the actual situation of Soviet society, but they retain their "transcendental" connotation, that is the image of a future which will compensate the individuals for their present sufferings and frustrations. Soviet ethics here contains a "safety valve": the image of the future seems to perform a function corresponding to that of the transcendental elements of Western ethics—in this image we seem to have a real Soviet substitute for religion. However, there is an essential

difference from which Soviet ethics derives much of its appeal. The transcendental goal
in Soviet ethics is a historical one, and the road to its attainment a historical
process—the result of a concrete social and political development. Final human fulfil-
ment and gratification are not oriented on the "inner self" or the hereafter, but on the
"next Stage" of the actual development of society. And the truth of this conception is to
be, not a matter of faith, but a matter of scientific analysis and reason—of necessity.[77]

Nyerere has taken a strong position against state infringement on the rights
of the individual. He rejects any justification of infringement on the grounds of
the scientific development toward a perfect future society.

It [*Ujamaa* socialism] is an assertion that there are not natural laws of human development which we have only to discover and apply in order to reach the Nirvana of a
perfect socialist society; on the contrary, that it is by deliberate design that men will
build socialist societies, and by deliberate designs that they will maintain socialist
principles in a form which seems to them to be good. It is an assertion of man's unity
and also his diversity; the validity of certain basic principles for social living, and the
variety of their expression. It is a statement that one will not recognize or define a
socialist society by its institutions or its statements, but by its fundamental characteristics of equality, co-operation, and freedom.[78]

NOTES

1. Julius K. Nyerere, *Ujamaa: Essays on Socialism* (Dar es Salaam: Oxford University Press,
1968), pp. 1ff.
2. Ibid., p. 9.
3. Ibid., pp. 3–4.
4. Julius K. Nyerere, *Freedom and Socialism* (Dar es Salaam: Oxford University Press, 1968),
p. 2.
5. Ibid., p. 16.
6. Nyerere, *Ujamaa: Essays on Socialism*, p. 6
7. Ibid.
8. Ibid., p. 5
9. Nyerere, *Freedom and Socialism*, p. 16.
10. Nyerere, *Ujamaa: Essays on Socialism*, p. 5.
11. Ibid., p. 9.
12. Ibid., p. 12.
13. Ibid., p. 11.
14. Ibid., p. 12.
15. Nyerere, *Freedom and Socialism*, p. 2.
16. Ibid.
17. Fred G. Burke, "Tanganyika: The Search for Ujamaa," *African Socialism*, ed. William H.
Friedland and Carl S. Rosberg, Jr. (Stanford: Stanford University Press, 1964), pp. 195–204.
18. Ibid., p. 219.
19. Nyerere, *Ujamaa: Essays on Socialism*, p. 1.
20. Ibid., p. 17.
21. Ibid., p. 1.

22. Nyerere gives the example of the diamond miners of Mwadui whose work yields greater financial profits to the community than that of the peasant farmers. "If, however, they went on to demand that they should therefore be given most of that extra profit for themselves, and that no share of it should be spent on helping the farmers, they would be potential capitalists: This is exactly where the attitude of mind comes in" (ibid., p. 10).

23. Ibid., p. 11.

24. Ibid., p. 89.

25. Chandler Morse, "The Economics of African Socialism," *African Socialism*, p. 36.

26. Nyerere, *Freedom and Socialism*, p. 4.

27. Ibid., p. 30.

28. Nyerere, *Ujamaa: Essays on Socialism*, p. 12.

29. Ibid., p. 29.

30. Julius K. Nyerere, *Freedom and Unity* (Dar es Salaam: Oxford University Press, 1966), p. 207.

31. Burke, "Tanganyika," p. 31.

32. Nyerere, *Freedom and Socialism*, p. 24.

33. Ibid.

34. Nyerere, *Ujamaa: Essays on Socialism*, p. 1.

35. Nyerere, *Freedom and Socialism*, p. 25.

36. Julius K. Nyerere, "From Uhuru to Ujamaa," *Africa Today* (Summer 1974), p. 6.

37. Nyerere, *Freedom and Socialism*, p. 24.

38. Julius K. Nyerere, "Stability and Change in Africa" (Toronto University, October 2, 1969), *Vital Speeches* 36 (November 1, 1969), p. 50.

39. Nyerere, *Freedom and Socialism*, p. 19.

40. Ibid., p. 40.

41. Julius K. Nyerere, *Freedom and Development* (London: Oxford University Press, 1973), p. 128.

42. Nyerere, *Ujamaa: Essays on Socialism*, p. 87.

43. Nyerere, *Freedom and Socialism*, p. 22.

44. Nyerere, *Ujamaa: Essays on Socialism*, p. 92.

45. Ibid., pp. 108–09.

46. Igor Koptoff, "Socialism and Traditional African Societies," *African Socialism*, p. 62.

47. Kwame Nkrumah, "African Socialism Revisited," *African Forum* 1 (1966), 3:5.

48. William H. Friedland, "Basic Social Trends," *African Socialism*, p. 17.

49. Ahmed Mohiddin, "Ujamaa: A Commentary on President Nyerere's Vision of Tanzanian Society," *African Affairs* 67 (April 1968), 267:137.

50. Ibid., p. 138.

51. Henry Bienen, *Party Transformation and Economic Development* (Princeton: Princeton University Press, 1970), pp. 244–45.

52. Gustave A. Wetter, *Soviet Ideology Today*, trans. Peter Heath (London: Heinemann, 1966), parts 1 and 2.

53. Nikolaj Buharin and E. Prebobrazhensky, *The ABC of Communism*, trans. Eden and Cedar Paul (Baltimore: Penguin Books, 1969), pp. 242–43.

54. Lenin used the word "communism" to mean the final stage of the evolution of society and also to signify the common ownership of the means of production ("The Professional Revolutionary," *Modern Socialism*, ed. M. Salvadori [New York: Harper Torchbooks], p. 195).

55. Nyerere, *Freedom and Socialism*, p. 14.

56. Ibid., p. 16.

57. Ibid., p. 3.

58. Bienen argues that the very foreignness of Marxism makes it appealing to Tanzanians (Bienen, *Party Transformation*, p. 252).

59. Nyerere, *Freedom and Socialism*, p. 14.

60. The dogmatism of Marxism can be seen in the Soviet repudiation of the Chinese communists. "It will be recalled that the Chinese leaders have put forward an ideological political platform of their own which is incompatible with Leninism on the key questions of international life and the world communist movement. . . . Our part has resolutely opposed the attempts to

distort the Marxist-Leninist teaching, and to split the international communist movement and the ranks of the fighters against imperialism" ("Report of the Central Committee of the Communist Party of the Soviet Union to the Twenty-Fourth Congress of the CPSU," delivered by L.I. Brezhnev, March 30, 1971; *Moscow News*, supplement to issue no. 14 (1971), 1057: 3).

61. Nyerere, *Freedom and Socialism*, p. 15.
62. I.I. Potekhin, "On African Socialism; A Soviet View," *African Socialism*, p. 108.
63. Ibid., p. 111.
64. For an analysis of the Soviet concept of individual freedom, see Herbert Marcuse, *Soviet Marxism: A Critical Analysis* (Middlesex, Eng.: Pelican Books, 1971), pp. 168–72.
65. Nyerere, *Freedom and Unity*, p. 201.
66. Nyerere, *Freedom and Socialism*, p. 5.
67. Buharin, *ABC of Communism*, p. 300.
68. Ibid., p. 299.
69. Ibid.
70. "The Constitution of the Union of Soviet Socialist Republics" (art. 124), in John N. Hazard, *The Soviet System of Government* (Chicago: University of Chicago Press, 1964).
71. George H. Hampsch, *The Theory of Communism* (New York: Philosophical Library, 1975), p. 122.
72. Nyerere, *Freedom and Socialism*, p. 12.
73. Peter Enahoro, "African Socialism" (an interview with Julius Nyerere), *Africa* 6 (1972): 60.
74. Buharin, *ABC of Communism*, p. 118.
75. Ibid., p. 119.
76. M. Salvadori, *Modern Socialism*, p. 100.
77. Marcuse, *Soviet Marxism*, p. 179.
78. Nyerere, *Freedom and Socialism*, p. 23.

CHAPTER 16

THE PRINCIPLES
OF NYERERE'S SOCIALISM

Nyerere is striving to build *Ujamaa* socialism on the basic assumption that the purpose of all social activity is the human person. "Nothing is more central to a socialist society than an acceptance that Man is its justification for existence."[1] Nyerere makes it clear that the word "man" implies two things: it means all the people in a society without exception and it means that all people are equal.[2] These assumptions are the unquestionable beliefs upon which *Ujamaa* is built.

Equality is violated by any discrimination among the people for reasons of parentage, place of birth, appearance, religious beliefs, or "anything other than their behaviour in relation to their fellows."[3] In building a society that has no discrimination, Tanzania has the added problems to overcome of the historical European-African discriminatory relationship as well as the traditional hostility in a nation formed of 120 different tribes, each with its own language and customs.

More positively, the equality of all means that, as society progresses, each person will share more nearly equally in the economic and political power. A society does not have equal members if one person's livelihood depends on the whim of another. A society does not have equal members if every member is not an equal participant in the government of the society.[4]

Tanzania is not yet a socialist society but, rather, it is in the process of building a socialist society in which all live in human dignity as equal members. The state has the function to organize "men's inequalities to serve their equality."[5] The equality of all people guarantees their rights, which in turn imposes certain duties.

Human Rights

Ujamaa socialism is a belief in the fundamental equality of all and that "without the acceptance of equality of all men there can be no socialism."[6] This basic assumption of the equality of all is a belief that every individual hopes to live in a society as a free person and to have a decent life in peace with one's neighbors.[7] It is a belief that it is wrong for one person to dominate or exploit another,[8] and that no persons should be ashamed of their poverty in the light of others' affluence.[9] It is a belief that every person has a right to a decent life before any individuals have a surplus above their needs.[10] The foundation of *Ujamaa* socialism, then, is the equality of all people, not the state or the flag,[11] not national grandeur or wealth as distinct from the well-being of the citizens.[12] All other characteristics of socialism follow from this basic belief in equality.[13]

In his independence address to the United Nations on December 14, 1961, Julius Nyerere stated that the equality of all and the corresponding rights embodied in the Universal Declaration of Human Rights were the goals rather than the de facto situation of Tanganyika.[14] But it is to these principles that his new country is committed and by which it intends to be judged.[15]

The specific rights guaranteed to each Tanzanian citizen have been listed in the Arusha Declaration, the official policy document of the TANU government. Beginning with the equality of all, the Arusha Declaration states that every person has the right to dignity and respect; the right to take an equal part in the government; the right to freedom of expression, of movement, of religious belief, and of association within the context of the law. Each citizen has the right to protection of life and of property held according to the law, and the right to receive a just return for labor.[16]

It is necessary to explain here what Nyerere understands by some of these rights. The meaning of the other rights will become clear in the development of the policies of *Ujamaa*.

The right to dignity and respect implies that a person be guaranteed the necessities of life. "There is no human dignity in extreme poverty or debilitating disease—nor in the ignorance which buttresses these things."[17] These evils—poverty, disease, ignorance—must be eliminated first.[18] Furthermore, the right to dignity and respect means equal opportunity to the goods of this world, to education, and to service for the country.[19]

On the other hand, when the right to dignity is denied, people will act without dignity. "If they are treated solely as a dispensable means of production, they will become soul-less 'hands' to whom life is a matter of doing as little work as possible and then escaping into the illusion of happiness and pride through vice."[20]

Democracy is another essential characteristic of *Ujamaa* socialism. "For the people's equality must be reflected in the political organization;

everyone must be an equal participant in the government of his society."[21]

Specifically this means that any patriotic citizen may run for any elected office;[22] that the people have complete freedom to choose their own representatives and legislators;[23] that the people have control over all the organs of the state on a basis of universal suffrage.[24]

Political freedom presupposes discussion, equality, and freedom.[25] It also admits the possibility of choosing wrongly. But for Nyerere, the really "wrong" government is not a government the people have elected; it is a government imposed on them by external force or by the will of the minority.[26] Nyerere admits that people can err in choosing an official but believes that their common sense will prevent them from repeating the mistake. "It is this common sense of man which makes democracy possible, and the whole essence of democracy is the will of the people and faith in the people."[27]

Nyerere has stated his government's position on religious liberty very clearly: "Socialism is concerned with man's life in this society. A man's relationship with his God is a personal matter for him and him alone; his beliefs about the hereafter are his own affair."[28] Because *Ujamaa* socialism is secular and has nothing to say about a person's relationship with God does not mean, on the other hand, that the government can require its citizens to be atheists.[29] In fact the necessity for religious tolerance arises out of the nature of socialism. "For a man's religious beliefs are important to him, and the purpose of socialism is Man."[30]

An example of religious freedom is that the government has guaranteed by law (Education Act 1969)[31] that religious bodies may conduct their own religious schools without interference; they may run private schools and they may give religious instruction in government schools.[32]

This does not mean that the government will support every religious enterprise. Nyerere has made it clear he will not support "priests with feudalistic ideas" who fear they will lose their privileges under *Ujamaa* socialism. "The Arusha Declaration says only children and old men can live on the sweat of others. We do not intend to add the word priests to that clause."[33]

A developing country's poverty forces it to limit some personal rights. For example, Tanzania has neither the money nor the manpower to give a complete primary education to every child, let alone a secondary education. A decision has to be made on who will be the fortunate person to be educated. "Decisions of this kind are not a choice between right and wrong, between justice and injustice. They are a choice between conflicting demands, both of which are right, but only one of which can be met."[34] These decisions must be made in the light of the kind of society Tanzania wants to build.[35]

More controversial is the restriction on the right of speech or of association when the government decides that the exercise of such freedom by some individuals endangers economic development or national security. Nyerere, after admitting the seriousness of imprisoning a person on circumstantial evidence, justifies his position as follows:

Yet, knowing these things, I have still supported the introduction of a law which gives the Government power to detain people without trial. I have myself signed Detention Orders. I have done these things as an inevitable part of my responsibilities as President of the Republic. For even on so important and fundamental an issue as this, other principles conflict. Our Union has neither the long tradition of nationhood, nor the strong physical means of national security, which older countries take for granted. While the vast mass of the people give full and active support to their country and its government, a handful of individuals can still put our nation into jeopardy, and reduce to ashes the effort of millions.[36]

The reason for restricting some rights at times is the government's desire to maintain a balance between various viewpoints on the direction of the country lest the whole society collapse.[37]

Duties of the Person

In a 1971 interview President Nyerere explained: "The West is just too individualistic. All the textbooks of Western countries talk about rights, rights, rights, and no duties. . . . Eastern countries have something Africa needs: a stress on duties."[38]

The first duty of a Tanzanian is to work. "There is no such thing as socialism without work."[39] The Arusha Declaration stresses the need of hard work from everyone as a necessity for development of Tanzania. "Industries will come and money will come but their foundation is the people and hard work."[40]

Besides the developmental needs, there is a more socialistic need for work. Work is required by all to avoid the rise of a class of "exploiters," people who make their livelihood off the work of others. Only small children, the aged, and the crippled have the right to be supported by others. This policy is succinctly stated in the Arusha Declaration.

A truly socialist state is one in which all people are workers and in which neither capitalism nor feudalism exists. It does not have two classes of people, a lower class composed of people who work for their living, and an upper class composed of people who live on the work of others. In a really socialist country no person exploits another; everyone who is physically able to work does so; every worker obtains a just return for the labor he performs; and the incomes derived from different types of work are not grossly divergent.[41]

William Friedland further explains how this duty to work differs, for a socialist, from the duty to work in capitalist countries that Max Weber notes in his theory of the Protestant ethic:

Classical socialism held that the exploitation of man by man was indefensible and that all men consequently had the obligation to labor. In this respect, the socialist obligation to work is different from that of the Protestant ethic, where the obligation to work is personal and success at accumulation confirms membership in God's elect.[42]

Besides the duty to work, Nyerere had also emphasized personal responsibility because, ultimately, the building up of Tanzania depends upon the people. "For any society is only what the people makes it."[43] The seriousness with which all people must accept their responsibilities can be seen in the sharpness by which the president speaks to peasant and educated alike.

Yet poverty is something that really only you can fight. If you have cotton unpicked on your shamba, if you have cultivated half an acre less than you could cultivate, if you are letting the soil run needlessly off your land, or if your shamba is full of weeds, if you deliberately ignore the advice given you by the agricultural experts, then you are a traitor in the battle.[44]

But with all this stress on his individual responsibility how can we at the same time safeguard the individual against the arrogance of looking upon himself as someone special, someone who has the right to make very heavy demands upon society, in return for which he will deign to make available the skills which that society has enabled him to acquire? In particular, what can a university do to ensure that its students regard themselves as "servants-in-training"?[45]

Function of the State

Concerning the function of the government, naturally the TANU government has to maintain the sovereignty of the state and protect the rights of its citizens. But over and above protecting the rights of the citizens the TANU government has an essentially socialist function, which will be explained more fully below. Briefly, the government has as its principal aims to participate directly in the economic development of the country whenever possible, to exercise effective control over the principal means of production, to expedite collective ownership of all natural resources, to prevent exploitation of one person by another or one group by another, to prevent the accumulation of wealth which is inconsistent with the existence of a classless society, and to cooperate with all political parties in Africa engaged in the liberation of Africa.[46]

Since the TANU government has such a strong role in the economic and political life of the community, the ancient question arises about the limits a state can impose on individuals' freedom before they are absorbed into the collectivity. Nyerere gives the principle by which his government decides.

This means that neither the good of the individual as such, nor the group as such, can always be the determining factor in society's decisions. Both have constantly to be served. Yet underlying everything must be a consciousness that the very purpose of society—its reason for existence—is and must be the individual man, his growth, his health, his security, his dignity, and, therefore, his happiness.[47]

Nyerere goes on to elaborate what he means by the individual man. "It is not any particular man who is the justification for society and all its problems. It is every man, equally with every other man."[48] In treating every person equally, *Ujamaa* socialism has as its purpose "to enlarge the real freedom of man, to expand his opportunity of living in dignity and peace."[49] The balance between individual freedom and the state's safeguarding the rights and equality of all will be seen in the policies of *Ujamaa* socialism.

NOTES

1. Julius K. Nyerere, *Freedom and Socialism* (Dar es Salaam: Oxford University Press, 1968), p. 5.
2. Ibid.
3. Ibid.
4. Ibid., pp. 5–9.
5. Ibid., p. 4.
6. Julius K. Nyerere, *Ujamaa: Essays on Socialism* (Dar es Salaam: Oxford University Press, 1968), p. 37.
7. Ibid., p. 92.
8. Ibid.
9. Ibid., p. 104.
10. Ibid., p. 103.
11. Ibid., p. 92.
12. Ibid.
13. Nyerere, *Freedom and Socialism*, p. 4.
14. Julius K. Nyerere, *Freedom and Unity* (Dar es Salaam: Oxford University Press, 1966), p. 146.
15. Ibid., p. 156.
16. Nyerere, *Ujamaa: Essays on Socialism*, pp. 13–14.
17. Nyerere, *Freedom and Unity*, p. 15.
18. Ibid., p. 139.
19. Ibid., p. 130.
20. Julius K. Nyerere, "Speech to the Maryknoll Congress in New York" (Dar es Salaam: Government Printer, 1970), p. 15.
21. Nyerere, *Freedom and Socialism*, p. 5.
22. Nyerere, *Freedom and Unity*, p. 207.
23. Ibid., p. 262.
24. Ibid.
25. Ibid., p. 103.
26. Nyerere, "Speech to Maryknoll," p. 15.
27. Ibid.
28. Nyerere, *Freedom and Socialism*, p. 12.
29. Ibid., p. 13.
30. Ibid.
31. Theodore Slaats, C.S.Sp., "The Nationalization of Schools in Tanzania," *IDOC International*, North American ed. (May 23, 1970), p. 33.

32. Ibid.
33. *The Nationalist* (Dar es Salaam), August 10, 1970, p. 1.
34. Nyerere, *Freedom and Unity*, p. 311.
35. Ibid., p. 6.
36. Ibid., p. 312.
37. Ibid., p. 313.
38. Edgar Smith, "Profiles: Julius K. Nyerere," part 3, *The New Yorker* (October 30, 1971), p. 53.
39. Nyerere, *Ujamaa: Essays on Socialism*, p. 6.
40. Nyerere, *Freedom and Unity*, p. 246.
41. Nyerere, *Ujamaa: Essays on Socialism*, p. 15.
42. William H. Friedland, "Basic Social Trends," *African Socialism* (Stanford: Stanford University Press, 1964), p. 18.
43. Nyerere, *Freedom and Socialism*, p. 32.
44. Nyerere, *Freedom and Unity*, pp. 114–15.
45. Nyerere, *Freedom and Socialism*, p. 185.
46. Nyerere, *Ujamaa: Essays on Socialism*, pp. 14–15.
47. Nyerere, *Freedom and Unity*, p. 7.
48. Ibid., p. 8.
49. Ibid.

CHAPTER 17

SOCIAL EQUALITY

Elimination of Exploitation

According to Nyerere, exploitation is making a living from the work of others;[1] it is making money out of proportion to the rest of society;[2] it is a rich person making a profit from a poor person;[3] it is the taking of more than one needs;[4] it is displaying a capitalistic attitude of mind;[5] it is acquisitiveness for the purpose of gaining power and prestige;[6] it is having control over those who are poor;[7] it is making money without working.[8] The elimination of this exploitation is so central to *Ujamaa* socialism that Nyerere has given many examples to pinpoint what he means.

Exploitation is a person with money making a profit from a person without money. "A man who can afford to buy only one loaf of bread a day contributes to the profit accruing to the owner of the bakery, despite the fact that the owner already has more money than he knows how to use."[9] A more lengthy example shows a cotton farmer who decides to double the acreage of his farm. To do so he must hire three people for only three months a year to pick the cotton. Nyerere considers this exploitation because:

The three men whose work at a crucial stage made this extra shs. 2,070/- possible, will have received between them shs. 900/- and for the rest of the year they will have to depend upon other kinds of wages employment or find some other way of getting minimum food, clothes and shelter. The one man (the owner of the farm) is progressing very fast—and with increasing speed—and the others are receiving less than they could receive if they worked on their own account.[10]

The source of this kind of exploitation is private ownership of the means of production. "For when one man controls the means by which another earns or obtains the food, clothing and shelter which are essential to life, then there is no equality. One man must call another 'master'— for he is the master of life as truly as if he had the power to kill with a gun."[11] In *Ujamaa* society there can be no "masters" who sit in idleness while others labor on "their" farms or in "their" factories.[12]

Exploitation is not all on the side of the more affluent. People can exploit their neighbors by laziness, dishonesty, cheating, or being uncooperative with development plans.[13] Town dwellers can be the exploiters of the peasants because most of the tax money is spent in towns in the building of roads, hospitals, electric plants, and water lines.[14] "Society has as much a right, and a duty, to prevent these kinds of exploitation as it has to prevent the exploitation which arises from individual ownership of the means of production and exchange."[15]

The justification for a strong government program to reduce and eventually to eliminate exploitation is the basic assumption that all people are equal.[16] This does not mean that Nyerere advocates a completely classless society with no extra rewards for people with special skills. He does, however, maintain there must be some reasonable proportion in the incomes of a poor country. "Can any one man do work which is 100 times more valuable than that of another?"[17] "Does anyone need a palace while another receives only a 'bedspace'?"[18] "There must be something wrong with a society where one man, however hard-working or clever he may be, can acquire as great a 'reward' as a thousand of his fellows can acquire between them."[19]

Human equality also means that persons must control their own means of production. The tools of production must be under the control of the one whose life depends on them.[20] It follows, then, that in larger enterprises it is necessary to have group ownership of the means of production to prevent the exploitation of one person by another.[21]

The root of the evil of exploitation is not that one person has more than he or she needs while another lacks the necessities of life but, rather, that one person has power over the life of another.[22] This power enables the rich to get richer while the poor become relatively poorer and less able to control their own future. This is why Nyerere will not have economic development at the expense of creating social inequalities. "Government understands that our people do not believe that it is better to be a wealthy slave than a poorer free man."[23]

This control of power is also true on the international level. For example, Nyerere points out that the United States has a per capita income of $3,200 versus approximately $80 for Tanzania. Although both countries may grow at the same rate, the per capita income of the United States will increase $60 yearly while Tanzania's increases only $2.[24] In reality the economic gap between a rich country and a poor country is widening every year, with the result that the poor country has less and less control over its own future.[25]

Moreover, if Tanzania were to go capitalistic, Nyerere does not believe it could compete with General Motors, Nippon Enterprises, or any other multinational corporation. Capitalism could not be developed in Tanzania without foreign money and expertise. And foreign capitalists will invest only to the extent it is profitable to them. Tanzania would be a "very junior partner."[26]

The rich country "exploits" by exerting great financial and political pressure. Financially, for example, the rich countries of North America and Western Europe have control over the market value of cash crops of a developing country. Politically a rich country can virtually dictate policy to a developing country which is dependent upon foreign aid.[27] It is in reaction to this neocolonial kind of exploitation that Nyerere has developed his policies of self-reliance and Pan-Africanism.

Specific Policies against Exploitation

In keeping with a socialist philosophy the first step in eliminating exploitation is to restrict capitalistic practices even though great advances in technology and economic growth have been made under capitalism. William Friedland and Carl Rosberg claim that this is a trend of all African socialist countries. "African entrepreneurs tend to þe regarded as self-interested rather than as contributors to the general welfare. . . . The accumulation of capital is seen as being primarily a responsibility of government."[28] Nyerere is more specific on why he is against capitalism in Tanzania:

But the decisions [under capitalism] as to what goods shall be produced, and how they shall be produced, are made by a small number of people who have control over land and capital. And the determining factor in all their decision-making is whether the activity will yield a monetary profit, or power, or prestige, to them as owners of the land and capital. The needs of mankind are secondary, if they are considered at all. . . . The result is . . . a few men living in great luxury. . . . At the same time masses of men, women, and children are reduced to beggary, squalor, and to the humiliation of that disease and soul-destroying insecurity which arises out of their enforced poverty.[29]

This determination to stop capitalism has necessitated the government's policies of nationalization and control over the means of production and exchange. One specific example, which applies to the 95 percent of the population who are farmers, is the hiring of farmhands to make larger farms possible.[30] Nyerere opposes the practice of one person hiring another because it breaks down equality and is the beginning of a class system.[31] Statistical increase of national wealth does not justify rural capitalistic development.[32] "They [the farmhands] will become a 'rural proletariat' depending on the decisions of other men for their existence, and subject in consequence to all the subservience, social and economic inequality, and insecurity, which such a position involves."[33]

The impact of Nyerere's determination to root out exploitation and capitalism can be seen in the resolution of the Arusha Declaration concerning positions of leadership in the government. No TANU or government leader, according to the Arusha Declaration, may be associated with capitalist or feudal practices, nor hold shares in any company, nor receive two or more salaries, nor own houses which are rented to others.[34] Nyerere sees these requirements as necessary for *Ujamaa* socialism and is relentless in upholding them. "Some people want it both ways. They want the opportunity to exploit the people, and at the same time they want the right to serve the people and lead them in the struggle against exploitation."[35] "A leader who gets fat on the sweat of others is little better than a thief, for while pretending to serve his master—that is, the people—he is really taking advantage of their trust to increase his own wealth by reducing theirs."[36] Furthermore, these policies admit no exception even for "lofty" motives. "Exploitation is still exploitation even if it is undertaken with the intention of assisting one's children."[37]

During the first years of the independence of Tanganyika, union workers were in a position to exploit the rest of the country had the government not intervened.[38] "Underlying this conflict is the concern of the TANU Government that the unions should not become a drag on economic development by continuing their consumptionist activities. During the course of this conflict, productionism has been urged on the unions by Mr. Nyerere."[39] Nyerere has stressed the responsibility of union workers to build *Ujamaa*.[40] This means that union workers must increase production, while avoiding strikes and slow-downs.[41]

The guidelines for a fair wage were explained by Nyerere. "It is one of the purposes of trade unions to ensure for the workers a fair share of the profits of their labor. But a 'fair' share must be fair in relation to the whole society."[42] The union workers' wages cannot increase at the expense of the farmers.[43]

As far back as 1958 Nyerere laid down the principles for the rent of land. "There are many Africans paying land rent . . . and house rent. The point which is basically wrong is for a man to pay rent to another person for using land which is a free gift of God to him and his neighbor."[44] This is the basis of the government's policy to own all land and to lease it to individuals as long as they use it (leasehold property).[45] But this system of leasehold property inaugurated by the TANU government did not prevent individuals from renting out buildings on their property. In April 1971 Nyerere, denouncing landlordism as theft, made all buildings costing over 5,000 (T) pounds (approximately $14,000) subject to nationalization.[46] All tenants would now pay their rent to the government.[47] Nyerere explains the reasoning behind the buildings being taken over: "No one can be rich by his own work unless he picks diamonds or exploits others. How can one afford to build projects without mustering the labor of other people?"[48] In an editorial the *Nationalist* commented: "Our struggle to end exploitation has been eliminated and socialism has been built."[49]

In common with many countries less socialistic, Tanzania has a graduated income tax. There are only ten people in all Tanzania who make over TShs 300,000 (approximately $43,000) a year and they pay over two-thirds in income tax.[50] In a country of over twelve million there are less than 35,000 people who make enough to pay any income tax at all.[51] This comparatively low amount of revenue from taxation gives impetus to Nyerere's policies of self-reliance. "However heavily we taxed the citizens of Tanzania and the aliens living here, the resulting revenue would not be enough to meet the costs of the development we want."[52]

Communal Ownership

In talking about private property a distinction has to be made between ownership which affects only the individual person and ownership which exerts some control over the lives of other people. Nyerere does not oppose ownership of property that pertains to the individual alone. "A farmer can own his own hoe, a carpenter can own his handsaw which he uses himself as a supplement to his own hands. Similarly, a family can own the house in which it lives, and so on."[53] In fact, one of the purposes of *Ujamaa* socialism is to ensure that persons control their own means of production so that their livelihood is not dependent on the whims of another.[54]

Property that is not subject to private ownership includes land and the means of production requiring the employment of workers. This kind of property, which is under the domain of public or communal ownership, has its roots in traditional tribal society.[55] Private ownership of land was a foreign concept introduced by colonialism.[56] It makes land a marketable commodity which allows exploitation through rents and speculation. "Landlords, in a society which recognizes individual ownership of land, can be, and usually are, in the same class as the loiterers, . . . the class of parasites."[57]

To minimize exploitation through private ownership of land, Tanzania adopted a system of leasehold land shortly after independence. All land is owned by the government.[58] "A member of society will be entitled to a piece of land on the condition he uses it."[59] The system of leasehold gives persons sufficient land, and security that they will not be evicted as long as they use the land.[60] This right to the use of land is necessary because otherwise a citizen "could not earn his living and one cannot have the right to live without also having the right to some means of maintaining life."[61] Leasehold land ensures that the land benefits the whole nation and not just a few people.[62]

As far back as 1963 Nyerere said in private that if he had a completely free hand, government policy would be to seek the complete elimination of private profit and substitute cooperative methods of sharing the rewards of enterprise.[63] He has pursued this ideal gradually. In the Arusha Declaration of February 1967, the TANU government committed itself to a policy of nationalization in order to control the principal means of production and exchange.[64] "To build and maintain socialism it is essential that all the major means of production and exchange in the nation are controlled and owned by the peasants through the machinery of their Government and their co-operatives."[65]

The following week Nyerere listed which companies were to be nationalized and which companies the government would take only majority control.[66] This takeover of these companies was an extension of the political control which Tanzanian people secured in 1961.[67] It ensures that the people of the country are able to decide development policies as well as obtain a large portion of the profits.[68]

The companies that were nationalized were to be paid full and fair compensation.[69] The reason some companies lost only majority control without being completely nationalized is, according to A.W. Bradley, that this partial nationalization cost the government less in compensation, and also experience shows these companies to be more profitable.[70] In a lengthy analysis of the legal aspects of nationalization in Tanzania, Bradley upholds the legality of the nationalization policies:

The nationalizations were carried out in pursuance of a policy of socialization approved and implemented by the country's political, administrative and legislative institutions; the nationalizations are not in breach of treaty obligations; the nationalizations do not seem discriminatory against alien interests; and the legislation provided for payment of compensation which does not seem to fall below the internationally accepted minimum standard of compensation.[71]

The policy of nationalization which Nyerere has implemented for greater control has been often criticized for economic reasons. Peter Temu summarizes the three principal objections to nationalization: "The inflow of foreign capital will be discouraged; scarce development capital will be wasted and people made to carry an intolerable repayment burden; the economy will collapse or stagnate because there will be an exodus of expatriate skills from the nationalized industries."[72] The other extreme has been expressed by A. Roe, who says the nationalization policy will not greatly affect companies because it is mainly political, "to reform attitudes which were so patently inappropriate to the development needs of the country."[73] A position more in the middle has been published in a study by economists in Kenya:

On balance the Tanzanians have evidently decided that the small amount of overseas aid and investment they were getting was not worth the price that had to be paid for it, in terms of its threat to self-reliance and egalitarianism and to "true independence." Some further investment will no doubt continue to flow, even on the stiffer terms offered in Tanzania. As an oversimplification, Tanzania appears to have chosen to follow the path of social cohesion at the expense of a slower rate of growth, while Kenya has chosen a policy of rapid growth, even at the risk of sacrificing some degree of social cohesion.[74]

This same study argues that the cost of compensation to industries nationalized is not an "intolerable repayment burden":

The cost of Tanzania's take-overs following the Arusha Declaration has been estimated at over 20 million (T) pounds. Spread over, say, a seven-year period, this could cost as little as 3 million (T) pounds a year, depending on terms agreed for compensation. The profits from the organizations concerned, if maintained at some 20 per cent of invested capital, might cover the cost in the period. Further profit would then accrue to finance further expansion.[75]

Finally, the nationalization of companies ensures that Tanzania is free from foreign domination of its economy without building up a new class of African entrepreneurs.[76] This has been a great concern of Nyerere and of the TANU government who had to take action as early as 1960 to undermine a small group of African entrepreneurs who were beginning to compete with Asian traders.[77] Nyerere has said that he has no intention of replacing one class of exploiters by another, even if they are African.[78]

One-Party Democracy

When Tanganyika became a republic in 1962, its constitution, based on the practices of democracy in Britain, called for a two-party system.[79] The following year Nyerere publicly spoke against the two-party system, which he claimed was alien to Tanganyikan background:

The European and American parties came into being as the result of existing social and economic divisions—the second party being formed to challenge the monopoly of the political power of some aristocratic or capitalistic group. Our own parties had a very different origin. They were not formed to challenge any ruling group of our own people; they were formed to challenge the foreigners who ruled over us. They were not, therefore, political "parties"—i.e., factions—but nationalist movements. And from the outset they represented the interests and aspirations of the whole nation.[80]

A two-party system based on class conflict is not a necessary part of democracy, nor is it desirable for *Ujamaa* socialism. "The two essentials for 'representative' democracy are the freedom of the individual, and the regular opportunity for him to join with his fellows in replacing, or reinstating, the government of his country by means of the ballot box."[81] Nyerere believes democracy can exist in Tanzania by a one-party system. His contention is that where there is a one-party system the foundations of democracy can be firmer and the people can have more opportunity for a real choice than in a system of two or more parties each representing sectional interests.[82] This assumes that the one-party system is identified with the nation as a whole. In a two-party state the people are voting only for the party policy, not the individual who will represent them.[83]

The one-party state is more in accord with traditional tribal methods of conducting affairs, namely, the elders sat under a tree and talked until they agreed.[84] Democracy in classless tribal life was more personal than institutional because the structure of society was an extension of the family. "When the word 'Government' was mentioned, the African thought of the chief; he did not, as does the Briton, think of a grand building in which a debate was taking place."[85] The democracy of tribal life is possible now only in a modified form in which freely elected spokesmen meet in a parliament on behalf of the people. The important thing is that the people are free to elect their personal representatives.[86] Based on this historical background of Tanzania, Nyerere sees a two-party state in a classless society as eventually being fatal to democracy.[87]

In July 1965 the National Assembly made a constitutional change making Tanzania a one-party state. Nyerere was criticized for denying freedom of dissent.[88] Two months later Tanzania had a general election in what outside observers called "the first real test in Africa of the possibility of a one-party democracy."[89] Nyerere, running unopposed, was reelected by over 98 percent of the vote, with over 50 percent of all possible voters voting.[90] However, sixteen out of thirty-two ministers of Parliament lost their positions. Henry Bienen, in his study of the 1965 elections, sees this not as a lack of confidence in TANU but as an expression of the freedom of the people. "These men were all defeated because they faced a 'throw-the-varmint-out' sentiment which feeds on seeing leaders living in high style."[91] In fact, Nyerere sees the one-party system as the best way to ensure a change of top leadership without recourse to violent means which result when all political opposition is regarded as treason.

Perhaps that [change of top leadership] is one advantage of our single-party system. If our party people felt that the top leadership should go, it will go! You can't call it treason. Some of our earlier leaders have gone. . . . I could go any time. It would not be regarded as treason.[92]

Perhaps the highest praise for the one-party system in Tanzania has come from the former British governor of Tanzania, Sir Richard Turnbull, when he commented in 1966: "None of us realized at the time that the one-party state is the natural and proper way of governing a country like Tanzania."[93]

TANU has continued to grow in power. In January 1975 TANU Central

Committee directed the government to set in motion machinery to amend the constitution so as to make the party supreme.[94] This would simply be making into law what was already happening in fact. In effect it means that TANU, not the government, is the real center of power and decisions, and will continue to build a socialist state.

NOTES

1. Julius K. Nyerere, *Ujamaa: Essays on Socialism* (Dar es Salaam: Oxford University Press, 1968), p. 15.

2. Ibid., p. 3.

3. Julius K. Nyerere, "Speech to the Maryknoll Congress in New York" (Dar es Salaam: Government Printer, 1970), pp. 14–15.

4. Nyerere, *Ujamaa: Essays on Socialism*, p. 10.

5. Ibid.

6. Ibid., p. 3.

7. Nyerere, "Speech to Maryknoll," p. 9.

8. Nyerere, *Ujamaa: Essays on Socialism*, pp. 15–16.

9. Nyerere, "Speech to Maryknoll," pp. 9–10.

10. Nyerere, *Ujamaa: Essays on Socialism*, pp. 114–15.

11. Julius K. Nyerere, *Freedom and Socialism* (Dar es Salaam: Oxford University Press, 1968), p. 304.

12. Ibid., p. 6.

13. Ibid., p. 7.

14. Ibid., pp. 242–43.

15. Ibid., p. 7.

16. Ibid., p. 316.

17. Ibid., p. 6.

18. Ibid., p. 7.

19. Nyerere, *Ujamaa: Essays on Socialism*, p. 3.

20. Nyerere, *Freedom and Socialism*, p. 305.

21. Ibid., pp. 305–06.

22. Nyerere, "Speech to Maryknoll," p. 9.

23. Nyerere, *Freedom and Socialism*, p. 200.

24. Nyerere, "Speech to Maryknoll," p. 11.

25. Ibid., p. 9.

26. Julius K. Nyerere, *Freedom and Development* (London: Oxford University Press, 1973), p. 384.

27. Nyerere, *Freedom and Socialism*, pp. 202–03.

28. William H. Friedland and Carl G. Rosberg, Jr., "Introduction," *African Socialism*, ed. William H. Friedland and Carl G. Rosberg, Jr. (Stanford: Stanford University Press, 1964), pp. 5–6.

29. Nyerere, "Speech to Maryknoll," p. 13.

30. Kamarch favors having larger plantations over small family farms for economic reasons. See *Economics of African Development* (London: Praeger, 1971, rev. ed.), pp. 161–64.

31. Nyerere, *Ujamaa: Essays on Socialism*, pp. 113–14.

32. Ibid., p. 115.

33. Ibid.

34. Ibid., p. 36.

35. Julius K. Nyerere, "The Arusha Declaration: Answers to Questions" (Dar es Salaam: Government Printer, 1967), p. 2.

36. Ibid., p. 10.

37. Ibid., p. 3.

38. Margaret Roberts, "A Socialist Looks at African Socialism," in *African Socialism*, p. 20.

39. William H. Friedland, "Basic Social Trends," in *African Socialism*, p. 20.
40. Nyerere, *Freedom and Socialism*, p. 311.
41. Ibid., p. 313.
42. Nyerere, *Ujamaa: Essays on Socialism*, p. 10.
43. Nyerere, *Freedom and Socialism*, p. 314.
44. Julius K. Nyerere, *Freedom and Unity* (Dar es Salaam: Oxford University Press, 1966), p. 58.
45. Nyerere, *Ujamaa: Essays on Socialism*, p. 84.
46. "Buildings Taken Over," *Tanzania News Service* 34 (June 1974): 1–3.
47. Ibid., p. 2.
48. Ibid., p. 1.
49. Ibid., p. 3.
50. Nyerere, *Ujamaa: Essays on Socialism*, p. 162.
51. Ibid., p. 163.
52. Ibid., p. 23.
53. Nyerere, *Freedom and Socialism*, p. 8.
54. Nyerere, *Ujamaa: Essays on Socialism*, p. 81.
55. Ibid., p. 84.
56. Ibid., p. 7.
57. Ibid.
58. Ibid., p. 85.
59. Ibid., p. 8.
60. Nyerere, *Freedom and Unity*, pp. 56–57.
61. Nyerere, *Ujamaa: Essays on Socialism*, p. 7.
62. Ibid., p. 33.
63. Harvey Glickman, "The Ideology of Julius Nyerere," *Boston University Papers on Africa*, ed. Jeffrey Butler and A.A. Castagno (London: Praeger, 1967), p. 203.
64. "The major means of production and exchange are such things as: land; forests; minerals; water; oil and electricity; news media; communications; banks, insurance, import and export trade, wholesale trade; iron and steel, machine-tool, arms, motor-car, cement, fertilizer, and textile industries; and any big factory on which a large section of the people depend for their living, or which provides essential components of other industries; large plantations, and especially those which provide raw materials essential to important industries" (The Arusha Declaration, in Nyerere, *Ujamaa: Essays on Socialism*, p. 16).
65. Ibid.
66. Nyerere, *Freedom and Socialism*, pp. 252–53.
67. Ibid., p. 262.
68. Ibid., p. 311.
69. Ibid., p. 253.
70. A.W. Bradley, "The Nationalization of Companies in Tanzania," *Private Enterprise and the East African Company*, ed. P. A. Thomas (Dar es Salaam: Tanzania Publishing House, 1969), p. 220.
71. A.W. Bradley, "Legal Aspects of Nationalization in Tanzania," *East African Law Journal* 3 (1967), 3:35.
72. Peter Temu, "Nationalization in Tanzania," *East Africa Journal* 4 (June 1967), 3:35.
73. A. Roe, "The Company in Tanzania: A Post Arusha Declaration Appraisal," *Private Enterprise and the East African Company*, pp. 257–58.
74. *Who Controls Industry in Kenya?* (Nairobi: East African Publishing House, 1968), p. 228.
75. Ibid., p. 229,
76. A.W. Bradley, "The Nationalization of Companies in Tanzania," p. 209.
77. William H. Friedland, "Basic Social Trends," p. 33.
78. Nyerere, *Ujamaa: Essays on Socialism*, pp. 82–83.
79. Nyerere, *Freedom and Socialism*, p. 37.
80. Ibid., p. 198,
81. Nyerere, *Freedom and Unity*, p. 106.
82. Ibid., p. 200.
83. Nyerere, *Freedom and Socialism*, p. 75.

84. Nyerere, *Freedom and Unity*, p. 195.

85. Ibid., p. 105.

86. Nyerere, *Freedom and Socialism*, p. 19.

87. Ibid., p. 20.

88. Ibid., p. 19.

89. Colin Legum, "One-Party State Passes Its Test," *Observer*, London (September 26, 1965), p. 4.

90. Henry Bienen, *Party Transformation and Economic Development* (Princeton: Princeton University Press, 1970), p. 404.

91. *Ibid.*, p. 394.

92. Peter Enahoro, "African Socialism" (an interview with Julius Nyerere), *Africa* 6 (1962):61.

93. Edgar Smith, "Profiles: Julius K. Nyerere," part 2, *The New Yorker* (October 23, 1971), pp. 52–53.

94. "Tanzania: TANU Supremacy," *Africa* (April 1975), p. 86.

CHAPTER 18

SELF-RELIANCE

Development Policy

Tanzanians do not live in isolation from the rest of the world. They see a better life and want it. "Is it possible for a mother to see the wonders of clean water from a tap and not want it for her child and for herself? Bicycles, bright clothes, education, aluminum cooking pots—all these things in the hands of others inevitably induce a discontent with the poverty which back-breaking work results in."[1]

The poverty of Tanzania is a yearly per capita income of approximately $80 to $100, a figure which is itself deceptive in that it includes estimates of production from subsistence agriculture.[2] The poverty is the fact that there are less than 400,000 Tanzanians working for wages, with almost half of these working on plantations.[3] The poverty is a total expenditure by the government of only $180 million in one year.[4] More graphically, the poverty of Tanzania is a life expectancy of thirty-eight years, an infant mortality rate of 154 per 1,000 births, one doctor for every 16,800 people, and a literacy rate of 15 to 20 percent.[5]

The wealth is simply not there. "If all the wealth of all the people in this country were put into one big heap, and then divided equally between all the people who live in Tanzania, each person would receive goods to the total value of shs 525/-."[6]

These are the actual conditions that concern President Nyerere. "There is no human dignity in extreme poverty or debilitating disease."[7] Justice and peace demand that the economic inequalities be corrected.[8] For Tanzanians to be free they must be free of their poverty.[9] "If we defeat poverty, we shall have achieved the means by which we can defeat ignorance and disease."[10] "I do not believe that it is impossible for these conditions of living to be changed; I believe that what is necessary is for us to make up our minds that they shall change, and attack the problem objectively and scientifically."[11]

In the beginning Nyerere favored receiving large amounts of foreign aid to overcome the crippling effects of extreme poverty in the shortest time.[12] He admits this was a mistake. "Even if all the prosperous nations were willing to help the needy countries, the assistance would still not suffice. But in any case the prosperous nations have not accepted a responsibility to fight world poverty."[13]

Past experience with foreign assistance plus the ever present reality of poverty has convinced Nyerere of the necessity of a development program based on self-reliance. "There is no choice. . . . The only people we can rely upon are ourselves."[14] Even if Tanzania could receive ample foreign aid, the foreign domination accompanying the aid would more than offset the economic advantages.[15] "Political independence is meaningless if a nation does not control the means by which the citizens can earn their living."[16] "Independence means self-reliance."[17]

In his first inaugural address as president, Nyerere expressed the purpose of nation-building:

To build a nation is not just a matter of producing tarmac roads, multi-storied buildings, luxury hotels, and so on. . . . To build a nation in the true sense . . . is to build the character of its people—of ourselves; to build an attitude of mind which will enable us to live together. . . . It is the dignity and well-being of all our people which is the beginning and the end of all our effort. . . . We [are] determined to build a country in which all her citizens are equal; where there is no division into rulers and ruled, rich and poor, educated and illiterate, those in distress and those in idle comfort. We determined that in this country all would be equal in dignity; all would have an equal right to respect, to the opportunity of acquiring a good education and the necessities of life; and all her citizens should have an equal opportunity of serving their country to the limit of their ability.[18]

Since the Arusha Declaration these social goals have been pursued by a self-reliant economic policy. Nyerere is not interested in another kind of economic program which may produce wealth for the country if it involves sacrificing the social and political development of the people.[19] These social and political objectives must be kept in mind in order to understand Nyerere's policy of economic self-reliance.

In a speech cited in *Second Five Year Plan*, Nyerere states succinctly the economic goals of *Ujamaa* socialism's program of self-reliance.[20]

Basically, if all Tanzanians: i) enjoy a healthy diet, ii) are adequately clothed, iii) enjoy acceptable housing conditions, and iv) have access to basic education and health facilities, Tanzania will have achieved more economic success than many supposed wealthy societies.[21]

This economic goal, which enables a person to live in dignity, can be achieved only by an increase of production. "There is no way of improving our income until and unless we improve our output."[22] To increase production, emphasis has been placed on economic planning rather than giving freedom to prevailing market forces favored by traditional Western economic theory.[23] The Arusha Declaration has called for an increase in government interventions to ensure what Goran Hyden calls transformative planning as distinct from allocative or economic planning.

Transformative planning, which is mainly political in character, seeks to legitimize new social objectives or to accomplish a major realignment of existing objectives. The emphasis is on management of change through manipulation of variables which are important to social action. Little attention is paid to whether the marginal returns obtained are equal. This is the primary concern of allocative planning. Transformative planning, then, aims at self-transformation of the society by creating new institutional relationships and concrete action programs. This, in my view, is also the essence of the Arusha Declaration.[24]

The patterns of Tanzania's economic transformative planning are now emerging. The government plans to go from a precapitalist society directly to a socialist structure, preventing the further expansion of indigenous capitalistic groups and curbing their political power.[25] Instead, government planning will stress cooperative farm communities with more social services.[26]

The first Five-Year Plan, in stressing the need of money for development, had emphasized urban development at the expense of the farmers.[27] Now the Arusha Declaration has made people, not money, the basis of development.[28] "The people have to be taught the meaning of self-reliance and its practice. They must become self-sufficient in food, serviceable clothes and good housing."[29] Only if each individual is self-reliant will each small village be self-reliant; only then will each district and each region be self-reliant, and finally the whole nation be self-reliant.[30]

Self-reliance is not some vague political slogan. It has meaning for every citizen, for every group, and for the nation as a whole. A self-reliant individual is one who co-operates with others, who is willing to help others and be helped by them, but who does not depend on anyone else for his food, clothing or shelter. He lives on what he earns, whether this be large or small, so that he is truly a free person beholden to no one. This is the position of the vast majority of our people now; it must be the position of all of us.[31]

Nyerere's plans to build a self-reliant nation are characterized by a gradual development. Negatively, this gradualism is above all opposed to violence as a means to effect social and economic change quickly.[32] Less drastically, gradualism also opposes rapid economic development at the expense of social goals.[33] More positively, gradualism looks to a deliberate policy of development using the resources that are available to the best advantage in accord with the philosophy of *Ujamaa* socialism. This means an approach to development which will emphasize equality, working together, and the good of all in contrast to economic classes, competition, and individualism.

With over 95 percent of the population peasant farmers, Nyerere sees Tanzania as having for a long time to come a predominantly rural economy which must be developed gradually.[34] "The jembe [hoe] will have to be eliminated by the ox-plough before the latter can be eliminated by the tractor. We cannot hope to eliminate the jembe by the tractor."[35] The Tanzanian peasant farmer is not ready now either financially or technically for the tractor.[36] And whatever financial merits large mechanized farms may yield, the resulting "proletarianization of our rural population" makes the program unacceptable to the ideals of *Ujamaa*.[37] The modernization of farming, as Nyerere envisions it, must begin with the oxen-plough and oxen-wagon and then gradually proceed to more advanced methods.[38]

The approach to gradualism will also apply to the industrialization of Tanzania. The development of the country will depend on farming, not industry for which there is neither the money nor skilled manpower to make it efficient and economical.[39] Foreign assistance is not the answer. "The policy of inviting a chain of capitalists to come and establish industries in our country might succeed in giving us all the industries we need, but it would also succeed in preventing the establishment of socialism unless we believe that without first building capitalism we cannot build socialism."[40] This is not to say that there will be no new industries, but to be realistic only a small percentage of the people will be able to work in a modern industry for years to come.[41] "What is here being proposed is that we in Tanzania should move from being a nation of individual peasant producers who are gradually adopting the incentives and ethics of the capitalist system. . . . Instead we should gradually become a nation of *Ujamaa* villages where the people co-operate directly in small groups and where these small groups co-operate together for joint enterprises."[42]

Nyerere believes that the education a child receives must reinforce the values of society and prepare the child to live and work in that society.[43] In that *Ujamaa* socialism is an attitude of mind requiring that the people care for each other's welfare, the educational system of Tanzania of the colonial past, based on the capitalist system, must be rejected. Not only did colonial education fail to prepare young Tanzanians for the service of their country,[44] but "it emphasized and encouraged the individualistic instincts of mankind, instead of his co-operative instincts. It led to the possession of individual material wealth being the major criterion of social merit and worth."[45] In effect this was replacing traditional tribal values with British values.[46]

With nearly 20 percent of the government's revenue being spent on education, Nyerere is concerned that the educational system uphold the principles of socialism and self-reliance of the Arusha Declaration and not develop a new class of exploiters who see their education in terms of more money and power.[47] Tanzanian education must promote the social goals of living and working together for the common good. It must inculcate a sense of commitment and service to the total community. And it must counteract the temptation to intellectual arrogance which has no place in a society of equal citizens.[48] "Education for a selected few must be education for service to the many. There can be no other justification for taxing the many to give education to only a few."[49]

Besides the social values of *Ujamaa*, Tanzanian education must develop self-reliant citizens. At the time of the Arusha Declaration only 13 percent of the children finishing primary school could attend secondary school. The other 87 percent not only finished school with a sense of failure but they also finished without learning any useful skills.[50] The curriculum according to the new policy must be geared to the needs of the vast majority who will not attend secondary school.[51] Furthermore, the new policy wants schools as a real part of the society and economy, which means the schools themselves must practice the precept of self-reliance.[52] In an address to headmasters, Nyerere clarified what he meant by education for self-reliance.[53]

It must be clear we are not introducing a new subject called "self-reliance," or "socialism" into the school curriculum. . . . What we are aiming at is converting our schools into economic communities as well as educational communities; in other words, into educational communities which are to a considerable extent self-reliant (financially). . . . It is while they are practicing this self-reliance—and as an important by-product of it—that the pupils will learn new skills which are relevant to their future life, and adopt a realistic attitude to getting their hands dirty by physical labor. . . . They will learn by doing. . . . [54]

In his address celebrating the tenth anniversary of independence Nyerere noted that the stress in education was on secondary education in order to train people to fill government jobs. Only 52 percent were able to attend primary schools.[55] Universal primary education was planned for 1985. Now from enormous pressure from certain elements within TANU the goal of universal primary education is set for 1977.[56]

Rural Socialism

The Arusha Declaration of 1967 stated that the basis of Tanzanian development would be agriculture. Seven months later President Nyerere published a policy booklet, *Socialism and Rural Development*, explaining the need for farming to be done in *Ujamaa* villages rather than individual farms or large corporation plantations. The individual farmers cannot hope to grow by themselves enough crops to rise above the subsistence level. Large plantations, with the aid of skilled managers and machinery, are economically profitable but they defeat goals of socialism by creating a "rural proletariat." By living in *Ujamaa* villages the people with technical and financial help from the government would be able to increase their output and thereby raise their standard of living without sacrificing the goals of socialism.

When Tanganyika was made independent in 1961, the vast majority of citizens were subsistence farmers working their own small farms with no implement beyond a hoe—the output depending entirely on the weather and the health of the individual farmer. "The net result was a life of poverty and insecurity for the masses of the people, while a small number of foreign companies or private farmers from Europe were obtaining a comfortable life—often at the expense of their exploited workers."[57]

In his first inaugural address Nyerere expressed the need to move into village communities. This was the only way the government could begin to provide drinking water, tractors, electricity, schools, and hospitals. But it wasn't until the Arusha Declaration that the government took a radically new step in committing itself to an extensive development program for the peasant farmers.[58]

The new philosophy meant a departure from the traditional post-colonial economics on the Kenya or Ivory Coast pattern. Resources would not be concentrated on those sectors that were doing best, or which showed the greatest export potential, or which led to the fastest accumulation of private capital, but would be an attempt to unleash the energies of the underemployed majority of the population in the countryside.[59]

This policy is in keeping with Nyerere's ideal of not sacrificing the social objectives of "no class system" for an economic objective of "production increase."[60] In fact, Nyerere sees the program of *Ujamaa* villages as a revival of traditional tribal life in which goods were held in common and no one went hungry while another had an abundance of food.[61]

Nyerere envisions an agricultural organization of cooperative living and working for the good of all.[62] The first step is to persuade people to move their houses into a single village. The second step is to persuade a village group of approximately ten families to start a small communal plot which they would work jointly, and at harvest time would share in the proceeds according to the work each has done.[63] The final stage develops only after the people have confidence in the idea. In this stage the people would have a community farm and invest all their effort in it.[64] The harvest would be divided according to the work each one did, thus preventing lazy people from exploiting the more industrious.[65]

As can be seen, the emphasis is on gradualism and persuasion and not force. Nyerere recognizes that such communities depend on a willingness to cooperate and an understanding of the different kind of life which can be obtained by the participants if they work together. Furthermore, experience in other countries had shown that force and intimidation would not work.[66]

Despite Nyerere's great personal effort to persuade peasants to move into villages, the *Ujamaa* village program after seven years could claim less than 20 percent of the rural population. In early 1974 the decision was made to move the entire rural population into villages by 1976, thus making the new adage "force if persuasion fails."[67] In the spring of 1975 Prime Minister Kawawa announced that 10 million of the nearly 15 million population were living in *Ujamaa* villages, with another 3.5 million on waiting lists to be moved into newly planned villages.[68]

So far *Ujamaa* villages have contributed little to Tanzania's economic growth but they have not been a burden on the government.[69] Nyerere explains, however, that it is a mistake to compare the standard of living of the past with the present standard of living solely in terms of economic growth.

For in reality every man has two pockets: one holds the money which he is free to spend on his private needs at his own will; the other holds his share of the public services. Thus, even if there has been no change over ten years in the amount a man has to spend on food, clothes, shelter and recreation each month, his standard of living may have improved. This will happen if, at the end of the period, but not at the beginning, he can go to a hospital or dispensary, or his children can go to school, or he himself to adult classes, or he can travel to work to get goods brought to him more safely, comfortably and cheaply, and so on. All these things are an improvement in condition of life—and are more vital to it than extra consumer goods like watches, carpets, or cars.[70]

Socio-politically the *Ujamaa* village program enabled the peasant farmers to improve their living standard without being exploited by landowners, that is, without the establishing of a class system of landowners and landless.[71] This socio-political aspect of rural development is essential if Tanzania is to be committed to socialism.[72] Rural life must be built on the basis of human equality. "There must be no masters and servants, but just people working together for the good of all and thus their own good."[73]

In the *Ujamaa* villages the people become their own masters, deciding for themselves what they will do. Every decision that relates exclusively to the village must be decided by the village and no one else. This, according to Nyerere, is the most important part of the *Ujamaa* living because it is building a socialist way of life.[74] "A nation of such villages would be a socialist nation."[75] Whether or not Tanzania can become such a nation, Nyerere says, it is too early to tell.[76]

National Self-Reliance

The first responsibility of the Tanzanian government is to protect its independence and its freedom to determine its own policies, both internally and externally.[77] Because Tanzania is economically poor, richer countries have attempted to use monetary aid as a political weapon to force Tanzania to take certain political positions. Nyerere has been criticized for refusing monetary gain for the sake of principle. The cases of West Germany and Britain are the most noted.

Prior to 1964 Tanganyika had diplomatic relations with West Germany, and Zanzibar with East Germany. After the union in April 1964 the new Republic of Tanzania wanted to recognize West Germany but allow East Germany to have a consulate general's office in Dar es Salaam. This compromise was used by Egypt and found acceptable to both Germanies. West Germany withdrew part of its aid and threatened to withdraw the rest if Tanzania did not change its policy. Nyerere, in turn, canceled all aid from West Germany. "The Government had little alternative if it was to uphold the dignity of our independent country."[78] This defense of principle perhaps cost Tanzania "many millions of pounds."[79]

A similar defense of principle occurred in June 1965 when Tanzania broke diplomatic relations with Britain over the Rhodesia issue. This decision cost Tanzania a 7.5 million pound interest-free loan.[80]

Part of the drive for political independence is the policy of nonalignment adopted immediately after independence in 1961.[81] This is consistent with the doctrine of self-reliance in that Tanzania, while avoiding political isolationism, is determined to rely on itself and not others.[82] Prior to independence Tanganyika was not nonaligned; it was part of the Western bloc, having no contact with the Eastern bloc. "If we are to be non-aligned we have to make friends with Eastern bloc countries. . . . "[83] Nyerere claims this does not mean Tanzania is "anti-West."[84] "We wish to live in friendship with all states and all peoples. . . . We shall not allow anyone to choose any of our friends or enemies for us."[85]

The Arusha Declaration was an admission that Tanzania was wrong to rely on foreign investment for development.[86] It was a mistake for two reasons: There was not enough money available, and even if there were enough, Tanzania would be sacrificing its independence.[87] Actually the foreign aid was only about one dollar per capita per year.[88] This aid had the bad effects of encouraging foreign political interference,[89] as well as promoting capitalism at home.[90]

To be self-reliant and free from foreign interference, Nyerere saw that a great change in the economic well-being was needed.[91] "A nation's real freedom depends on its capacity to do things, not on the legal rights conferred by its internationally recognized sovereignty."[92] This is the reasoning behind the new emphasis on development through agriculture.[93]

In reality an unexpected two-year drought, a quadrupling of the price of imported oil, and the corresponding impact of inflation have hindered the efforts toward economic independence. In 1975 two-thirds of Tanzania's total budget was financed by foreign loans and grants.[94]

Pan-Africanism. George Padmore spoke of Pan-Africanism as government of Africans, by Africans, and for Africans which would be characterized by democratic socialism and state control of production and distribution.[95] Padmore envisioned a "United States of Africa" to ensure equality and freedom for all.[96] Almost all African socialists in various countries have followed Padmore's continental perspective as an essential for achieving progress.[97]

Nyerere has been a strong promoter of Pan-Africanism. To implement a supranational organization Nyerere has taken a pragmatic position of avoiding any preconceived political structure to embody the Pan-African ideal.[98] He has cautioned against strong nationalism.[99] He has advocated that the present boundaries, the result of arbitrary colonial decisions, lose their significance and become merely demarcations of administrative areas within larger units. He has condemned one African state fighting against another as the most real danger to Africa.[100] He has warned about the futility of inter-African economic competition.[101] He has worked gradually for Pan-Africanism by promoting the East African Community and the Organization of African Unity.[102] The only solution is for all African countries to unite. "Together we are too big for even the giants to pick up and use."[103] Not to unite will lead to a further breakup into smaller units perhaps based on tribes. Such division makes another period of foreign domination inevitable.[104]

In an interview on the tenth anniversary of independence, Nyerere reflected on the development of his thought on a realistic approach to African unity:

Well, at one time we were—when I say "we" I mean a number of African leaders—we were very ambitious; and we hoped that we would move the continent more quickly to greater unity. I think we should admit that we have not succeeded. If we are going to move to unity in Africa at all, it's going to be a slow process. And I think we probably have to admit that we have to work regionally. We have to move as we are trying to move in East Africa. And I think this kind of movement should take place all over the continent; and perhaps that will be the right way to move towards greater unity.[105]

The 1974 Pan-African Congress, the first since 1945, was highlighted by its united support for the liberation of Africa from both colonialism and neo-colonialism. In giving the opening address Nyerere reiterated his theme of establishing just societies. "If it is not the case [that free black countries are just societies], can we remain quiet and still demand support for our fight against racism and oppression when it is practiced against us by others?"[106]

NOTES

1. Julius K. Nyerere, *Freedom and Unity* (Dar es Salaam: Oxford University Press, 1966), p. 235.

2. Joan E. Wicken, "The United Republic of Tanzania," *Africa Handbook*, ed. Colin Legum (Middlesex, Eng.: Penguin Books, 1969), p. 190. The International Monetary Fund (*Survey of African Economics*) listed the per capita income of mainland Tanzania in 1966 as 25 pounds (approximately 60 dollars) against 29 pounds on Zanzibar. Bienen estimates that nonmonetary subsistence farming figures for one-third of the per capita income. He also estimates that the native African Tanzanian has a per capita money income of between 17 and 22 dollars a year. Tanzania is in the lower third of African countries in per capita income (*Party Transformation and Economic Development*, pp. 266–67).

3. Wicken, *Tanzania*, p. 191.

4. Nyerere writes: "The total wealth available to be spent by the people of Tanzania during one year is much less than the amount which the Government of the United States of America spends on its military forces in one week" (*Freedom and Socialism* [Dar es Salaam: Oxford University Press, 1968], p. 397).

5. *AID: African Regional* (Washington, D.C.: U.S. Government Printing Office), pp. 7–10.

6. Nyerere, *Freedom and Socialism*, p. 397.

7. Nyerere, *Freedom and Unity*, p. 15.

8. Ibid., p. 235.

9. Nyerere, *Freedom and Socialism*, p. 134.

10. Nyerere, *Freedom and Unity*, p. 114.

11. Ibid., p. 235.

12. Ibid., p. 240.

13. Julius K. Nyerere, *Ujamaa: Essays on Socialism* (Dar es Salaam: Oxford University Press, 1968), p. 23.

14. Nyerere, *Freedom and Socialism*, p. 167.

15. Nyerere, *Ujamaa: Essays on Socialism*, p. 25.

16. Julius K. Nyerere, "Speech to the Maryknoll Congress in New York" (Dar es Salaam: Government Printer, 1970), p. 12.

17. Nyerere, *Ujamaa: Essays on Socialism*, p. 23.

18. Nyerere, *Freedom and Unity*, p. 178.

19. Seidman explains Nyerere's concern for social and political goals: "Development theory, by its very nature, cannot be positivistic. It cannot exclude value judgements since it implicitly incorporates the concept of the goal of the development process: economic development must be going in *some* direction (or standing still which is itself a direction); the determination as to whether that direction is desirable implies a value judgement. If the goal is not explicit, it will nevertheless be implicit in any development theory ("Comparative Development Strategies in East Africa," *East Africa Journal* 7 [April 1970]: 14).

20. Specific economic goals can be found in *Tanzania: Second Five Year Plan for Economic and Social Development, 1 July 1969—30 June 1974* (Dar es Salaam: Government Printer, 1969).

21. Ibid., vol. I, p. 2: "Speech by the President, Mwalimu Julius K. Nyerere to the TANU Conference on May 28, 1969."

22. Nyerere, *Ujamaa: Essays on Socialism*, p. 165.

23. As Seidman explains: "Only the State can mobilize the capital and manpower resources to reshape existing institutional patterns in the manner required to reallocate resources to attain the desired goals. A political corollary appears to be that the State may only be expected to take the necessary measures in this direction if the political apparatus is so designed as to ensure that it represents the interests of the majority of the poorer peasants . . . " ("Development Strategies," p. 18).

24. Goran Hyden, "Planning in Tanzania: Lessons of Experience," *East Africa Journal* 6 (October 1969), 10:0.17.

25. Lionel Cliffe, "Tanzania: Socialist Transformation and Party Development," *The African Review* 1 (March 1971): 121.

26. Cliffe pinpoints the toughest problem for the government. It is what agency will persuade,

encourage, and guide the rural populations so that they will revolutionize their modes of production and their way of living ("Tanzania," p. 122).

27. Nyerere, *Ujamaa: Essays on Socialism*, pp. 26–27.

28. Ibid., p. 28.

29. Ibid., p. 33.

30. Ibid., p. 34.

31. Ibid., pp. 151–52.

32. See chapter 15.

33. A less gradual approach to development can be seen in a report of some economists from Nairobi: "While we accept that rapid Kenyanization now and in the coming years may require some restriction on competition between citizens, we see no reason why the Government should not follow a policy of giving maximum opportunity to and encouraging maximum competition among citizens themselves" (Aldington et al., "The Economics of Kenyanization: Some Professional Comments and Recommendations, *East Africa Journal*, March 1968, p. 21).

34. Nyerere, *Ujamaa: Essays on Socialism*, p. 51.

35. Ibid., p. 97.

36. Ibid., p. 150.

37. Ibid., p. 97.

38. Ibid., p. 151.

39. Ibid., p. 97.

40. Ibid., p. 26.

41. Ibid., p. 51.

42. Ibid., p. 143.

43. Ibid., p. 46.

44. Nyerere explains the inadequacy of colonial education: "So little education had been provided that in December, 1961, we had too few people with the necessary educational qualifications even to man the administration of Government as it was then, much less undertake the big economic and social development work which was essential. Neither was the school population in 1961 large enough to allow for any expectation that this situation would be speedily corrected. On top of that, education was based upon race, whereas the whole moral case of the independence movement had been based upon a rejection of racial distinctions" (*Education for Self-Reliance* [Dar es Salaam: Government Printer, 1967], pp. 47–48).

45. Ibid., p. 47.

46. Ibid.

47. Ibid., p. 44.

48. Ibid., p. 52. Van de Laar explains the problems of British schooling: "Whatever the merits of the existing educational system, moulded after British patterns, it is unmistakable that it has not contributed to imbuing in pupils and students egalitarian attitudes. Nor is their social responsibility very great. Education in well-catered-for boarding schools, the factual selection and continual admonishments as the 'leaders of tomorrow' have only sharpened the sense of indispensability, exclusiveness and power in the selected" ("Arusha: Before and After," *East Africa Journal*, November 1968, p. 18).

49. Nyerere, *Ujamaa: Essays on Socialism*, p. 62.

50. Ibid., p. 54.

51. Ibid., p. 63.

52. Ibid., p. 64.

53. Resnick, in "Manpower Development in Tanzania," *The Journal of Modern African Studies* (1967), points out that Tanzania is one of the few African countries that has an educational system geared for supplying the manpower requirements of the nation (p. 107).

54. Nyerere, *Freedom and Socialism*, pp. 410–11.

55. Julius K. Nyerere, *Freedom and Development* (London: Oxford University Press, 1973), p. 297.

56. David Ottaway, "Tanzania: Peasants on the Move," *Washington Post*, May 18, 1975.

57. Julius K. Nyerere, *Tanzania Ten Years after Independence* (Dar es Salaam: TANU General Conference, 1971), p. 2.

58. Friedland and Rosberg argue that this stress on village development is the most characteristic feature of Nyerere's socialism which distinguishes his from other African socialisms

210   *Part Two:* Ujamaa *Socialism*

("Introduction," *African Socialism*, ed. William H. Friedland and Carl G. Rosberg, Jr. [Stanford: Stanford University Press, 1964], p. 3).

59. Alan Rake, "Brave Economic Experiment," *The Financial Times* (London), December 9, 1971, p. 28.
60. Nyerere, *Freedom and Unity*, p. 237.
61. Nyerere, *Ujamaa: Essays on Socialism*, p. 107.
62. Ibid., p. 124.
63. Ibid., p. 132.
64. Ibid., p. 135.
65. Ibid.
66. Nyerere, *Freedom and Development*, p. 190.
67. Ottaway, "Peasants on the Move."
68. David Ottaway, "Letter from Tanzania," *Washington Post*, May 24, 1975.
69. Rake, "Brave Economic Experiment," p. 28.
70. Nyerere, *Tanzania Ten Years after Independence*, pp. 22–23.
71. Nyerere, *Ujamaa: Essays on Socialism*, pp. 117–18.
72. Ibid., p. 118.
73. Ibid., p. 119.
74. Ibid., p. 136.
75. Ibid., p. 127.
76. Nyerere, *Tanzania Ten Years after Independence*, p. 41.
77. Nyerere, *Freedom and Socialism*, p. 189.
78. Ibid., p. 190.
79. Ibid., p. 202.
80. Ibid., p. 203.
81. Friedland and Rosberg explain that nonalignment is characteristic of African socialism in order that it may reject political domination by either East or West (*African Socialism*, p. 9).
82. Nyerere, *Ujamaa: Essays on Socialism*, p. 99.
83. Nyerere, *Freedom and Socialism*, p. 51.
84. Ibid., p. 368.
85. Ibid., p. 369.
86. In *Who Controls Industry in Kenya?* it is explained that all modern countries are interdependent economically. What is usually meant by "economic independence" is "economic viability" or "economic self-determination." "What is at stake is that a country should be able to deal with others from a position of strength" (p. 223).
87. Nyerere, *Ujamaa: Essays on Socialism*, pp. 22–25.
88. Henry Bienen, *Tanzania: Party Transformation and Economic Development* (Princeton: Princeton University Press, 1967), p. 413.
89. Nyerere, *Ujamaa: Essays on Socialism*, p. 25.
90. Bienen, *Party Transformation*, p. 414.
91. Julius K. Nyerere, "Stability and Change in Africa" (Toronto University, October 2, 1969), *Vital Speeches* 36 (November 1, 1969): 48.
92. Nyerere, *Tanzania Ten Years after Independence*, p. 1.
93. Nyerere, *Ujamaa: Essays on Socialism*, p. 93.
94. Ottaway, "Peasants on the Move."
95. George Padmore, *Pan-Africanism or Communism?* (London: Dobson, 1956), pp. 21–22.
96. Colin Legum, "The Roots of Pan-Africanism," *Africa Handbook*, p. 553.
97. Dorothy Nelkin, "Socialist Sources of Pan-African Ideology," *African Socialism*, p. 72.
98. Ibid., p. 78.
99. Nyerere, *Freedom and Socialism*, p. 212.
100. Ibid., pp. 220–21.
101. Ibid., p. 210.
102. Ibid., p. 193.
103. Ibid., p. 219.
104. Ibid., p. 209.
105. Peter Enahoro, "African Socialism" (an interview with Julius Nyerere), *Africa* 6 (1972): 61.
106. Magaga Alot, "Dar es Salaam Notebook," *African Affairs* (August 1974), p. 17.

CHAPTER 19

THE STARTING POINT
FOR THE CHURCH'S
SOCIAL TEACHINGS

Having examined the principles and policies of Nyerere's approach to a just society, the plan now is to analyze the Catholic Church's teaching on social justice in order to have some kind of standard for comparison. This is not to say that the Church has all the answers for concrete situations or that the Church is the leading agent of social change. Rather it is an investigation of how the Church, reflecting on the gospel and its own tradition, establishes general and middle principles as some kind of guide for evaluating concrete activity.

Signs of the Times

Pope John XXIII in convoking the Vatican Council II on December 25, 1961, used the phrase "the signs of the times."[1] This biblical phrase was to become the focal point for a new era of Church teaching on social issues.[2] "Signs" represented a new leap forward, a leap which does not break continuity with the past.[3] To appreciate this new leap forward it is necessary first to take a glance at the past.

Modern social teaching of the Catholic Church begins in 1891 with the revolutionary encyclical *Rerum Novarum.*[4] Written in an era when liberal capitalism was flourishing, the encyclical was the first time the Church specifically treated the cause of "working-men, surrendered, isolated and helpless, to the hardheartedness of employers and the greed of unchecked competition."[5] Rejecting a solution from the extremes of liberalism and socialism, Leo XIII based his teachings on principles rooted in the natural law. Stressing the dignity of the worker as a human being, the pope proclaimed certain basic rights, which included: the right of the workers to a just wage; the right of the workers to organize for group protection; the right and necessity of private ownership for all; and the right of the state to intervene in private industry for the protection of workers. In *Rerum Novarum* "for the first time [there] was a complete synthesis of social principles, formulated as to be of permanent value to Christendom."[6] Although it has been updated by subsequent papal writings, *Rerum Novarum* remains the Magna Carta of the Church's social teaching.[7]

The many debates in the formulation of Vatican II's Pastoral Constitution *Gaudium et Spes* give us an insight into the new trends in the development of the Church's teaching on social problems. Beginning with the seventy schemata of the conciliar preparatory commissions, it was clear that Vatican Council II was going to be almost exclusively a domestic affair of the Church.[8] The impulse for change came, according to Charles Moeller, from a Latin American Council Father, Dom Helder Camara, who asked during the first session of the Council: "Are we to spend our whole time discussing internal Church problems while two-thirds of mankind is dying of hunger? What have we to say on the problem of underdevelopment? Will the Council express its concern about the great problems of mankind?"[9]

Toward the end of the same session of the Council (December 4, 1962) Cardinal Suenens suggested that the Fathers "examine the Church in her dialogue with the world . . . so that the world might better understand and accept the Church, so that Christ might more and more become, for present-day man, 'the way, the truth, the life.' "[10]

This motion was supported by Cardinals Montini, Lercaro, Lienart, and Leger and paved the way for Schema 17 (later to be called Schema 13, or the Pastoral Constitution on the Church in the Modern World, or simply *Gaudium et Spes*).[11]

The first drafts of Schema 17 (Text 2 and the Malines text) did little more than compile the various teachings of the social encyclicals of the previous fifty years.[12] The Malines text, while very scholarly and precise, was rejected because "it was too dry, too didactic, too wrapped up in theological terminology to be understood by the uninitiated."[13] This rejection brought to focus the aim of Schema 17.

The real question was not to promulgate a social doctrine, a catalogue of principles to be applied to a given situation; the real question was to delineate the root principles and the basic laws governing the existence of the Church in the world and in history.[14]

The next draft (first Zurich text), it was decided, would not begin from a theological position but, rather, from gospel truths laying stress on reading the signs of the times.[15] The expression "signs of the times" which formed the basis of the pastoral constitution was defined by Bishop McGrath's subcommission as: "The phenomena which occur so frequently and so pervasively that they characterize a given epoch and seem to express the needs and aspirations of contemporary humanity."[16]

These signs of the times include socialization; advances in technology and the behavioral sciences; the awareness of inequalities and the imbalances among peoples and nations; psychological, moral, and religious changes; the desire of all peoples to share in the benefits of culture and the goods of the earth; and a thirst for a full and free life worthy of man.[17] These general phenomena are "signs" in that they bring about a new sense of awareness in human history. The primary thing is not the phenomenon itself but the flash of awareness it launches, the energies and hopes of a human community it fans, the sign of a new leap forward for humanity.[18]

The most authoritative commentary on the concept of the signs of the times is an address of Pope Paul on April 16, 1969, in which he treats this question exclusively. He points out that the phrase "signs of the times" has now taken on a new meaning, that of the theological interpretation of contemporary history.[19] The pope explains that there have always been attempts to discover the divine plan in human history, but such syntheses, often of questionable value, were made after the events are past. "Now, on the contrary, modern thought is invited to decipher in historical reality, particularly the present, the 'signs,' that is, the indications of a meaning that goes further than the one recorded by the passive observer."[20] The "signs" give us some indication of the workings of providence and the needs of apostolic action.[21] The discovery of these signs of the times is a fact of Christian conscience.[22]

It is the duty of the Church to scrutinize the signs of the times and to interpret them in the light of the gospel in order to respond to the perennial questions people ask about this life and the life to come.[23] This approach has become the basis of a new methodology developing in the Church toward social problems. Recent papal teachings have elaborated on values presupposed by this new method.

First, the new method toward the problems in the world is characterized by an attitude of humility. Gone is the paternalism of *Quadragesimo Anno* in which the social doctrine of the Church is presented as the exclusive dominion of the hierarchy and in which the laity adapt to modern needs "the unchanging and unchangeable doctrine of the Church."[24] Rather, today the Church, guided by the ideal of Christ, joins with all humankind in search for the answers to the complex questions of our times.[25] In his apostolic letter *Octogesima Adveniens*, Pope Paul has explicitly stated that it is neither his ambition nor his mission to make a universally valid solution for all the problems facing humankind. Rather, it is the duty of Christians and all people of goodwill "to discern the options and commitments which are called for in order to bring about the social, political and economic changes seen in many cases to be urgently needed."[26]

An indication of this human search for social justice is that, beginning with the encyclical *Pacem in Terris*, all social teachings have been addressed not just to the members of the Church but to all people of goodwill. Furthermore, beginning with *Gaudium et Spes*, which adopted the suggestion of Monsignor Pavan, all Church social teaching has begun by first identifying the concern of the Church for the problems facing humankind instead of first offering solutions.[27] "The Christian must turn to these new perceptions in order to take on responsibility, together with the rest of men, for a destiny which from now on is shared by all."[28]

In searching for answers for the problems of the times secular pursuits are seen as having a value in themselves.[29] Yves Congar explains the significance of this point of view:

It is plainly a matter of recognizing the historicity of the world and of the Church herself which, though separated from the world, is also bound to it. The events of the world must have an echo in the Church, at least to the extent that they raise questions for her. She will not have adequate and ready-made answers for every question, but will realize that the answers of a given moment cannot simply be repeated over and over again. When we speak of signs of the times we are saying that the times themselves have something to teach us.[30]

Gaudium et Spes declares that humanity has passed from a static concept of reality to a more dynamic, evolutionary one. Consequently a new analysis of the problems of mankind is called for.[31] Pope Paul's encyclical *Populorum Progressio*, following this line of thinking, is future orientated.[32] Similarly, *Octogesima Adveniens* is more concerned with the future than with the past; more with humankind than with the internal Church. This dynamism can be seen in that the term "Church doctrine"—a static concept based on logical deductions from a universal and immutable Christian philosophy—has been replaced by "Church teaching," a more forward-looking, dynamic term.[33]

This dynamism can also be seen in the approach to social questions. For example, in *Populorum Progressio* and especially in *Octogesima Adveniens* we can see the traditional notion of social questions based on the conflict of capital and labor surpassed by social questions seen in "the wider context of a new civilization."[34]

Octogesima Adveniens has stressed the diversity of the problems, many of which are restricted to certain parts of the world, and yet all are the concern of everyone.

Some new problems include: the many evils of rapid urbanization (new forms of exploitation, dehumanizing living conditions, lack of employment, the new loneliness of an anonymous crowd, drugs and eroticism); the role of youth; the rights of women; the various groups on the fringe of society; the victims of discrimination; the responsibility of social communications; ecology.[35] As in *Populorum Progressio* Pope Paul has presented these problems not with specific solutions in mind but, rather, with a view of presenting a method for solving them.[36]

This method analyzes the historical situation objectively. Then it interprets the problems from a historical and technical viewpoint and also from the light of the gospels and Church teaching.[37] The choice to be made will necessarily be characterized by a pluralism of options. "In concrete situations, and taking account of solidarity of each person's life, one must recognize a legitimate variety of possible options."[38]

Pope Paul has cautioned against four methods in discerning the signs of the times. The first warning is against a superficial or artificial superimposing of religious thought on the signs of the times by a forced comparison of faith in order to be able to see a step forward for the kingdom of God in the human kingdom. Rather, we have "to see where these cases postulate, by their intrinsic dynamism, by their very obscurity, sometimes by their immorality, a ray of faith, an evangelical word, that classifies them, that redeems them."[39]

A second danger is a charismatic prophetism that may degenerate into bigoted fancy, conferring miraculous interpretations on chance and often insignificant coincidences. Not everyone has the gift of wise insight.[40] A third caution is against a purely phenomenological observation of the facts which may happen when the facts are surveyed and classified in a purely technical and sociological manner. The signs cannot be interpreted independently of a moral criterion.[41] A final warning is against considering the historical aspect of the signs of the times as predominant without looking to the future.[42]

In showing concern for the methodology, the Holy Father wishes to emphasize the importance of the signs of the times "which are to bestow sagacity and modernity on our Christian judgement and our apostolate in the midst of the flood of transformations sweeping over the contemporary world."[43]

Socialization

John XXIII singled out socialization as one of the most characteristic marks of our times.[44] Since it is a term that has been used in many ways, Pope John said precisely what he meant. Socialization is the ensemble of "those mutual relationships, daily on the increase, which have introduced into the lives and activities of men, a close network of social bonds, generally respected by public and private law."[45] Socialization is not a theory but a socio-cultural phenomenon, an observable fact.[46] It has been caused mainly by scientific and technical progress, greater productive efficiency, and a higher standard of living.[47]

Socialization has many advantages. "It makes it possible for the individual to exercise many of his personal rights, especially those which we call economic and social and which pertain to the necessities of life, health care, education on a more extensive and improved basis, a more thorough professional training, housing, work, and suitable leisure and recreation."[48] These benefits, furthermore, are being extended to people all over the world through the new developments in communication.

At the same time these increased social relations also infringe on a person's freedom of action. This does not reduce the person to a mere automaton, because the growth of social life is not a product of natural forces working by blind impulse.[49] The aspect of the fact of socialization that Pope John wants to make clear is that "the development of these social relationships, therefore, can and ought to be realized in a way best calculated to promote its inherent advantages and to preclude, or at least diminish, its attendant disadvantages."[50]

Gaudium et Spes reiterated Pope John's teaching on socialization, but whereas *Mater et Magistra* judges it favorably, the Council, concerned about possible dangers, does not express an evaluative opinion.[51] Further, while *Mater et Magistra* considered socialization primarily under its phenomenological or existential aspect, *Gaudium et Spes* treats socialization under a more fundamental and essential aspect of the actual causes of socio-cultural development.[52] "What is the meaning and value of this feverish activity? . . . To the achievement of what goal are the strivings of individuals and societies heading?"[53] In offering a solution to the essential aspect of socialization, the Council implies a dynamic view of history.[54] "The Pastoral Constitution makes it clear that the Christian who believes in the resurrection of the body and the transfiguration of the world, may also believe in the consummation of technical achievement in the transformed world and in the fulfillment, in the communion of saints, of the socialization brought about by technology."[55]

Socialization, then, is the name of a process by which the Church recognizes that human existence in society is historical, developing, and has a direction. The increasing social and institutional configurations are seen as more and more important to preserve human dignity in general and basic human rights in particular.

Human Dignity

In the debates during the drawing up of *Gaudium et Spes*, Monsignor Haubtmann described the orientation of the schema. "It starts off with truths which, though they belong to the order of faith, are commonly held by non-Christians; then it moves on to the deepest truths of faith that are summed up in Christ the Lord."[56]

Following this approach, *Gaudium et Spes* takes as a basic assumption the dignity of the human person because this has a wider acceptance than a doctrine of the person stated in religious terms. "According to the almost unanimous opinion of believers and unbelievers alike, all things on earth should be related to man as their center and crown."[57] This is immediately followed by a phenomenological description of man, which is more in accord with history, rather than a philosophical doctrine of man along the lines of the neoscholastic tradition, which was thought to be too static.[58] Then from a scriptural perspective man's dignity is seen in that he is made in the image of God.[59] But the fullness of our human dignity comes in our identification in Christ. "He has lavished life upon us so that, as sons in the Son, we can cry out in the Spirit: Abba, Father."[60]

Gaudium et Spes, defining man first of all by his responsibility to others, is permeated with the consequences of our human dignity. "Everyone must consider his every neighbor without exception as another self, taking into account first of all his life and the means necessary to living it with dignity, so as not to imitate the rich man who had no concern for the poor man Lazarus."[61] The dignity of man requires that he have decent housing,[62] not be discriminated against, and share in the benefits of culture.[63] Human dignity requires that a person be free to choose.[64] This includes freedom of conscience. "For man has in his heart a law written by God. To obey it is the very dignity of man; according to it he will be judged."[65] Dignity means respect for the human body.[66] The equality of human dignity demands that excessive economic and social differences between the members of the human family be eliminated.[67] Human dignity is violated by subhuman living conditions, arbitrary imprisonment, deportation, slavery, prostitution, the selling of women and children, and exploitative working conditions.[68] "There is a growing awareness of the exalted dignity proper to the human person, since he stands above all things, and his rights and duties are universal and inviolable."[69] This is an incentive for a better political order;[70] the basis of economic and social life;[71] a necessity for mutual respect;[72] and an essential for peace.[73] A person never loses his dignity as a person even when in error.[74] Human dignity is the foundation of religious freedom.[75]

Finally it was the expressed purpose of *Gaudium et Spes* to look for assistance from believers and unbelievers alike in order "to help men gain a sharper insight into their full destiny, so that they can fashion the world more to man's surpassing dignity, search for a brotherhood which is universal and more deeply rooted, and meet the urgencies of our age with a gallant and unified effort born of love."[76]

The stress on human dignity has deepened the value of human activity, giving it a value in itself.[77] The norm of human activity is that it should harmonize with the genuine good of the human race, and allow persons as individuals and as members of society to pursue their total vocation and fulfill it.[78] For the person of faith, even the most ordinary everyday activities have taken on a new importance because the person, created in God's image, has received a mandate to subject to himself the earth and all it contains, and to govern the world with justice and holiness.[79]

Human Rights

The first systematic declaration on human rights by the magisterium is Pope John's encyclical *Pacem in Terris.*[80] Most of these teachings can be traced back to the teachings of Pius XII.[81] Pope John gives the foundation for human rights in the following principle:

Each individual man is truly a person. His is a nature that is endowed with intelligence and free will. As such he has rights and duties, which together flow from his nature. These rights and duties are universal and inviolable, and therefore altogether inalienable.[82]

Man has the right to live, including the means necessary for the proper development of life, namely, food, clothing, shelter, medical care, rest, and necessary social services.[83] Man has the natural right to a good name, to freedom of speech, press, and choice of profession. He has a right to be informed accurately about public events.[84] He has a right to share in the benefits of culture, including a good general education.[85] "Also among man's rights is that of being able to worship God in accordance with the right dictates of his own conscience, and to profess his religion both in private and in public."[86]

Man has a right to found a family[87] and to support and educate the children.[88] Man has the right to work with both initiative and responsibility.[89] He has a natural right to ownership of private property, including the means of production.[90] Because he is by nature social, man has the right of meeting and association.[91] He has the right to emigrate and immigrate.[92] By his personal dignity man has a right to an active part in public life,[93] and to legal protection of his rights, which must be effective, unbiased, and strictly just.[94]

Gaudium et Spes reaffirmed these rights. As human interdependence grows "there is a growing awareness of the exalted dignity proper to the human person, since he stands above all things, and his rights and duties are universal and inviolable."[95] It is the duty of the Church to protect and support these rights.[96] Confronting the difficulties stemming from rapid population growth, the Council stressed the right to marry and have children as inalienable.[97]

The Roman Synod of Bishops, following the teaching of *Populorum Progressio,* emphasized the right to development.

This aspiring to justice asserts itself in advancing the threshold at which begins a consciousness of enhancement of personal worth with both regard to the whole of man and the whole of mankind. The right to development must be seen as a dynamic interpenetration of all those fundamental human rights upon which the aspiration of individuals and nations are based.[98]

The Synod has also called for all governments to ratify the United Nations Declaration on Human Rights.[99]

The 1974 Roman Synod of Bishops called attention in some detail to certain rights most threatened today: the right to life; the right to eat; socio-economic rights; politico-cultural rights; and the right to religious liberty. All these rights are based on human dignity, which is "rooted in the image and reflection of God in each of us."[100] This 1974 Synod thus continues the process of articulating more clearly human rights in our day.

Duties of the Person

Pacem in Terris, reasoning from the natural law, sees a person's duties as following from his rights. "The possession of rights involves the duty of implementing those rights, for they are the expression of a man's personal dignity. And the possession of rights also involves their recognition and respect by other people."[101] It follows that a person has the duty to respect the rights of others.[102]

The right a person has to provide a livelihood for himself and his family imposes on him the duty to work.[103]

The right to freedom gives every person the duty to act on his own initiative, conviction, and sense of responsibility.[104] The right to live involves the duty to preserve one's life; the right to a decent standard of living, the duty to live in a becoming fashion; the right to be free to seek out the truth, the duty to devote oneself to an ever deeper and wider search for it.[105]

In speaking about man's duties, the Council addresses itself to Christians. The Fathers warn Christians against shirking their earthly responsibilities. "They are mistaken . . . who think that religion consists in acts of worship alone and in the discharge of certain moral obligations, and who imagine they can plunge themselves into earthly affairs in such a way as to imply that these are altogether divorced from religious life."[106] The Fathers go on to warn that the Christian who neglects his temporal duties neglects his duties toward his neighbor and even God.[107]

Populorum Progressio expresses man's duties in terms of his vocation to self-fulfillment. "Endowed with intelligence and freedom, he is responsible for his fulfillment as he is for his salvation."[108] Self-fulfillment is not optional. Man must orientate himself to God. Highest fulfillment comes from union in Christ. "Thus it is that human fulfillment constitutes, as it were, a summary of our duties."[109] Since all people are obliged to self-fulfillment, each person has the duty toward others in helping them go from less human conditions to more human ones.[110]

For Catholic laymen this means to take the initiative freely and to infuse a Christian spirit into the mentality, customs, laws, and structures of the community in which he lives without waiting passively for orders and directions from the hierarchy.[111] Fellow Christians are called upon to join in a cooperative effort to help humankind banish selfishness, pride, and injustices and to work for a world with a better human life in which each will be loved and treated as a brother.[112] Men of goodwill are called to take a responsible position to make known to men, and to awaken their consciences to, the plight of the poor.[113] All men of learning are given the duty: "Open the paths which lead to mutual assistance among peoples, to a deepening of heart, to a more brotherly way of living within a truly universal human society."[114] All these tasks reflect the duty the Holy Father feels himself to have, that is, the responsibility to awaken the conscience of the world.[115]

Octogesima Adveniens gives several specific examples of duties. "The most important duty in the realm of justice is to allow each country to promote its own development, within the framework of a cooperation free from any spirit of domination, whether economic or political."[116] Admitting the complexity of the problem, the Holy Father nevertheless has called for a change in people's attitudes so that they may realize the prior call of international duty.

Another area is the field of politics. After briefly explaining the good that politics can bring about, Pope Paul exhorts:

To take politics seriously at its different levels—local, regional, national and worldwide—is to affirm the duty of man, of every man, to recognize the concrete reality and the value of the freedom of choice that is offered to him to seek to bring about both the good of the city and of the nation of mankind.[117]

Politics is a way of living the Christian commitment of service to others in that, without attempting to solve every problem, it endeavors to apply solutions to the relationship men have with one another.[118]

The 1971 Synod of Bishops begins its analyses of justice and world society by describing the crisis of universal solidarity. The principle of solidarity comes from solidarism, a nineteenth-century French socio-philosophical theory which expounded a system of securing social order that was equally opposed to both individualism and collectivism.[119] Stating the concept of solidarism another way, all individuals are involved as members of the social totality in the common social destiny of this totality (society or community); similarly the totality is involved in the destiny of the members. A practical consequence follows in that each individual must stand responsible for each and every member. The principle of solidarity expresses this ethical content of common responsibility. According to this principle each person must be prepared to make up for the defective or absent performance of others.

Pius XI first used the principle of solidarity by name in Church teaching, applying it to the economic order.[120] *Mater et Magistra* applied it to rural farm workers and to wealthy nations.[121] Pope John called for an education of conscience to a sense of responsibility because "we are all equally responsible for the undernourished people."[122] *Pacem in Terris* stated that men "are meant to live with others and to work for one another's welfare."[123] Vatican II has greatly delineated this principle. "Among the signs of our times, the irresistibly increasing sense of solidarity among all people is especially noteworthy."[124]

Although the world of today has a very vivid sense of its unity and of how one man depends on another in needful solidarity, it is most grievously torn into opposing camps by conflicting forces. For political, social, economic, racial, and ideological disputes still continue bitterly, and with them the peril of war that would reduce everything to ashes.[125]

Because of these problems that characterize our times, the Council has stressed the universal scope of solidarity. Men must look to "the welfare of the whole human family, which is tied together by the manifold bonds linking races, peoples, and nations."[126] This is one of the primary duties of modern man.[127]

Populorum Progressio has reasserted that solidarity in action at this turning point in history is a matter of urgency.[128] Pope Paul extends the principle of solidarity to responsibility for future generations.

Humanity is advancing along the path of history like the waves of a rising tide encroaching gradually on the shore. We have inherited from past generations, and we have an obligation toward all, and we cannot refuse to interest ourselves in those who will come after us to enlarge the human family. The reality of human solidarity, which is a benefit for us, also imposes a duty.[129]

The development of all humanity in the spirit of solidarity is an essential condition for progress. This duty of solidarity not only exists for individuals but for nations in that nations have a very heavy obligation to help the developing countries.[130] In concluding, Pope Paul appeals again to the urgency of the tasks and the cooperation of all people:

We have desired to remind all men how crucial is the present moment, how urgent the work to be done. The hour for action has sounded. At stake are the survival of so many innocent children, for so many families overcome by misery, the access to conditions fit for human beings; at stake are the peace of the world and the future of civilization. It is time for all men and all peoples to face up to their responsibilities.[131]

Octogesima Adveniens called for a renewed education in the principle of solidarity.[132] Speaking to Christians, Pope Paul warns that it is not enough to recall principles, state intentions, point to injustices, and utter prophetic denunciations. "It is too easy to throw back on others responsibility for injustices, if at the same time one does not realize how each one shares in it personally, and how personal conversion is needed first."[133] Furthermore, the Christian must constantly clarify his motives lest in the name of solidarity he violate true humanism by leaning to selfish particularism or oppressive totalitarianism.[134]

The 1971 Synod describes the injustices which result from sinful social structures and calls us to a renewed solidarity with the voiceless victims of injustice. New functions and new duties must pervade every sector of human activity, but especially world society, if justice is to be put into practice.

The exercise of rights and duties in a society immediately calls to mind the ancient debate of what is the common good. John XXIII defined it as follows: "The common good comprises all the conditions of social life through which men may better and more easily attain their own personal fulfillment."[135] In *Pacem in Terris* Pope John stressed more the personalist aspect of the common good. "It is agreed that in our time the common good is chiefly guaranteed when personal rights and duties are maintained. . . . For to safeguard the inviolable right of the human person and to facilitate the fulfillment of his duties should be the essential office of every public authority."[136] The term "individual" applies to an instrument of production or a possessor of property, whereas the term "person" is in legal terminology a substance of which rights and duties are attributes.[137] But beyond the legal concept, the term "person" denotes an intrinsic dignity that takes priority over every form of political association.[138] Whereas an individual can rest on his right to acquire, Pope John has made it clear that a person has the duty of giving and sharing.[139]

Pope John, contrary to the theory of individualism, has upheld the government's right to intervene in the economy.[140] Stressing the value of the person, the Pope said that the economic prosperity of a nation is not so much in the total assets of wealth and property as it is in the distribution of this wealth.[141] And no nation can conceive of the common good apart from its relations with other nations.[142] Furthermore, the fact of socialization which Pope John had stressed makes it clear that the common good cannot be limited to a fixed social condition. The norms for the common good must be determined by having regard for the human person.[143]

Vatican II described the common good several times, always stressing the value of the person:

The common welfare of society consists in the entirety of those conditions of social life under which men enjoy the possibility of achieving their own perfection in a certain fullness of measure and also with some relative ease. Hence this welfare consists chiefly in the protection of the rights, and in the performance of the duties, of the human person.[144]

   The Council also noted that as a result of the increasing human interdependence, the common good today takes on an increasing universal complexion involving rights and duties with respect to the whole human race.[145] Stressing the changing times the Council urged:

The universal common good needs to be intelligently pursued and more effectively achieved. Hence it is now necessary for the family of nations to create for themselves an order which corresponds to modern obligation, particularly with reference to those numerous regions still laboring under intolerable need.[146]

Octogesima Adveniens, after discussing various political ideologies, concludes that any political power must have as its aim the common good, that is, while respecting the legitimate liberties of individuals, families, and subsidiary groups, it acts in such a way as to create, effectively and for the well-being of all, the conditions required for attaining man's true and complete good.[147] Pope Paul notes that this political power can vary from people to people and country to country, but it can never destroy or absorb the individual member.[148]

Summary of Nyerere's Position

   Even in a cursory reading of Nyerere's writings and the Church's teachings, certain parallels immediately present themselves. There are in both a primary emphasis on human dignity, a concern for human rights (especially for the weak), a responsibility in solidarity, a duty to work, an orientation to the future, and a desire for development. But as Herbert Marcuse notes, these same principles are upheld by Soviet Marxist ideology.[149] It would seem, therefore, that any evaluation of Nyerere's position must be made in light of concrete applications of these ideals and in light of the social and cultural background of Tanzania today.
   This approach to the problem of social justice is certainly the mind of Paul VI as noted in *Octogesima Adveniens*.[150] The Holy Father has urged all Christians in cooperation with all people of goodwill to analyze objectively the situations of their own country in order to bring about a more just social order. The Church in light of the gospel can give norms of judgment and principles of reflection, but the Church has neither the intention nor the ambition to put forward a solution which has universal validity.[151] The solutions will vary according to regions, socio-political systems, and cultures.
   A case in point is the statement by the 1971 Synod of Bishops urging all nations who have not done so to ratify and observe the United Nations Declaration on Human Rights.[152] But as early as 1961, Nyerere stated frankly that it is one thing to ratify the Declaration on Human Rights and another to

see that all people enjoy such rights. "The Declaration confirms the right of every individual to many things, which we cannot yet provide for the citizens of our country. In that respect this document, the Universal Declaration on Human Rights, represents our goal rather than something we have already achieved."[153] The question is, Who will enjoy these rights? On one extreme is the Soviet Union, a collaborator in the formulation of the Universal Declaration on Human Rights.[154] Yet the Marxist ideology was condemned in *Octogesima Adveniens,*[155] and more recently by the Chilean bishops,[156] as violating these basic rights. The other extreme can be seen in the writings of the economist Milton Friedman, an advocate of liberal capitalism. Friedman sees any restriction on economic life as an unwarranted violation of personal freedom.[157]

Seen in terms of the common good, Soviet Marxism sees the social interest (represented by the state) standing at present over and above the individual's interest, with the two interests eventually becoming identified according to the inevitable scientific historical process.[158] The liberal capitalist sees the common good as the sum of the individual goods.[159] Both extremes claim to represent the best interests of all and both have been condemned by papal teaching.

Nyerere's approach to human rights avoids both extremes. Taking as a basic assumption the dignity and the quality of the person, Nyerere set out to build a country in which all the people would enjoy the basic human rights. Economic development would not be obtained at the expense of social development. From a capitalist point of view this meant a restriction on some of the rights of other people. "But any apparent deviation from the articles of the Declaration [on Human Rights] will be an honest attempt on our part to balance conflicting interests while preserving the major principle itself."[160] These "conflicting interests" were any groups in the country who had the power to exploit others.

In applying the principles of *Ujamaa*, certain conflicts of rights appear with regard to Church teaching.[161] One is the question of the trade unions, which have received so much attention in papal encyclicals. But the social conditions of a country must be taken into account. The union workers of industrial countries are not in the same social condition as workers from developing countries. A Tanzanian union worker is in a privileged position in which he can easily exploit the 95 percent of peasant farmers. Therefore the common good demands that the government restrict their bargaining powers.

More controversial is the question of the right of free speech and expression. Tanzanians do not enjoy the same freedom as do citizens of the United States and England. Nyerere admits this, saying Tanzania does not have the long tradition of freedom. There are some forty-one states on the African mainland south of the Sahara. Some have white minority rule; a few are virtually puppet states of South Africa; most have military dictators. The rest have a strong central government with varying degrees of freedom. A strong government is needed to overcome tribal factions, as can be seen in Kenya and Uganda.

Nyerere's justification for the restriction of the freedom of some in Tanzania is for the development of actual freedom for the overwhelmingly vast majority. The reason for restricting some rights at times is the government's desire to maintain a balance between various viewpoints on the direction of the country lest the whole society collapse.[162] Stated another way, the policy is to restrict the peripheral rights of a few to safeguard the more basic rights of the masses.

Nyerere has laid great stress on the responsibilities of the person, particularly his duty to work to build up the society. This responsibility is rooted in the conviction that *Ujamaa* is an attitude of mind demanding the practical acceptance of the equality of all. The parallels with the Church's concept of the principle of solidarity are obvious. But what Nyerere has done is the difficult task of taking the principles and applying them to concrete situations. The results have to be judged in light of what he is trying to do. Reflecting in 1974 on the twentieth anniversary of TANU, Nyerere admitted the probability of making tactical mistakes in executing policies: "But we shall continue as we have begun—trying to create a society in which all citizens work together in freedom, dignity and equality, for their common good."[163]

Not least in showing an attitude of responsibility for others is the example Nyerere himself gives. At a time when the Holy Father has been urging greater simplicity in the lifestyle of churchmen, Nyerere has given the personal standard for government officials. "Nyerere is probably one of the most Spartan of African heads of state with almost no tangible assets and a monthly salarly of about $570. His small home belongs to the state and he has no car of his own."[164] He accepts no title except *Mwalimu* (Teacher), the title he had as a village schoolmaster. Writing against confusing dignity with pomposity[165] and forbidding by law his officials' using their positions for personal financial gain,[166] Nyerere has set the example to show that the purpose of the government is to serve the people, all the people.

NOTES

1. "Humanae Salutis," in Walter M. Abbott, S.J., ed., *The Documents of Vatican II* (New York: Herder and Herder, 1966), p. 704.

2. The phrase "signs of the times" was subsequently used in *Pacem in Terris, Ecclesiam Suam* (no. 52), *Gaudium et Spes* (no. 4), *Populorum Progressio* (no. 13), and the Synod of Bishops' *Justice in the World* (no. 2).

3. M. Chenu, O.P., "The Signs of the Times," trans. John Drury, in *The Church Today*, ed. Group 2000 (New York: Newman Press, 1968), p. 52.

4. Healy, in his study of the social teaching of the 150 years previous to *Rerum Novarum*, shows how revolutionary the teaching of Leo XIII was (*The Just Wage, 1750–1890* [The Hague: Martinus Nijhoff, 1966]).

5. Leo XIII, *Rerum Novarum*, May 15, 1891 (New York: Paulist Press, 1939), no. 2.

6. John XXIII, *Mater et Magistra*, in *The Pope Speaks*, 7 (1962), 4:295–343, no. 15. Text also included in *The Gospel of Peace and Justice: Catholic Social Teaching since Pope John*, presented by Joseph Gremillion (Maryknoll, N.Y.: Orbis Books, 1976).

7. Pius XI, *Quadragesimo Anno*, May 15, 1931, in *The Social Order* (London: Catholic Truth Society, 1960), no. 29; see *Mater et Magistra*, no. 26.

8. Charles Moeller, "History of the Constitution," *Commentary on the Documents of Vatican II,* ed. H. Vorgrimler (New York: Herder and Herder, 1969), vol. 5, p. 2.

9. Ibid., pp. 10–11.

10. Henri de Riedmatten, O.P., "Introduction: History of the Pastoral Constitution," *The Church Today,* p. 3.

11. Moeller, "History," p. 11.

12. Chenu, "Signs," p. 46.

13. Riedmatten, "Introduction," p. 21.

14. Chenu, "Signs," p. 46.

15. Moeller, "History," p. 26.

16. Chenu, "Signs," p. 48.

17. *Gaudium et Spes,* nos. 4–10; text in *Documents of Vatican II,* and *Gospel of Peace and Justice.*

18. Chenu, "Signs," pp. 51–52.

19. *The Teachings of Pope Paul VI,* 3 vols. (Vatican: Liveria Editrice, 1968–70), vol. 2, p. 80.

20. Ibid.

21. Ibid., p. 61.

22. Ibid.

23. *Gaudium et Spes,* no. 4.

24. *Quadragesimo Anno,* no. 18.

25. *Gaudium et Spes,* no. 46.

26. Paul VI, *Octogesima Adveniens,* May 14, 1971 (On the Occasion of the Eightieth Anniversary of the Encyclical, "Rerum Novarum"), no. 4; text in *Gospel of Peace and Justice.*

27. Synod of Bishops, *Justice in the World,* nos. 1–28; text in *Gospel of Peace and Justice.*

28. *Octogesima Adveniens,* no. 21.

29. *Gaudium et Spes,* no. 11.

30. Chenu, "Signs," p. 49.

31. *Gaudium et Spes,* no. 5.

32. Roger Heckel, S.J., "Lettre Apostolique de Paul VI sur le 80e anniversaire de Rerum Novarum," *Cahiers* 23 (October 15, 1971), p. 584.

33. Bartolomeo Sorge, S.J., "L'apporto Dottrinale della Lettera Apostolica, 'Octogesima Adveniens,' " *Civiltà Cattolica* 2 (1967), pp. 420–22.

34. Ibid., p. 422.

35. *Octogesima Adveniens,* nos. 8–21.

36. Bartolomeo Sorge, S.J., "Il Dibattito Sinodale sulla Guistizia nel Mondo," *Civiltà Cattolica* 4 (1971), p. 114.

37. *Octogesima Adveniens,* no. 47.

38. Ibid., no. 50.

39. *Teachings of Pope Paul VI,* vol. 2, p. 81.

40. Ibid., p. 82.

41. Ibid., p. 81.

42. Ibid.

43. Ibid., p. 83.

44. *Mater et Magistra,* no. 59.

45. Ibid.

46. Jean-Yves Calvez, S.J., *The Social Thought of John XXIII,* trans. G. McKenzie (Chicago: Henry Regnery, 1964), p. 6.

47. *Mater et Magistra,* no. 59.

48. Ibid., no. 61.

49. Ibid., no. 63.

50. Ibid., no. 64.

51. Oswald von Nell-Breuning, "The Life of the Political Community," in *Commentary on the Documents of Vatican II,* p. 322.

52. Roberto Tucci, "Development of Culture," in *Commentary on the Documents of Vatican II,* p. 259.

53. *Gaudium et Spes,* no. 33.

54. Alphonse Auer, "Man's Activity in the World," in *Commentary on the Documents of Vatican II,* p. 185.

55. Ibid., p. 197.

56. Riedmatten, "Introduction," p. 31.

57. *Gaudium et Spes*, no. 12.

58. Joseph Ratzinger, "Dignity of the Human Person," in *Commentary on the Documents of Vatican II*, p. 31.

59. Moeller sees the theme *imago Dei* as important as the themes of collegiality and "People of God." The theme of the image of God was inserted in the perspective of man's dominion over the world, which is expressly connected with the divine image that radiates his countenance ("History," p. 5).

60. *Gaudium et Spes*, no. 22.

61. Ibid., no. 27.

62. Ibid., nos. 31 and 66.

63. Ibid., no. 60.

64. Ibid., no. 17.

65. Ibid., no. 16.

66. Ibid., nos. 14 and 41.

67. Ibid., no. 29.

68. Ibid., no. 27.

69. Ibid., no. 26.

70. Ibid., no. 73.

71. Ibid., no. 63.

72. Ibid., no. 23.

73. Ibid., no. 78.

74. Ibid., no. 28,

75. *Dignitatis Humanae*, nos. 2, 9, 12; text in *Documents of Vatican II* and *Gospel of Peace and Justice*.

76. *Gaudium et Spes*, no. 91.

77. Ibid., no. 11.

78. Ibid., no. 35.

79. Ibid., no. 34.

80. José Díez-Alegría, "The Rights of Man," in *Sacramentum Mundi*, ed. Karl Rahner (1969), vol. 5, p. 366.

81. Every paragraph except one in *Pacem in Terris* refers to Pius XII.

82. John XXIII, *Pacem in Terris*, April 11, 1963 in *The Pope Speaks* 9 (1963), no. 9; text also in *Gospel of Peace and Justice*.

83. Ibid., no. 11.

84. Ibid., no. 12.

85. Ibid., no. 13.

86. Ibid., no. 14.

87. Ibid., no. 15.

88. Ibid., no. 17.

89. Ibid., nos. 18, 20.

90. Ibid., no. 21.

91. Ibid., no. 23.

92. Ibid., no. 25.

93. Ibid., no. 26.

94. Ibid., no. 27.

95. Ibid., no. 26.

96. *Gaudium et Spes*, no. 41.

97. Ibid., no. 87.

98. *Justice in the World*, no. 15.

99. Ibid., no. 64.

100. Synod of Bishops (1974), "Human Rights and Reconciliation," October 23, 1974.

101. *Pacem in Terris*, no. 44.

102. Ibid., no. 30.

103. Ibid., no. 20.

104. Ibid., no. 34.

105. Ibid., no. 29.

106. *Gaudium et Spes*, no. 43.

107. Ibid., no. 43.

108. Paul VI, *Populorum Progressio*, March 26, 1967 (Glen Rock, N.J.: Paulist Press, 1967), no. 15; text also in *Gospel of Peace and Justice*.
109. Ibid., no. 16.
110. Ibid., nos. 17, 20.
111. Ibid., no. 81.
112. Ibid., no. 82.
113. Ibid., no. 83.
114. Ibid., no. 85.
115. Poupard, "Introduction to Populorum Progressio," *Lo Sviluppo dei Popoli* (Brescia: Queriniana, 1968), p. 17.
116. *Gaudium et Spes*, no. 43.
117. *Octogesima Adveniens*, no. 46.
118. Ibid.
119. Nell-Breuning, "Christian Social Doctrine," *Sacramentum Mundi*, vol. 6, pp. 113–14.
120. *Quadragesimo Anno*, no. 88.
121. *Mater et Magistra*, nos. 146, 157.
122. Ibid., no. 158.
123. *Pacem in Terris*, no. 31.
124. *Apostolicam Actuositatem*, no. 14; text in *Documents of Vatican II*.
125. *Gaudium et Spes*, no. 4.
126. Ibid., no. 75.
127. Ibid., no. 30.
128. *Populorum Progressio*, no. 1.
129. Ibid., no. 17.
130. Ibid., no. 48.
131. Ibid., no. 80.
132. *Octogesima Adveniens*, no. 23.
133. Ibid., no. 48.
134. Ibid., no. 49.
135. *Mater et Magistra*, no. 65.
136. *Pacem in Terris*, no. 60.
137. José Díez-Alegría, "Common Good," in *Sacramentum Mundum*, vol. 4, p. 18.
138. Ibid.
139. *Pacem in Terris*, no. 60.
140. *Mater et Magistra*, no. 60.
141. Ibid., no. 74.
142. *Pacem in Terris*, no. 131.
143. Ibid., no. 139.
144. *Dignitatis Humanae*, no. 6; also see *Gaudium et Spes*, nos. 26, 74.
145. *Gaudium et Spes*, no. 26.
146. Ibid., no. 84.
147. *Octogesima Adveniens*, no. 46.
148. Ibid.
149. Herbert Marcuse, *Soviet Marxism: A Critical Analysis* (Middlesex, England: Pelican Books, 1971), pp. 161–203.
150. *Octogesima Adveniens*, no. 4.
151. Ibid.
152. *Justice in the World*, no. 64.
153. Julius K. Nyerere, *Freedom and Unity* (Dar es Salaam: Oxford University Press, 1966), p. 146.
154. *The Rights and Freedoms* (New York: United Nations Publications, 1950).
155. *Octogesima Adveniens*, no. 26.
156. "List Marxist Dangers," *National Catholic Reporter*, January 7, 1972, p. 2.
157. Milton Friedman, *Capitalism and Freedom* (Chicago: University of Chicago Press, 1962), pp. 1–21.
158. Marcuse, *Soviet Marxism*, p. 100.

159. Friedman, *Capitalism*, pp. 1–2.

160. Nyerere, *Freedom and Unity*, p. 146.

161. The question of private property and the means of production will be treated in a separate chapter.

162. Nyerere, *Freedom and Unity*, p. 312.

163. Nyerere, "From Uhuru to Ujamaa," *Africa Today* (Summer 1974), p. 8.

164. *Newsweek*, September 20, 1971, p. 54.

165. Nyerere, *Freedom and Unity*, pp. 223–26.

166. Julius K. Nyerere, *Ujamaa: Essays on Socialism* (Dar es Salaam: Oxford University Press, 1968), pp. 36–37.

CHAPTER 20

THE CHURCH'S TEACHING
ON DEVELOPMENT

Since World War II a great amount of foreign aid has gone to developing countries—most of it unsatisfactory. The Synod of Bishops summarized the failure in their report of 1971 on justice in the world:

In the last twenty-five years a hope has spread through the human race that economic growth would bring about such a quantity of goods that it would be possible to feed the hungry at least with the crumbs falling from the table, but this has proved a vain hope in underdeveloped areas and in pockets of poverty in wealthier areas, because of the rapid growth of population and of the labour force, because of rural stagnation and the lack of agrarian reform, and because of the massive migratory flow to the cities, where the industries, even though endowed with huge sums of money, nevertheless provide so few jobs that not infrequently one worker in four is left unemployed. These stifling oppressions constantly give rise to great numbers of "marginal" persons, ill-fed, inhumanly housed, illiterate and deprived of political power as well as of the suitable means of acquiring responsibility and moral dignity.[1]

To avoid these evils and to build a society that will raise the quality of life for all, Nyerere has pursued a program of development in accord with *Ujamaa* socialism. It is a program that considers not only the economic and social situations within Tanzania but also the interrelation of Tanzania with other countries. But any specific development program is formed in the light of the socialist tenets that the purpose of all activity is the human person and that all people are equal. This chapter treats the practical implications of human development in a developing country.

Defining Development

Recent ecclesial statements have spoken often about development. Any definition will have to include these insights. Furthermore, development is a continually growing concept which cannot be limited by a definition, because the basic principles of justice under the driving force of the gospel must be applied anew to the changing situations of the world.[2] A description of development as found in ecclesial writings, then, will have many aspects.

Pope Paul has spoken of development in terms of the economically poorer countries. "By development is meant the human, civil, temporal advancement of those people who, by contrast with modern civilization and with the help that it can provide, are becoming more aware of themselves and are setting out on the road to higher levels of culture and prosperity."[3] Development, according to Paul VI, goes beyond economic growth to promote the good of the whole man.[4] Development is liberation from poverty, disease, exploitation, social inequalities, ignorance, oppressive social structures, lack of culture, and egoism.[5]

Development is growth in human fulfillment by which the human being, becoming more a person, enhances his personal worth.[6] Development is a search for a new humanism that will embrace the higher values of love and friendship, prayer and contemplation, because "this will permit the fulness of authentic development, a development which is for each and all a transformation from less human conditions to those which are more human."[7]

Development is both personal and communal; the person has both the obligation to better himself and, since he is a member of society, to work for the betterment of all.[8] This implies a global vision of the person, and of the human race.[9] Basing itself on the teaching of *Populorum Progressio*, the Association of Episcopal Conferences in Eastern Africa (AMECEA) defined development as:

the growth of the whole man and of all men in solidarity with the whole human race. It is therefore the progressive humanization of life embracing liberation from all servitude and domination. It goes further to embrace that integral human development which includes the higher values of love and friendship, prayer and contemplation and in Christ, the perfector of men, finds ultimate fulfillment in communion with God Himself.[10]

From this concept of development certain other characteristics follow. Development will be marked by bold transformation which will change the structures of society rather than treat the symptoms.[11] The going from the less human to the more human means that development will have a future orientation. Development must meet the "rising expectations" of the human race.[12] People are today aspiring to do more, know more, and have more in order to be more.[13] "Development in fact means a movement towards a goal, in which the original value becomes reaffirmed in deeper, purer, and more explicit terms."[14] The aspect of the future was again stressed in *Octogesima Adveniens.*[15]

Pluralism is another characteristic, because development will not be a single, homogenous growth.[16] In concrete situations there can be a variety of possible options. Christians are invited "to take up a double task of inspiring and of innovating, in order to make structures evolve, so as to adapt them to the real needs of today."[17]

The importance of development in Church teaching can be seen in that Pope Paul equates it with peace.[18] "Peace cannot be limited to a mere absence of war. . . . No, peace is something built up day after day, in the pursuit of an order intended by God, which implies a more perfect form of justice among men."[19] The most important duty in the realm of justice is to allow each country to promote its own development free from political and economic domination.[20] This invitation to work for development and peace does not ignore the practical difficulty of first defining justice and then attaining it.[21]

It is important to understand clearly what the Church means by development, because every person has the right to development, a right guaranteed by his own personal dignity.[22] The freedom to exercise this right is a matter of justice.[23] Elaborating on this right, the Synod of Bishops (1971) declared: "The right to development must be seen as a dynamic interpenetration of all those fundamental human rights upon which the aspirations of individuals and nations are based."[24]

This right to development implies that the people have the right to take an active part in the shaping of their own lives, to be artisans of their own destiny.[25] "By taking their future into their own hands through a determined will for progress, the developing peoples—even if they do not achieve the final goal—will authentically manifest their own personalization."[26] In light of this right of all people to development, the aid of the rich to the poor is not charity but a duty in solidarity.[27] Furthermore, this right to development entails a cessation of various kinds of exploitation: colonialism and neocolonialism with its economic and political domination;[28] racial and ideological discrimination;[29] and unregulated competition in which the poor cannot ·compete.[30] This right to development based on human dignity demands a new understanding for our times. As the Synod of Bishops summarized in 1971:

The strong drive towards global unity, the unequal distribution which places decisions concerning three quarters of income, investment and trade in the hands of one third of the human race, namely the more highly developed part, the insufficiency of a merely economic progress, and the new recognition of the material limits of the biosphere—all this makes us aware of the fact that in today's world new modes of understanding human dignity are arising.[31]

To see more clearly the Church's understanding of development and how it correlates with *Ujamaa* socialism, we will see it divided into certain aspects: as economic advancement, as liberation, and as humanization.

Development as Economic Advancement

At one time it may have been quite possible that a traditional African society would not have looked on itself as underdeveloped even though it lacked nearly all civilized refinements and conveniences. "However, such an evaluation offers no appeal today, even to the African himself, because he finds himself incorporated de facto in an all-embracing socio-economic complex in which his particular way of life must appear 'underdeveloped' culturally and technologically."[32] *Gaudium et Spes*, acknowledging the growing awareness among the underdeveloped countries of their lack of material goods and also noting their "rising expectations" to overcome these economic inequalities, has called for numerous reforms on the socio-economic level.[33]

The Church has been a strong advocate of economic development.[34] Certainly economic development is development in a narrow sense, and in Church teaching it is as a prerequisite for a more fully human development, that is, not only material needs but intellectual, moral, and spiritual needs as well.[35] But Father Lebret notes in his commentary on *Gaudium et Spes:* "Economic progress, far from being a despicable thing, is an urgent necessity."[36]

Economic development is necessary because it produces the material basis required for decent human existence. Pope Paul states some of these basic requirements: freedom from hunger, misery, and endemic disease; freedom from situations that do violence to human dignity; better education; health; and security in obtaining food, shelter, and employment.[37]

Another way Church teaching has stressed the urgent necessity of economic development is by stressing the importance of reducing economic inequality. While the Council did not advocate rigid egalitarianism, it did establish a criterion for determining inequality: "While an enormous mass of people still lack the absolute necessities of life, some, even in less advanced countries, live sumptuously or squander wealth."[38] But *Gaudium et Spes* did not give specific criteria distinguishing strict justice from works of supererogation.[39] Such practical applications of the demands of justice must be made by the local community.[40] The Pastoral Constitution did draw attention to the plight of the farmers who are so easily exploited.[41] Justice and equity demand they be given a fair return for their work.[42] Becoming more specific, Pope Paul asks each person to examine his conscience to see if he is ready to pay a higher price for imported goods so that the producers may be more justly rewarded.[43]

The seriousness of these needs expresses in itself the urgency of development. Imposing a special obligation on wealthy nations,[44] Pope Paul called for a planned program for systematic development[45] and the establishment of a world fund.[46] Such a fund under an international authority would eliminate fears in developing nations of neocolonialism in the form of political pressures and economic domination.[47] "Would that those in authority listen to our words before it is too late!"[48] "The task must be undertaken without delay; at stake are the very life of poor nations, civil peace in developing countries, and world peace itself."[49]

Populorum Progressio stressed the evils of inequality on the international level in calling on rich countries to be at the service of the poor ones.[50] But the responsibilities of wealthy nations do not relieve the developing nations of their own duties. The peoples themselves make their own future, and therefore have the prime responsibility to work for their own development.[51]

The Synod of Bishops came out very strongly on the necessity of economic development: "It is impossible to conceive true progress without recognizing the necessity—within the political system chosen—of a development composed both of economic growth and participation."[52] Certainly development is much more than economic growth, but at the same time any political system must provide economic growth as a prerequisite for social development.

The possibility of *Ujamaa* socialism providing economic development for the citizens of Tanzania has been criticized as unrealistic. Albert Meister in his book, *East Africa: The Past in Chains, the Future in Pawn,* summarizes the criticism:

Development is not so important in itself; what counts is "the progress of men," their "fulfillment," . . . "harmonious development." The second difficulty consists in precisely this jump out of reality; the increasingly burning question is NOT to fulfill—or even to develop—but to enable man to survive.[53]

The seriousness of these charges is acknowledged by Nyerere. In a 1972 interview he was asked what he thought Tanzania's greatest achievement was in ten years of independence. Nyerere answered frankly: "We have survived."[54]

It is beyond the scope of this chapter to give an economic analysis of Tanzania under *Ujamaa* socialism.[55] But a few economic considerations must be made to understand better Nyerere's goals. First and foremost, any economic consideration must be seen in light of the overall philosophy of *Ujamaa* socialism, which strives to make social equality a reality for all citizens. "We are not simply trying to organize increased production; we are trying to introduce a whole new way of life for the majority of our people."[56]

Economic development has been committed to a policy of self-reliance. "There is no choice. . . . The only people we can rely upon are ourselves."[57] The decision of the United States Senate to cut foreign aid[58] would seem to bear out Nyerere's prophecy that Tanzania could never get enough foreign assistance to meet its development needs.[59] More specifically, the decision to rely primarily on agriculture for economic development[60] has support from a recent study by the Food and Agriculture Organization of the United Nations.[61]

Finally, economic growth is often measured by an increased per capita income.[62] Apart from the difficulty of obtaining reliable per capita income statistics in developing countries, Henry Bienen noted some other difficulties in his study on the Tanzanian economy.[63] Per capita statistics do not include the work of subsistence farmers who, because they do not produce cash crops, do not enter into the monetary sector. In Tanzania this is over 25 percent of the people. Furthermore, the per capita income statistics are obtained by dividing the national monetary output by the number of people. They say nothing on how the national income is distributed.[64] In Kenya, for example, with its emphasis on development from foreign investment, it is estimated that all the Africans have only 50 percent of the national income to divide among themselves.[65] This means the other half of the wealth is being distributed to relatively few people. Nyerere is trying to eliminate these inequalities in Tanzania.

To repeat, any economic evaluation of Tanzania must include the goals of *Ujamaa* socialism: greater distribution of wealth, freedom from foreign domination, and social development of all the people.

Development as Liberation

Twenty years ago most colonial powers believed their colonies would need decades of assistance before they had the economic capacity for statehood.[66] Development was thought of as overcoming poverty by means of modern technology, some patience, and a great deal of money.[67] In accord with this kind of thinking, development was measured in terms of an increased gross national product (GNP) or an increased per capita income for the developing country. In other words, development became synonymous with economic growth.

However, this type of development proved unsatisfactory. The developing countries, while having more money, saw themselves being exploited in a new way. The colonial system kept the colonies producing agricultural products and minerals and at the same time this system denied them the advantages of industrialization.[68] The gap between developed countries and developing countries continued to increase despite development aid.[69] In 1971, after decades of developmental aid, the Peruvian bishops spoke out for liberation because:

With the nations of the Third World we share the fact that we are the victims of systems that exploit our natural resources, that control our political decisions, that impose on us the cultural domination of their values and their consumer civilization. This situation [is] . . . reinforced and supported by the internal structures of our own nation, where there is increasing economic, social and cultural inequality, where politics are perverted so that instead of serving the common good, only a few are favored.[70]

Development in the past, promoted as economic growth, did not attack the roots of the evil of the disparity between rich nations and poor nations.[71] Instead, after generating "rising expectations," it produced only more frustration and bitterness. Dom Helder Camara analyzed the situation: "If you open their eyes and if the structural changes are not being made fast enough, you are preparing for revolution."[72] This failure of previous development efforts has promoted the concept of liberation.

In Church teachings the theme of liberation by name first appears in *Gaudium et Spes.*[73] Liberation was mentioned twice, both times in the negative context of lamenting those who see liberation only in terms of human effort.[74] *Populorum Progressio,* while denouncing many forms of exploitation and encouraging man to be the artisan of his own destiny, uses the terminology of liberation only once.

The struggle against destitution . . . is not enough. It is a question, rather, of building a world where every man, no matter what his race, religion, or nationality, can live a fully human life, freed from servitude imposed on him by other men or by natural forces over which he has not sufficient control. . . . [75]

In *Octogesima Adveniens* the concept of liberation is more prominent. "The most important duty in the realm of justice is to allow each country to promote its own development, whether economic or political."[76] In a spirit of human solidarity the structures of society must be changed to reverse the ever increasing form of exploitation.[77] But the concept of liberation goes beyond the suppressed peoples of developing countries. Pope Paul has made it clear that all people are called to a continual liberation.

Today men yearn to free themselves from need and dependence. But this liberation starts with the interior freedom that men must find again with regard to their goods and their powers; they will never reach it except through a transcendent love for man, and, in consequence, through a genuine readiness to serve. Otherwise, as one can see only too clearly, the most revolutionary ideologies lead only to a change of masters.[78]

Liberation in this interior sense applies to all people, not just to those in developing countries. It is a call for continual purification of selfishness. Furthermore, it lends itself to profound theological implications. "Christ has liberated us so that we might enjoy freedom" (Gal. 5:1). More practical, liberation in this sense implies that things do not happen by chance, that behind an unjust structure there is a personal or collective guilt. "It suggests, likewise, that a social transformation, no matter how radical it may be, does not automatically achieve the suppression of all evils."[79]

However, the difficult decisions arise from the concept of liberation in the exterior sense, that is, freedom from outside forces. The Interamerican bishops declared in a statement in February 1970: "Liberation in its broadest meaning is the process of freeing man from all that prevents him from developing his potentialities and his obligations as a person who is created in the image of God."[80] In reality this process of freeing man is a call for a radical change of structure of society, because development cannot take place within the present structure.

Attempts to bring about changes within the existing order have proven futile. We find ourselves analyzing a situation at the level of scientific rationality. Only a radical breakdown of the present state of affairs, a profound transformation of the system of property-owning, with access to power by the exploited class, and a social revolution that would break the dependence, would allow for the evolution of a new society, or at least make it possible for a new society to exist.[81]

The necessity of the concept of liberation can perhaps best be seen in the statement by the bishops of Peru in preparation for the Synod of Bishops in 1971. They have been the most vocal in stressing the need of liberation from present structures as the only way to bring about a more truly human existence. Specifically, they called for a structural change in education, distribution of property, banking and investment practices, communications, foreign aid policies of developed nations, and even in the image of the Church itself.[82] More controversially, the Peruvian bishops upheld a person's right to fight for liberation.

In the face of the repressive policies of any government, particularly when, in the name of Christian civilization, any government uses violence and even torture on the men who are fighting for liberation of their peoples, we propose that the church condemn these repressive methods, that it recognize the right these men have to fight for justice, and that it should manifest solidarity with their ideals, even though it may not always approve of their methods.[83]

What the Peruvian bishops say specifically for South America applies generally to the whole Third World.[84] True development cannot take place until people are freed from suppressive economic, social, and political structures. Obviously the structures of each country must be analyzed independently. But liberation implies that development cannot take place if people are denied freedom by oppressive economic, social, and political strutures.

The Synod of Bishops in 1971, dominated by Third World bishops, stressed that in the signs of the times "there is arising a new awareness which shakes them [the victims of injustice] out of any fatalistic rejection and which spurs them on to liberate themselves and to be responsible for their own destiny."[85]

These victims of injustice in developing countries must attain liberation through development or face the dangers of new forms of injustice through neocolonialism.[86] This struggle for liberation is not foreign to the dynamism of the gospel, but is properly the work of the Church.

Action on behalf of justice and participation in the transformation of the world fully appear to us as a constitutive dimension of the preaching of the Gospel, or, in other words, of the Church's mission for the redemption of the human race and its liberation from every oppressive situation.[87]

The 1974 Roman Synod also treated liberation in connection with evangelization. Noting the Church's responsibility to the elimination of deviations in the political, social, and economic spheres, the Synod stressed the Church's primary responsibility of liberating people from sin, from individual or collective selfishness, so that they may enjoy the freedom of communion with God. "In this way the Church, in her evangelical way, promotes the true and complete liberation of all men, groups and peoples."[88]

Nyerere believes that Tanzania's lack of development while under British domination has actually been a blessing in disguise. Tanzania, unlike neighboring Uganda and Kenya, does not have to liberate itself as much from the effects of capitalism: competition over cooperation, a strong entrepreneurial class, huge inequalities of income, individualism at the expense of the common good, and widespread exploitation by the use of money or land. The growing disappointment and frustration of Latin American countries with developmental aid in the last twenty years has supported Nyerere's conviction that:

the reality and depth of the problem arises because the man who is rich has power over the lives of those who are poor, and the rich nation has power over the policies of those which are not rich. And even more important is that our social and economic system, nationally and internationally, supports these divisions and constantly increases them, so that the rich get ever richer and more powerful, while the poor get relatively poorer and less able to control their own future. This continues despite all the talk of human equality, the fight against poverty, and of development.[89]

As an alternative to a capitalistic system, *Ujamaa* socialism strives for economic development while preserving the values of traditional tribal life: equality and dignity of all, work by all, cooperation, sharing, and no exploitation of one person by another. In this way economic development helps all the citizens to go from the less human to the more human.

But the kind of liberation Nyerere is primarily concerned with is not from these external forces but with what Pope Paul calls "interior freedom," the first step of liberation which opens a person to the needs of others.[90] *Ujamaa* socialism is fundamentally this attitude of mind in which one sees every person as his brother.[91] "A socialist society can only be built by those who believe in, and who practice, the principles of socialism."[92] This, then, is the liberation that Nyerere is striving for—a peaceful, interior liberation to free people from selfish individualism. It is a liberation that cannot be legislated or forced; it has to be made convincing. The need and difficulty of persuasion was made very clear by Nyerere in an impromptu answer to a question following his Mary-knoll speech (1970):

We are thirteen million people. Less than half a million live in towns. The rest in those rural areas. Those are Tanzanians. Now how do you change them? We could have done what the Russians did—increase the army and police, and then say to everybody: "Ya, this is the way you do it. You understand?" And if they don't do it, well they get into trouble. Well, we are not doing it for two reasons. One, we are saying development is of the people and by the people. Who are we to say to the people: "Do it or else!" This is not development. This is a different form of slavery, that's all. Secondly, even if we wanted to do it we're not as efficient as the Russians! Even dictatorships need an efficiency and we lack that kind of development. We are not as developed as all that. So we have to persuade, and persuading is not an easy thing.[93]

Although Nyerere's policies of self-reliance and nonalignment have preserved Tanzania from many external political pressures, there is one force that needs mentioning. Nyerere has supported military measures to liberate Tanzania and all Africa from the influence of white, minority-controlled Africa, beginning with neighboring Mozambique.[94]

Nyerere is basically against violence. "For violence cannot be welcomed by those who care."[95] But as a last resort, he has supported the Freedom Fighters, stating the seriousness of the case before the United Nations.

Until now, we have not acted in support of our verbal condemnations of apartheid and colonialism. We have given the peoples of Southern Africa no hope of change. So they have begun to take up arms in their own defence—in defence of their manhood and their right to life which is more than brutal existence. . . . For Africa there is no choice. We have to support the freedom fighters. . . . Yet if this right to self-determination existed for Tanzania, then it does not exist for Southern Africa—and if it does not exist for those peoples, then it does not exist for us either. This is recognized both by South Africa, and by Tanzania. It is the root cause of the conflict between the free states of Africa and the apartheid regime of South Africa. For apartheid is the modern form of slavery—and Africa can no more survive half-slave, half-free, than could the United States of America.[96]

If one accepts Nyerere's contention that all other means have failed to solve the apartheid problem, then Nyerere's backing of the Freedom Fighters has, in principle, support in Church teaching.

We concur with Vatican II, with the unanimous tradition of Catholic doctrine since Augustine (who for his part reflects the view of the major part of the early Church) and with the great majority of theologians, in holding that Christ did emphatically propound his dynamic ideal of non-violence but did not mean it absolutely to forbid Christians any recourse to legitimate defence, especially when this appears absolutely necessary for the defence of the innocent.[97]

Development as Humanization

While liberation is usually thought of as the means to development, humanization answers the most fundamental question: Why development? The theme of humanization has been progressively developing in papal teaching.[98]

Mater et Magistra, written at a time when development was thought of only as economic growth,[99] does not admit a separation between economic development and social growth, neither in determining the purpose nor in achieving the various stages of development. "Economic progress must be accomplished by a corresponding social progress, so that all classes of citizens can participate in the increased productivity."[100] Citing Pius XII's statement that the sole purpose of the economy is to provide the person with the material means which he needs to develop fully, Pope John declared that it is the equitable division and distribution of this wealth "which guarantees the personal development of the members of society, which is the true goal of a nation's economy."[101] While personal development means development of the whole person,[102] Pope John does not elaborate except to emphasize the view of man as a creature and son of God.[103]

Gaudium et Spes greatly amplifies the theme of development as humanization in an appeal to all men of goodwill. "The norm of human activity is this: that in accord with the divine plan and will, it should harmonize with the genuine good of the human race, and allow men as individuals and as members of society to pursue their total vocation and fulfill it."[104] The Council, while admitting that the process of socialization has increased the qualities of the human person,[105] repudiated any concept of development that is equated with mere economic growth or that does not eliminate social inequalities.[106] Man must be the purpose of all economic and social life[107] and social institutions.[108] Man can come to a true and full humanity only through culture, that is, through the cultivation of the natural goods and values by which man refines and unfolds his manifold spiritual and bodily qualities.[109] The fullness of human development culminates by incorporation into the mysteries of Christ.[110]

In *Populorum Progressio* development as humanization is more dynamically presented as a process of growth, going from the less human to the more human.[111] Every man is capable of becoming more a person.[112] Condemning excessive economic inequalities,[113] and cautioning against a view of development which is stifled by materialism,[114] Pope Paul prompts man to search for "a new humanism which will enable modern man to find himself anew by embracing the higher values of love and friendship, prayer and contemplation."[115] This is a transcendent humanism in which the person is continually called to surpass himself.

In order to make clear what he means by the development of the person, Pope Paul presents a scale of values.

Less human conditions first affect those who are so poor as to lack the minimum essentials for life, or who are menaced by the moral deficiencies to which they have succumbed through selfishness; then they affect those who are oppressed by social structures which have been created by abuses of ownership or by abuses of power, by the exploitation of the workers or by unfair business deals. On the other hand, more human conditions of life clearly imply passage from want to the possession of necessities, overcoming social evils, increase of knowledge and acquisition of culture. Other more human conditions are increased esteem for the dignity of others, a turning toward the spirit of poverty, cooperation for the common good and the will for peace. Then comes the acknowledgment by man of supreme values and of God, their source and finality. Finally, and above all, are faith, a gift of God accepted by man's goodwill, and unity in the charity of Christ, who calls us all to share as sons in the life of the living God, the Father of all men.[116]

Humanization, then, is a continual process of going from the less human to the more human. This theme was again stressed in *Octogesima Adveniens* and the Synod of Bishops' *Justice in the World*.[117]

While virtually all nations recognize in theory that the purpose of development is man, Church teaching has repeatedly pointed out that development cannot be limited to mere economic achievement without concern for the genuine welfare of all the people.[118] Economic development does not necessarily mean human development. "Never has the human race enjoyed such an abundance of wealth, resources, and economic power. Yet a huge proportion of the world's citizens is still tormented by hunger and poverty, while countless numbers suffer from total illiteracy."[119] The Church has spoken out often against this false notion of development because the evils are so prevalent: hunger, misery, diseases, ignorance, unemployment, lack of human dignity, selfish individualism, discrimination.[120] These evils breed new dangers of violent insurrections and totalitarian ideologies.[121]

Octogesima Adveniens singles out some new social problems "which because of their urgency, extent and complexity must in the years to come take first place among the preoccupations of Christians, so that with other men the latter may dedicate themselves to solving the new difficulties which put the very future of man in jeopardy."[122] Chief among these urgent new problems is urbanization:

In this disordered growth, new proletariats are born. . . . They dwell on the outskirts—which become a belt of misery besieging in a still silent protest the luxury which blatantly cries out from centres of consumption and waste. Behind the facades, much misery is hidden, unsuspected even by the closest neighbors; other forms of misery spread where human dignity founders; deliquency, criminality, abuse of drugs and eroticism.[123]

Without attempting to exhaust the list of evils cited in papal teaching, it is evident that the Church attributes these evils to false notions of development. If these evils are to be overcome, we must have a new vision of man.

What must be aimed at is complete humanism. And what is that if not the fully-rounded development of the whole man and of all men? A humanism closed in on itself, and not open to the values of the spirit and to God who is their source, could achieve only apparent success. True, man can organize the world apart from God, but without God man can organize it in the end only to man's detriment. An isolated humanism is an inhuman humanism. There is no true humanism but that which is open to the absolute and is conscious of a vocation which gives human life its true meaning.[124]

"For in a Tanzania which is implementing the Arusha Declaration, the purpose of all social, economic and political activity must be man—the citizens, and all the citizens of the country."[125] While this priority on man has been a consistent emphasis in the ideology of Nyerere,[126] the important thing is to see what this means in reality.

First of all Nyerere is trying to build a certain quality of life. Because *Ujamaa* socialism is person-centered, it rejects the concept of national grandeur as distinct from the well-being of its citizens.[127] In practice, Nyerere has had to resist the political pressure to follow the Soviet policy of concentrating more on heavy industry.[128] His criterion for rejecting heavy industry in favor of light industry and agriculture is that heavy industry does not justify the expenditure it requires.[129] Heavy industry, while perhaps giving national prestige, would not noticeably improve the quality of life of the people.

Nyerere, while recognizing that a strong nationalist spirit was necessary for obtaining independence, has rejected strong nationalism as detrimental to the good of the citizens.[130] National boundaries must fade so that all Africans can work in cooperation for the good of all.[131] This position certainly finds support in papal teaching.

Nationalism isolates people from their true good. It would be especially harmful where the weakness of national economic demands rather the pooling of efforts, of knowledge and of funds, in order to implement programs of development and to increase commercial and cultural exchange.[132]

More controversial is Nyerere's program to improve the quality of life of the people primarily through small-scale agriculture. With over 95 percent of the population peasant farmers, any realistic approach for improving the quality of life must give first place to agriculture. Starting with the assumption of human equality, Nyerere is building a nation of *Ujamaa* villages in which the farmers can improve their standard of living without being exploited by landowners or city-dwellers.[133] *Ujamaa* socialism envisions the peasant farmers living on an equal basis with the other citizens. The boldness of this vision can be seen in that the farmers, even in economically advanced countries, are frequently the exploited class.[134]

The *Ujamaa* village program also offers a positive solution to what Pope John asks: "What can be done to persuade agricultural workers that, far from being inferior to other people, they have every opportunity of developing their personality through their work, and can look forward to the future with confidence?"[135] Furthermore the *Ujamaa* village program is a positive effort to combat what Pope Paul calls a major phenomenon of our time caused by "this unceasing flight from the land"—urbanization, which destroys the quality of life by new forms of exploitation.[136] The village development program gives the people an alternative to living on the "fringe" of the city.

The basic assumption that a better quality of life is meant for *all* the citizens has been the major influence in all of Nyerere's policies. In itself, the assumption of the equality of all has been stated so often, including in Church teaching, that it can be given such a wide variety of interpretations as to render it virtually meaningless. What does it mean when the Council Fathers say: "Since all men possess a rational soul and are created in God's likeness, since they have the same nature and origin, have been redeemed by Christ, and enjoy the same calling and destiny, the basic equality of all must receive increasingly greater recognition"?[137] Nyerere summarizes the problem: "But equality in law—even the theory of equality in the making of law—is not sufficient by itself. For the fact is that equality is indivisible. In practice it is not possible to be equal in some respects but not in others."[138]

Ujamaa socialism is a conviction that human equality implies a reasonable economic equality. "The essence of socialism is the practical acceptance of human equality. That is to say, every man's equal right to a decent life before any individual has a surplus above his needs."[139] In practice this means that minority groups in privileged positions (e.g., trade union workers, city-dwellers, the educated, property owners, politicians) are not given the opportunity to "exploit" the people through "glaring income differentials."[140] The real evil of such disproportions of wealth is that the rich person has power over the poor person.[141] The poor person therefore is not equal because he is not free.[142] This right of all citizens to economic equality is a prerequisite to the greater human development of social and political freedom.[143]

The process for achieving equality for all will be gradual "in order to make structures evolve, so as to adapt them to the real needs of today."[144] Stating that the economic structure inherited from the British cannot be changed overnight, Nyerere has given a program of "revolution by evolution."[145] "Our change will, therefore, be effected almost entirely by the emphasis of our new development and by the gradual conversion of existing institutions into others more in accordance with our new philosophy."[146]

NOTES

1. Synod of Bishops, *Justice in the World*, no. 10; text in *The Gospel of Peace and Justice: Catholic Social Teaching since Pope John*, presented by Joseph Gremillion (Maryknoll, New York: Orbis Books, 1976).

2. Paul VI, *Octogesima Adveniens*, May 14, 1971 (On the Occasion of the Eightieth Anniversary of the Encyclical "Rerum Novarum" [Vatican: Typis Polyglottis Vaticanus, 1971]), no. 42; text also in *Gospel of Peace and Justice*.

3. Paul VI, "Message for Mission Sunday," June 5, 1970, *The Teachings of Pope Paul VI*, vol. 3, p. 240.

4. Paul VI, *Populorum Progressio*, March 26, 1967 (Glen Rock, N.J.: Paulist Press, 1967), no. 14; text also in *Gospel of Peace and Justice*.

5. *Populorum Progressio*, no. 21.

6. Ibid., no. 15

7. Ibid., no. 20.

8. Ibid., nos. 16–17.

9. Ibid., no. 13.

10. *The Church and Development*, proceedings of the December 1970 Amecea-Misereor Seminar (Nairobi: Amecea, 1971), p. 13.

11. *Populorum Progressio*, no. 32; *Octogesima Adveniens*, no. 43.

12. *Gaudium et Spes*, December 7, 1965, in *The Documents of Vatican II*, ed. William Abbott, S.J. (New York: America Press, 1966), no. 64; text also in *Gospel of Peace and Justice*.

13. *Populorum Progressio*, no. 6.

14. Zoltan Alszeghy, S.J., and Maurizio Flick, S.J., "Theology of Development: A Question of Method," *Theology Meets Progress*, ed. Philip Land, S.J. (Rome: Gregorian University Press, 1971), p. 14.

15. *Octogesima Adveniens*, nos. 7, 42.

16. *Populorum Progressio*, no. 39.

17. *Octogesima Adveniens*, no. 50.

18. *Populorum Progressio*, no. 87.

19. Ibid., no. 75.

20. *Octogesima Adveniens*, no. 43.

21. Paul VI, "Messaggio per la Giornata della Pace," January 1, 1972.

22. *Justice in the World*, no. 15.

23. Paul VI, "Message of the Church to the Peoples of Africa," August 1, 1969, in *The Teachings of Pope Paul VI* (1970), vol. 2, p. 208.

24. *Justice in the World*, no. 15.

25. *Populorum Progressio*, no. 65.

26. *Justice in the World*, no. 17.

27. *Populorum Progressio*, no. 43; *Octogesima Adveniens*, no. 23.

28. *Populorum Progressio*, no. 7.

29. Ibid., no. 63; *Octogesima Adveniens*, no. 16.

30. *Populorum Progressio*, no. 58; *Octogesima Adveniens*, no. 44.

31. *Justice in the World*, no. 12.

32. Peter Henrici, S.J., "From Progress to Development: A History of Ideas," *Theology Meets Progress*, p. 76.

33. *Gaudium et Spes*, nos. 63–64.

34. John XXIII, *Mater et Magistra*, May 15, 1961, in *The Pope Speaks* 7 (1962); text also in *Gospel of Peace and Justice; Gaudium et Spes*, no. 63; *Populorum Progressio*, no. 6.

35. *Mater et Magistra*, no. 83; *Gaudium et Spes*, no. 64; *Populorum Progressio*, no. 14; *Octogesima Adveniens*, no. 46.

36. L.J. Lebret, O.P., "Economic and Social Life: The Community of Nations," *The Church Today*, ed. Group 2000 (New York: Newman Press, 1967), p. 177.

37. *Populorum Progressio*, nos. 1, 6.

38. *Gaudium et Spes*, no. 63.

39. "A precise delimitation of concepts of that sort could not in any case be translated directly into practice, for in practice limits are blurred and can scarcely ever be sharply drawn. It will not be possible to prevent less being done (in justice and charity) by strict conceptual definition of the extent of the obligation" (Oswald von Nell-Breuning, "Socio-Economic Life," *Commentary on the Documents of Vatican II*, ed. H. Vorgrimler (New York: Herder and Herder, 1969), vol. 5, p. 294.

40. *Octogesima Adveniens*, no. 4.

41. *Mater et Magistra* (nos. 122–49) had made an extensive plea for farmers. "Nearly every country, therefore, is faced with this fundamental problem: What can be done to ensure that agricultural living standards approximate as closely as possible those enjoyed by city dwellers who draw their resources either from industry or from the services in which they are engaged?" (*Mater et Magistra*, no. 125).

42. *Gaudium et Spes*, no. 66.

43. *Populorum Progressio*, no. 47.

44. Cardinal Roy, president of the Pontifical Commission Justice and Peace, comments: "Pope Paul underlines in his encyclical Populorum Progressio that the unfettered working of the market, operating between 'partners' of grossly unequal strength, does not secure anything like a proper distribution of the fruits of economic development. In the modern economy, with its premium on skill, drive, capacity and investment, it is the intelligent, the tough, the energetic and the already rich that tend to take all the profits, unless strong political and social policies accompany moderation in order to secure greater justice and greater participation" ("Second Development Decade," no. 10; text in *Gospel of Justice and Peace*).

45. *Populorum Progressio*, no. 50.

46. Ibid., no. 51.

47. Ibid., no. 52.

48. Ibid., no. 53.

49. Ibid., no. 55.

50. Ibid., no. 49.

51. Ibid., no. 77.

52. *Justice in the World*, no. 18.

53. New York: Walker and Co., 1966, p. 239. Also see Giovanni Arrighi and John Saul, "Socialism and Economic Development in Tropical Africa," *The Journal of Modern African Studies* 6 (1968), 2:168; and Andrew Mamarck, *The Economics of African Development* (London: Praeger, 1971), ch. 12.

54. Peter Enharo, "African Socialism" (an interview with Julius Nyerere) *Africa* 6 (1972), p. 63.

55. Economic information on Tanzania can be found in United Nations *Yearbook of Nation Account Statistics.*

56. Julius K. Nyerere, *Ujamaa: Essays on Socialism* (Dar es Salaam: Oxford University Press, 1968), p. 174.

57. Julius K. Nyerere, *Freedom and Socialism* (Dar es Salaam: Oxford University Press, 1968), p. 167.

58. Frank Church, "Farewell to Foreign Aid," *Vital Speeches* 38 (November 15, 1971), 3:66–73.

59. Nyerere, *Ujamaa: Essays on Socialism*, p. 23.

60. Ibid., p. 97.

61. *Provisional Indicative World Plan for Agricultural Development. Summary and Main Conclusions* (Rome: Food and Agriculture Organization of the United Nations, 1970).

62. Andrew M. Kamarck, *The Economics of African Development* (London: Praeger, 1971), p. 296.

63. Henry Bienen, *Party Transformation and Economic Development* (Princeton: Princeton University Press, 1970), pp. 266–67.

64. For example, according to the statistics of the United States government published in *AID: African Regional* (Washington, D.C., 1970), the per capita income of Libya in 1968 was $1,644, while Tanzania's, in the same year, was $74. Although statistically Libyans' per capita income is

more than twenty times as great, their life expectancy in 1968 was less and their infant mortality was almost double that of Tanzania.

65. Bienen, *Party Transformation*, p. 267.

66. In 1950 there were only three independent African countries: Ethiopia, Liberia, and United Arab Republic.

67. Lester Pearson, chairman, *Partners in Development: Report of the Commission on International Development* (London: Pall Mall Press, 1969), p. 233.

68. Ibid., p. 234.

69. Rubem Alves explains why the economic structures perpetuate this gap. "Development and underdevelopment, far from being successive *phases* of the same development process, are rather interdependent poles of the same structure, in which underdevelopment is both caused by and the cause of development, and development is the cause of and depends on underdevelopment" ("Theology and Liberation of Man," *In Search of a Theology of Development* (Lausanne: La Concorde, 1969), p. 85.

70. Bishops of Peru, "Justice in the World," *IDOC International* 37 (December 11, 1971), pp. 2–3.

71. Gustavo Gutiérrez, "Liberation and Development," *Cross Currents* 21 (Summer 1971), p. 246.

72. Cited in "The Role of the Church in Development" by Archbishop Angelo Fernandes, *Catholic Mind* 59 (May 1971), p. 34.

73. In treating the theme of development, both *Mater et Magistra* and *Pacem in Terris* express the urgent need to do away with existing injustices, but the terminology of liberation is not used.

74. *Gaudium et Spes*, nos. 10, 20.

75. *Populorum Progressio*, no. 47.

76. *Octogesima Adveniens*, no. 43.

77. Ibid., nos. 43–44.

78. Ibid., no. 45.

79. Gutiérrez, "Liberation," p. 253.

80. Cited in "Liberation of Men and Nations" by William F. Ryan, S.J., and Joseph Komochak, Interamerican Bishops' Meeting, Mexico City, May 18–21, 1971 (Washington: NCCB, 1971), p. 8.

81. Gutiérrez, "Liberation," p. 247.

82. Bishops of Peru, "Justice in the World," passim.

83. Ibid., p. 9. There is no intention here of going into the complicated question of the use of violence to obtain a just social order. For an analysis of this problem, see *A Theology of Protest* by Bernard Häring (New York: Farrar, Straus and Giroux, 1970) and "Violent Revolution", a dissertation by Dennis M. Regan (Rome: Academia Alfonsiana, 1970).

84. Most of these ideas are found in *Populorum Progressio* and *Octogesima Adveniens*, but not in the language of liberation.

85. *Justice in the World*, no. 4.

86. Ibid., no. 16.

87. Ibid., no. 6.

88. Synod of Bishops (1974), "Declaration," October 25, 1974.

89. Nyerere, *Speech to the Maryknoll Congress in New York* (Dar es Salaam: Government Printer, 1970), p. 9.

90. *Octogesima Adveniens*, no. 45.

91. Nyerere, *Ujamaa: Essays on Socialism*, pp. 1, 5.

92. Ibid., p. 17.

93. "Questions and Answers following the Maryknoll Address," October 16, 1970 (mimeographed).

94. For example, Rev. Theodore Slaats, C.S.Sp., of Morogoro College has publicly stated that Nyerere's position here cannot be in accord with papal teaching, which is in principle against all violence as a means of redressing injustice ("International Relations," in *Arusha Declaration and Christian Socialism* [Dar es Salaam: Tanzania Publishing House, 1969], p. 53).

95. Nyerere, *Freedom and Socialism*, p. 24.

96. Julius K. Nyerere "Speech to the United Nations General Assembly" (Dar es Salaam: Government Printer, 1970), p. 4.

97. René Coste, "Peace and Community of Nations," *Commentary on the Documents of Vatican II*, ed. H. Vorgrimler (New York: Herder and Herder, 1969), vol. 5, p. 351.

98. "Humanization" is an older term than "liberation." Father Lebret was emphasizing the theme of humanization in the early 1950s, while the theme of liberation did not appear strongly until the early 1960s with the trouble in Latin America (Charles Elliott, *The Development Debate* [London: SCM Press, 1971], p. 59).

99. Pearson, *Partners in Development*, p. 233.

100. This is an attack on the theory that uneven distribution of income favors savings and investment and therefore economic development (Jean-Yves Calvez, *The Social Thought of John XXIII* (Chicago: Regnery, 1964), pp. 72–73.

101. *Mater et Magistra*, no. 74.

102. Ibid., nos. 213–14.

103. Ibid., nos. 215–17.

104. *Gaudium et Spes*, no. 35.

105. Ibid., no. 25.

106. Ibid., no. 63.

107. Ibid.

108. Ibid., no. 25.

109. Ibid., no. 53.

110. Ibid., no. 39.

111. *Populorum Progressio*, no. 20.

112. Ibid., no. 15.

113. Ibid., no. 76.

114. Ibid., nos. 18–19.

115. Ibid., no. 20.

116. Ibid., no. 21.

117. *Justice in the World*, no. 71.

118. *Mater et Magistra*, no. 73; *Pacem in Terris*, no. 123; *Gaudium et Spes*, no. 66; *Populorum Progressio*, no. 14; *Octogesima Adveniens*, no. 41; *Justice in the World*, no. 18.

119. Even in a country as wealthy as the United States, it is estimated that one-fourth of the people go hungry (Michael Harrington, *The Other America* [New York: Macmillan, 1962]).

120. *Populorum Progressio*, nos. 1, 6.

121. Ibid., no. 11.

122. *Octogesima Adveniens*, no. 7.

123. Ibid., no. 10.

124. *Populorum Progressio*, no. 42.

125. Nyerere, *Ujamaa: Essays on Socialism*, p. 92.

126. Ibid., p. 1.

127. Ibid., p. 92.

128. Bienen, *Party Transformation*, p. 459.

129. Nyerere, *Ujamaa: Essays on Socialism*, pp. 95–96.

130. Nyerere, *Freedom and Socialism*, p. 212.

131. Ibid., pp. 209–10.

132. *Populorum Progressio*, no. 62.

133. Nyerere, *Ujamaa: Essays on Socialism*, pp. 117–18.

134. *Mater et Magistra*, no. 125.

135. Ibid.

136. *Octogesima Adveniens*, nos. 8, 10.

137. *Gaudium et Spes*, no. 29.

138. Nyerere, *Freedom and Socialism*, p. 304.

139. Nyerere, *Ujamaa: Essays on Socialism*, p. 103.

140. Ibid.

141. Nyerere, *Freedom and Socialism*, p. 304.

142. Ibid., p. 305.

143. Ibid., p. 200.

144. *Octogesima Adveniens*, no. 50.

145. Nyerere, *Ujamaa: Essays on Socialism*, p. 104.

146. Ibid.

CHAPTER 21

THE CHURCH'S POSITION ON PRIVATE PROPERTY

President Nyerere is not opposed in principle to the private ownership of property including the means of production. In fact, one of the purposes of *Ujamaa* socialism is to make it possible for everyone to control his own means of production so that his livelihood is not dependent on the whims of another.[1] But to ensure that the overwhelmingly vast majority of the people can control their own means of production, the government must regulate the amount of *productive* property that any one individual can possess. There is no question that the state has this right and duty.[2] The question is the extent to which the state should allow an individual to control productive property. The criterion for judgment is the demands of the common good.[3] This chapter presents the argument that the principles and policies of *Ujamaa* socialism implement to a very high degree the Christian ideal, often formulated in Church teachings, that the goods of this earth are intended for the use of every human being.

The Defense of Private Property

In writing *Mater et Magistra*, Pope John prefaces his teaching on property by noting the changing conditions which attack the right to private property. The attack on the need of private property comes especially from an increasing number of social institutions (e.g., insurance groups, social security programs), which provide security for the future, and also from an increasing value of labor, which guarantees a steady income.[4] This income and security was formerly guaranteed by the possession of a certain amount of property. In view of the changing times, with less stress on the need for private property,

Pope John asks if there has been a change in "man's natural right to own private property, including productive goods."[5] In answering, he reaffirms the traditional teaching of the Church on the right to own private property.

The right of private ownership of goods [*jus privati dominii*], including productive goods, has permanent validity. It is part of the natural order, which teaches that the individual is prior to society and society must be ordered to the good of the individual.[6]

An understanding of what Pope John means by a natural right to private property must include previous Church teaching. The concept of the natural right to property, so strongly stated in *Rerum Novarum* and *Quadragesimo Anno*,[7] is based on the teaching of St. Thomas.[8] Man, according to St. Thomas, has a natural dominion over all external things, and so he has the right to use them.[9] This is a natural right in the strict sense. In considering the question of an individual possessing a given object as his own, St. Thomas distinguishes property from the use of property.[10] St. Thomas sees private property useful for three reasons: people take better care of what is their own; there is better order among people; and private property leads to peace when each person is content with what he has.[11] The actual distribution of property is a matter of positive law.[12]

Pius XII repeated the teaching of St. Thomas, subjecting the right of private property to the higher right of all to have the use of material goods. Pius XII also defended the right of the state to regulate the control over property.

Every man, as a living being gifted with reason, has in fact from nature the fundamental right to make use of the material goods of the earth, while it is left to the will of man and to the juridical statutes of nations to regulate in greater detail the actuation of this right. This individual right cannot in any way be suppressed, even by other clear and undisputed rights over material goods. Undoubtedly the material order, deriving from God, demands also private property and the free reciprocal commerce of goods by interchange and gift, as well as the functioning of the State as a control over both these institutions. But all this remains subordinated to the natural scope of material goods and cannot emancipate itself from the first and fundamental right which concedes their use to all men; but it should rather serve to make possible the actuation of this right in conformity with its scope. Only thus can we and must we secure that private property and the use of material goods bring to society peace and prosperity and long life.[13]

In a radio message on September 1, 1944, Pius XII elaborated on the intervention of the state in matters of private property. He said that the state is able to intervene for the common good and to regulate the use of private property, and also that the state, when other means are not possible, is able to expropriate property, fitting indemnity being given.[14]

This background must be kept in mind while reading *Mater et Magistra*. The right to private property is regulated by the higher right of all to the use of material goods.[15] The right to private property is not an absolute right. If private property were an absolute natural right, the state would have no right to intervene, which is contrary to the teaching of Pius XII.[16] Furthermore, *Mater et Magistra* does not exclude the legitimacy of the necessity of positive law for determining the control of private property.[17]

Pope John has upheld the right to private property as an efficacious means of asserting one's personality[18] and as a guarantee of the essential freedom of the individual.[19]

Further, history and experience testify that in those political regimes which do not recognize the rights of private ownership of goods, productive included, the exercise of freedom in almost every other direction is suppressed or stifled. This suggests, surely, that the exercise of freedom finds its guarantee and incentive in the right of ownership.[20]

Mater et Magistra teaches that it is not enough to assert the right to own private property but it is necessary to "insist on the extension of this right in practice to all classes of citizens."[21] In calling for the widest possible distribution, Pope John gave examples: durable consumer goods, houses, land, tools and equipment, and shares in medium and large business concerns.[22]

Limitations to the Right to Private Property

Beginning with *Gaudium et Spes* there is a new approach in the Church's teaching on property. The stress is not on a person's right to property. In fact, the Council Fathers avoided any reference to a natural right to own property. Rather, the stress is on a person's responsibility in solidarity based on the absolute principle that the goods of the earth are meant for all.

God intended the earth and all that it contains for the use of every human being and people. . . . Whatever the form of ownership may be, as adapted to the legitimate institutions of people according to diverse and changeable circumstances, attention must always be paid to the universal purpose for which created goods are meant. In using them, therefore, a man should regard his lawful possessions not merely as his own but also as common property in the sense that they should accrue to the benefit of not only himself but of others. . . . According to their ability, let all individuals and governments undertake a genuine sharing of their goods. Let them use these goods especially to provide individuals and nations with the means for helping and developing themselves.[23]

With these traditional principles in mind the Council explained the right to property. In new language the Council said that "ownership and other forms of private control" contribute to the expression of personality, facilitate man's participation in society and the economy, provide an area of independence, provide an incentive to do one's duty, and are "a kind of prerequisite for civil liberties."[24]

This is a further evolution in Church thinking on property.[25] In contrast to Pope John's listing of specific things to be privately owned,[26] *Gaudium et Spes* is much more open to other forms of control over material goods, calling simply for "the right to have a share of earthly goods sufficient for oneself and one's family."[27] And avoiding the confusion and the restriction of the term "private property,"[28] the Council called for "ownership and other forms of private control over material goods."[29] Furthermore, "the forms of such dominion or ownership are varied today and are becoming increasingly diversified."[30] Special mention is made of the distribution of goods in developing countries, which is very appropriate to a country like Tanzania with its tribal traditions. "In economically less advanced societies, it is not rare for the communal purpose of earthly goods to be partially satisfied through customs and traditions proper to a community."[31] A further modification is that the need of private property for security has been reduced "in the face of the public funds, rights, and services provided by society."[32] This is a much more adaptive approach to the changeable forms of society and it stands in sharp contrast to *Mater et Magistra*'s reassertion of the permanent validity of the natural right to private property despite the changes in society.[33]

While earlier papal teachings promoted private property as a natural right, the Council Fathers stressed the changeable forms of control over material goods, forms that are historically conditioned and determined by the will of the people (e.g., communal property in certain tribal societies). While these forms of control over material goods are contingent and depend on positive laws, the underlying purpose of these forms of control is not contingent but absolute, namely, a person's natural right to use the things of this world.[34] This purpose is of the metaphysical order and hence of the immutable natural law. The Council, in stressing the necessity of various forms of control over material goods, is promoting, as did previous papal teaching, the fundamental, absolute, natural right of all to use the things of this earth.[35]

Such is the basis in the very law of nature for the most primary and inalienable function of the goods of earth. They are basically social and their most fundamental function is social. Nor is their social character lost after they are portioned out as particular private possession. The common gifts of the one Heavenly Father still retain their social function even though they are owned legitimately by individuals as their private possessions.[36]

This common purpose of created things is prior to an individual's right to ownership of particular created goods. The ideal to be pursued is that *all* may have a greater share in the goods of this world.

Populorum Progressio does not continue the line of development elaborated by *Mater et Magistra* and *Gaudium et Spes*, but speaks of the rights of property strictly in connection with development.[37] It adds little to what has already been taught in *Gaudium et Spes*.[38] After declaring that private property is for no one an absolute and unconditional right, it reaffirms the social obligation that arises from the universal destination of material goods.[39] This is a specific rebuff to economic theories that lean to the liberal capitalism which "consider material gain the key motive for economic progress, competition as the supreme law of economics, and private ownership of the means of production as an absolute right that has no limits and carries no corresponding social obligation."[40]

Concerning landed estates, *Populorum Progressio* has taken a stronger position than previous Church teachings. The Council said that whenever the common good requires expropriation, compensation "must be reckoned in equity after all the circumstances have been weighed."[41] *Populorum Progressio* is stronger in calling for expropriation and without explicitly mentioning compensation as necessary.

The common good sometimes demands the expropriation of certain landed estates if they impede the general prosperity because they are extensive, unused or poorly used, or because they bring hardship to peoples or are detrimental to the interests of the country.[42]

Father Lebret states some of the problems involved in determining just compensation for expropriation or nationalization. In the first place, the distinction must be made between laws transferring property from the private to the public sector and laws that prevent land speculation on agricultural and construction property.[43] Who should profit most from increased value of land, the land speculator or the nation? If the government does not redistribute the surplus wealth of the rich, will it not end up impoverished itself? Is a government bound to pay compensation when it does not have the resources to establish the necessary structures for developing the country's economy? Lebret, noting that the Council did not go into much detail, concludes that the local episcopate will have to take a stand on these questions.[44]

Octogesima Adveniens does not treat ownership directly, but it does give the guidelines for determining the use of property based on the principle of solidarity.

The more fortunate should renounce some of their rights so as to place their goods more generously at the service of others. If beyond legal rules, there is really no deeper feeling of respect for and service to others, then even equality before the law can serve as an alibi for flagrant discrimination, continued exploitation and actual contempt. With renewed education in solidarity, an overemphasis of equality can give rise to an individualism in which each one claims his own rights without wishing to be answerable for the common good.[45]

This same theme was continued in the 1971 Synod, which saw "the unequal distribution which places decisions concerning three quarters of income, investment and trade in the hands of one third of the human race" as a major cause of social sin which oppresses the dignity of man.[46]

Summary of Nyerere's Position

Every government regulates some control over the means of production.[47] Of special note to Tanzania have been the policies of leasehold land and extensive nationalization. The leasehold system allows all citizens to have a section of land as long as they use it. It prevents one person from exploiting another by "renting to him that which is a free gift of God."[48] The freehold system, the system used by tribal culture, avoids the evils of landed estates, while at the same time it provides land for all.

As explained in chapter 17, Nyerere has an extensive policy of nationalization with the purpose to ensure that all share in the wealth they helped create. What general guidelines does the Church give to tell if nationalization has gone too far or, conversely, not far enough? *Octogesima Adveniens* gives the two extremes in contrasting Marxist economics against liberal capitalism.

For others, [Marxism] is first and foremost the collective exercise of political and economic power under the direction of a single party, which would be the sole expression and guarantee of the welfare of all, and would deprive individuals and other groups of any possibility of initiative and choice.[49]

Certainly, says Pope Paul, personal initiative must be maintained and developed but not to the extent fostered by liberal capitalism.[50]

. . . Nor can [the Christian] adhere to the liberal ideology which believes it exalts individual freedom by withdrawing it from every limitation, by stimulating it through exclusive seeking of interests and power, and by considering social solidarities as more or less automatic consequences of individual initiative, not as an aim and a major criterion of the value of the social organization.[51]

Within these extremes each state must decide what amount and what kind of control it will exercise for the best interest of the common good. Pope John gave some specific guidelines. Noting the necessity of a wider sphere of activity for public authority, he gave the principle of subsidiarity as a norm to determine competence:

The State and other agencies of public law must not extend their ownership beyond what is clearly required by considerations of the common good properly understood, and even then there must be safeguards. Otherwise private ownership could be reduced beyond measure, or, even worse, completely destroyed.[52]

Oswald von Nell-Breuning, in analyzing this principle, notes that, the danger of power attendant upon centralization notwithstanding, it is ultimately up to the government itself to decide the extent of the government's sphere of activity.[53]

In evaluating nationalization in Tanzania in light of principles given by Church teaching, the question, then, is not: "Is the TANU government going beyond its competence?" but: "How do the nationalization policies work for the common good?" As explained in previous chapters, the policy of nationalization in accord with the overall philosophy of *Ujamaa* socialism not only is trying to raise the living standard of all the people, but is trying to prevent the exploitation of one person by another in which one person has economic control over the life of another. *Ujamaa* socialism is striving to give every person control over his own means of production. The nationalization policies as well as the program of leasehold property are designed not only to prevent the vast majority of citizens from being controlled against their will by a powerful few, but to provide all people with property, including control over the means of production, so that they can live in freedom and security. In ecclesial language, the policies of *Ujamaa* socialism are striving to reduce the "undeserved hardship" of farmers and to eliminate the "scandal of glaring inequalities not merely in the enjoyment of possession but even more in the exercise of power."[54] More positively, these programs are providing for the vast majority a greater role in society and in the economy,[55] more stable independence, an increase of human freedom, and an incentive for carrying on one's functions and duty.[56]

NOTES

1. Julius K. Nyerere, *Ujamaa: Essays on Socialism* (Dar es Salaam: Oxford University Press, 1968), p. 81.

2. Vatican Council II, *Gaudium et Spes*, December 7, 1965, no. 71; text in *The Documents of Vatican II*, ed. Walter Abbott, S.J. (New York: America Press, 1966), and in *The Gospel of Peace and Justice: Catholic Social Teaching since Pope John*, presented by Joseph Gremillion (Maryknoll, New York: Orbis Books, 1976). See also Paul VI, *Populorum Progressio*, March 26, 1967 (Glen Rock, N.J.: Paulist Press, 1967), no. 23; text also in *Gospel of Peace and Justice*.

3. *Gaudium et Spes*, no. 69; *Populorum Progressio*, no. 24.

4. John XXIII, *Mater et Magistra*, May 15, 1961, *The Pope Speaks* (1962), nos. 104–07; text also in *Gospel of Peace and Justice*.

5. Ibid., no. 108.

6. Ibid., no. 109. "As a further consequence of man's nature, he has the right to the private ownership of property, including productive goods" (*Pacem in Terris*, in *The Pope Speaks*, 9 [1963], no. 21; text also in *Gospel of Peace and Justice*).

7. *Mater et Magistra*, nos. 19, 30.

8. *Summa Theologiae*, II/II, q. 66, a. 1–2.

9. Ibid., a. 1.

10. Ibid., a. 2.

11. Papal teaching since Leo XIII added other reasons for defending private property: defense against public power (*Quadragesimo Anno*, no. 49); defense of human dignity (*Rerum Novarum*, no. 5); security for future (*Rerum Novarum*, no. 6); security for the family (*Mater et Magistra*, no. 112); and deproletarianization of workers (*Quadragesimo Anno*, no. 61).

12. *Summa Theologiae*, II/II, q. 66, a. 2, ad. 1.

13. *Acta Apostolicae Sedis* (1941), p. 221.

14. Ibid. (1944), p. 254.

15. Frans Kluber explains the distinction between an absolute and a relative norm. "Since, however, this stand in favor of private property is based on empirical facts and changing historical experience, and not on metaphysical arguments, it belongs—in contrast to the principle of the social purpose of property—not to the unchangeable (absolute) norms of natural law but to the relative norms, according to scholastic terminology to the positive law of the *jus gentium*. The system of private property remains a precept of changeable natural law as long as the empirical facts on which it is based retain their validity" (*Sacramentum Mundi*, vol. 5, p. 110).

16. Jean-Yves Calvez, S.J., *The Social Thought of John XXIII*, trans. George McKenzie (Chicago: Henry Regnery, 1964), p. 21.

17. *Mater et Magistra*, nos. 117, 120.

18. Ibid., no. 112.

19. Ibid., no. 111.

20. Calvez says that the political significance of private property "is doubtless the most novel characteristic of John XXIII's teaching" (*Social Thought*, p. 24).

21. *Mater et Magistra*, no. 113.

22. Ibid., no. 115.

23. *Gaudium et Spes*, no. 69.

24. Ibid., no. 71.

25. Georges Jarlot, S.J., "La Dottrina della Propietà di Pio XII al Populorum Progressio," *Civiltà Cattolica* 2 (1967), p. 353.

26. " . . . To pursue an economic and social policy which facilitates the widest possible distribution of private property in terms of durable consumer goods, houses, land, tools, and equipment (in case of craftsmen and owners of family farms), and shares in medium and large business concerns" (*Mater et Magistra*, no. 115).

27. *Gaudium et Spes*, no. 69.

28. Father Lebret says that the whole notion of "property" has become analogous and ambiguous and could create an impasse for the Church's social doctrine. It should be replaced by the term "control over goods" or "power over goods." "The word 'property' no longer permits us to talk precisely about man's various rights today: over the means and instruments of production; over collective social assets; over social security; over durable and non-durable goods for consumer use" ("Economic and Social Life: The Community of Nations," *The Church Today*, ed. Group 2000 [New York: Newman Press, 1967], p. 188).

29. "Cum proprietas ac aliae bona exteriora dominii privati formae" (*Gaudium et Spes*, no. 71).

30. *Gaudium et Spes*, no. 71.

31. Ibid., no. 69.

32. Ibid., no. 71. But this socialization of security for the individual and the family does not eliminate ownership or other forms of control over goods, nor is socialization of security provision without danger of citizens falling "into a kind of sluggishness toward society" (*Gaudium et Spes*, no. 69).

33. *Mater et Magistra*, no. 109.

34. Jarlot, "La Dottrina," p. 355.

35. "God intended the earth and all that it contains for the use of every human being and people" (*Gaudium et Spes*, no. 69).

36. Bernard Häring, C.Ss.R., *The Law of Christ* (Westminster, Md.: Newman Press, 1966), vol. 3, p. 499.

37. Jarlot, "La Dottrina," p. 356.

38. José Díez-Alegría, "Problemi di Etica Sociale" (Rome: Pontifica Università Gregoriana, n.d.), p. 49.

39. *Populorum Progressio*, no. 23.

40. Ibid., no. 26.

41. *Gaudium et Spes*, no. 71.

42. *Populorum Progressio*, no. 24.

43. Lebret, "Economic and Social Life," p. 189.

44. Ibid., p. 190.

45. Paul VI, *Octogesima Adveniens*, May 14, 1971, On the Occasion of the Eightieth Anniversary

of the Encyclical Rerum Novarum (Vatican Typis Polyglottis Vaticanis, 1971), no. 23; text in *Gospel of Peace and Justice.*

46. Ibid., no. 25.

47. John Kenneth Galbraith in *The New Industrial State* notes how much government control there is in even such an avowedly free enterprise country as the United States. "The services of Federal, state and local governments now account for between a fifth and a quarter of all economic activity. In 1929 it was about eight percent. This far exceeds the government share in such an avowedly socialist state as India, considerably exceeds that in the anciently social democratic kingdoms of Sweden and Norway, and is not wholly incommensurate with the share in Poland, a Communist country which, however, is heavily agricultural and which has left its agriculture in private ownership. A very large part (between one-third and one-half) of public activity is concerned with national defense and the exploration of space. This is not regarded even by conservatives as socialism. Elsewhere the nomenclature is less certain" (New York: Signet, 1967, p. 14.)

48. Julius K. Nyerere, *Freedom and Unity* (Dar es Salaam: Oxford University Press, 1966), p. 58.

49. *Octogesima Adveniens,* no. 33.

50. Ibid., no. 35.

51. Ibid., no. 26.

52. *Mater et Magistra,* no. 117.

53. "Those who hold ultimate responsibility for the well-being of the whole community must be in a position to regulate competence and to vest in themselves those competences that they require in order to be able to offer to the members who make up the whole community the assistance due to them" (Nell-Breuning, "Social Movements," in *Sacramentum Mundi,* vol. 6, p. 115.)

54. *Populorum Progressio,* no. 9.

55. *Gaudium et Spes,* no. 71.

56. Ibid.

CHAPTER 22

CHURCH TEACHING
ON SOCIALISM

Tanzania from the beginning of its independence has been a socialist country. " 'Ujamaa,' then, or 'Familyhood,' describes our socialism."[1] To a Christian socialist it may seem obvious that this does not equate *Ujamaa* with communism.[2] However, in 1970 after almost ten years of independence under *Ujamaa* socialism, Nyerere found it necessary to attack critics who implied his government was communistic. He said:

Then before we left Tabora, somebody showed me the booklet, *Huu Ndio Uhuru*. It is a translation of *Divini Redemptoris*, the Encyclical on Communism issued by Pope Pius XI. This is the point I want to make. The booklet is published in 1970; and I ask now—why should the Catholic Church be preaching against Communism in 1970? The Encyclical was written in 1932. Why make propaganda against Communism? The booklet has the picture of Mwenge [the Torch which is the symbol of the TANU Party] on the cover and so one might think that it is published by TANU! I still ask why not publish and preach *Populorum Progressio*? I am sorry about my own Church: she is negative instead of being positive. If she preached social justice positively, there would be no Communism. If she just condemns Communism by words, this is no solution.[3]

A year later at the Episcopal Conference in Dar es Salaam, in July 1971, Father Bernard Joinet spent a major part of his talk, "The Role of the Church in Politics," explaining that *Ujamaa* socialism is not the same as communism.[4] According to Father Joinet, the fears and confusions over *Ujamaa* socialism have been increased since the Acquisition Act of April 1971.[5] In February

1972 Nyerere complained about the lack of support among Christians for *Ujamaa* socialism. In addressing a group of priests he said that the word "socialism" has intimidated and confused people, especially the Christians, from whom he would have expected the fullest and most cordial support.[6]

This chapter will treat the Church's position and how it correlates with *Ujamaa* socialism.

Quadragesimo Anno

The Church's teaching on socialism was virtually unchanged from *Quadragesimo Anno* until *Octogesima Adveniens*.[7] *Mater et Magistra* repeated the judgment of Pius XI, and Vatican Council II[8] and *Populorum Progressio* did not explicitly treat the subject.[9] For an understanding, therefore, of the Church's teaching today on socialism it is necessary to go back to *Quadragesimo Anno*.

Although Leo XIII strongly attacked the theory of socialism,[10] socialism in the late 1800s was not a major political power. By 1931, however, socialism had been entrenched in Russia for almost a quarter century and was continuing to spread and to assume many new forms. In its extreme form, socialism pursued a twofold aim: "merciless class warfare, and complete abolition of private ownership; and this it does, not in secret and by hidden methods, but openly, publicly, and by every means even the most violent."[11] More moderate socialism advocates abolition of private property and "sometimes closely approaches the just demands of Christian social reformers."[12] Pius XI condemned socialism, even in its moderate form, because "it conceives human society in a way utterly alien to Christian truth."[13] Rather than seeing the purpose of society as a place where man "may cultivate and evolve to the full all his faculties to the praise and glory of his Creator, [socialism], entirely ignorant of and unconcerned about this sublime end both of individuals and of society, affirms that human society was instituted merely for the sake of material well-being."[14] Besides seeing society as being established merely for material well-being, socialism, according to Pius XI, argues that economic activity must be carried on collectively; it demands that all of man's higher goods, including liberty, must be sacrificed to the needs of higher production; and that the necessary loss of human dignity will be compensated for by the abundance of goods socially produced.[15]

This is a restricted concept of socialism. According to Oswald von Nell-Breuning, the definition of socialism used by Pius XI was that made by Gustav Gundlach, S.J.: Socialism is "a movement affecting the whole of life, essentially a feature of the capitalistic age by reason of its scale of values and its methods, which seeks to secure the freedom and earthly happiness of all on a permanent basis by anchoring these in the institutions of an expertly organized human society from which all trace of heteronomy is banished."[16] Such a concept of socialism is against Christian faith. "Religious socialism, Christian socialism, are contradictory terms. No one can be at the same time a good Catholic and a true socialist."[17]

Given this concept of socialism, the question becomes: "Does a particular socialism in practice correspond to the socialism described by Pius XI?" Cardinal Bourne, archbishop of Westminster, quickly pointed out that it did not apply to the socialism of the British Labour Party.[18] Most democratic socialists would not identify with the socialism described by Pius XI.[19]

Mater et Magistra repeated Pius XI's condemnation of socialism in the section of the encyclical reviewing the teaching of *Quadragesimo Anno*, but did not treat socialism in the doctrinal part of the encyclical.[20] Pierre Bigo interprets the silence of Pope John on socialism as a desire to avoid an all-embracing pro- nouncement on socialism and to leave it up to Christians to interpret each separate socialism.[21]

Pacem in Terris

In *Pacem in Terris*, Pope John made a distinction between the ideology itself and the practical activities or undertakings of the ideology. According to Bartolomeo Sorge, this distinction prepared the way for two new doctrinal pronouncements on socialism in *Octogesima Adveniens:* namely, a new attitude of investigation into contemporary ideologies, particularly socialism; and the specific contribution to the construction of a new society, but not any longer presented as a "third way" between socialism and liberalism.[22] The following distinction between ideology and activity, made by Pope John, was quoted in its entirety in *Octogesima Adveniens*[23] and this distinction was used in the apostolic letter at least six times.[24]

Neither can false philosophical teachings regarding the nature, origin and destiny of the universe and of man be identified with historical movements that have economic, social, cultural or political ends, not even when these movements have drawn and still draw inspiration therefrom. Because the teachings, once they are drawn up and defined, remain always the same, while the movements, being concerned with histori- cal situations in constant evolution, cannot but be influenced by these latter and cannot avoid, therefore, being subject to changes, even of a profound nature. Besides, who can deny that those movements, in so far as they conform to the dictates of right reason and are interpreters of the lawful aspirations of the human person, contain elements that are positive and deserving of approval?[25]

Octogesima Adveniens

The foregoing passage of John XXIII was quoted in *Octogesima Adveniens* in calling for a new attitude of investigation into contemporary ideologies.[26] And this distinction of Pope John's was made again in different words calling the

Christian to his duty to investigate: " . . . The search goes on between ideological and pragmatic tendencies. The Christian has the duty to take part in the search and in the organization and life of political society."[27] The reason the search for a better model for society is so pressing today is that people are aspiring for a more democratic type of society with greater equality and participation, and so far there is no model of society that gives complete satisfaction.[28]

For Christians engaging in political activity, Pope Paul warns against identifying the activity with the false ideology of Marxism or with the other extreme—liberal ideology—which exalts the individual's freedom without limitation. The Holy Father is very specific in what he condemns in Marxist ideology.

He [the Christian] cannot adhere to the Marxist ideology, to its atheistic materialism, to its dialectic of violence and to the way it absorbs individual freedom in the collectivity, at the same time denying all transcendence to man and his personal and collective history.[29]

The realm of the state or political party is political activity. It is beyond the competence of the state or the political party to impose "an ideology by means that would lead to a dictatorship over minds."[30]

In speaking about socialism itself, Pope Paul notes the ambiguity in the present-day understanding of the word and he calls for distinguishing between the various levels of expression of socialism to guide concrete choices.[31] The distinction must be made between political organizations with generous aspirations for a more just society and ideologies which claim a complete and self-sufficient picture of the human person, always keeping in mind that these distinctions are completely separate and independent. "This insight will enable Christians to see the degree of commitment possible along these lines, while safeguarding the values, especially those of liberty, responsibility, and openness to the spiritual, which guarantees the integral development of man."[32] Father Sorge sees this as the first time a papal document explicitly admits, although with reserve and due guarantees, the possibility that a Christian might adhere to a determined historical movement of socialism.[33]

In *Rerum Novarum*, Leo XIII outlined a solution to social problems midway between the two extremes of laissez-faire liberalism and socialism.[34] In *Quadragesimo Anno* Pius XI treated the possibility of a middle course or "third way" between Christian principles and socialism. Considering the possibility of such a middle course strictly on an ideological level, Pius XI declared that socialism, however mitigated, could not ever be brought into harmony with the dogmas of the Catholic Church because it conceives human society in a way utterly alien to Christian truth.[35] And staying on the ideological level, Pius XI urged "those who wish to be apostles amongst the socialists . . . let their first endeavour be to convince socialists that their demands, in so far as they are just, are defended much more cogently by the principle of Christian faith, and are promoted much more efficaciously by the power of Christian charity."[36]

In *Octogesima Adveniens*, Paul VI, having made the distinction between ideology and concrete activity, calls Christians not to form a new ideology but "to go beyond every system and every ideology."[37] "The Church invites all Christians to take up a double task of inspiring and of innovating, in order to make structures evolve, so as to adapt them to the real needs of today."[38] The Church today does not intend to intervene "to authenticate a given structure or to propose a ready-made model."[39] Rather than authenticating a given structure, the Church under the driving force of the gospel must become a conscience to "the changing situations of this world."[40] These changes, especially the change of ever increasing technocracy, will have to be counterbalanced by ever new forms of democracy, making it possible for each person to express himself and have a greater part in shared responsibility.[41] Rather than proposing an ideological synthesis between liberalism and socialism, Pope Paul is stressing the responsibility of Christians to overcome ideologies and to work with others for a more just world.[42]

In calling Christians to fulfill their responsibilities toward society, Pope Paul warns not only against adhering to false ideologies but also against looking for "utopias" which claim to resolve the political problems of modern society better than the ideologies. "The appeal to a utopia is often a convenient excuse for those who wish to escape from concrete tasks in order to take refuge in an imaginary world. To live in a hypothetical future is a facile alibi for rejecting immediate responsibilities."[43] The Christian "animated by the power of the Spirit of Jesus Christ" has the responsibility to "involve himself in the building up of the human city."[44] Concretely, this means a greater involvement in political activity because in the social and economic field, the ultimate decision rests with the political power.

To take politics seriously ·at its different levels—local, regional, national and worldwide—is to affirm the duty of man, of every man, to recognize the concrete reality and the value of the freedom of choice that is offered to him to seek to bring about both the good of the city and of the nation and of mankind. Politics are a demanding manner—but not the only one—of living the Christian commitment to the service of others. Without of course solving every problem, it endeavors to apply solutions to the relationships men have with one another. The domain of politics is wide and comprehensive, but not exclusive. An attitude of encroachment, which would tend to set up politics as an absolute value, would bring serious danger. While recognizing the autonomy of the reality of politics, Christians who are invited to take up political activity should try to make their choices consistent with the Gospel and, in the framework of a legitimate plurality, to give both personal and collective witness to the seriousness of their faith by effective and disinterested service of men.[45]

With this stress on political activity, Pope Paul has extended the principle of subsidiarity beyond the economic field[46] into the social and political sphere.[47]

"This legitimate aspiration [for a greater sharing in responsibility and in decision-making] becomes more evident as the cultural level rises, as the sense of freedom develops and as man becomes more aware of how, in a world facing an uncertain future, the choices today already condition the life of tomorrow."[48]

The teaching of Paul VI on socialism can be seen reflected concretely in the teaching of the bishops of Peru. The Peruvian bishops, in rejecting the economic expression and ideological basis of capitalism, called for the creation of a qualitatively different society.[49] Citing the different levels of socialism in *Octogesima Adveniens,* they called for a more just society that values freedom, responsibility, openness to things spiritual, and which will guarantee the development of man.[50] More specifically, the bishops called for democracy made real through political participation, through the human concept and realization of work, and through the submission of capital to the needs of the whole society. "Consequently, a society so understood excludes certain historical socialisms which we do not accept because of their bureaucracy, their totalitarianism, or their militant atheism."[51]

In summary, the Church's attitude toward socialism today is characterized by a desire to cooperate with all in searching for ways to build a more just society.[52] As an ideology the Church condemns as contrary to Christian faith a socialism which denies all transcendence to the person or holds a dialectic of violence or absorbs individual freedom in the collectivity, just as it condemns any liberalism which exalts human freedom without limits. As a concrete political activity, the Church does not authenticate any given structure but urges Christians to cooperate with all people in working for the common good by making structures evolve so as to meet the needs of today.

Summary of Nyerere's Position

Following the distinction emphasized by Pope Paul, *Ujamaa* socialism can be viewed as either an ideology or a concrete program of action. As an ideology, it is easier to say what *Ujamaa* is not. It is not a historical socialism born of European class struggle; it does not deny God; it is not rooted in dialectical materialism; it rejects Marxist dogmatism as well as communist suppression of individual freedom; it does not advocate violent class struggle. It is really not an ideology.[53] Rather, it is an attitude of mind. "In a socialist society it is the socialist attitude of mind, and not the right adherence to a standard political pattern [ideology], which is needed to ensure that the people care for each other's welfare."[54]

As a concrete activity, *Ujamaa* socialism implements policies that are guided by certain values: namely, the purpose of all social activity is the person; all people are equal in theory and in practice; society must uphold human dignity; society must be governed democratically; everyone must work and receive a return in proportion to his efforts; and there must be no exploitation of one person by another. "All these things together are the hallmark of a socialist society."[55] Nyerere points out that these values cannot be legislated but they have to be built. Tanzania is not now a socialist country; it is only a country whose people have firmly committed themselves to building socialism.[56]

In contrasting *Ujamaa* socialism with recent Church teaching on socialism, the question becomes, then, not one of agreement but, How well does *Ujamaa* build up a society that is more just? The value of a specific program must be determined in the concrete situation by its contribution to the common good.[57] And these programs will continually have to evolve to meet the needs of the times.[58] But even more important than any political outlook, according to Paul VI, is the Christian's acceptance of his own responsibility for building up a more just society.

Let each one examine himself, to see what he has done up to now, and what he ought to do. It is not enough to recall principles, state intentions, point to crying injustices and utter prophetic denunciations; these words will lack real weight unless they are accompanied for each individual by a livelier awareness of responsibility and by effective action. It is too easy to throw back on others responsibility for injustices, if at the same time one does not realize how each one shares in it personally, and how personal conviction is needed first. This basic humility will rid action of all inflexibility and sectarianism; it will also avoid discouragement in the face of a task which seems limitless in size.[59]

NOTES

1. Julius K. Nyerere, *Ujamaa: Essays on Socialism* (Dar es Salaam: Oxford University Press, 1968), p. 12.

2. Bernard Häring, *The Law of Christ* (Westminster, Md.: Newman Press, 1966), vol. 3, p. 520.

3. "President Nyerere and the Role of Priests in Tanzania" (a transcript between President Nyerere and Father Robert Rweyemasu, secretary of the Tanzania Episcopal Conference, on August 3, 1970; mimeographed), p. 3.

4. Bernard Joinet, W.F., "The Role of the Church in Politics" (address to the Tanzania Episcopal Conference in Dar es Salaam, July, 1971; mimeographed), pp. 5–10.

5. Ibid., pp. 1–2.

6. *Osservatore Romano*, February 23, 1972, p. 6.

7. Bartolomeo Sorge, S.J., "L'Apporto Dottrinale della Lettera Apostolica 'Octogesima Adveniens,' " *Civiltà Cattolica* 2 (1971), p. 425.

8. The Council Fathers did not discuss socialism but communism under the topic of atheism. They finally decided neither to condemn communism afresh, nor even to mention it in the final text (Joseph Ratzinger, "Dignity of Human Person," *Commentary on the Documents of Vatican II*, ed. H. Vorgrimler (New York: Herder and Herder, 1969), vol. 5, pp. 143–50.

9. Sorge "L'Apporto," p. 426.

10. Leo XIII, *Rerum Novarum*, May 15, 1891 (New York: Paulist Press, 1939), nos. 3, 11, 12.

11. Pius XI, *Quadragesimo Anno*, May 15, 1931, in *The Social Order* (London: Catholic Truth Society, 1960), no. 112.

12. Ibid., no. 113.

13. Ibid., no. 117.

14. Ibid., no. 118.

15. Ibid., no. 119.

16. Oswald von Nell-Breuning, "Social Movements," *Sacramentum Mundi*, ed. Karl Rahner (New York: Herder and Herder, 1970), vol. 6, p. 102.

17. *Quadragesimo Anno*, no. 120.

18. Nell-Breuning, "Social Movements," p. 102.

19. Ibid.

20. John XXIII, *Mater et Magistra*, May 15, 1961, no. 34; text in *The Pope Speaks* 7 (1962), and in *The Gospel of Peace and Justice: Catholic Social Teaching Since Pope John*, presented by Joseph Gremillion (Maryknoll, New York: Orbis Books, 1976).

21. Pierre Bigo, *La Doctrine Sociale de l'Eglise* (Paris: PUF, 1965), p. 178. Bigo concludes that to understand how Pope John really understood socialism it is necessary to analyze all his pronouncements on the structure of economics in society.

22. Sorge, "L'Apporto," pp. 419–20. In explaining what he means by the new doctrinal contributions, Father Sorge says that the newness is not in the sense that these are points of doctrine which up to now have not been discussed, but the newness is in the fact they have acquired in a definite way in the social thought of the Church a position of great importance both on the theoretical and the practical level concerning problems of our day which are much discussed and debated (p. 419).

23. *Octogesima Adveniens*, no. 30.

24. Ibid., nos. 24, 25, 26, 30, 31, 37.

25. *Pacem in Terris*, no. 115.

26. *Octogesima Adveniens*, no. 30.

27. Ibid., no. 24.

28. Ibid.

29. Ibid., no. 26.

30. Ibid., no. 25.

31. Ibid., no. 31.

32. Ibid.

33. Sorge, "L'Apporto," p. 426.

34. *Rerum Novarum*, nos. 2, 3; *Quadragesimo Anno*, no. 101.

35. *Quadragesimo Anno*, no. 177. An American commentator, Raymond Miller, C.Ss.R., in *Forty Years After: Pius XI and the Social Order*, which was written in a time of great anticommunist sentiment, said: "Note that the Socialism referred to here by the Pope is not one single party; it is the term he uses to cover all the various shades of 'pink' " (St. Paul: Radio Replies Press, 1947, pp. 251–52).

36. *Quadragesimo Anno*, no. 116.

37. Johannes Metz in *Theology in the World* explains why theology cannot be presented as ideology. Historically, the Enlightenment, and later, Marxism, approached "religion as an ideology, seeking to unmask it as a function, as the ideological superstructure of definite societal usages and power structures." The result is that the Christian message of salvation and sociopolitical reality move farther and farther apart (New York: Herder and Herder, 1969, p. 108).

38. *Octogesima Adveniens*, no. 50.

39. Ibid., no. 42.

40. Ibid.

41. Ibid., no. 47.

42. Sorge, "L'Apporto," p. 428.

43. *Octogesima Adveniens*, no. 37.

44. Ibid.

45. Ibid., no. 46.

46. John XXIII, *Mater et Magistra*, May 15, 1961, no. 117; text in *The Pope Speaks* 7 (1962), and in *Gospel of Peace and Justice*.

47. *Octogesima Adveniens*, no. 47.

48. Ibid.

49. Bishops of Peru, "Justice in the World," *IDOC International* 37 (December 11, 1971), p. 7.

50. Ibid., pp. 7–8.

51. Ibid., p. 8.

52. The language of *Octogesima Adveniens* stands in sharp contrast to the paternalism of

Quadragesimo Anno: "This is a question which holds many in suspense; and many are Catholic who, realizing clearly that Christian principles can never be either sacrificed or minimized, seem to be raising their eyes towards the Holy See, and earnestly beseeching Us to decide whether or not this form of socialism has retracted so far its false doctrines that it can now be accepted. In Our fatherly solicitude We desire to satisfy these petitions, and Our pronouncement is as follows" (*Quadragesimo Anno*, no. 117).

53. Werner Post says that it is almost impossible to give a strict definition of "ideology," because it has been used in so many ways ("Ideology," *Sacramentum Mundi*, vol. 3, p. 95). Roger Heckel notes that the word "ideology" is not used the same throughout *Octogesima Adveniens* (*Cahiers*, January 15, 1972, pp. 60, 62). According to Karl Rahner the word "ideology" today has a pejorative meaning in that it is a system of thought which refuses to recognize the demands of reality which contradict its assumptions by "arbitrary obduracy, purely speculative evasiveness and intolerance" ("Theology," *Sacramentum Mundi*, vol. 6, p. 239). That Nyerere bases *Ujamaa* on unprovable assumptions of the equality of man and that the purpose of society is man does not make it an ideology. As Siebel and Martin note: "If every universal view of things, every form of group consciousness is termed an ideology, this lends itself to a relativism for which the distinction between ideology and truth is a matter of indifference" ("Sociology," *Sacramentum Mundi*, vol. 6, p. 135).

54. Nyerere, *Ujamaa: Essays on Socialism*, p. 1.

55. Julius K. Nyerere, *Freedom and Socialism* (Dar es Salaam: Oxford University Press, 1968), p. 9.

56. Julius K. Nyerere, "From Uhuru to Ujamaa," *Africa Today* (Summer 1974), p. 6.

57. *Octogesima Adveniens*, no. 24.

58. Ibid., no. 50.

59. Ibid., no. 48.

CHAPTER 23

CONCLUSION

In contrasting the principles of *Ujamaa* socialism with the social teaching of the Church there is obviously no conflict. But the more difficult part is evaluating these principles in concrete situations. Principles have no meaning if they are not applied. Nyerere has demonstrated a course of action for improving the quality of life in accord with the fundamental principle that society exists for the good of all people equally. While its programs are progressive there is careful monitoring from a continent increasingly inclined toward socialism to see if they will work. The *Ujamaa* village program has long been seen as a testing ground for African socialist theories.

Nyerere is the first to admit that Tanzania has not achieved socialism (the country is still too poor) or self-reliance.[1] They are still goals. Any judgment of the justice of a particular program must be seen in the overall goals of *Ujamaa* and in the unique situation of the Tanzanian people, a situation made more difficult by a severe two-year drought, quadrupling prices for imported oil, and runaway inflation beyond their control. This background must be kept in mind in trying to evaluate the recent uprooting of millions of peasants to *Ujamaa* villages at a speed that seems to violate the Arusha Declaration's policy of "the gradual conversion of existing institutions into others more in accordance with our philosophy." Whether Tanzania can make a "rural breakthrough" on a continent of falling agricultural production remains to be seen, and the experts are watching closely.[2] At the height of the drought in 1974 Nyerere reflected on his government's decisions: "We shall probably continue to make mistakes in tactics, and in the execution of our policies. But we shall continue as we have begun—trying to create a society in which all citizens work together in freedom, dignity, and equality, for their common good."[3]

Nyerere's *Ujamaa* socialism has value beyond the limits of Tanzania. As

266

Pope Paul has noted, the social problem has become increasingly worldwide. And the recent Roman Synods have stressed our need for global unity and international justice. In this regard, Nyerere articulates well the plight of a poor country whose people are on the short end of a worldwide economic system that gives 80 percent of the wealth to only 20 percent of the people. Besides moving our conscience, Tanzania can teach us in the "developed" countries about the quality of life, responsibility to others, the overcoming of an individual ethic, and the lifestyle of a leader who puts service before prestige. Perhaps the importance of Nyerere's vision can best be seen in his own words in a reply to a question on whether he was long on idealism and short on pragmatism:

True idealism goes together with realism; they are obverse sides of the same coin. One represents the vision—the goal. The other represents the road to that goal, and the obstacles. It is no good being so concerned about the obstacles on the road that you allow yourself to be deflected from the goal. But it's also no good to go along without a realistic look at the road ahead. Either way brings disaster. As for whether I myself overemphasize one fault or the other—that is for history to say! And I do think that the greater danger in the modern world is to forget what the struggle is all about.[4]

NOTES

1. Julius K. Nyerere, "From Uhuru to Ujamaa," *Africa Today* (Summer 1974), p. 6.
2. David Ottaway, "Tanzania: Peasants on the Move," *Washington Post*, May 18, 1975.
3. Nyerere, "From Uhuru to Ujamaa," p. 8.
4. Peter Webb, "Nyerere: Operation Bootstrap or Backstep?" *Newsweek*, March 6, 1967, p. 47.

BIBLIOGRAPHY

PART ONE

To the authors, editors and publishers of the following books, periodicals, newspapers, pamphlets, and official documents, the author gratefully acknowledges valued help in the factual presentation and analytical background of this book.—W.R.D.

BOOKS

Bienen, Henry. *Party Transformation and Economic Development*. Princeton: Princeton University Press, 1970.

Burton, Sir Richard. *First Footsteps in East Africa*. London: Routledge, Kegan Paul, 1966.

Chidzero, B.T.G. *Tanganyika: An International Trusteeship*. London: Oxford University Press, 1961.

Coupland, R. *East Africa and Its Invaders*. Oxford: Clarendon Press, 1938.

Delf, George. *Asians in East Africa*. London: Oxford University Press, 1963.

Duggan, William R. *Socio-Economic Profile of South Africa*. New York: Praeger Publishers, 1973.

Filesi, Teobaldo. *China and Africa in the Middle Ages*. London: Cass & Co., 1972.

Gardner, Brian. *German East*. London: Cassell, 1963.

Hamilton, Genesta. *Princes of Zinj*. London: Hutchinson, 1957.

Hancock, W.K. *Smuts*, vol. 1: *The Sanguine Years—1870-1919*. Cambridge: Cambridge University Press, 1962.

Hill, M.F. *Permanent Way*, vol. 2: *Story of the Tanganyika Railways*. Nairobi: East African Railways & Harbours, 1957.

Hughes, A.J. *East Africa: The Search for Unity*. Baltimore: Penguin Books, 1963.

Ingham, Kenneth. *History of East Africa*. London: Longmans, Green, 1962.

Kinambo, I.N. and A.J. Temu, eds. *History of Tanzania*. Evanston, Ill.: Northwestern University Press, 1969.

Leslie, J.K. *Survey of Dar Es Salaam*. London: Oxford University Press, 1963.

Ley, Charles D., ed. *Portuguese Voyages—1498-1663*. New York: E.P. Dutton, 1947.

Liebenow, J. Gus. *Colonial Rule and Political Development in Tanzania: The Case of the Makonde*. Evanston, Ill.: Northwestern University Press, 1971.

Listowel, Judith. *The Making of Tanganyika*. London: Chatto & Windus, 1965.

MacDonald, Alexander. *Tanzania: Young Nation in a Hurry*. New York: Hawthorn Books, 1966.

Middleton, J., and J. Campbell. *Zanzibar, Its Society and Its Politics*. London: Oxford University Press, 1965.

Moffett, J.P., ed. *Handbook of Tanganyika*. Dar es Salaam: Government Printers, 1958.

Nyerere, Julius K. *Freedom and Development*. London: Oxford University Press, 1968.

———. *Freedom and Socialism*. London: Oxford University Press, 1960.

————. *Freedom and Unity*. London: Oxford University Press, 1967.

Okello, John. *Revolution in Zanzibar*. Nairobi: East Africa Publishing House, 1967.

Oliver, Roland. *Missionary Factor in East Africa*. London: Longmans, Green, 1952.

Richards, Audrey, ed. *East African Chiefs*. London: Faber & Faber, 1960.

Smith, Hadley E., ed. *Readings on Economic Development and Administration in Tanzania*. London: Oxford University Press, 1966.

Steer, G.L. *Judgement on German East Africa*. London: Hodder, Stoughton, 1939.

Taylor, J.C. *The Political Development of Tanganyika*. Stanford, Calif.: Stanford University Press, 1963.

Wilson, Monica and Leonard Thompson, eds. *Oxford History of South Africa*, vol. 1. London: Oxford University Press, 1969.

Young, Roland and Henry Fosbrooke. *Smoke in the Hills*. Evanston, Ill.: Northwestern University Press, 1960.

PERIODICALS

Africa Report
African Studies Review
Atlantic
Economist
Foreign Affairs
Journal of Modern African Studies
National Geographic
New Yorker
Newsweek
Southern Africa
Tanganyika Notes & Records (Dar es Salaam)
Time
West Africa

NEWSPAPERS

Amsterdam News (New York City)
Baltimore Sun
Christian Science Monitor
Courier-Journal (Louisville)
Daily Nation (Nairobi)
East African Standard (Nairobi)
Evening Star-News (Washington)
Guardian
Journal of Commerce
Le Monde
London Observer
Los Angeles Times
Nationalist (Dar es Salaam)
New York Times
Oregonian
Tanganyika Standard (Dar es Salaam)
Times (London)
Washington Post

PAMPHLETS AND DOCUMENTS

Background Notes on Tanzania, Department of State, Washington, D.C.

Benton, Massell. *East African Economic Union: An Evaluation and Some Implications for Policy*. Santa Monica, Calif.: Rand Corporation, 1963.

International Monetary Fund and IBRD (World Bank) statistical information and documentation.

Nyerere, Julius K. *Democracy & the Party System.* Dar es Salaam: Tanganyika Standard, n.d.

——. *The Second Scramble.* Dar es Salaam: Tanganyika Standard, 1962.

Overseas Business Reports, Department of Commerce, Washington, D.C.

Tanganyika Legislative Council Proceedings (Hansard), Government Printer, Dar es Salaam.

United Nations General Assembly and Trusteeship Council Documents.

PART TWO

SELECTED SPEECHES AND WRITINGS OF JULIUS K. NYERERE

"Arusha Declaration: Answers to Questions." Dar es Salaam: Government Printer, 1967.

"Arusha Declaration Parliament" (July 6, 1970). Dar es Salaam: Government Printer, 1970.

"Development: Another Name for Peace" (a shortened form of the Maryknoll Address). *Tablet* 225 (January 23, 1971), 6816: 92–95.

Freedom and Development. London: Oxford University Press, 1973.

Freedom and Socialism (a selection of forty-one speeches and writings from 1965 to 1967). London: Oxford University Press, 1968.

Freedom and Unity (a selection of seventy-one speeches and writings from 1952 to 1965). London: Oxford University Press, 1967.

"From Uhuru to Ujamaa," *Africa Today* (Summer 1974), pp. 3–8.

"Speech as Chancellor at the Inauguration of the University of Dar es Salaam." Dar es Salaam: Ministry of Information and Tourism, 1970.

"Speech at the Commonwealth Conference at Singapore" (January 20, 1971). Dar es Salaam: Government Printer, 1971.

"Speech by the President, Mwalimu Julius K. Nyerere, to the TANU Conference on May 28, 1969." Tanzania: *Second Five-Year Plan for Economic and Social Development, 1 July 1969–30 June 1974,* vol. 1: *General Analysis,* pp. vii–xxiii. Dar es Salaam: Government Printer, 1969.

"Speech to the Maryknoll Congress in New York." Dar es Salaam: Government Printer, 1978.

"Speech to the United Nations General Assembly." Dar es Salaam: Government Printer, 1970.

"Stability and Change in Africa" (Toronto University, October 2, 1969). *Vital Speeches* 36 (November 1, 1969):48–53.

"A Statement of Policies," *Punch* (March 16, 1966):370–72.

Tanzania Ten Years after Independence. Dar es Salaam: TANU National Conference, 1971.

"Tanzania's Second Five-Year Development Plan," *East Africa Journal* 6 (October 1969) 10:6–12.

Ujamaa: Essays on Socialism. London: Oxford University Press, 1968.

WORKS PERTAINING TO NYERERE'S UJAMAA SOCIALISM

Aldington, T., et al. "The Economics of Kenyanization: Some Professional Comments and Recommendations." *East Africa Journal* 5 (March 1963)3:21–36.

Alot, Magoza. "Dar es Salaam Notebook." *Africa* (August 1974):17–18.

Andrain, C.J. "Democracy and Socialism: Ideologies of African Leaders," *Ideology and Discontent,* ed. D. Apter, pp. 155–205. London: Free Press of Glencoe, 1964.

——. "Patterns of African Socialist Thought," *African Forum* 1 (1966)3:41–60.

Apter, D., ed. *Ideology and Discontent.* London: Free Press of Glencoe, 1964.

Arrighi, Giovanni and John S. Saul. "Socialism and Economic Development, Tropical Africa." *The Journal of Modern African Studies* 6 (1968)2:141–69.

Babu, Hon. Abdulrahman M. "A New Strategy for Development." *Financial Times* (London), December 9, 1971.

Bakula, B.B. "The Effect of Traditionalism on Rural Development: The Omurunazi Ujamaa Village, Bukoba," *Building Ujamaa Villages in Tanzania,* ed. J.H. Proctor, pp. 15–32. Dar es Salaam: Tanzania Publishing House, 1971.

Berg, E. "Socialism and Economic Development in Tropical Africa," *The Quarterly Journal of Economics,* Cambridge, Mass.

Bienen, Henry. "An Ideology for Africa," *Foreign Affairs* 47 (1969)3:545–59.

————. *Party Transformation and Economic Development.* Princeton: Princeton University Press, 1970.

Bloom, Bridget. "Tanzania: Model for Development," *The Financial Times* (London), December 9, 1971.

Bradley, A.W. "Legal Aspects of Nationalization in Tanzania," *East African Law Journal* 3 (1967) 3:149–76.

————, "The Nationalisation of Companies in Tanzania," *Private Enterprise and the East African Company,* ed. P.A. Thomas, pp. 207–28. Dar es Salaam: Tanzania Publishing House, 1969.

Bucharin, Nikolaj, and E. Prebobrazhensky, *The ABC of Communism,* trans. Eden and Cedar Paul. Baltimore: Penguin Books, 1969 (originally published in England in 1922).

"Buildings Taken Over," *Tanzania News Service* 34 (June 1971):1–3.

Bukenya, A.S. "Preface," *The Arusha Declaration and Christian Socialism,* pp. vii–ix. Dar es Salaam: Tanzania Publishing House, 1969.

Burke, Fred G. "Tanganyika: The Search for Ujamaa," *African Socialism,* ed. William H. Friedland and Carl S. Rosberg, Jr., pp. 194–222. Stanford: Stanford University Press, 1964.

Carthew, John. "Andy Capp, 'The Nationalist' and the Tanzania National Ethic." *East Africa Journal* 6 (December 1969)12:5–12.

The Challenge of Development. Nairobi: East African Publishing House, 1968.

Church, Frank. "Farewell to Foreign Aid," *Vital Speeches* 38 (November 15, 1971)3:66–73.

Clarke, Adam. "Another Look at Tanzania," *African Development* 1 (1967)9:3.

Cliffe, Lionel. "Tanzania: Socialist Transformation and Party Development," *The African Review* 1 (March 1971)1:119–35.

Darja, A.W.M. "The Tanzanian Pattern of Rural Development: Some Administrative Problems," *Building Ujamaa Villages in Tanzania,* ed. J.H. Proctor, pp. 48–54. Dar es Salaam: Tanzania Publishing House, 1971.

Dumont, René. *Tanzanian Agriculture after the Arusha Declaration* (Ministry of Economic Affairs and Development Planning). Dar es Salaam: Government Printer, 1969.

Ellman, A.O. "Progress, Problems and Prospects in Ujamaa Development in Tanzania." Dar es Salaam: East African Agricultural Economics Society Conference, March 31–April 4, 1970.

Enaharo, Peter. "African Socialism" (an interview with Julius Nyerere), *Africa* 6 (1972):55–63.

Franken, John, C.S.Sp. "African Socialism Is an Attitude of Mind," *Arusha Declaration and Christian Socialism,* pp. 20–38. Dar es Salaam: Tanzania Publishing House, 1969.

Friedland, William H., and Carl G. Rosberg, Jr., eds. *African Socialism,* Stanford: Stanford University Press, 1964. See especially "Basic Social Trends," pp. 15–34, and "Introduction: The Anatomy of African Socialism," pp. 1–14.

Friedman, Milton. *Capitalism and Freedom.* Chicago: University of Chicago Press, 1962.

Galbraith, John Kenneth. *The New Industrial State.* New York: Signet Books, 1968.

Gallina, Ernesto. *Africa Present.* London: Geoffrey Chapman, 1970.

Ghai, Dharam. "The Concept and Strategies of Economic Independence in African Countries" (mimeographed). Dar es Salaam: Universities of East Africa Social Science Conference, December 27–31, 1970.

Glickman, Harvey. "The Ideology of Julius Nyerere," *Boston University Papers on Africa*, ed. Jeffrey Butler and A.A. Castagno, pp. 195–223. London: Frederick A. Praeger, 1967.

Green, Reginald H., and Ann Seidman. *Unity or Poverty? The Economics of Pan-Africanism*. Baltimore: Penguin Books, 1968.

Guruli, Kassim. "The Struggle for Socialism in Tanzania" (mimeographed). Dar es Salaam: Universities of East Africa Social Science Conference, December 27–31, 1970.

———. "Toward an Independent and Equal East African Common Market," *East Africa Journal* 8 (September 1971):25–32.

Hampsch, George H. *The Theory of Communism*. New York: Philosophical Library, 1965.

Harrington, Michael. *The Other America*. New York: Macmillan, 1962.

Hastings, Adrian. "Tanzania's Lonely Leader," *Tablet* 225 (July 17, 1971):688.

Helleiner, G.K. "Tanzania's Second Plan: Socialism and Self-Reliance," *East Africa Journal* 5 (December 1968) 12:41–50.

Herrick, Allison, B., et al. *Area Handbook for Tanzania*. Washington, D.C.: U.S. Government Printing Office, 1968.

Honeybone, Reginald C. "The Nature, Scope and Function of Education for Development," *Nation-Building in Tanzania*, ed. Anthony Rweyamamu. Nairobi: East African Publishing House, 1970.

Hudson, G.F. *Fifty Years of Communism: Theory and Practice, 1917–1967*. Baltimore: Pelican Books, 1968.

Hughes, A.J. *East Africa*. Baltimore: Penguin Books, 1969.

Hyden, Goran. "Planning in Tanzania: Lessons of Experience." *East Africa Journal* 6 (October 1969)10:13–17.

Ifill, Max B. *Regional Economic Planning: Report to the Government of Tanzania*. Rome: Food and Agriculture Organization of the United Nations, 1970.

Illife, John. *Agricultural Change in Modern Tanganyika: An Outline History* (mimeographed). Dar es Salaam: Universities of East Africa Social Science Conference, December 27–31, 1970.

Jumba-Masagazi, A.H.K. *African Socialism: A Bibliography and a Short Summary*. Nairobi: East African Academy, 1970.

Kamarck, Andrew M. *The Economics of African Development* (rev. ed.). London: Praeger Publishers, 1971.

Kambona, Oscar S. *Tanzania and Problems of African Unity*. London: Oscar S. Kambona, 7 Glenloch Court, 1968.

Kawawa, R.R. "Toward African Unity." Dar es Salaam: Tanganyika Information Service, 1963.

Kimambo, I.N. and A.J. Temu, eds. *A History of Tanzania*. Nairobi: East African Publishing House, 1969.

Kopytoff, Igor. "Socialism and Traditional African Societies," *African Socialism*, ed. William H. Friedland and Carl G. Rosberg, Jr., pp. 53–62. Stanford: Stanford University Press, 1964.

Kunsanje, Mamisi. "Tanzania: La Défense d'Accuser: Differences between Oscar S. Kambona and President Julius Nyerere." London: Debemoja, 1970.

Lacy, Creighton. "Christian Socialism in Tanzania," *The Christian Century*, 89 (March 1, 1972).

Lavoie, John, W.F. "The University Student and Nation-Building in Modern Africa," *Arusha Declaration and Christian Socialism*, pp. 11–19. Dar es Salaam: Tanzania Publishing House, 1969.

Legum, Colin. "One-Party State Passes Its Test." *London Observer*, September 26, 1965.

———. *Africa Handbook*. Middlesex, Eng.: Penguin, 1969.

Lenin, V.I., "The Professional Revolutionary," *Modern Socialism*, Ed. Salvadori, pp. 181–99. New York: Harper Torchbooks, 1968.

Leontyev, L. *Fundamentals of Marxist Political Thought*. Moscow: Novosti Press, 1970.

Lewis, William H. "Tanzania: Commitment to Self-Reliance," *Current History* 58 (March, 1970):160.

Listowel, Judith. "The Making of President Nyerere," *Tablet* 225 (January 23, 1971) 6816:76–77.

——. *The Making of Tanganyika*. London: Chatto & Windus, 1965.

Maguire, G. Andrew. *Toward "Uhuru" in Tanzania: The Politics of Participation*. Cambridge: Cambridge University Press, 1969.

Marcuse, Herbert. *One-Dimensional Man*. London: Sphere Books, 1968.

——. *Soviet Marxism: A Critical Analysis*. Middlesex, England: Pelican Books, 1971.

Martin, David. "Tanu: the Architect of Future Policy." *Financial Times* (London), December 9, 1971.

Mashauri, R.K. "Leadership Structure and Functions in an Ujamaa Village: A Case Study of Gullu," *Building Ujamaa Villages in Tanzania*, ed. J.H. Proctor, pp. 55–63. Dar es Salaam: Tanzania Publishing House, 1971.

Mbilinyi, S.M. "Enormous Dependence on Agriculture." *Financial Times* (London), December 9, 1971.

Mboya, G.R. "The Feasibility of Ujamaa Villages in Kilimanjaro," *Building Ujamaa Villages in Tanzania*, ed. J.H. Proctor, pp. 64–69. Dar es Salaam: Tanzania Publishing House, 1971.

Meister, Albert. *East Africa: The Past in Chains, the Future in Pawn*, trans. P.N. Ott. New York: Walker and Co., 1966.

Melady, Thomas Patrick. "African Socialism: A Bibliographic Essay." *African Forum* 1 (1966)3:61–65.

Mohiddin, Ahmed. "Uhuru Na Umoja" (Freedom and Unity), *Présence Africaine* 1 (1969) 69:160–62.

——. "Ujamaa: A Commentary on President Nyerere's Vision of Tanzanian Society." *African Affairs*, 67 (April 1968):267, 130–43.

Morse, Chandler. "The Economics of African Socialism," *African Socialism*, ed. William H. Friedland and Carl S. Rosberg, Jr., pp. 35–52. Stanford: Stanford University Press, 1964.

Mumby, Denys, ed. *World Development*. Washington, D.C.: Corpus Books, 1969, p. 208.

Musoke, I.K.S. "Building Socialism in Bukoba: The Establishment of Rugazi (Nyerere) Ujamaa Village," *Building Ujamaa Villages in Tanzania*, ed. J.H. Proctor, pp. 1–14. Dar es Salaam: Tanzania Publishing House, 1971.

Myrdal, Gunnar. *Beyond the Welfare State*. New York: Bantam Books, 1960.

Nelkin, Dorothy. "Socialist Sources of Pan-African Ideology," *African Socialism*, ed. William H. Friedland and Carl S. Rosberg, Jr. pp. 63–79. Stanford: Stanford University Press, 1964.

Nellis, John. *A Theory of Ideology: The Tanzanian Example*. London: Oxford University Press, 1972.

Ngororo, Abdulla. " 'Ujamaa' Meets Success." *Financial Times* (London), December 9, 1971.

Nkrumah, Kwame. "African Socialism Revisited," *African Forum* 1 (1966) 3:4–5.

Novati, Gianpaolo Calchi. "Un'ideologia Rivoluzionaria," *Socialismo in Tanzania*, pp. 7–12. Bologna: II Mulino, 1970.

Ntirukigwa, E.N. "The Land Tenure System and the Building of Ujamaa Villages in Geita: A Case Study of Kalebezo," *Building Ujamaa Villages in Tanzania*, ed. J.H. Proctor, pp. 33–47. Dar es Salaam: Tanzania Publishing House, 1971.

Ogot, B.A. "Traditional Communalism and European Socialism in African Politics," *East Africa Journal* 4 (December 1967)8:31–36.

Omari, C.K. "Tanzania's Emerging Rural Development Policy," *Africa Today* (Summer 1974):9–14.

Onuoha, Bede. *The Elements of African Socialism*. London: Andre Deutsch, 1965.

Othman, H.M. "The Arusha Declaration and the 'Triangle Principles' of Tanzania Foreign Policy." *East Africa Journal* 7 (May 1970)5:35–42.

Ottaway, David. "Letter from Tanzania," *Washington Post,* May 25, 1975.

———. "Tanzania: Peasants on the Move," *Washington Post,* May 18, 1975.

Padmore, George. *Pan-Africanism or Communism?* London: Dobson, 1956.

Pearson, Lester B., chairman. *Partners in Development: Report of the Commission on International Development.* London: Pall Mall Press, 1969.

Phillips, Sir Henry. "Venture Capital: Its New Role in Developing Africa," *African Affairs* 70 (October 1971) 281:395–403.

Potekhin, I.I. "On African Socialism: A Soviet View," *African Socialism,* ed. William H. Friedland and Carl S. Rosberg, Jr., pp. 97–112. Stanford: Stanford Universtiy Press, 1964.

Proctor, J.H. ed. *Building Ujamaa Villages in Tanzania.* Dar es Salaam: Tanzania Publishing House, 1971.

———. *The Cell System of the Tanganyika African Union.* Dar es Salaam: Tanzania Publishing House, 1971.

Provisional Indicative World Plan for Agricultural Development: Summary and Main Conclusions. Rome: Food and Agriculture Organization of the United Nations, 1970.

Quarterly Economic Review: Tanzania, Zambia, April 1971, no. 2.

Rejai, Mostafa. "African Socialism: An Appraisal," *International Philosophical Quarterly* 10 (September 1970):458–67.

"Report on the Central Committee of the Communist Party of the Soviet Union to the Twenty-Fourth Congress of the CPSU," March 30, 1971, *Moscow News* 14 (April 3, 1971) 105:supplement, pp. 1–23.

Resnick, Idrian N. "Manpower Development in Tanzania." *The Journal of Modern African Studies* 1 (1967)5:107–23.

———. "Socialist Policy Analysis." Dar es Salaam: Universities of East Africa Social Science Conference, December 27–31, 1970.

The Rights and Freedoms. New York: United Nations Publications, 1950.

Roberts, Margaret. "A Socialist Looks at African Socialism." *African Socialism,* ed. William H. Friedland and Carl S. Rosberg, Jr., pp. 80–96. Stanford: Stanford University Press, 1964.

Roe, A. "The Company in Tanzania: A Post Arusha Declaration Appraisal," *Private Enterprises and the East African Company,* pp. 229–261. Dar es Salaam: Tanzania Publishing House, 1969.

———. "The Future of the Company in Tanzanian Development," *The Journal of Modern African Studies* 7 (1969)1:47–67.

Rweyamamu, Anthony. "An Overview of Nation-Building: Problems and Issues." *Nation-Building in Tanzania,* ed. A. Rweyamamu, pp. 1–8. Nairobi: East African Publishing House, 1970.

———. "Socialism in Operation," *Financial Times* (London), December 9, 1971, pp. 30–31.

Salvador, Massimo, ed. *Modern Socialism.* New York: Harper Torchbooks, 1968.

Saul, John. "Who Is the Immediate Enemy?" Dar es Salaam: Universities of East Africa Social Science Conference, December 27–31, 1970.

Seidman, A.W. "Comparative Development Strategies in East Africa" (part 1), *East Africa Journal* 7 (April 1970) 4:13–18.

Shivji, Issa G. "Tanzania—the Silent Class Struggle." Dar es Salaam: Universities of East Africa Social Science Conference, December 27–31, 1970.

Siebel, Wigand and Norbert Martin. "Sociology," *Sacramentum Mundi,* vol. 3, pp. 133–35. New York: Herder and Herder, 1969.

Sigmund, Paul E., ed. *The Ideologies of the Developing Nations.* London: Frederick A. Praeger, 1967, rev. edn.

Singleton, Seth. "Africa's Boldest Experiment," *Africa Report* 16 (December 1971)9:10–14.

Slaats, Theodore, C.S.Sp. "International Relations," *Arusha Declaration and Christian Socialism*, pp. 44–54. Dar es Salaam: Tanzania Publishing House, 1969.

————. "The Nationalization of Schools in Tanzania," *IDOC International*, North American edn. (May 23, 1970):28–36.

Smith, William Edgett. "Profiles: Julius K. Nyerere," part 1, *New Yorker* (October 16, 1971), pp. 44–100; part 2, *New Yorker* (October 23, 1971), pp. 47–109; part 3, *New Yorker* (October 30, 1971), pp. 53–99.

————. "Spotlight on Tanzania," *Africa* (December 1974).

————. "Standard Solution," *The Economist* 240 (August 7, 1971) 6676:37–38.

Surveys of African Economics. Washington, D.C.: International Monetary Fund, 1969.

Svendsen, Knud Erik. "The Present Stage of Economic Planning in Tanzania," *Nation-Building in Tanzania*, ed. Anthony Rweyamamu. Nairobi: East African Publishing House, 1970.

————. "Socialist Problems after the Arusha Declaration." *East African Journal* 4 (May 1967) 2:9–15.

"TANU Supremacy," *Africa* (April 1975), p. 86.

"Tanzania," *Deadline Data on World Affairs*. Greenwich, Conn.: Deadline Data, Inc. (September 13, 1968).

"Tanzania: Education and Leadership," *Africa* (February 1975), p. 33.

"Tanzania: Twenty Years After," *African Development*, London (July 1974).

Temu, Peter. "Nationalization in Tanzania," *East Africa Journal* 4 (June 1967)3:35–41.

Thomas, Gary. "Agricultural Capitalism and Rural Development in Tanzania," *East Africa Journal* 4 (November 1967)7:29-36.

Uba, Sam. "Opposition in Africa," *Africa* 6 (1972):15–17.

Van de Laar, Art. "Arusha: Before and After." *East Africa Journal* 5 (November 1968) 11:13–68.

Webb, Peter. "Nyerere: Operation Bootstrap—or Backstep? *Newsweek* (March 6, 1967), p. 47.

Wetter, Gustave, S.J. *Soviet Ideology Today*, trans. Peter Heath. London: Heinemann, 1966.

Whelan, Anthony. "A Preliminary Approach to Tanzanian Socialism," *African Ecclesiastical Review* 11 (January 1969)1:88–91.

Wicken, Joan E. "The United Republic of Tanzania: Tanganyika," *Africa Handbook*, ed. Colin Legum, pp. 165–94. Middlesex, England: Penguin Books, 1969.

Who Controls Industry in Kenya? (report of the Working Party, under the auspices of the Department of Education and Training of the National Christian Council of Kenya). Nairobi: East African Publishing House, 1968.

Zolberg, Aristide R. "The Dakar Colloquium: The Search for a Doctrine." *African Socialism*, ed. William Friedland and Carl S. Rosberg, Jr. pp. 113–30. Stanford: Stanford University Press, 1964.

SELECTED CHURCH DOCUMENTS
(listed in order of promulgation)

Leo XIII, *Rerum Novarum* (encyclical on the conditions of labor), May 15, 1891. English translation in *Rerum Novarum*. New York: Paulist Press, 1939.

Pius XI, *Quadragesimo Anno* (encyclical on the reconstruction of the social order), May 15, 1931. English translation in *The Social Order*. London: Catholic Truth Society, 1960.

Pius XII, "Discourse on the Feast of Pentecost," June 1, 1941. *Acta Apostolcae Sedis* 33 (1941):216–27.

John XXIII, *Mater et Magistra* (encyclical on Christianity and social progress), May 15, 1961. English translation in *The Pope Speaks* 7 (1962)4:295–343, and in *The Gospel of Peace and Justice:*

Catholic Social Teaching since Pope John, presented by Joseph Gremillion. Maryknoll, New York; Orbis Books, 1976.

———, *Pacem in Terris* (encyclical on peace), April 11, 1963. English translation in *The Pope Speaks* 9 (1963)1:13–48, and in *Gospel of Peace and Justice.*

Vatican Council II, *Gaudium et Spes* (Pastoral Constitution on the Church in the Modern World), December 7, 1965. English translation in William Abbott, S.J., *The Documents of Vatican II.* New York: America Press, 1966, and in *Gospel of Peace and Justice.*

Paul VI, *Populorum Progressio* (encyclical on development), March 26, 1967. English translation in *Encyclical Letter of His Holiness Pope Paul VI,* Glen Rock, New Jersey: Paulist Press, 1967, and in *Gospel of Peace and Justice.*

———, *Octogesima Adveniens* (Apostolic Letter to Cardinal Roy), May 14, 1971. English translation in *On the Occasion of the Eightieth Anniversary of the Encyclical Rerum Novarum.* Vatican: Typis Polyglottis Vaticanis, 1971, and in *Gospel of Peace and Justice.*

WORKS PERTAINING TO THE CHURCH'S TEACHING ON SOCIAL JUSTICE

Alszeghy, Zoltan, S.J. and Maurizio Flick, S.J. "Theology of Development: A Question of Method," *Theology Meets Progress,* ed. Philip Land, S.J., pp. 105–44. Rome: Gregorian University Press, 1971.

Alves, Rubem A. "Theology and Liberation of Man," *In Search of a Theology of Development* (a Sodepax Report of November 1969), pp. 75–92. Lausanne: La Concorde, 1969.

Bauer, Gerhard. "A Systematic Bibliography of Theology of Development," *Theology Meets Progress,* ed. Philip Land, S.J., pp. 289–346. Rome: Gregorian University Press, 1971.

———. *Toward a Theology of Development: An Annotated Bibliography for Sodepax.* Geneva: Committee on Society, Development, and Peace, 1969.

Bigo, Pierre. *La Doctrine Sociale de l'Eglise.* Paris: PUF, 1965.

Bishops of Paraguay. "A Letter on Liberation" (December 8, 1970). *Catholic Mind* 59 (May 1971):13–14.

Bishops of Peru. "Justice in the World," *IDOC International,* North American edn., 37 (December 11, 1971):2–18.

Blomjous, Bishop Joseph, W.F. (former bishop of Mwanza, Tanzania). "The Church in a Developing World," *Cross Currents* 20 (1970)3:287–300.

Butler, Christopher. *In the Light of the Council.* London: Darton, Longman and Todd, 1969.

Calvez, J.Y. and J. Perring. *The Church and Social Justice.* London: Burns and Oates, 1961.

Calvez, Jean-Yves, S.J. "Eglise et développement." *Gregorianum* 49 (1968):623–36.

———. *The Social Thought of John XXIII,* trans. George J.M. McKenzie, S.M. Chicago: Henry Regnery Co., 1964.

Camara, Dom Helder. *The Church and Colonialism: The Betrayal of the Third World.* Denville, N.J.: Dimension Books, 1969.

Caprille, Giovanni, ed. *Concilio Vaticano II* (chronicle of the Second Vatican Council in eight volumes). Rome: Edizioni La Civiltà Cattolica, 1966–69.

Catao, Francisco. "Justice in the World," *IDOC International* (N. American edn.), June 26, 1971, pp. 51–61.

Chenu, M.D., O.P. "The Signs of the Times," trans. John Drury, in *The Church Today,* ed. Group 2000, pp. 43–59. New York: Newman Press, 1968.

Coste, René. "Peace and Community of Nations," *Commentary on the Documents of Vatican II,* ed. Herbert Vorgrimler, vol. 5, pp. 347–69. New York: Herder and Herder, 1969.

De Riematten, Heinrich, et al. *La Chiesa nel Mondo contemporaneo.* Brescia: Queriniana, 1966.

Deretz, Jacques and Adrien Nocent. *Dictionary of the Council.* London: Geoffrey Chapman, 1968.

Díez-Alegría, José, S.J. "A Christian View of Progress through Violence." *Theology Meets Progress,* ed. Philip Land, S.J., pp. 171–206. Rome: Gregorian University Press, 1971.

————. "Common Good," *Sacramentum Mundi*, ed. Karl Rahner, vol. 6, pp. 128–30. New York: Herder and Herder, 1970.

————. "Problemi di Etica Sociale." Rome: Pontificia Universita Gregoriana, n.d.

————."The Rights of Men," *Sacramentum Mundi*, ed. Karl Rahner, vol. 5, pp. 365–68. New York: Herder and Herder, 1969.

Discorsi, Messaggi, Colloqui del Santo Padre Giovanni XXIII, 6 vols. Vaticana: Tipografia Poliglotta, 1963–1967.

Dulles, Avery, S.J. "The Dilemmas of the Church in the World," *Origins* (February 20, 1975):548–51.

Elliott, Charles. *The Development Debate*. London: SCM Press, 1971.

The Encyclicals and Other Messages of John XXIII, ed. the staff of *The Pope Speaks* magazine. Washington, D.C.: TPS Press, 1964.

Fernandes, Archbishop Angelo. "The Role of the Church in Development," *Catholic Mind* 59 (May 1971):30–53.

The Gospel of Peace and Justice: Catholic Social Teaching since Pope John, presented by Joseph Gremillion. Maryknoll, New York: Orbis Books, 1976.

Gremillion, Joseph. *The Other Dialogue*. Garden City, N.Y.: Doubleday, 1965.

Gutiérrez, Gustavo. "Liberation and Development," *Cross Currents* 21 (Summer 1971)3:243–56.

Häring, Bernard, C.SS.R. *The Law of Christ*, vol. 3, trans. Edwin Kaiser, C.PP.S. Westminster, Md.: Newman Press, 1966.

————. "L'uomo in cerca di Liberazione nella Comunità," *Liberazione dell'Uomo: Relatà di Oggi e Storia della Salvezza*, ed. Viktor Schurr and Bernard Häring, pp. 71–97. Rome: Edizioni Paoline, 1969.

————. *A Theology of Protest*. New York: Farrar, Straus, and Giroux, 1970.

Hastings, Adrian. "Christian Faith and Social Commitment," *Arusha Declaration and Christian Socialism*, pp. 1–10. Dar es Salaam: Tanzania Publishing House, 1969.

Healy, James, S.J. *The Just Wage: 1750–1890*. The Hague: Martinus Nijhoff, 1966.

Heckel, Roger, S.J. "Lettre Apostolique de Paul VI sur le 80e anniversaire de Rerum Novarum," *Cahiers* (a series of commentaries beginning October 1, 1971.)

Henrici, Peter, S.J. "From Progress to Development: A History of Ideas," *Theology Meets Progress*, ed. Philip Land, S.J., pp. 37–84. Rome: Gregorian University Press, 1971.

Herder-Dorneich, Philip. "How Can the Church Provide Guidelines in Social Ethics?" *Concilium* 5 (May 1968) 4:42–48.

Höffner, Joseph. *Fundamentals of Christian Sociology*, trans. Geoffrey-Stevens. Cork: Mercier Press, 1962.

In Search of a Theology of Development. Geneva: Committee of Society, Development and Peace, 1969.

Insegnamenti di Paolo VI. Vatican: Tipografia Poliglotta Vaticana, 1965.

Jarlot, Georges, S.J. "La Dottrina della Proprietà di Pio XII alla Populorum Progressio," *Civiltà Cattolica* 2 (1967):341–59.

————. "L'elaborazione progressiva della dottrina della Proprietà privata nell' insegnamento Pontificio," *Civiltà Cattolica* 2 (1967):224–37.

Joblin, Joseph, S.J. "Chiesa e sviluppo nella 'Populorum Progressio,' " *Civiltà Cattolica* 1 (1968):437–49.

Joinet, Bernard, W.F. "The Role of the Church in Politics" (mimeographed paper of the Tanzania Episcopal Conference, July 13–16, 1971, Dar es Salaam).

Klüber, Franz. "Property," *Sacramentum Mundi*, ed. Karl Rahner, vol. 5, pp. 108–10. New York: Herder and Herder, 1970.

Land, Philip, S.J. "Theology for Church Action in Development," *The Church and Development* (proceedings of the December 1970 Amecea-Misereor Seminar), pp. 23–29. Nairobi: Amecea, 1971.

———. *Theology Meets Progress.* Rome: Gregorian University Press, 1971. See especially "Social and Economic Processes of Development," pp. 1–36.

Lebret, L.J., O.P. "Economic and Social Life: The Community of Nations," *The Church Today*, trans. John Drury, ed. Group 2000, pp. 154–91. New York: Newman Press, 1967.

———. *The Last Revolution*, trans. John Morgan. Dublin: Logos Books, Gill and Son, 1965.

Levi, Virgilio, ed. *Di Fronte alla Contestazione.* Testi di Paolo VI. Milan: Rusconi, 1970.

"List Marxist Dangers" (statement by Chilean Bishops), *National Catholic Reporter*, January 7, 1972.

Lutti, Gerard. "Justice in the World," *IDOC International*, North American edn. (June 26, 1971):62–68.

Mercatali, Andrea. *La Promozione della Persona nei Documenti Conciliari.* Brescia: La Scuola Editrice, 1971.

Messineo, Antonio, S.J. "L'Umanesimo Plenario e lo Sviluppo Integrale del Popolo." *Civiltà Cattolica* (1968):213–26.

Metz, Johannes. *Theology in the World*, trans. William Glen-Doepel. New York: Herder and Herder, 1969.

Moeller, Charles. "History of the Constitution," *Commentary on the Documents of Vatican II*, ed. H. Vorgrimler, vol. 5, pp. 1–76. New York: Herder and Herder, 1969.

———. "Preface and Introductory Statement," *Commentary on the Documents of Vatican II*, ed. H. Vorgrimler, vol. 5, pp. 77–114. New York: Herder and Herder, 1969.

Murray, Francis, M.M. "Agriculture, the Arusha Declaration and Mater et Magistra," *Arusha Declaration and Christian Socialism*, pp. 35–43. Dar es Salaam: Tanzania Publishing House, 1969.

Mwoleka, Bishop Christopher. "Cooperation of the Church with the Government" (mimeographed). Rulenge, Tanzania: Diocese of Rulenge, March 1971.

———. "Nation-Building in Vatican II as Applied to Tanzania" (mimeographed). Rulenge, Tanzania: Diocese of Rulenge, September 1970.

Nell-Breuning, Oswald von. "Chiesa Cattolica e Critica Marxiana del Capitalismo," *Aggiornamento Sociale* (May 1968):385–96.

———. "Christian Social Doctrine," *Sacramentum Mundi*, ed. Karl Rahner, vol. 6, pp. 108–16. New York: Herder and Herder, 1970.

———. "The Life of the Political Community," *Commentary on the Documents of Vatican II*, ed. H. Vorgrimler, pp. 315–27. New York: Herder and Herder, 1969.

Ochoa Xaverius. *Index Verborum cum Documentis Concilii Vaticani Secundi.* Rome: Commentarium pro Religionis, 1967.

Pavan, Pietro. "Dominio sul Mondo e Liberazione dell'uomo," *Liberazione dell'uomo: Realtà di Oggi e Storia della Salvezza*, ed. Viktor Schurr and Bernard Häring, pp. 11–69. Rome: Edizioni Paoline, 1969.

———. "Papal Social Thought," *New Catholic Encyclopedia* (1967) vol. 13, pp. 354–61.

Payne, Denis, ed. *African Independence and Christian Freedom.* London: Oxford University Press, 1965.

Pontifical Commission Justice and Peace, "Justice in the World," *IDOC International*, North American edn. 37 (December, 1971):19–34.

Post, Werner. "Ideology," *Sacramentum Mundi*, ed. Karl Rahner, vol. 6, pp. 233–46. New York: Herder and Herder, 1970.

Poupard, P. "Introduction to Populorum Progressio," *Lo Sviluppo dei Popoli*, pp. 11–29. Brescia: Queriniana, 1968.

Rahner, Karl, S.J. "Theology," *Sacramentum Mundi*, vol. 6, pp. 233–46. New York: Herder and Herder, 1970.

Ratzinger, Joseph. "Dignity of Human Person," *Commentary on the Documents of Vatican II*, ed. H. Vorgrimler, vol. 5, pp. 115–63. New York: Herder and Herder, 1969.

Regan, Dennis M. *Violent Revolution*. Rome: Academia Alfonsiana, 1970.

Rendtorff, Trutz. "Christian Foundation and Worldly Commitment," *Theology Meets Progress*, ed. Philip Land, S.J., pp. 85–104. Rome: Gregorian University Press, 1971.

Riedmatten, Henri de, O.P. "Introduction: History of the Pastoral Constitution," trans. John Drury. *The Church Today*, ed. Group 2000, pp. 3–40. New York: Newman Press, 1968.

Riga, Peter J. *The Church and Revolution: Some Reflections on the Modern World*. Milwaukee: Bruce, 1967.

———. *The Church of the Poor* (commentary on *Populorum Progressio*). Techny, Ill.: Divine Word Publications, 1967.

Roy, Maurice Cardinal. *"Second Development Decade"* (November 19, 1970), *IDOC International*, North American edn. (February 13, 1971):66–74.

Ryan, William F. and Joseph Komochak. "The Liberation of Men and Nations" (Interamerican Bishops' Meeting, Mexico City, May 18–21). Washington: NCCB, 1971.

Simons, F. (bishop of Indore, India). "Communism and Democracy," *IDOC International*, North American edn. (June 26, 1971):72–76.

Sipendi, Joseph (bishop of Moshi, Tanzania). "Christian Concepts of Socialism and the Arusha Declaration," *Arusha Declaration and Christian Socialism*, pp. 29–34. Dar es Salaam: Tanzania Publishing House, 1969.

Sorge, Bartolomeo, S.J. "L'Apporto Dottrinale della Lettera Apostolica 'Octogesima Adveniens,' "*Civiltà Cattolica* 2 (1971): 417–28.

———. "Come leggere l'Enciclica Populorum Progressio," *Civiltà Cattolica* 2 (1967):209–23.

———. "La Mater et Magistra di Fronte ai Socialismi Contemporanei," *Civiltà Cattolica* 11 (1963):545–56.

———. "I Sinodo e la Giustizia nel Mondo," *Civiltà Cattolica* 6 (December 18, 1971):525–42.

———. "Socializzazione e Socialismo," *Civiltà Cattolica* 1 (1963):326–37.

———. "Sviluppo Economico e Ordine Morale," *Civiltà Cattolica* 4 (1966):133–39.

———. "Teología e historia en la Enciclica 'Populorum Progresso,' " *Criterio* 4 (1963):558–64.

———. "La Vita Economica nel Magistero della Chiesa," *Civiltà Cattolica* 4 (1966):569–71.

Synod of Bishops. "Justice in the World," Vatican: Polyglot Press, 1971.

Synod of Bishops. 1974. Washington, D.C.: USCC Publications, 1975.

Synod Secretariat for Synod of Bishops. "Justice in the World," *IDOC International*, North American edn. (June 26, 1971):31–50.

The Teachings of Pope Paul VI. Vatican: Libreria Editrice, 1968–.

Tucci, Roberto, et al. *La Chiesa nel Mondo Contemporaneo*. Turin: Elle di Ci, 1968, 3rd. edn.

———. "Development of Culture," *Commentary on the Documents of Vatican II*, ed. H. Vorgrimler, vol 5, pp. 246–87. New York: Herder and Herder, 1969.

Tufari, Paolo, S.J. "The Church between Ideology and Utopia," *Theology Meets Progress*, ed. Philip Land, S.J., pp. 249–88. Rome: Gregorian University Press, 1971.

Villot, Jean Cardinal. "I Poveri nella Società Ricca," *Aggiornamento Sociale* (January 1971):61–64.

Vorgrimler, Herbert, ed. *Commentary on the Documents of Vatican II*, 5 vols. New York: Herder and Herder, 1967–69.

Ward, Barbara. *The Angry Seventies*. Rome: Justice and Peace, 1970.

———. "Structures for World Justice," *IDOC International*, North American edn. 37 (December 11, 1971):39–43.

INDEX

Abdulla, 76
Aboriginal Bushmen, 11
Africa Report, 102
African Independent Church, 120, 121
African Liberation Committee (ALC), 133, 134, 141
African National Congress (ANC), 74, 134–35
Africanization policy, 75, 81–82
Afro-Shirazi Party, 58, 59, 76, 103
Afro-Shirazi peoples, 12
Agnosticism, 120
Agriculture (Tanzanian), 107–8, *see also Ujamaa*
  socialism: rural economy; villagization
  program
Ahidjo, Ahadou, 3
AID projects (U.S.), 151
Airways, *see* Transport
Albuquerque, Duke of, 17
ALC, *see* African Liberation Committee
Alexander the Great, 15
Algeria, 40
Alvarez Cabral, Pedro, 17
Amin, Idi, 98–100, 138, 160
ANC, *see* African National Congress
Angola, 141, 173
  civil war in, 136
Animism, 120
Apartheid, 132
Arabs in East Africa, 10, 12, 13, 15, 16, 17–20
Aristotle, 15, 50
Arusha, Tanzania, 91, 99, 138
Arusha Declaration, 43, 66, 73, 266
  and agricultural development, 203
  and capitalism, 191
  and economic transformative planning, 201
  implementation of, 57–58, 92–94
  and influence on educational system, 123
  issued by TANU, 57
  and means of production and exchange, 197n64
  and nationalization of business and industry, 193
  and need for work, 184

on rights of Tanzanians, 182
  and villagization program, 128
Asian Association, 52
Asians in East Africa, 10, 12–13, 15, 16–17
Association of Episcopal Conferences in Eastern Africa, 231
Aswan Dam, Egypt, 89
Atlantic, 95

Babu, *see* Rahman Mohammed, Sheikh Abdull
Bagamoyo, Tanzania, 15, 17, 20
Bahaya tribe, 10
Balewa, Sir Abubakar, 146
Baltimore Sun, 135
Banda, Hastings, 70, 135, 139
Bantu peoples, 11–12, 14
Barghash, 18, 19
Battersill, Sir William, 31
Belgian Congo, 20, 80, 136; *see also* Zaire
Belgium, 19, 20
Benedictines, 121
Berlin, Treaty of (1884), 19
Bevin, Ernest, 29
Bienen, Henry, 195, 235
Bigo, Pierre, 259
Boer War, 22
Bomani, Paul, 55
Botswana, 2
Bourguiba, Habib, 3
Bourne, Cardinal, 259
Bradley, A.W., 193
Brazil, 17
Britain
  exploration in East Africa, 17, 18, 19, 21, 22
  and relations with Tanzania, 68–69, 88, 140, 144–46, 206
British Cameroons, 28
British Labour Party, 259
British Togo, 28
Bryceson, Derek, 55
Bunche, Ralph, 70
Burton, Sir Richard, 16

281

Burundi, 20, 25
  and relations with Tanzania, 138–39
Bushmen, *see* Aboriginal Bushmen
Butiama, Tanzania, 44
Buxton, Thomas, 18
Byatt, Sir Horace, 25, 26

Callaghan, James, 146
Camara, Dom Helder, 212, 236
Cameron, Sir Donald, 26–27, 32, 45, 47, 51
Cameroon, United Republic of, 3
Canada
  and relations with Tanzania, 147–48
Capetown, South Africa, 67
Capitalism in Tanzania, 189–91, 238
Capuchins, 121
Carlucci, Frank, 150
Carter, Beverly, 151
Catholic Church teachings, *see* Social justice
  teachings of the Catholic Church
Central Intelligence Agency, 151
Chagga people, 10, 12, 55
Chagula, Wilbert, 55
Chaka Chaka, Tanzania, 16
China
  in East Africa, 13, 15, 16–17
  and relations with Tanzania, 84–86, 153–55;
    see also Tan-Zam railway
  and relations with Zanzibar, 154
Chou En-lai
  visit to Tanzania of, 85
Christianity, 45, 120–21
Chronicles of Kilwa, 16
Church teachings, *see* Social justice teachings of
  the Catholic Church
Churchill, Winston, 43
Civil liberties, 63
Civil service, 65
  Africanization of, 74, 75
Collins, Fr. William J., 45, 49
Colonialism
  and decolonization in Africa, 1–5
  effect of, on Africa, 53–54
Commerce, 112–13
Common good
  Church teachings on, 222–23
Communications media, 125–26
Communism
  Chinese vs. Soviet, 179n60
  Lenin on, 179n54
  vs. *Ujamaa* socialism, 257
  see also Marxism-Leninism
Congar, Yves, 214
Constitution (Tanzanian), 60, 61, 62, 64
  Bill of Rights of, 63

Constitutional Conference (Tanzania), 68
Constitutional Conference (Zanzibar), 77
Cooperatives, growth of, 126–27
Creech-Jones, Arthur, 28, 91
Cuba, 79

Daily News (Tanzania), 125
Dar es Salaam, Tanzania, 9, 11, 13, 16, 17, 18,
  20, 23, 29, 38, 44, 49, 66, 67, 68, 76, 79, 80,
  88, 114, 132, 206, 257
  exile groups in, 134–35
  meaning of name of, 1
Dar es Salaam, University of, 89, 122, 124
  law faculty of, 64
Decolonization, *see* Colonialism
Development (in Church teaching)
  defined, 231–33
  as economic advancement, 233–35
  as humanization, 240–44
  as liberation, 235–40
Development plans (Tanzanian)
  first (1964–69), 116–17
  second (1969–74), 117
  third (1975–80), 117
Dhow, origins of, 16
Divini Redemptoris, 257
Dodoma, Tanzania, as capital, 66
Dulles, John Foster, 34

East Africa, *see names of individual countries*
East African Common Services Organization,
  91
East African Community, 91, 99, 114, 138,
  160, 207
East African High Commission, 91
East African University, 99
Economist (London), 84, 100, 103
Edinburgh University, 45, 51
Education, 121–23; *see also* Dar es Salaam, Uni-
  versity of; East African University; Makerere
  University; *Ujamaa* socialism
Egypt, 2
Eliufoo, Solomon, 55
Ethiopia, 2, 11, 27
Eyasi, Lake, 11

Familyhood, *see* Ujamaa
Filesi, Teobalso
  China and Africa in the Middle Ages, 17
Finances (Tanzanian), 114–16
Food and Agriculture Organization, 131, 235
Ford, Gerald, 43
FRELIMO, *see* Mozambique Liberation Front